UNIVERSITY OF
GLOUCESTERSHIRE
at Cheltenham and Gloucester

E-learning is becoming integral to on-site education in learning institutions worldwide, and the rapid explosion of interest in the subject means that this timely, cutting-edge book will be an instant and indispensable resource. Among educators, the development of reusable learning objects made accessible via the Internet is ever more important to teaching and learning.

This book provides a comprehensive look at state-of-the-art online education, and presents advice on the creation, adaptation and implementation of learning objects and metadata. Including articles written by some of the leading innovators in the field, this book takes the reader through:

- designing effective learning objects;
- creating learning objects;
- transforming existing content into reusable learning objects;
- building a metadata management system.

This book will be essential reference material for course developers at universities, postgraduate students, teachers and learners in the field of e-learning.

Rory McGreal is Associate Vice President Research at Athabasca University, Canada.

Open and Flexible Learning series
Series Editors: Fred Lockwood, Tony Bates and Som Naidu

Activities in Self-Instructional Texts, Fred Lockwood
Assessing Open and Distance Learners, Chris Morgan and Meg O'Reilly
Changing University Teaching, Terry Evans and Daryl Nation
The Costs and Economics of Open and Distance Learning, Greville Rumble
Delivering Digitally, Alistair Inglis, Peter Ling and Vera Joosten
Delivering Learning on the Net: The Why, What and How of Online Education, Martin Weller
The Design and Production of Self-Instructional Materials, Fred Lockwood
Developing Innovation in Online Learning: An Action Research Framework, Maggie McPherson and Miguel Baptista Nunes
Exploring Open and Distance Learning, Derek Rowntree
Flexible Learning in a Digital World, Betty Collis and Jef Moonen
Improving Your Students' Learning, Alistair Morgan
Innovation in Open and Distance Learning, Fred Lockwood and Anne Gooley
Integrated E-Learning: Implications for Pedagogy, Technology and Organization, Wim Jochems, Jeroen van Merriënboer and Rob Koper
Key Terms and Issues in Open and Distance Learning, Barbara Hodgson
The Knowledge Web: Learning and Collaborating on the Net, Marc Eisenstadt and Tom Vincent
Learning and Teaching in Distance Education, Edited by Som Naidu
Making Materials-Based Learning Work, Derek Rowntree
Managing Open Systems, Richard Freeman
Mega-Universities and Knowledge Media, John S Daniel
Objectives, Competencies and Learning Outcomes, Reginald F Melton
The Open Classroom: Distance Learning In and Out of Schools, Edited by Jo Bradley
Online Education Using Learning Objects, Edited by Rory McGreal
Open and Distance Learning: Case Studies from Education, Industry and Commerce, Stephen Brown
Open and Flexible Learning in Vocational Education and Training, Judith Calder and Ann McCollum
Planning and Management in Distance Education, Santosh Panda
Preparing Materials for Open, Distance and Flexible Learning, Derek Rowntree
Programme Evaluation and Quality, Judith Calder
Reforming Open and Distance Learning, Terry Evans and Daryl Nation
Reusing Online Resources, Alison Littlejohn
Student Retention in Online, Open and Distance Learning, Ormond Simpson
Supporting Students in Online, Open and Distance Learning, 2nd Edition, Ormond Simpson
Teaching with Audio in Open and Distance Learning, Derek Rowntree
Teaching Through Projects, Jane Henry
Towards More Effective Open and Distance Learning, Perc Marland
Understanding Learners in Open and Distance Education, Terry Evans
Using Communications Media in Open and Flexible Learning, Robin Mason
The Virtual University, Steve Ryan, Bernard Scott, Howard Freeman and Daxa Patel

Online Education using Learning Objects

Edited by

Rory McGreal

RoutledgeFalmer
Taylor & Francis Group

LONDON AND NEW YORK

First published 2004 by Routledge
Reprinted in paperback 2006 by Routledge
2 Park Square, Milton Park, Abingdon, Oxon, OX14 4RN

Simultaneously published in the USA and Canada
by Routledge
270 Madison Avenue, New York, NY 10016

Transferred to Digital Printing 2005

Routledge is an imprint of the Taylor & Francis Group

© 2004 Edited by Rory McGreal

Typeset in Times
by Florence Production Ltd, Stoodleigh, Devon
Printed and bound in Great Britain by
Antony Rowe Ltd, Chippenham, Wiltshire

British Library Cataloguing in Publication Data
A catalogue record for this book is available from the British Library

Library of Congress Cataloging in Publication Data
   Online education using learning objects/(edited by) Rory McGreal.
      p. cm.
   Includes bibliographical references.
   1. Internet in higher education.   2. Education, Higher – Electronic
   information resources.   3. Education, Higher – Computer-assisted
   instruction.   I. McGreal, Rory, 1950–
   LB2395.7.O65 2004
   378.1'734 – dc22   2003023345

ISBN 0–415–33512–4 (hbk)
ISBN 0–415–41660-4 (pbk)

Contents

Figures

Tables

Contributors

Heidrun Allert, Learning Laboratory, Lower Saxony, Germany, allert@learninglab.de

Mohamed Ally, Computer Science and Information Studies, Athabasca University, Canada, mohameda@athabascau.ca

Terry Anderson, Canada Research Chair, Athabasca University, Canada, terrya@athabascau.ca

Luis Anido, Universidade de Vigo, Spain, lanido@det.uvigo.es

Karen Belfer, Simon Fraser University, Surrey, Canada, kbelfer@sfu.ca

Jan Daniels, Open University of the Netherlands, jan.daniels@ou.nl

Hadhami Dhraief, Learning Laboratory, Lower Saxony, Germany, dhraief @learninglab.de

Monique Doorten, Open University of the Netherlands, Monique.doorten@ou.nl

Stephen Downes, National Research Council Canada, Moncton, New Brunswick, stephen@downes.ca

Erik Duval, ARIADNE, Dept. Computerwetenschappen, K. U. Leuven, Belgium, erik.duval@cs.kuleuven.ac.be

René van Es, Educational Technology Expertise Centre, Open University of the Netherlands, rene.vanes@ou.nl

Norm Friesen, CanCore/EduSource Project, Athabasca University, Canada, normf@athabascau.ca

Bas Giesbers, Open University of the Netherlands, bas.giesbers@ou.nl

Louis Guérette, Télé université du Québec, lguerette@licef.teluq.uquebec.ca

Marek Hatala, Assistant Professor, Simon Fraser University, Surrey, Canada, mhatala@sfu.ca

Susan Hesemeier, CanCore/EduSource Project, Athabasca University, Canada, susanh@athabascau.ca

Wayne Hodgins, Learnativity.com, USA, wayne.hodgins@autodesk.com

José Janssen, Open University of the Netherlands, jose.janssen@ou.nl

Pythagoras Karampiperis, Informatics and Telematics Institute (ITI), Center for Research and Technology – Hellas (CERTH), Greece, karampiperis@iti.gr

Neil R. Kestner, Charles Barré Professor of Chemistry and Former President of the Faculty Senate, Louisiana State University, Baton Rouge, LA, USA, kestner@lsu.edu

Rob Koper, Educational Technology Expertise Centre, Open University of the Netherlands, rob.koper@ou.nl

Fuhua Oscar Lin, Computer Science and Information Studies, Athabasca University, Canada, oscarl@athabascau.ca

Karin Lundgren-Cayrol, Téléuniversité du Québec, kayrol@licef.teluq.uquebec.ca

Jon Mason, Executive Consultant, Education Au Limited, Australia, jmason@educationau.edn.au

Rory McGreal, Associate Vice President, Research, Athabasca University, rory@athabascau.ca

Alexis Miara, Téléuniversité du Québec, amiara@licef.teluq.uquebec.ca

Wolfgang Nejdl, Researcher, Learning Laboratory, Lower Saxony, Germany, nejdl@learninglab.de

John C. Nesbit, Simon Fraser University, Surrey, Canada, jnesbit@sfu.ca

Mikael Nilsson, Knowledge Management Research Group, Royal Institute of Technology, Stockholm, Sweden, mini@nada.knth.se

Sean B. Palmer, Web developer, Infomesh.net, UK, sean@mysterylights.com

Gilbert Paquette, Canada Research Chair, Télé-université du Québec, gpaquette@licef.teluq.uquebec.ca

Anita Petrinjak, EduSource, Athabasca University, Canada, anitah@athabascau.ca

Pithamber R. Polsani, Assistant Professor, University of Arizona, USA, pithamber@email.arizona.edu

Griff Richards, Instructor, British Columbia Institute of Technology, Canada, griff@sfu.ca

Christoph Richter, Researcher, Learning Laboratory, Lower Saxony, Germany, richter@learninglab.de

Anthony Roberts, TeleCampus, TeleEducation NB, Canada, toni@tele-campus.edu

Robby Robson, Chair, IEEE Metadata Standards Committee, USA, rrobson@eduworks.com

Demetrios G. Sampson, Informatics and Telematics Institute (ITI), Center for Research and Technology – Hellas (CERTH), Greece, sampson@iti.gr

Peter B. Sloep, Open University of the Netherlands, Fontys University of Professional Education, Netherlands, peter.sloep@ou.nl

Mike Sosteric, Athabasca University, Canada, mikes@athabascau.ca

Series Editor's Foreword

We are told we are entering the knowledge economy; where knowledge is power and where the future prosperity of whole countries will depend upon the knowledge and skills of their workforce. To compete internationally we are told an investment in people, in their education and training, and exploitation of the new media is vital. The Consultation Document *Towards a Unified e-Learning Strategy*, UK Government Department for Education and Skills [http://www.dfes.gov.uk/elearningstrategy], launched in June 2003, illustrates one national initiative – an initiative being repeated in many countries.

Certainly, higher education is expanding rapidly around the world, but the consensus is that the resources and facilities needed are insufficient to meet this demand, even in developed countries. For example, it is estimated that today there are about 70 million learners in higher education and that this number will more than double to 160 million in 2025. Many believe that it will not be possible to simply *scale up* current provision, to build more institutions, to train more teachers and to replicate more courses. Many believe that to meet the challenge we will need to teach differently, to embrace the new technologies, to exploit cost effective ways of teaching and learning and empower learners. The growth of open, distance and flexible learning programmes and use of Communications and Information Technology is evidence of institutions striving to meet these challenges – of teaching differently. The reuse of existing materials – to make best use of the time and resources available to teachers and thus to learners is an obvious strategy and the basis of this book *Online Education using Learning Objects* by Rory McGreal; it complements the book *Reusing Online Resources: A sustainable approach to e-learning* by Allison Littlejohn published last year.

Rory McGreal has brought together an authoritative group of colleagues, from around the world, who are both theoreticians and practitioners and who are united in their desire to share current thinking and good practice. Their chapters span this rapidly developing field, from the creation of learning objects, current applications to future developments. The scope of the book, attention to detail and clarity will not only demystify the activities of these pioneers but will reassure many who have *recycled* materials for different audiences and made them available for others. For most readers the concepts behind reusing Learning Objects are not new – but their operation on the scales envisaged is both exciting and challenging.

I am sure you will find this book an invaluable resource and that your learners will reap the rewards that exploiting Learning Objects will bring.

Fred Lockwood
May 2004

Preface

Interest in learning objects (LOs) in education has been growing steadily since the late 1990s. This interest is coming primarily from educators who have experience in putting their course materials or their entire courses online. This book can serve as a manual for these educators and other researchers and practitioners who wish to know more about what is happening in the field of learning objects and metadata. Its principal goal is to provide readers with an overview of the field and an understanding of the basic terms, the ongoing discussions among the experts, the creation of learning objects, some of the current applications being used and how all this might fit into the future development of the Semantic Web.

This book will serve as a good reference source for both researchers and practitioners involved in the business of putting learning resources online. Readers should profit from a general introduction to the field of LOs and from the more in-depth investigation of some specific areas of discussion and application which follow.

The contents should be of interest to teachers, course developers, instructional designers, librarians, knowledge engineers, students of e-learning and other educational professionals. Knowledge of LOs and metadata is becoming recognized as essential for educators concerned with developing and delivering learning content for the World Wide Web. This book is a resource for a growing number of course developers in universities, community colleges, schools, private training institutes and the workplace. As course developers become more sophisticated in their e-learning skills, they are coming to recognize the relevance of applying metadata to well-conceived and constructed digital LOs. The book is also relevant for postgraduate or upper level undergraduate courses in instructional design and course development for programmes in educational technology, distance education, and so on.

The book is divided into five parts:

1. Learning Objects and Metadata
2. Constructing and Creating Learning Objects

3. Contextualization and Standardization of Learning Objects
4. Learning Object Profiles, Applications and Models
5. From the Semantic Web to EML and Instructional Engineering

The first part – Learning Objects and Metadata – launches the discussion with a variety of opinions on what LOs are at the theoretical and practical levels. It raises some objections to the use of LOs and introduces the notion of pedagogical design and educational modelling languages. The section concludes by introducing the concept of a taxonomy of learning objects and their components.

In the second part – Constructing and Creating Learning Objects – some of the challenges of creating and using LOs are presented along with some approaches to their design. Drawing on concepts from computer science, it further describes LOs from a simple technical perspective. Peirce's theory of signs is put forward as one approach to designing them. Another chapter addresses the question of how to deal with the reuse of existing course materials, on both the individual and organizational levels. The pedagogical inner structure of learning objects is also described, based on recently developed pedagogical meta-languages. This section concludes with a review of evaluation models that can be applied to LOs in which a convergent participation model is assessed in relation to other models of software evaluation.

In part three – Contextualization and Standardization of Learning Objects – the different contributors explore how information products or resources become LOs. This section highlights the issue of context in determining what might best inform the next generation of metadata schema that will in turn best support learning, education and training. It presents ideas for the use of LOs guided by different models of learning and instructional design using different interfaces. The issue of standardization is also raised with a view to enabling the reuse and interoperation of LOs among diverse systems. The section concludes with a description of a Learning Object Metadata Management System (LOMMS).

The fourth part – Learning Object Profiles, Applications and Models – introduces a metadata application profile, some peer-to-peer tools, a learning content management system (LCMS) and a LO repository. CanCore is a metadata application profile that provides simple recommendations for implementing the semantics and syntax for the international metadata standard, the IEEE LOM. POOL and Edutella are two examples of peer-to-peer (P2P) networks for exchanging information about LOs. An overview of the management functions of Explor@2, a third-generation LCMS system, is described. And the MERLOT LOR review process is examined.

The fifth section, From the Semantic Web to EML and Instructional Engineering, introduces more complex issues beginning with the Semantic Web and educational modelling languages (EMLs). Reparitory interoperability issues are raised and a proposed solution based on connector architecture is discussed. Intelligent agents are introduced along with a methodology for modelling and managing knowledge for web-based adaptive course generation. Finally, an instructional engineering approach is introduced, supporting the analysis, creation, production and delivery planning of a learning system.

An Appendix provides a listing of many of the organizations involved in the LOs and metadata community. This listing is also available online at http://www.irrodl.org/content/v3.2/tech11.html.

Acknowledgements

I would like to thank the people and organizations that have helped in realizing the publication of this book. Foremost in my mind are the contributors of the different chapters, who so willingly share their knowledge in this volume. I also wish to express my gratitude to Athabasca University and Alan Davis, Vice President Academic for his encouragement in my position, supporting my work on this research project, and to Alice Tieulie for her special assistance. Other organizations and people who have contributed to the success of this publication include: the Netera Alliance: Doug Macleod; CANARIE: Jamie Rossiter; Industry Canada: Michael Nadler, Mary DaCosta and David Beattie (School Net); and Alberta Learning: Garry Popowich. Special thanks to Terry Anderson, Canada Research Chair in Distance Education, and James O'Driscoll for his advice and encouragement. And I would like to especially thank Kathleen Fay for her extensive help in editing and formatting the chapters.

I also wish to thank the following publications and organizations that have given permission to authors to adapt articles or use figures for publication in this book:

Athabasca University's Centre for Distance Education for permission to publish Chapters 1, 2, 7 and Appendix. These chapters are partially based on articles published in the *International Review of Research in Open and Distance Learning*. Chapter 1 is partially based on an article originally published as:

Downes, S. (2000, 22 May). (accessed 28 April 2003). The Need for and Nature of Learning Objects: Some Assumptions and a Premise, (Online) http://www. newstrolls.com/news/dev/downes/column000523_1.htm.

Chapter 2 is based on an article, originally published as:

Sosteric, M. and Hesemeier, S. (accessed 1 December 2002) When is a learning object not an object: A first step towards a theory of learning objects, *International Review of Research in Open and Distance Learning*, **3** (2), (Online) http://www. irrodl.org/content/v3.2/index.html.

The image in Figure 2.1 An example of a learning object, is printed with permission from the CAREO Repository. It is available at http://aloha. netera.ca/uploads/crdc/unt5049b.jpg.

Steve Slosser of the Joint ADL Co-Laboratory has granted permission to use his diagram in Figure 4.1 ADL and the sharable content object reference model. The Association for Media and Technology in Education of Canada (AMTEC) grants permission for Chapter 11, which is based on this article:

Nesbit, J. C., Belfer, K. and Vargo, J. (2002) A convergent participation model for evaluation of LOs, *Canadian Journal of Learning and Technology*, **28** (3): 105–120.

Chapter 7 is partially based on:

Downes, S. (2001). (accessed 29 April 2003). Learning Objects: Resources for distance education worldwide. International Review of Research in Open and Distance Education, 2(1) (Online) http://www.irrodl.org/content/v2.1/downes.html

Chapter 18 is based on work presented at the IS2002, Informing Science + IT Education Conference, June, 2002, Cork, Ireland. It is published with the permission of the IS2002 organization (IS2002, 2003) as:

Richards, G., McGreal, R. and Friesen, N. (2002) Learning object repository technologies for telelearning: The evolution of POOL and CANCORE, *Proceedings of the Informing Science + IT Education Conference*, IS 2002, Cork, Ireland.

Chapter 24 was supported in part by the Canadian TeleLearning Network of Centres of Excellence through a grant to Dr Tom Calvert at Simon Fraser University, and through the CANARIE e-Learning Program. Dr Hatala's work is supported by a grant from Canada's National Sciences and Engineering Sciences Research Council.

The IEEE Intellectual Property Rights Office grants permission for the use of Figure 25.5 An example of topic trees.

Acronyms and abbreviations

ADDIE	Assess needs, Design, Develop, Implement and Evaluate
ADISA	un atelier distribué d'ingénierie d'un système d'apprentissage [a distributed engineering workshop for a learning system]
ADL	Advanced Distributed Learning
ANSI	American National Standards Institute
API	Application Programming Interface
ARIADNE	Alliance of Remote Instructional Authoring and Distribution Networks for Europe
AU	Athabasca University
BELLE	Broadband Enabled Lifelong Learning Environment
CANARIE	Canadian Network for Advanced Research for Industry and Education
CanCore	Canadian Core
CAREO	Campus Alberta Repository of Educational Objects
CASE	Computer-Aided Software Engineering
CEdMA	Computer Education Management Association
CEN/ISSS	Comité Européen de Normalisation/Information Society Standardization System
CEN/ISSS/LT	CEN/ISSS Learning Technologies
CORBA	Common Object Request Broker Architecture
CS	Computer Science
CUBER	CUrriculum BuildER
DAML+OIL	DARPA Agent Markup Language + Ontology Inference Layer
DARPA	Defense Advanced Research Projects Agency
DC	Dublin Core
DCG	Dynamic Course Generation
DCMES	Dublin Core Metadata Element Set
DCMI	Dublin Core Metadata Initiative

DCQ	Dublin Core Qualified
DIN	Deutsches Institut für Normung (German Institute of Standardization)
DIN-EBN	DIN Entwicklungsbegleitende Normung (Research & Development Phase Standardization)
DLS	Distributed Learning System
DTD	Data Type Definition
EAC	Encoded Archival Content
EAD	Encoded Archival Description
ECL	eduSource Communication Layer
ECP	Educational Content Provider
EML	Educational Modelling Language
EPSS	Electronic Performance Support Systems
ERC	Electronic Resource Citation
ESP	Educational Service Provider
FAQ	Frequently Asked Questions
FOAF	Friend Of A Friend (an RDFWeb project)
FOPL	First Order Predicate Logic
FTP	File Transfer Protocol
GEM	Gateway to Educational Materials
GESTALT	Getting Educational Systems Talking Across Leading-edge Technologies
HTML	Hypertext Markup Language
HTTP	Hypertext Transfer Protocol
ICOM-CIDOC	International Committee for Documentation of the International Council of Museums – Comité International pour la Documentation du Conseil
ID	Instructional Design
IE	Instructional Engineering
IEEE	Institute of Electrical and Electronics Engineers
IEEE LTSC	IEEE Learning Technology Standards Committee
IMS	formerly Instructional Management System
IMS DRI	IMS Digital Repository Interoperability Group
IMS LD	IMS Learning Design
ISD	Instructional System Design
ISO	International Standards Organization
ISO/IEC JTC1	ISO/International Electrotechnical Commission Joint Technical Committee 1
JXTA	Juxtapose; a project to explore a vision of distributed network computing using peer-to-peer topology
K12	Kindergarten to Grade 12 (US primary and secondary schools)
LAN	Local Area Network
LCD	Learner-Centered Design

LCMS	Learning Content Management System
LD	Learning Design (IMS specification)
LMS	Learning Management System
LO	Learning Object
LOM	Learning Object Metadata
LOMMS	Learning Object Metadata Management Systems
LOR	Learning Object Repository
LORI	Learning Object Rating Instrument
LP	Learning Plan
LP-net	Learning Plan network
LTSA	Learning Technology Systems Architecture
LU	Learning Unit
MERLOT	Multimedia Educational Resource for Learning and Online Teaching
METS	Metadata Encoding Transmission Standard
MISA	méthode d'ingénierie d'un système d'apprentissage [Learning Systems Engineering Method]
MLE	Managed Learning Environment
NCSA	National Center for Supercomputing Applications
NSDL	National Science Digital Library
N-Triples	A line-based, plain text format for encoding an RDF graph
OAI	Open Archives Initiative
OAI PMH	OAI Protocol for Metadata Harvesting
OIL	Ontology Inference Layer
OKI	Open Knowledge Initiative
OLR	Open Learning Repository
OOP	Object-Oriented Programming
OUNL	Open University of the Netherlands (Dutch Open University)
OUNL EML	OUNL Educational Modelling Language
OWL	Web Ontology Language (Successor to DARPA-OIL)
OSI	Open System Interconnection
P2P	Peer-to-Peer
PALO	Spanish EML
PMH	Protocol for Metadata Harvesting
PN	Petri Nets
POND	A repository using the POOL protocol or simply a larger, community implementation of SPLASH
POOL	Portal for Online Objects in Learning; a web-based client server repository using the CanCore guidelines
QoS	Quality of Service
QT&I	Question and TestInteroperability; an IMS specification
RAD	Rapid Application Design

RDF	Resource Description Framework
RDFS	RDF Schema Specification 1.0; describes how to use RDF to describe RDF vocabularies; the specification also describes a basic vocabulary
RDF Schema	A general-purpose web language
RIO	Reusable Information Object
RLO	Reusable Learning Object
SCORM	Sharable Content Object Reference Model
SeSDL	Scottish electronic Staff Development Library
SIF	Schools Interoperability Framework
SingCore	Singapore Metadata application profile
SiRPAC	Simple RDF Parser & Compiler; a reference implementation of an RDF parser which does a compilation process from XML encoding syntax to the triples (3-tables) of the underlying data models
SMETE	Science, Mathematics, Engineering and Technology Education
SMIL	Synchronized Multimedia Integration Language
SOAP	Simple Open Access Protocol
SPLASH	A desktop client communicating with other peers via the peer-to-peer POOL protocol
SWEBOK	Software Engineering Body of Knowledge
TL-NCE	Telelearning Network of Centers of Excellence
UML	Unified Modelling Language
URI	Uniform Resource Identifier
URL	Uniform Resource Locator
URN	Uniform Resource Name
VLC	Virtual Learning Center
VRP	Validating RDF Parser; a tool for analysing, validating and processing RDF schemas and resource descriptions
W3C	World Wide Web Consortium
XHTML	XML + HTML
XML	Extensible Markup Language
WYSIWYG	What You See Is What You Get
Z39.50	A library metadata standard IS

Introduction

Roll over Napster and make way for Learnster. With the emergence of new internationally recognized metadata specifications, the peer-to-peer exchange of lessons and courses by learners, instructors and course developers is becoming possible. Imagine having seamless access to a vast store of learning resources such as animations, videos, simulations, educational games, and multimedia texts in the same way that Napster users have access to music files. Learning objects (LOs) are what make this happen.

LOs are sometimes defined as being educational resources that can be employed in technology-supported learning. With appropriate metadata descriptions, they can become modular units that can be assembled together to form lessons and courses. A LO can be based on an electronic text, a simulation, a website, a .gif graphic image, a Quicktime movie, a Java applet or any other resource that can be used in learning.

Learning object '-abilities'

Online LOs enable a range of '-abilities'. These include:

- Accessibility: instructional components can be accessed from one remote location and delivered to many other locations;
- Interoperability: instructional components can be developed in one location with one set of tools (or platform) or in another location with a different set of tools (or platform);
- Adaptability: instruction can be tailored to individual and situational needs;
- Reusability: instructional components can be incorporated into multiple applications;
- Durability: instructional components can be used when base technology changes, without the need for redesigning or recoding;
- Affordability: learning effectiveness can be significantly increased, while reducing time and costs;

- Assessability: pedagogical effectiveness, price, and usability can be assessed;
- Discoverability: components can be easily found using simple under-standable search terms;
- Interchangeability: one component can be substituted for another;
- Manageability: components can be handily found, inserted, replaced and substituted;
- Reliability: the other 'abilities' can be counted on to work when needed; and
- Retrieveability: components can be retrieved when and where you want them.

(List expanded from Parmentier, 1999)

Learning object granularity

Online, LOs exist and interoperate at different levels of granularity. The simplest level is the content, information or knowledge object. This could be a simple text document, a photograph, a video clip, a 3D image, a Java applet or any other object that might be used for online learning.

For example, a video clip from the Pope's visit to Cuba would be an example of a simple media object. It becomes more useful for learners when a lesson is added to it. Many different lessons can be created from one component. This one video clip could form part of lessons in religion, politics, history, ethics, and media studies. And many other subjects could be created from this one video clip.

Longer learning experiences or groupings of lessons are considered to be modules. A module normally comprises less than 10 hours of learning. When lessons are longer than 10 hours or if they consist of more than one module, they are considered to be a course. A group of courses that lead towards a certificate or diploma is considered to be a programme. These are all LOs at different levels of granularity as shown in Figure 0.1.

The importance of learning objects

In the past, craftsmen, known as cobblers, created shoes on request for individuals. Shoes were very rare and many people did not have enough money to buy them. With mass production, shoes could be produced very cheaply so that everyone could afford to buy a pair. However, they were all the same, and people had to fit into standard sizes and styles. Now, mass-customization is possible because with the aid of technology, one-off products can be produced much more cheaply.

Education is following a similar path. In the past only the rich could afford to pay tutors or send their children to private schools. With mass education, students are trained in large groups of cohorts, who all learn the same things at the same time. With technology, learning can now be

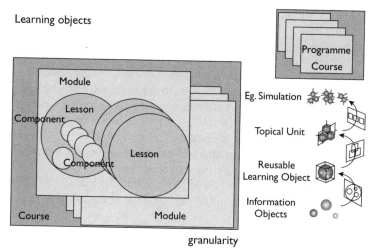

Figure 0.1 Learning object granularity

individualized and mass-customized. LOs can be used by course developers to engineer courses and assemble them to meet the needs of individual students. Moreover, independent students can construct their own courses by assembling LOs relevant to their own needs. We are moving from a one-size-fits-all generic approach to learning, towards one that is more individualized and focused.

However, this development does not mean that every course for every different individual needs to be designed from scratch. Many institutions and organizations presently develop lessons, modules and courses on common topics. Large numbers of similar lessons are being adapted for online delivery. This process can be very time consuming and expensive, making sharing essential.

Downes (2000b) argues that the world does not need tens of thousands of similar learning topics. Just as a cobbler did not go out and kill an animal, skin it, select the desired pieces of hide, and tan them for every single commission, but rather had various pieces in stock from which he could assemble to order, so a dozen well designed multimedia LOs could be used in thousands of courses. Online courses should therefore be designed as a collection of LOs rather than as whole, inseparable, long courses. In order to search for and find these LOs, descriptions of their characteristics are needed. For this you need metadata that describe their many features. Metadata are essential for addressing LOs.

Metadata

It is at this point that metadata come in. In order to search for and find LOs, which might be ideal for a particular course, descriptions of their *many* characteristics are needed. This is what metadata do. They are essential for addressing LOs.

Metadata are often described as being 'data about data'. This description is not particularly useful without examples. Have you tried to find a house when there are no street signs or house numbers? These indicators may not be necessary in small villages, but in large cities, they become essential. Street names and house numbers are widely accepted descriptors that make it easier for people to find a particular building. The street names and numbers are a form of metadata.

Another example of metadata is a date that can be described in a number of different formats or specifications, for example: March 2, 2001, 2001-05-02, 02-05-2001. A library card is another commonly known type of metadata. The author, title, ISBN code are all fields in this standard metadata format (see Figure 0.2).

Metadata can be either objective as in the example of a library card that gives basic factual information, or subjective, providing opinions and evaluations. The opinions supplied by readers at the Amazon.com site are good examples of subjective metadata. Online lessons and courses could have both objective metadata such as the course name and description, and subjective metadata made up of student opinions or professional ratings.

Metadata characteristics

Metadata includes a listing of commonly defined fields for each LO. These fields conform to an accepted set of rules. These rules provide a means

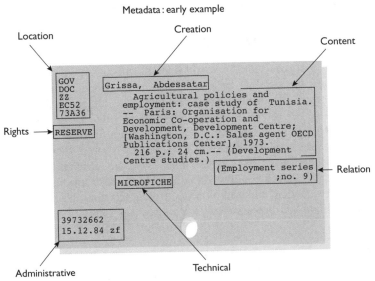

Figure 0.2 A library card showing metadata

of creating, handling and storing data and electronically transferring information using common standards that enable international interoperability. Institutions normally insist on a subset of mandatory fields. These are often accompanied by a larger listing of optional fields. Addition fields can normally be added, so that the specifications are generally extensible.

Metadata specifications

The principal metadata standard for LOs is IEEE LTSC LOM <http://ltsc. ieee.org/index.html>. Many organizations such as ADL, ARIADNE, and IMS have been involved either directly or indirectly in the development of the specifications on which this standard is based. A variety of application profiles for the implementation of these standards such as SCORM, CanCore and SingCore have been developed. A list of the different organizations involved along with an explanation of the difference between a standard, a specification, and an application profile is available in the Appendix.

Learning object analogies

Several analogies or metaphors have been used to elucidate the context for using LOs. These include the following:

- Lego blocks (Hartnett, 2002; Hodgins and Conner, 2000; Sheperd, 2000);
- building materials (Duval and Hodgins, Chapter 5 in this book; Hodgins (cited in Trondsen, 2002);
- atoms/molecules (Wiley, 1999);
- organic entities such as cells or more complex organisms (Paquette and Rosca, 2002).

The Lego blocks analogy was taken from a metaphor that has frequently been used in object-oriented programming. Sheperd (2000) and Trondsen (2002) credit Hodgins as being among the first to use this analogy for LOs. It compares them to small uniform building blocks that can be assembled together to form different types of constructions. The analogy arises from the concept that any Lego block can be assembled/combined with any other Lego block in an infinite number of ways. This can be done so simply that even a child can create things with them.

The limitations of this rather generalized Lego analogy become apparent to anyone who has experimented with course construction. The most important of these stems from the lack of uniformity in LOs, which can be quite different in terms of content, quality and size. They cannot always be easily assembled/combined like Lego blocks with every other LO. SCORM and Cisco's RLO proponents aim to do this, but it is all too often problematic. Far from a child being able to assemble them, the assembly/combination of LOs can sometimes test the skills of a professional educator or even educational technologist.

Duval and Hodgins in Chapter 5 prefer the analogy of the construction industry in which up to 85 per cent of the building materials consist of standardized components such as bathroom fixtures, windows, doors, stairs, and so on. They note that attempts to provide entire kitchens or bathrooms as components have never caught on because they were not flexible enough to fit into tailor-made buildings. Likewise, they believe that smaller LOs are useful, but that large LOs comprising entire courses will not catch on. This construction analogy is superior to the Lego one as it allows for the complexity of different types of objects and points to their dependence on skilled professionals for implementation.

Wiley (1999) sees even greater complexity in LO implementations. He prefers the analogy of atoms and molecules. Some LOs, like atoms, cannot be broken down into smaller units without considerable effort; other LOs, like some atoms and molecules, do not fit well together. The nature of LOs may restrict what can be created with them. They are the basic components of online courses, but different ones function in different ways. Like atoms and molecules, only certain LOs can be assembled or combined together and they fit together only in limited ways. For example, a LO on statistics may fit into a variety of different contexts, but not all. It may work well in sociology and psychology courses, but may find no place in a literature course. It would probably combine better with other LOs on statistics, but it might also combine well with lessons on a wide variety of other topics. As with the chemistry professional combining molecules, it can require the hands of an experienced learning professional to know which combinations work and which ones do not.

Paquette and Rosca (2002) introduce an organic metaphor for LOs, in which cells can be combined to form simple or complex organisms, in which the whole is greater than the parts. They refer to this as an ecology of educational organisms. They see the ideal LO as being the equivalent of a complete organism on its own that nevertheless can be subsumed and well integrated into another entity when aggregated into a larger organism. A LO should be autonomous, yet possess the necessary plasticity to combine with other LOs to create something greater than a collection of parts. As with living organisms, some LOs are capable of existing alone, while others need to exist in combination with other complementary LOs.

Learning objects: A definition?

One would expect that a book about LOs would be able to provide the reader with a commonly accepted definitive definition. At present, this is proving very difficult. The scholars contributing to this volume and others conducting research in the field are finding it remarkably difficult to come up with a common definition. Nor is there any agreement even on the terms used to describe LOs.

The terminology

Different terms used in defining LOs include:

- asset (Wiley, 2000);
- component (Ip *et al.*, 1997; Koutlis, Roschelle and Reppening, 1999; Quinn and Hobbs, 2000; Roschelle *et al.*, 1999);
- content object (ADL, 2003; OASIS, 2003; Shabajee, 2002; Slosser, 2001);
- educational object (Ilich, 1971; EOE, 2003; Friesen, 2001);
- information object (Epsilon Learning Systems, 2003; Wieseler, 1999; Wiley, 1999);
- knowledge object (Merrill, 1999; Paquette and Rosca, 2002);
- learning object (generic) term credited to W. Hodgins (Jacobsen, 2001);
- learning resource (IMS Global Learning Consortium, 2000; Koper, 2003; Papatheodorou, Vassiliou and Simon, 2002; Paquette and Rosca, 2002);
- media object (ADL, 2001; Shabajee, 2002);
- raw media element (CanCore, 2003; Duval and Hodgins, Chapter 5);
- RIO (reusable information object) (Cisco Systems Reusable Information Object strategy, 1999; Wieseler, 1999);
- RLO (reusable learning object) (Barritt and Lewis, 2002; Cisco Systems, 2001; MERLOT, 2002);
- unit of learning (Sloep, Chapter 10);
- unit of study (Koper, 2001).

An examination of the various terms reveals that despite the differences of opinion, four general types of meaning can be discerned. These are shown in Table 0.1. They range from the general to the particular. There are (1) objects that could be anything; (2) objects that could be anything

Table 0.1 Learning object terminology

Anything	Anything digital	Anything for learning	Specific learning environment
Asset	Content object	Educational object	RLO
Component	Information object	Learning object	Unit of learning
Learning resource	Knowledge object		Unit of study
	Media object		
	Raw media element		
	RIO		

digital; (3) digital objects that have been designed with an ostensible learning purpose or outcome; and (4) other objects specific to a single approach or proprietary standard like those of SCORM or Cisco's RLOs (Barritt *et al.*, 1999; OASIS, 2003). Figure 0.3 shows how they fit together. The smaller circles are more specific with meanings fitting within the definitions of the larger more general circles.

Definition landscape

In line with the terminology, the assortment of what can be considered to be a LO ranges from anything and everything, through anything digital, to only objects that have an ostensible learning purpose, to those that support learning only in a particular or specific context. Among the definitions proposed are the following, moving from the general to the specific:

1. Anything and everything (Downes, 2003; Friesen, 2001; Mortimer, 2002);
2. Anything digital, whether it has an educational purpose or not (Wiley, 1999);
3. Anything that has an educational purpose (Doorten, Giesbers, Janssen *et al.*, Chapter 9; Quinn and Hobbs, 2000);
4. Only digital objects that have a formal educational purpose (Dunning, 2002; Koper, 2003; Sosteric and Hesemeier, Chapter 2; and Polsani, Chapter 8); and

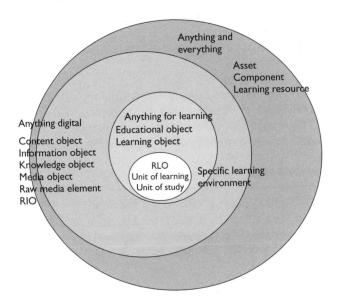

Figure 0.3 Terminology for learning objects

5. Only digital objects that are marked in a specific way for educational purposes (Alberta Learning, 2002; Cisco Systems, 2001; Koper, 2001; Rehak and Mason, 2003; Wieseler, 1999; Koper and van Es, Chapter 3; and Sloep, Chapter 10).

A diagram of these views of LOs is available in Figure 0.4. The north–south line represents the digital only/digital + anything dichotomy and the east–west axis represents the learning specific to generic continuum. The bottom left quadrant shows the extreme position of a LO as being anything while the opposite quadrant includes both digital LOs with an ostensible learning focus and the more explicit digital LOs for specific implementations. The top left quadrant shows LOs as anything digital, opposing the bottom right quadrant showing LOs with a learning focus including non-digital objects.

Figure 0.5 shows the same information in which the narrower definitions form subsets of the more generic ones. Note that the 'Anything for learning' circle is transparent as it overlaps the digital and non-digital domains.

Anything and everything

In most discussions of LOs, participants can agree that LOs are digital, reusable, and are intended to support learning. The IEEE (2002) defines LOs as 'any entity, digital or non-digital, which can be used, reused or

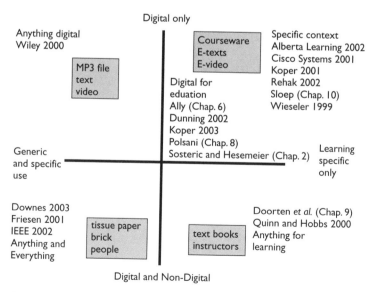

Figure 0.4 Learning object definitions quadrant

referenced during technology supported learning'. This definition is so broad as to encompass anything and everything. Merrill (2002) notes that it is 'as small as a drop and as big as the ocean'.

Downes (2003) uses the example of tissue paper to argue that anything and everything can be used for learning and therefore must be considered to be a LO. He argues that there is no reason to restrict a priori what counts as a LO.

> Whether something counts as a LO, depends on whether it can be used to teach or learn, and this can only be determined by its use, not by its nature. People will want to use a wide variety of objects, including even (in at least one case) a used tissue, in order to teach or learn. No good will come, therefore, of limiting a priori what objects will count as LOs and what objects will not.
>
> (Downes, 2003)

Anything digital

This approach argues that the terms 'learning object' and 'educational object' should not be used to encompass non-digital entities such as a book or even an instructor. The word 'object' in this term comes directly from object-oriented programming (OOP). This is not a coincidence. The term 'learning object' has grown out of the OOP movement (Quinn and Hobbs, 2000). The concept of LOs has been developed from OOP, much

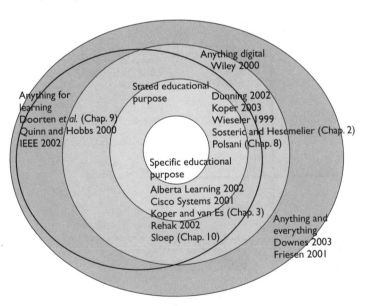

Figure 0.5 Learning object definitions from specific to generic

to the consternation of some (see Sosteric and Hesemeier, Chapter 2 and Friesen, Chapter 4). Therefore, it does make sense to limit the use of the term to digital entities only.

Wiley (2000) settles on a definition of a LO as 'any digital resource that can be reused to support learning'. Even so, as Wiley comments, 'the definition is broad enough to include the estimated 15 terabytes of information available on the publicly accessible Internet'. Thus, even restricting the definition of LOs to digital resources still does not narrow down the meaning enough for it to be useful.

Anything that has an educational purpose

Doorten *et al.* in Chapter 9 define LOs as any reusable resource, digital or non-digital that can be used to support learning activities. They point out that as long as an object is addressable it can be used. They mention examples such as web pages, applications, textbooks, calculators and microscopes. Quinn and Hobbs (2000) take this broader view also and describe LOs as 'chunks of educational content' that could be of any media type, digital or non-digital.

In contrast to Wiley (2000), who focuses on the digital or 'object' aspect of the definition of LOs, discounting the 'learning', Doorten *et al.*, Chapter 9 and Quinn and Hobbs (2000) choose to focus on the 'learning' aspect and disregard the 'object' (even though Quinn and Hobbs write about the link of LOs to OOP). I believe that the reality lies in accepting the limitation that LOs must be digital learning resources. This does not necessarily preclude LOs from referring to external non-digital objects although this might seriously affect their usability.

Digital objects that have a formal educational purpose

Sosteric and Hesemeier in Chapter 2 emphasize the intent of the object more than the structure. According to them, a LO is 'a digital file (image, movie, etc.) intended to be used for pedagogical purposes, which includes, either internally or via association, suggestions on the appropriate context within which to utilize the object'. They claim that a newspaper article would not be considered to be a LO simply because it could be used for learning. It must be linked to 'pedagogical purposes'. Polsani in Chapter 8, using Peirce's theory of signs, defines a LO as 'a form of organized knowledge content . . . involving learning purpose and reusable value'.

The triadic elements are sign, object and the interpretant. In recommending the use of Peirce's theory, Polsani accepts that a LO must fulfil a 'learning purpose'.

According to these authors, an information object becomes a LO when it is designed to be used by itself or in combination with other media objects to facilitate or promote learning. This learning should be demonstrable and testable through assessment and observation. To be a LO it must be packaged and made available for distribution as a lesson of some kind.

In Chapter 5, Duval and Hodgins refer to LOs as containing information objects, which in turn might contain raw media elements. They refer to aggregate assemblies that contain LOs and other aggregate assemblies.

Dunning (2002) not only accepts that LOs are digital objects that facilitate learning, but he seems to limit them to interactive practice exercises used to demonstrate content mastery by applying learnt content. He makes the further stipulation that the LO must also promote critical thinking through linkages to a larger course. In the same vein, Koper (2003) refers to LOs as 'units of learning' defined as digital objects with a specific educational purpose. However, he specifically excludes full courses from his definition. Ally, in Chapter 6, defines a LO as 'any digital resource that can be used and reused to achieve a specific learning outcome or outcomes'. The three key words in this definition are digital, reusable, and learning outcome.

Digital objects that are marked for specific educational purposes

Some LO proponents go further than accepting a generic digital LO approach and add special conditions to their definitions. These conditions either address problems specific to the particular users or just outline a common approach to some of the more precise operations of LOs as online applications.

Alberta Learning defines a LO for its own use:

> One or more digital assets combined and sequenced to create or support a learning experience addressing a curricular outcome(s) for an identified audience(s). A learning object can be identified, tracked, referenced, used and reused for a variety of learning experiences.
>
> (Alberta Learning, 2002)

With this meaning, Alberta Learning creates a specific definition of a LO to suit their needs. Cisco Systems (2001) also chooses a specific designation for their Reusable Learning Objects, providing detailed instructions on their formation (see also Wieseler, 1999).

In explaining SCORM, Rehak (2002) points out that it has been designed to support LOs with a particular use in mind. 'SCORM is essentially about a single-learner, self-paced and self-directed. It has a limited pedagogical model unsuited for some environments.' The initiators of SCORM – the US government and the Department of Defense – have designed SCORM to meet their particular needs for workplace training on job applications and machines. Rehak does not consider SCORM to be suitable for either the K12 or higher education environments.

Koper (2001) and Sloep, Chapter 10 referring to LOs as 'units of study' or 'units of learning' respectively, believe that an educational modelling language (EML) is necessary to get full power from the learning resources. Their EML now forms the basis of the IMS Learning Design specification and so could become acceptable more widely as being essential for the implementation of LOs in various learning contexts.

Conclusion and proposal

There are good reasons for restricting which information objects should count as LOs and which will not. When a LO has a formal, expressed learning purpose, the object becomes useful to learners. Learning can be accidental or fortuitous, but it is generally more efficient when it is focused and directed. Learners cannot always be expected to discern the learning possibilities of any accessed component. That is why we have instructional design. That is why we change information or knowledge objects to LOs. Moreover, the usefulness of a LO can best be evaluated once it has been placed in at least one specific learning context. Once it has been proven to work in one context, it can be better expected to be of some use in others.

In this way, learners can be more easily directed in their learning. This can in turn make it easier for them to achieve an unambiguous learning objective. It can be argued that this brings about an improvement in learning efficiency, which many would consider to be a good thing. In addition, the categorization and standardization of types of learning units allows the same lessons to be learnt by many different players. I suggest that such consistency in learning is of relevance in many situations, for example in skills training, such as learning a sport or a foreign language. Distinguishing between information objects that have no ostensible learning objective and LOs is useful. It could be argued that all human knowledge is based on limiting and categorizing the reality that surrounds us.

It can also be seen as a matter of practicality for educators. Professional practice is best served by limiting the definition of LOs to what practitioners typically work with. So it's a matter of usefulness to educators as much as learners.

I propose that a good working definition of LOs should be developed from the two last typologies listed earlier: digital objects that have a stated educational purpose; and digital objects that are marked for specific educational purposes. LOs can be defined as any reusable digital resource that is encapsulated in a lesson or assemblage of lessons grouped in units, modules, courses and even programmes. A lesson can be defined as a piece of instruction, normally including a learning purpose or purposes. This definition incorporates the top right quadrant of the chart in Figure 0.4. It is closer to the 'Digital for Education' group being broad enough to incorporate the 'Specific Context' group.

Summary

As course developers gain experience and as the number of online courses grows, the importance and necessity of LOs and the metadata standards that support them become more apparent. The terminology, definitions and context described in this introduction should help readers to get the most out of the chapters that follow. Efficient learning using the ever-expanding multimedia resources of the Internet will require the creation of LOs and the metadata to describe them. From anything and everything to specific digital learning resources, the future of learning is inextricably linked to the development of quality LOs.

References

ADL (2001) (accessed 26 April 2003) Sharable content object reference model Version 1.2: The SCORM overview, (Online) http://www.adlnet.org/ADLDOCS/Documents/SCORM_1.2_Overview.pdf.

ADL (2003) (accessed 28 April 2003) Sharable Content Object Reference Model (SCORM), (Online) http://www.adlnet.org/ADLDOCS/Documents/SCORM_1.2_ConformanceReq.pdf.

Alberta Learning (2002) (accessed 17 April 2003) Learn Alberta glossary, *Author*, (Online) http://www.learnalberta.ca/l.

Barritt, C., Lewis, D. and Wieseler, W. (1999) (accessed 23 April 2003) *Cisco Systems – Reusable information strategy*, (Online) http://www.cisco.com/warp/public/779/ibs/solutions/publishing/whitepapers/.

Barritt, C. and Lewis, D. (2002) (accessed 10 December 2002) Reusable learning object strategy, (Online) http://www.cisco.com/warp/public/10/wwtraining/elearning/implement/rlo_strategy_v3–1.pdf.

CanCore (2003) (accessed 17 April 2003) (Online) http://www.cancore.ca.

Cisco Systems (2001) (accessed 18 May 2002) Reusable learning object strategy. Designing information and learning objects through concept, fact, procedure, process, and principle templates, (Online) http://www.cisco.com/warp/public/10/wwtraining/elearning/implement/rlo_strategy.pdf.

Cisco Systems Reusable Information Object strategy (1999) (accessed 19 May 2003) *Cisco Systems*, (Online) http://www.cisco.com/warp/public/779/ibs/solutions/learning/whitepapers/el_cisco_rio.pdf.

Downes, S. (2000a) (accessed 20 May 2003) Exploring new directions in online learning, in *WebNet 2000*, University of New Brunswick, Fredericton, NB, (Online) http://www.atl.ualberta.ca/downes/home.html.

Downes, S. (2000b) (accessed 28 April 2003) The Need for and Nature of Learning Objects: Some Assumptions and a Premise, *News Trolls Inc.*, (Online) http://www.newstrolls.com/news/dev/downes/column000523_1.htm.

Downes, S. (2003) (accessed 5 April 2003) Paper tissue argument, *Downes blog*, (Online) http://www.downes.ca/cgibin/website/refer.cgi?item=1049084977&sender=.

Dunning, J. (2002) (accessed 18 April 2003) *Talon learning object system*, (Online) http://www.indiana.edu/~scstest/jd/learningobjects.html.

EOE (2003) (accessed 21 February 2003) *Educational object economy foundation*, (Online) http://www.eoe.org.

Epsilon Learning Systems (2003) (accessed 27 April 2003) Learning objects, *Author*, (Online) http://www.epsilonlearning.com/objects.htm.

Friesen, N. (2001) (accessed 18 April 2003) What are educational objects?, *Interactive Learning Environments*, **9** (3): 219–30, (Online) http://www.careo.org/documents/objects.html.

GESTALT (accessed 23 November 2001) (Online) http://www.fdgroup.co.uk/gestalt.

Hartnett, J. (2002) (accessed 24 April 2003) Where have all the Legos gone?, *Online Learning Magazine*, 21 February, (Online) http://www.onlinelearningmag.com/training/search/search_display.jsp?vnu_content_id=1278802.

Hodgins, W. and Conner, M. (2000) (accessed 17 April 2003) Everything you wanted to know about learning objects but were afraid to ask, *LineZine*, (Fall), (Online) http://www.linezine.com/2.1/features/wheyewtkls.htm.

IEEE (2002) (accessed 16 March 2003) *Draft standard for Learning Object Metadata (LOM)*, (Online) http://ltsc.ieee.org/doc/wg12/LOM_WD6_4.pdf.

Ilich, I. (1971) (accessed 20 April 2003) *Deschooling society* (Electronic version), http://philosophy.la.psu.edu/illich/deschool/intro.html.

IMS Global Learning Consortium (2000) (accessed 17 Apwwril 2003) IMS learning resource meta-data best practices and implementation guide, (Online) http://www.imsglobal.org/metadata/imsmdv1p2p1/imsmd_bestv1p2p1.html.

Ip, A. *et al.* (1997) Enabling re-useability of courseware components with Web-based virtual apparatus, in *What works and why, ASCILITE '97. Proceedings of the Australian Society for Computers in Learning in Tertiary Education Annual Conference*, eds R. Kevill, R. Oliver and R. Phillips, pp. 286–91, Academic Computing Services: Curtin University of Technology, Perth.

Jacobsen, P. (2001) (accessed 4 December 2001) Reusable learning objects – What does the future hold?, *E-Learning Magazine*, (Online) http://www.ltimagazine.com/ltimagazine/article/articleDetail.jsp?id=5043.

Koper, R. (2001) (accessed 28 June 2002) Modelling units of study from a peda-gogical perspective: The pedagogical meta-model behind EML, Heerlen, Open University of the Netherlands, (Online) http://eml.ou.nl/introduction/docs/ped-metamodel.pdf.

Koper, R. (2003) Combining reusable learning resources and services with peda-gogical purposeful units of learning, in *Reusing Online Resources*, ed. A. Littlejohn, pp. 46–59, Kogan Page, London.

Koutlis, M., Roschelle, J. and Reppening, A. (1999) Developing educational soft-ware components, *IEEE Computer*, **32**: 50–58.

MERLOT (2002) (accessed 23 March 2003) Multimedia educational resource for learning and online teaching, (Online) www.merlot.org.

Merrill, M. D. (1999) Instructional Transaction Theory (ITT): Instructional design based on knowledge objects, in *Instructional-design theories and models: a new paradigm of instructional theory*, ed. C. M. Reigeluth, pp. 397–424, Lawrence Erlbaum Associates, Mahwah.

Merrill, M. D. (2002) (accessed 2 June 2003) Mental models, knowledge objects, and instructional design, Brigham Young University, (Online) http://zola.byu.edu/id2scorm/2002/abstracts/merrill.html.

Mortimer, L. (2002) (accessed 1 June 2003) (Learning) objects of desire: Promise and practicality, *Learning Circuits*, (Online) http://www.learningcircuits.org/2002/apr2002/mortimer.html.

OASIS (2003) (accessed 21 February 2003) Sharable Content Object Reference Model initiative (SCORM), (Online) http://xml.coverpages.org/scorm.html.

Papatheodorou, C., Vassiliou, A. and Simon, B. (2002) (accessed 1 December 2003) Discovery of ontologies for learning resources using word-based clustering, in *ED-MEDIA 2002 Conference*, August, Denver, (Online) http://www.wu-wien.ac.at/usr/wi/bsimon/publikationen/EDMEDIA2002.pdf.

Paquette, G. and Rosca, I. (2002) (accessed 18 May 2003) Organic aggregation of knowledge objects in educational systems, *Canadian Journal of Learning Technologies* (Electronic version), **28** (3), (Online) http://www.cjlt.ca/content/vol 28.3/paquette_rosca.html.

Parmentier, M. (1999) (accessed 10 May 2001) The ABILITIES list of content enablers, *Internet Time*, (Online) http://www.internettime.com/itimegroup/astd_web/capture.htm.

Quinn, C. and Hobbs, S. (2000) (accessed 13 August 2002) Learning objects and instructional components, *Educational Technology and Society*, **3** (2), (Online) http://ifets.ieee.org/periodical/vol_2_2000/discuss_summary_0200.html.

Rehak, D. (2002) (accessed 25 March 2003) SCORM is not for everyone, *The Centre for Educational Technology Interoperability Standards*, (Online) http://www.cetis.ac.uk/content/20021002000737.

Rehak, D. and Mason, R. (2003) Keeping the learning in learning objects, in *Reusing online resources: A sustainable approach to e-learning*, ed. A. Littlejohn, pp. 20–34, Kogan, London.

Roschelle, J., DiGiano, C., Koutlis, M., Repenning, A., Jackiw, N. and Suthers, D. (1999) *Developing educational software components, IEEE Computer*, **32** (9): 50–58.

Shabajee, P. (2002) (accessed 26 April 2003) Primary multimedia objects and 'educational metadata' – A fundamental dilemma for developers of multimedia archives, *D-Lib Magazine*, **8** (6), (Online) http://www.dlib.org/dlib/june02/shabajee/06shabajee.html.

Sheperd, C. (2000) (accessed 1 June 2003) Objects of interest, *Fastrak Consulting Ltd.*, (Online) http://www.fastrak-consulting.co.uk/tactix/features/objects/objects.htm.

Slosser, S. (2001) (accessed 1 December 2003) ADL and the sharable content object reference model, *Joint ADL Co-laboratory*, (Online) http://www.nectec.or.th/courseware/pdf-documents/adl-scorm.pdf.

Trondsen, E. (2002) (accessed 1 June 2003) Learning objects symposium September 5 & 6, *SRI Consulting*, (Online) http://www.sric-bi.com/LoD/meetings/2002–09-05/LoDSymposiumNotes.pdf.

Wieseler, W. (1999) (accessed 9 May 2000) RIO: A standards-based approach for reusable information objects, *Cisco Systems*, (Online) http://www.cisco.com/warp/public/779/ibs/solutions/publishing/whitepapers/.

Wiley, D. A. (1999) (accessed 17 April 2003) The Post-LEGO Learning Object, *Author*, (Online) http://wiley.ed.usu.edu/docs/post-lego/.

Wiley, D. A. (2000) (accessed 17 April 2003) Connecting learning objects to instructional design theory: A definition, a metaphor, and a taxonomy, in *The instructional use of learning objects: Online version*, (Online) http://reusability.org/read/chapters/wiley.doc.

Part I

Learning Objects and Metadata

As pointed out in the Introduction, there are many views of LOs. In this part, the view that LOs are necessary course components is contrasted with others that are suspicious of the engineering and military origins of the LO concept. Pedagogical methodology is introduced using the educational modelling language approach, and followed by the model of taxonomies and the concept of granularity.

Stephen Downes of the National Research Council of Canada begins with a basic explanation of learning objects as digital materials that are used to create online courses accessible over the Internet through different types of repositories. He presents a solid case for the need for LOs, while explaining the costs of online learning. He argues that LOs can drastically reduce the costs of content development by facilitating sharing among students, institutions and instructors. He suggests that smaller units than courses will be shared, arguing that courses are too large and do not deliver the flexibility of smaller modules, which are more interoperable. Learning Object Repositories, Downes argues, will become networked using common standards enabling discoverability.

In Chapter 2 Sosteric and Hesemeier of Athabasca University argue that while learning objects may be revolutionary in the long term, in the short term, definition problems and conceptual confusion undermine our ability to understand and critically evaluate them. This chapter attempts to reduce the definition of learning objects to the bare essentials. In particular, they question the reliance of educators on Object-Oriented Programming (OOP), arguing that its applicability to learning objects is minor and possibly even counterproductive. They claim that much-needed time and energy are involved in trying to fit LOs into the OOP framework. They claim that even limiting OOP theory to just the reusability feature of LOs is not enough, pointing to development psychology, sociology and non-OOP areas of computation for direction in refining our understanding of LOs.

LOs, the authors assume, come equipped with features that make them not only pedagogically advantageous, but also economically and politically useful. And LO users, whether they be instructors or learners, have high expectations regarding their appropriateness and value. However, they lament the inability of present-day users to evaluate the claims.

They call for proper evaluative mechanisms to be put in place. This involves the development of theories of LOs in order to find the means to criticize and evaluate them. They suggest importing theories from other fields such as instructional design, or theories modified and distilled from eclectic sources. Their call for proper evaluation techniques is answered in one way by Nesbit and Belfer in Chapter 11 and in another approach by Kestner in Chapter 21.

As Sosteric and Hesemeier suggest, educators must relentlessly test the theories and standards using the LOs themselves. Theories must be based on lessons learnt in the actual implementation details and research conducted on the instructional effectiveness of LOs. Then, the LO research can contribute new knowledge to pedagogical theory and practice.

In Chapter 3, Koper and van Es of the Open University of the Netherlands (OUN) address the topic of pedagogical design of learning experiences. Their analysis of pedagogical models provides a meta-model from which course developers can build a notation for units of study using an educational modelling language (EML). They refer to the pedagogical meta-model behind EML/IMS LD, analysing the limitations and weaknesses in popular conceptions of LOs.

They go on to describe a containing framework for typed LOs in order to ensure a valid structure. But, they argue, such a framework is not sufficient because it lacks any pedagogical design. These theories form the basis for the design of the meta-model behind EML/IMS LD. On the other hand, the designs themselves are not enough to guarantee high-quality designs. They tend to be defined at too abstract a level, not providing enough details for the real structuring work that must be done when developing real units of learning.

EML/IMS LD makes the use of pedagogical models explicit. This is one of the factors needed to enhance the quality of a pedagogical design. So the combination of good design and good structuring of the design in a notation brings out the quality of learning. EML/IMS LD provides a framework too for communication. It can make the building of learning management systems easier and their use more effective.

Athabasca University's Norm Friesen, in Chapter 4, outlines three problems associated with the implementation of LOs, all of which are related to the dependence on technical and specialized concepts within the learning context. In particular, he focuses on the reliance on these concepts in the context of public education. The benefits of LOs such as 'systems interoperability', 'resource reusability' and 'application profiles' can appear strange when seen in many educational contexts.

Friesen's first objection is with the term 'learning object' itself, arguing that using these two words together is 'incongruous and incommensurable', one being pedagogical and the other technological. His second objection is based on the abstruseness of the term, noting that new concepts must be presented in terms that are meaningful to practitioners. His third objection is to the claim put forward by proponents of SCORM and other LO profiles for 'pedagogical neutrality', when the model may not be suitable for some learning environments and could even in some cases present a barrier. He warns us of the 'imprint of the ideology and culture of the American military-industrial complex', which he considers 'antithetical' to education.

In Chapter 5, Erik Duval and Wayne Hodgins investigate advanced and innovative interpretations of the basic concepts underlying the learning object (LO) paradigm. They consider a taxonomy of LOs and their components. This leads to a component architecture for structuring composite LOs based on the concept of granularity. This includes the processes of aggregation and disassembly to produce new or repurpose existing LOs. They then suggest factors that support the efficiency and effectiveness of LO repurposing, and how these can be influenced by appropriate design methodologies.

The authors point to the limited vision of many LO implementers, noting that they confine their view of LOs to traditional documents or software applications (e.g. simulations). They remind us that the current state of technology allows for a much smaller level of granularity facilitating a finer, more flexible repurposing of content. In support of this they recommend, for example, that authors design their content for reuse from the beginning by not inserting explicit references to other components.

Chapter 1

Learning objects

Resources for learning worldwide

Stephen Downes

This chapter describes the need for learning objects (LOs) and the importance of sharing, and then offers a definition of LOs drawn from the description of that need.

Learning, n.
1. The act, process, or experience of gaining knowledge or skill.
2. Knowledge or skill gained through schooling or study.
3. Psychology. Behavioural modification especially through experience or conditioning.

Object, n.
1. Something perceptible by one or more of the senses, especially by vision or touch; a material thing.
2. A focus of attention, feeling, thought, or action: an object of contempt.
3. The purpose, aim, or goal of a specific action or effort: the object of the game.
4. Grammar.
    a. A noun, pronoun, or noun phrase that receives or is affected by the action of a verb within a sentence.
    b. A noun or substantive governed by a preposition.
5. Philosophy. Something intelligible or perceptible by the mind.
6. Computer Science. A discrete item that can be selected and manoeuvered, such as an onscreen graphic. In object-oriented programming, objects include data and the procedures necessary to operate on that data.

The idea of learning objects

There is no consensus on the definition of LOs, as is addressed in the editor's Introduction to this book. Definitions abound and numerous analogies are employed to elucidate the concept. The basic idea, by virtue of its simplicity, allows wide latitude for interpretation. LOs are intended to support online learning. They are intended to be created once and used numerous times. Because they are delivered online, they are intended to be digital objects. And because they are used in learning, they are intended to have an educational component. Probably no definition of LOs will ever be sufficient; there will always be those who say the definition allows too much or too little. Part of the purpose of this chapter is to approach the subject of LOs from a different direction: rather than trying to say what they are, this chapter attempts to show the problems LOs are intended to solve and the manner in which they are used, providing a *functional definition* of LOs.

The case for online learning

We need accessible and affordable learning. The need for and usefulness of online learning is today no longer in question, but to understand the need for LOs, it is useful to reflect on the factors that led to the development of online learning. And, though the availability of the technology was a key factor, the primary driver behind the development was (and continues to be) a widespread need for accessible and affordable learning.

Dimensions of accessibility. In a world where many or most people have access to the Internet, online learning promises to make learning more accessible. Accessibility has numerous dimensions. Among the best known are timeliness (online learning may be used any time of the day or night), accessibility (online learning many be accessed from almost anywhere), and flexibility (online learners can proceed at their own pace).

Accessibility as choice. To a large degree, accessibility may be defined as choice. Vail (2001) wrote that students turning to online classes have one thing in common. They all want something that's not easily available on site. Rural students can study subjects such as Latin or calculus that their schools are too small to offer. Sick students can keep up in their lessons, as can gifted or travelling students.

Accessibility as lifelong learning. Accessibility may also be defined as having the opportunity to continue learning while being employed. In an article titled 'OU attracting more young people', published in the *Guardian*, 22 January 2002, Lee Elliott Major (referring to an Open University study) noted, for example, that, generally, learners prefer not to study for three years and then start their careers, but choose to both work and study immediately after graduation. Human Resources Development Canada (HRDC, 2002) has emphasized that broad-based, accessible adult lifelong learning is crucial for economic development.

The cost of online learning

Traditional courses are typically created by a single artisan. Though instructors in traditional classrooms use common course materials such as textbooks and journal articles, each time a course is offered by a school, college or university, it is created from scratch. And although instructors sometimes use core curricula and often use the same course outline from one year to the next, these are adapted and localized on a case-by-case basis. The task of creating a course in the traditional classroom, therefore, resembles what may be described as a cottage craft industry: it depends on and reflects the skills and inclinations of an individual artisan.

Online courses are also typically created by an individual artisan. Modern schools, colleges and universities developing courses for online delivery have migrated this strategy into their Internet offerings. Although supported by teams of designers and web specialists, courses are essentially the product of individual teachers or professors. And, though common materials such as course packs or other online learning resources may be used, the online course is essentially created from scratch each time it is delivered. Like traditional teaching, online teaching today is labour intensive and, therefore, expensive. Bates (2000) estimates a typical 45-hour course cost at US $24,400. Kurtis (2001) puts the cost at closer to US $60,000. Kruse (2002) suggests an even higher cost of $350,000.

Online courses are therefore at least as expensive to develop as traditional courses. Most online course developers use the design model Bates (2000) describes. It involves a course being developed from scratch, using nothing more than a traditional university course or a good textbook as a guide. The course author typically authors *all* the content, including examples and demonstrations, quizzes and tests. Because of the cost of development, there is little use of course-specific software or multimedia. The course is then offered to a small number of students over a limited time, resulting in course costs that are comparable to, if not greater than, traditional university course costs.

We can do so much better than this. We need to design online courses, even university courses, in such a way as to reduce these costs without diminishing the value of a university education. We need to do this by extracting what these courses have *in common* and by making these common elements available online.

We can create better online course materials. Consider *The Teacher's Guide to the Holocaust*. This site consists of dozens of resources on the Holocaust <http://fcit.coedu.usf.edu/holocaust/>. The site may be used and reused by any teacher. Each of the 'class activities' could be treated as an individual LO. The Holocaust is a very large subject and is appropriately divided into many components. But it is far easier, and of far greater quality, to assemble a lesson or series of lessons from these materials, than to create something from scratch.

Example: *Hamlet*. There is not a single description of *Hamlet*, yet there is only one standard text of the play *Hamlet*. It is not unreasonable to envision a definitive online multimedia edition. A course specializing in

Hamlet would employ the digital *Hamlet* as a central resource, and incorporate essays, discussions and articles from scholars around the world. Such an edition would contain not only the text, but would also contain video clips, audio clips, commentary from selected sources, pop-up glossaries, and more.

We can lower the cost of learning. Imagine a multimedia company spending a million dollars on such a production. Assume that *Hamlet* is taught in 10,000 schools, colleges or universities around the world (hardly a stretch). Assume 20 students per class (an underestimate, to be sure!). At \$5 per student, the company would make its million dollars back in one year! The economics are very good, and this excellent resource would be cheaper than even the book alone.

The argument for learning objects

Define LOs by defining the problems they solve. What are LOs? A good approach to answering this question is to describe what problems LOs are intended to solve, and thereby, to describe what LOs are designed to do.

The problem: Online educational content is expensive to produce. Online educational content is not cheap. Even a plain web page, authored by a mathematics professor, can cost hundreds of dollars if you take into account server costs and the professor's salary. Include graphics and a little animation and the price can double. Add an interactive exercise and the price can be quadrupled.

If each institution produces its own materials, the cost multiplies. Suppose that *one* description of *the sine wave function* is produced. A high quality and fully interactive piece of learning material could be produced for, say, a thousand dollars. If a thousand institutions share this one item, the cost is a dollar per institution. But if *each* of a thousand institutions produces a similar item, then each institution must pay a thousand dollars, or the institutions, collectively, must pay a million dollars. For one lesson! In one course!

The cost is reduced by sharing similar learning materials among institutions. The economics are relentless. It makes no financial sense to spend millions of dollars producing multiple versions of similar LOs when single versions of the same objects could be shared at a much lower cost per institution. There will be sharing, because no institution producing its own materials on its own could compete with institutions sharing learning materials.

To solve the problem of cost, learning materials will be shared. Economics, then, dictate that we need to be able to share learning materials between institutions over the Internet. But this raises a host of issues. What sort of materials can be shared? How might they be created? How do we account for the content that does change from one institution to the next? And from the millions of objects on the Internet, how can we find the one item we need for a particular course at a particular time? These issues and more need to be resolved, so we need to look at the problem of sharing more closely.

Courses? No, not courses

The problem: What will be shared? If we accept the premise that institutions will share learning materials, then we need to ask, what will they share? What size will the materials be? This is sometimes known as the problem of the *granularity* of LOs.

Postulation: We will share courses. The answer that intuitively offers itself is: *courses*. Existing listings of online learning materials, such as TeleCampus <http://telecampus.ca> list only courses. As good listings, they are divided into subject areas, where each subject page contains a list of similar courses offered by different institutions.

Courses are what students purchase from institutions. These directories are at the service of potential consumers of learning materials, that is, students. Students are typically motivated by an interest in a topic and they select courses from the list of offerings in that topic. Moreover, students are typically *offered* learning materials in course-sized units, and attempt to complete degree or diploma programmes defined as sets of related courses.

Institutions already share some courses. Why, then, would institutions not share them all? To a certain degree, they already do so. Most colleges and universities define course articulation policies, whereby a course completed at one institution is accepted for credit at another institution. A good example is the Baccalaureate Core Course Equivalency defined by Oregon State University for courses at thirteen regional community colleges <http://www.orst.edu/Dept/admindb/arttable/scr1140_arttab.htm>.

Course articulation is an example of sharing courses. Course articulations are the result of complex negotiations between teams of academics. Consider, for example, the information contained in the Illinois Mathematics and Computer Science Articulation Guide <http://www.imacc.org/articulation/>. To count as equivalent credit for a trigonometry course, for example, a candidate course must require certain prerequisites and must contain material covering a certain set of topics.

However, course articulation is complex and regional. It is notable that Oregon State University has made no attempt to articulate courses offered by community colleges in Florida. Because of the regional nature of course articulations and because of the detailed topic-by-topic definition of articulation agreements, course sharing between institutions is difficult to define and maintain. It is unlikely that *any* course could be shared by any significant number of institutions in different states or different nations.

Courses offered by institutions vary widely. We see this variety reflected in online course listings. Returning to the TeleCampus directory, it houses pointers to more than twenty separate history courses. No two of the courses share the same name. And though a number of courses focus on the same region and time period, no two of the courses share the same content. This is more or less true across all subjects and all institutions. Although courses may share elements in common, it is rare to find two courses from two institutions that share the same, and only the same, set of elements.

So we will not share courses. Courses themselves are *not* suitable candidates for sharing. Yet the dominant form of online education today is the course. So, it should come as no surprise that there is very little sharing of educational resources, even online resources, despite the tremendous potential cost savings.

So, we will share *parts* of courses. What needs to be shared may be best described as parts of courses, or more accurately, course *components*. From this it follows that we need not only collections of course components but also some mechanism for assembling course components into complete courses. This may be thought of as the problem of *packaging* LOs. Shortly we will first explore the idea of what sorts of things can be shared as course components, and then we will look at the problem of packaging.

Sharing the old way

We best understand sharing by looking at existing examples of sharing. To best understand the concept of sharing course components, and gain an intuitive understanding of what may constitute a LO, it is useful to look at how and why learning materials are shared in traditional classrooms. It is important to review the 'old ways' of sharing resources, not only to show that resource sharing is an established fact in today's classrooms, but also to point to some of the elements of resource sharing already in place.

Today's classrooms already share learning materials. If we describe 'sharing' as meaning 'one centrally produced resource used by many', then today's classroom is already an example of extensive resource sharing. Various publishers and content producers create resources centrally and distribute them to classes around the world. And while many of these resources are distributed for free, the majority of shared resources in classrooms are purchased from their respective producers or intermediaries.

An example of sharing: the textbook. The clearest example of resource sharing 'the old way' in today's classrooms occurs through the use of textbooks. These resources bear all the hallmarks of sharing: they are produced in publishing houses and obtained as needed by classroom instructors around the world. In many cases, the information in textbooks is so commonly used that the work becomes standard.

An example of sharing: classroom displays. But textbooks are just one type of item among many that are shared by classes around the world. No K12 school is complete without a set of wall maps in geography classes, periodical tables of the elements in science classes, and sets of large block letters for the early years. A rich and useful set of classroom displays is distributed by organizations as varied as astronomical societies, museums, and publishing companies.

An example of sharing: multimedia. In the area of multimedia, teachers employ a wide variety of published materials including filmstrips and videos, CD-ROMs and other software, presentation graphics and even complete learning resources, such as the Plato programme.

Sharing today involves the buying and selling of learning materials. Neither the producers nor the consumers of those resources would describe the distribution of textbooks, classroom displays or multimedia as 'sharing'. Textbook publishing and sales, especially, is a lucrative industry. The National Association of College Stores estimated US/Canadian college store sales to be US \$10.68 billion for the 2000–2001 academic year (NACS, 2002). Nonetheless these classes are sharing resources as defined. They are produced by a relatively small number of publishers and used by many institutions.

Sharing today involves decomposition. Instructors frequently employ only components of purchased learning materials in their classes. Many course syllabi require that students obtain more than one textbook. They may use, for example, only a few chapters out of a textbook. In class, they reassemble these selected materials in a way that meets their instructional goals (Wiley, 2000).

Sharing today involves sharing parts of courses. In many cases, the resources sold by publishers and distributed to classrooms are not entire courses, but rather, components of courses. This is most clearly the case for classroom aids such as wall maps and posters. Sometimes also students purchase only parts of courses, such as lecture notes or workbooks. And students frequently photocopy only parts of books (or parts of journals) in their research and reading.

Contemporary online sharing

Many agencies offer educational materials for sharing, but problems exist. In the traditional classroom, course components such as textbooks, classroom aids and multimedia are bought and sold and then combined by teachers and students to support classroom instruction. On the Internet, though most educational institutions offer complete courses only, many other agencies have started offering smaller, more portable learning materials. These materials fall short of what the author would define as 'learning objects', but they do offer some insight as to the direction and potential of online resources. Examples of these resources are provided in the repositories described near the end of this chapter.

While being among the leading learning resource sites on the Internet, they all have their limitations. SchoolNet links only to institutional home pages, and not to learning resources directly. MERLOT is difficult to search. And both MarcoPolo and XanEdu are closed to consortia members only.

Problem: It is difficult to locate relevant learning materials. The Internet contains a wealth of learning materials. But even with the help of portals, these learning materials are hard to find and hard to use. The portals need more robust mechanisms for updating and submissions. They need much better systems of categorization and searching. They need to be tied more closely to learning objectives, but in such a way as not to be tied to a specific curriculum. This would allow materials directly relevant to a given course topic to be quickly located (Schatz, 2000).

Problem: Existing portals offer access to only a fraction of available materials. Though the resources offered by learning materials portals are very good, and in some cases very comprehensive, no portal offers more than a fraction of the materials available on the Internet. Materials available from one portal are not available from other portals. And, because publishers sign exclusive agreements with certain portals, they are blocked from wider access except through that portal.

Problem: There is no consistency in the materials offered. An even greater weakness appears when we look at the collective set of learning resources (or applications, as MERLOT calls them) offered by these. It is almost impossible to identify consistency in format, scope, methodology, educational level or presentations. Some resources include lesson plans, but many others do not. Some are authored in Java, others in HTML, and others in a hybrid mixture known only to the author. Some involve ten minutes of student time, while others would occupy an entire day. And there is no structured means for an instructor to know which is which.

What we need

Learning objects are defined by the problems they solve. What would we need to implement the interoperability of course components online? We need something similar to the initiatives described in the previous section, but that addresses the weaknesses of existing learning web portals. The description of an online entity that addresses these problems forms the basis for a definition of LOs.

Learning objects are sharable. By 'sharable', we mean that a LO may be produced centrally and used in many different courses. Sometimes people speak of this criterion by saying that LOs must be *reusable*. This is accurate to the degree that it means that LOs may be used over and over again. But equally important is the idea that they are *interoperable*, capable of being used by *different* educational institutions using different systems.

Learning objects are digital. By 'digital', we mean that they can be distributed using the Internet. While some people could talk of physical entities (such as textbooks or maps) as LOs, such objects cannot be used online and therefore are not part of a fully online course.

Learning objects are modular. A LO is not an entire course. It is a part of a course. Therefore, in order to create an online course, LOs must be assembled or packaged into a larger entity. This is what we mean by 'modular', indicating that collections of LOs may be assembled into a single, larger unit. This in turn means that, as Longmire (2000) asserts, LOs must be free-standing, nonsequential, coherent and unitary.

Learning objects are interoperable. By 'interoperable', we mean that LOs produced by different publishers, or available through different repositories, may be packaged together into a single course. An instructor creating a course using LOs must be able to select from all available LOs, not merely a selected subset of proprietary learning materials offered by a single provider. Singh (2000) wrote that the framework must allow data to be exchanged using separate tools and systems connected on the Internet.

Learning objects are discoverable. By 'discoverable', we mean that the appropriate LO for any given instructional application can be located in a reasonable amount of time by a person who is not necessarily an expert at searching the Internet. Just as an average person could go into a library and, using the catalogue system, locate a particularly useful book, so also an average person should be able to go online and locate a particularly useful educational resource.

Learning object repositories

Learning object repositories are what make the LOs discoverable. Repositories are collections of LOs and metadata. There are two major types of repositories: those containing both the LOs and LO metadata, and those containing metadata only. In the latter case, the LOs themselves are located at a remote location and the repository is used as a tool to *locate* LOs. In the former, the repository may be used to both *locate and deliver* the LO.

Repositories are either stand-alone or included in another service. Most well known LO repositories are stand-alone. These repositories function like *portals*, containing a web-based user interface, a search mechanism and a category listing. Another major class of LO repositories functions more like a *database* attached to another product. A Learning Content

Management System (LCMS), for example, may contain a LO repository intended for its exclusive use.

Repositories may be centralized or distributed. Two major models for LO repositories exist. The most common form is a *centralized* form in which the LO metadata are located on a single server or website (the LOs themselves may be located somewhere else). An alternative model is the *distributed* LO, in which the LO metadata are contained in a number of connected servers or websites. Distributed LO repositories typically employ a *peer-to-peer* architecture to allow any number of servers or websites to communicate with each other.

Many LO repositories, and especially stand-alone repositories, are former online course portals (discussed earlier). These repositories are in a state of transition, listing and offering both courses and LOs. Some examples of repositories are:

- Canada's SchoolNet <http://www.schoolnet.ca/>
- CAREO <http://www.careo.org/>
- MERLOT <http://www.merlot.org>
- MarcoPolo <http://marcopolo.worldcom.com/>
- Universal Brokerage Platform <http://www.educanext.org/ UNIVERSAL/servlet/Universal>
- XanEdu <http://www.xanedu.com/>

Conclusion

Learning objects are digital materials used to create online courses where these materials are modular, interoperable, reusable and discoverable. They are accessible over the Internet through different types of repositories. These can be used by teachers and students to access the LOs and assemble viable lessons, units and courses and share them between different institutions and systems.

References

Bates, A. W. (2000) Managing technological change: Strategies for college and university administrators, Jossey-Bass, San Francisco.

HRDC (2002) (accessed 28 April 2003) Knowledge matters: Skills and learning for Canadians, (Online) http://www.hrdc-drhc.gc.ca/sp-ps/sl-ca/doc/toc.shtml.

Kruse, K. (2002) (accessed 24 April 2003) Measuring the total cost of e-learning, (Online) http://www.e-learningguru.com/articles/art5_2.htm.

Kurtis, R. (2001) (accessed 28 April 2003) Return on investment (ROI) from e-learning, CBT and WBT, *School for Champions*, (Online) http://www.school-for-champions.com/elearning/roi.htm.

Longmire, W. (2000) (accessed 21 May 2000) A primer on learning objects: Exerpt from learning without limits, *Learning Circuits*, (Online) http://www.learningcircuits.org/mar2000/primer.html.

Major, L. E. (2002) OU attracting more young people, *Guardian*, (Online) http://education.guardian.co.uk/universityaccess/story/0,10670,637574,00.html.

NACS (2002) (accessed 25 February 2003) Size of the college store market, (Online) http://www.nacs.org/public/research/higher_ed_retail.asp.

Schatz, S. (2000) (accessed 28 April 2003) Paradigm shifts and challenges for instructional designers, *IMS Project*, (Online) http://www.imsproject.org/feature/kb/knowledgebits.html.

Singh, H. (2000) (accessed 28 April 2003) Achieving interoperability in e-learning, *Learning Circuits*, (Online) http://www.learningcircuits.org/mar2000/singh.html.

Vail, K. (2001) (accessed 28 April 2003) Online learning grows up, *Electronic School*, (Online) http://www.electronic-school.com/2001/09/0901f1.html.

Wiley, D. A. (2000) Connecting learning objects to instructional design theory: A definition, a metaphor, and a taxonomy, in *The instructional use of learning objects: Online version*, (Online) http://reusability.org/read/chapters/wiley.doc.

Chapter 2

A first step towards a theory of learning objects

Mike Sosteric and Susan Hesemeier

With the advent of the Internet, it is not hyperbole to say we now live in a connected society where free access to information has become a necessary feature of life for many of those benefiting from the use of information technologies. New communication options have opened up our society, creating new opportunities for leisure activities, commerce and social development, to name only a few. This chapter is concerned with information technology as it is applied to the educational process. But our concern is not with information technology and education in general, but with a specific example of information technology that is being created to bolster the educational system (elementary schools and post-secondary), known as the learning object (LO).

What is a LO? Good definitions are difficult to find, and to begin to provide an adequate definition any inappropriate theoretical formations must be jettisoned and the definition of LO should be simplified. For the purposes of introduction, a LO is a digital file used in educational settings to support instruction, from elementary and secondary schools, and all levels of post-secondary instruction. Later in this chapter, a discussion will be introduced on how LOs have special characteristics that distinguish them from the more common learning resources with which most educators would be familiar.

LOs have been on the educational agenda for several years now (IEEE, 1998). Nevertheless, the corpus of research on LOs is less than satisfying. This does not mean that research has not been conducted. Organizations such as the IMS Global Learning Consortium (IMS) and the IEEE have contributed significantly by helping to define indexing and metadata standards for object search and retrieval. There has also been some commercial (Baron, 2000) and educational work accomplished (CAREO, 2000), but there remains a vacuum in descriptive, analytical and critical examinations of LO technologies.

This chapter is one entry into what will hopefully be a dynamic and energetic fray. In an attempt to capture their true nature, an overview of LOs is provided. In order to evaluate the usefulness of thinking about LOs in terms of Computer Science (CS) programming techniques, we start by looking at past attempts to define LOs, and then continue by looking at the ostensible link between LOs and Object-Oriented Programming (OOP) theory. This examination of OOP theory ends by concluding that CS OOP theory has little to offer in our attempt to define and understand LOs. Finally, this chapter concludes with a short working definition of LOs, and suggestions as to where future work is needed in the fleshing out of our understanding of LOs.

What is a learning object?

More than a few words have been written with the aim to give a clear picture of what LOs are all about. Yet confusion is apparent in the literature, as no consistent definition of LOs seems to exist. A recent article in *Learning Circuits* highlights this difficulty. LOs are different things to different e-learning professionals. In fact, there seems to be as many definitions as there are people to ask (ASTD and SmartForce, 2002).

Several problems have made defining LOs difficult. One bothersome difficulty is that existing definitions are far too general to be of any use in identifying, developing, or criticizing LOs. As an example, ASTD and SmartForce (2002) begin with the following definition of a LO: 'At its most basic level, a LO is a piece of content that's smaller than a course.' Compare this definition with that of the IEEE, which defines a LO as 'any entity, digital or non-digital, which can be used, re-used or referenced during technology supported learning'. The Learning Technology Standards Committee (LTSC) provides examples of these objects, including multimedia content, instructional content, learning objectives, instructional software and software tools, and persons, organizations, or events referenced during technology supported learning (IEEE, 1998).

The definition lumps all digital and non-digital 'things' into the LO category. But a definition that includes 'everything' is not a definition at all. There is nothing in such a definition to suggest how it might distinguish a LO from more mundane technological support or any other learning resource such as a computer or a keyboard, for example, and there is certainly nothing to assist the investigators if they want to develop a LO. All that is known from this definition is that LOs are 'something' used in some sort of learning environment.

Of course, one might say that anything digital *could* be used as a LO. For example, a picture of a rose (or the actual rose itself) could be used in various scientific disciplines to illustrate biological, chemical, or psychological processes. However, this loose definition is problematic for two reasons. On the one hand, most authors seem to assume that objects are more than mere digital files. As will be seen shortly, most authors like to attribute several special features to LOs such as reusability, searchability, and so on. At the least, our definition needs to include these special features, but including specific features may have the net result of excluding those digital files that do not have the required features.

'Things', on the other hand (and this includes more common materials used as traditional learning resources), do not become useful in learning environments until a context is attached to them. Consider the picture in Figure 2.1, which exists inside a Canadian learning repository as a LO. This image is a piece of multimedia content that can be used during technology-supported learning. However, just looking at the picture teaches us nothing. Are we to learn something about religious devotion, or respect for elders, or multiculturalism, or foreign languages, or the creation of posters? We do not know this from casual observation. What would make the image a LO is the addition of contextual information that would allow an instructor or instructional designer, and perhaps even an automated program, to know how to use the object in an educational setting.

In the low-tech world, the instructor normally provides this contextual information by harvesting objects and putting them onto projection screens, or passing the objects around to students while engaging in a lengthy description about them. In addition to providing contextual information, instructors interpret objects and creatively reorganize their context – a process that requires a vast amount of background information. This is a critical function of instructors and its importance is recognized in LO literature. By developing LO metadata standards that provide the necessary context for the educational resource, the IMS (2001) and the IEEE have

Figure 2.1 An example of a learning object

helped to provide the necessary infrastructure for contextualized LOs that has, in the past, been provided almost solely by instructors.

Though the importance of context is not in question in the literature on LOs, 'context' has not been emphasized in definitions of LOs. A LO is not just *any* digital file or any object. At the least, anything that could be considered a LO would need associated instructional information. This occurs even with ordinary classroom 'objects'. Images are often placed in textbooks, but the images themselves are always captioned and explanatory material is provided in the text. Of course, in technological settings where the goal is to use these objects in semi-automated instructional systems, the provision of this type of instructional context is critical.

Although authors tend to want to include digital and non-digital content as LOs, it is not clear that this is useful. As they are applied in the real world, LOs are clearly digital objects. Repositories and standards, and all the work being conducted on LOs, refer to digital objects. It makes little sense to include a universe of learning resources when there does not seem to be any real intention to include them in practical work.

To clarify the definition of LOs, a look at the pedagogical intention behind the production of objects is also necessary. Although many digital objects *could* be construed as LOs, not all digital files are LOs. Pornography is one obvious example. Other objects may or may not become LOs, as pedagogical intent is required for an object to become a LO. For example, a Unix utility program for listing files may be a LO. But it would only become a LO if someone decided to use it as one. Intent is necessary, as is the inclusion of associated metadata, and we have already seen that files are not useful as LOs without the provision of context. A rose might be a rose by any other name, but it is not a learning object unless some discourse is associated with it.

Armed with this initially simplistic perspective on LOs, let us now take a first stab at providing a definition. A LO is a digital file (image, movie, etc.) intended to be used for pedagogical purposes, which includes, either internally or via association, suggestions on the appropriate context in which to use the object.

There is reasonable clarity in this definition, as it usefully limits the universe of LOs and flows from current literature and practice. If writers in this area stopped at this definition, our current understanding of LOs would be acceptable. However, writers on LOs seem to want to make LOs 'sexier' than they really are. As a result, several attempts have been made to dress up the definition of LOs. One of the most counterproductive attempts is evident in theorists' use of the discipline of computing science and, in particular, Object-Oriented Programming (OOP) for additional theoretical grist. The reason behind the attempt to connect LOs to code objects is simple. There is a grammatical affinity between the term 'object' used in 'learning object' and object-oriented programming theory.

However, a grammatical affinity is not sufficient justification to draw from object-oriented programming theory. This can be seen in the following definition by Quinn and Hobbs (2000):

> The learning object (LO) model is characterized by the belief that we can create independent chunks of educational content that provide an educational experience for some pedagogical purpose. Drawing on the object-oriented programming (OOP) model, this approach asserts that these chunks are self contained, though they may contain references to other objects; and they may be combined or sequenced to form longer educational interactions. These chunks of educational content may be of any type – interactive, passive – and they may be of any format or media type. A LO is not necessarily a digital object . . .
>
> (Quinn and Hobbs, 2000)

Note again the tendency to define anything as a LO. But putting this aside, our real concern is to assess whether or not we can usefully extract a sensible understanding of what a LO might be from CS definitions of objects. According to Quinn and Hobbs's definition, LOs are: (a) self-contained, (b) modular (i.e. they can be sequenced, combined, etc.), and (c) interactive or passive.

The definitional extensions provided by Quinn and Hobbs are less than satisfactory. The problem is that even though Quinn and Hobbs make a connection to OOP theory, the definition of a LO is reduced to a thin description of features (e.g. objects can be combined and sequenced, and contain 'references') that do not contribute to our ability to understand or visualize LOs.

We could ignore the inadequate definition of LOs just given if it were the only such instance. But other authors also provide similarly thin definitions linked to OOP theory. Robson (1999), for example, begins his definition by stating that LOs are learning resources in an 'object-oriented model', and then continues, like Quinn and Hobbs, to provide terse feature sets for LOs:

> Learning resources are objects in an object-oriented model. They have methods and properties. Typically methods include rendering and assessment methods. Typical properties include content and relationships to other resources.
>
> (Robson, 1999)

As with Quinn and Hobbs's definition, the problem with Robson's definition involves depth. His definition may be useful only to someone who has experience with object-oriented programming methodology. Without significant background knowledge, we have no way to know what exactly a method is, what the properties are, and what these technical features of LOs provide in the way of functionality for LOs. In short, without knowing more about CS's application of object-oriented programming, we cannot assess the appropriateness of applying CS theory to our understanding of LOs.

This is a significant problem: authors toss around theoretical connections to object-oriented theory with insufficient theoretical rigour. Although there is nothing wrong with borrowing concepts from object theory to develop our ideas about LOs, we must do so carefully. We cannot just adopt the concept of 'objects', and its related terminology such as 'references', 'methods', and so on, without carefully specifying whether or not a method for a LO is the same as a method for a code object.

We believe that most authors will admit when pressed that code objects really do not provide suitable guidance for us in theorizing and creating LOs. As Friesen (2001) notes, not only is there conceptual confusion in the literature and no general agreement on how to map the features of OOP programming objects to LOs, but the fit between the two also seems to be counterintuitive:

> What senses of the word 'object' are (*sic*) can be profitably applied to the notion of 'educational objects'? The separation (*sic*) educational object and metadata seems to run counter to the combination of code and data that is said to define software objects.
>
> (Friesen, 2001)

We believe the confusion in this passage demonstrates that object-oriented theory should be discarded altogether when defining LOs, and that we should proceed to define LOs on their own terms. However, recognizing that there may be some resistance to this strategy, in the next section we take a more detailed look at the core concepts of OOP theory to see how well they apply to LOs.

The etiology of learning objects

> Object-orientation is a new technology based on objects and classes. It presently represents the best methodological framework for software engineering and its pragmatics provides the foundation for a systematic engineering discipline. By providing first class support for the objects and classes of objects of an application domain, the object oriented paradigm precepts better modeling and implementation of systems. Objects provide a canonical focus throughout analysis, design, and implementation by emphasizing the state, behavior, and interaction of objects in its models, providing the desirable property of seamlessness between activities.
>
> (Hathaway III, 2002)

As noted earlier, the concept of an 'object' is taken from CS theory, where it has a precise, if evolving, meaning. One of the most succinct definitions of computing objects we have found to date is provided by Conway (2000), who notes: 'An object is an access mechanism for data. In most object-oriented languages that means that objects act as containers for data or, at least, containers for pointers to data. But in the more general sense, *anything* that provides access to data – a variable, a subroutine, a file handle – may be thought of as an object.'

This is a useful starting point in describing object-oriented programming languages: objects are containers of data. This does not contradict our definition of LOs, i.e. that they have pedagogical intent, associated metadata, are a digital file, and so on, nor does it enhance the definition we have set up so far for the LO. Our definition that LOs are digital files implies, without needing comment, that these objects would contain data.

But a container of data, digital or otherwise, is somewhat useless unless there is a way to access and manipulate the data. OOP theory thus extends the definition of objects to include access methods. In computing science, objects are always written to provide encapsulated access to the attributes (data) of an object.

Friesen (2001) summarizes the thinking in the literature on how computing science objects map to LOs, when he notes that authors 'most often identify "modularity", "interoperability", [and] "discoverability" as important attributes of educational objects'. However, examining these features only emphasizes the theoretical morass. Not only are interoperability and discoverability decidedly not features of OOP, there is no general agreement on how each of these items should be conceived or mapped when it comes to LOs themselves.

To complicate matters further, Friesen (2001) points to three more or less distinct definitions of the term *modularity* in the literature. Ironically, none of these definitions seems to be at all helpful in theorizing LOs. Educational objects, as Longmire describes them, must be modular, 'free standing, non-sequential, coherent and unitary'. Others describe the same idea using slightly different terms. Roschelle *et al.* (1998) state that the object must be adaptable 'without the help of the original developers to meet unforeseen needs'. According to Ip *et al.* (1997), the object must be constructed in such a way that its users 'need not worry about the component's inner complexity'. The educational object, in other words, should be a 'black box' in the sense described in the theory of object-oriented design.

The above definitions are not helpful, as some parts of the conceptual paradigm, such as the requirement that LOs be free-standing, non-sequential, coherent, or adaptable, do not map to OOP theory at all. A programming object *may* have some or all of these properties, depending upon what the original authors might mean by these definitions. A programming object may or may not be free-standing and non-sequential, and some objects may, for example, be useful only in the restricted context of the program or sub-program for which they were designed. As may be recalled, the real nature of CS objects comes from the way in which they encapsulate code and data. As for the modifiability of an object by other than the original developer, that is a desideratum of *all* program code and is not the exclusive domain of OOP theory.

To be fair, there is a correspondence between the notion of modularity in the concept of a black box and a LO. But here the link to computing science objects actually reduces our understanding by introducing concepts that confuse the layperson and require considerable explanation and modification before they can become useful. Friesen quotes Berard (1993):

> Specifically, the underlying implementations of objects are hidden from those that use the object. In object-oriented systems, it is only the producer (creator, designer, or builder) of an object that knows the details about the internal construction of that object. The consumers (users) of an object are denied knowledge of the inner workings of the object.

This is precise in terms of the understanding of a CS object. Here the consumers are other programmers, and it is not necessary for them to understand the inner workings of code. They simply call the black box within the appropriate parameters. However, in the case of a CS object, the notion of the consumer is strictly associated with the programmer. The consumer of the preceding method could be the original programmer using her own code object or a third-party programmer, who is part of a development team working on a larger project. The consumer could even be an unknown programmer making use of some more generic library of code.

Confusion enters the world of the LO when we search for a consumer of a LO as required by CS theory. Here, in looking for an appropriate mirror concept, we end up trying to incorporate even more unnecessary concepts from OOP theory, thus clouding our understanding even further. One example is in the concept of interface, which does not map outside of the internal workings of the Java applet or OOP theory. Programs can have *interfaces*, but they are not the same types of interfaces referred to in OOP theory when we speak of an object having an interface. There is little meaning in trying to connect the two. In OOP theory, and OOP practice, an object's 'interface' connotes, simply, the methods that are available for manipulating the object's data. For example, a user object might have the following interface:

```
Public $user->rename()
Public $user->delete()
Public $user->archive()
```

```
Public $user->copy
Public $user->move()
Public $user->email()
Private $user->frobnicate()
Private $user->dbConnect()
Private $user->dbDisconnect
```

The object interface here refers to *all* the methods that the programmer created for manipulating data.

There are good reasons for hiding some methods from the user. However, it is sufficient to say that hiding unnecessary functions from programmers reduces bugs and enhances the object's long-term utility to the programmer. By exposing only certain methods, and by guaranteeing that the prototype of these methods never changes, programmers can rest assured that future modifications to the way an object is implemented will not affect the programs into which they have incorporated the object.

Conclusion – to object or not to object

Although OOP theory has many interesting concepts wrapped up in many fancy words, the applicability of OOP theory and/or methods to our under-standing of LOs is marginal at best, and counterproductive at worst. This can be clearly seen when we consider that few concepts of OOP theory have anything at all to do with LOs, and concepts that are somewhat rele-vant have marginal applicability and may actually create further confusion. In short, we end up wasting considerable time and energy trying to force LOs into an object-oriented model.

This is not exactly an original insight. Other authors recognize these difficulties and have even suggested the need to jettison most of the borrowing from OOP theory. Friesen (2001), for example, ultimately reduces the contribution of OOP only to providing the notion of reusability of objects. But even this is not satisfactory, because we really connote something different when we talk about the reusability of LOs. There is a rich literature in developmental psychology, sociology, and even compu-tation that deals directly with issues relevant to our understanding of LOs, and it is in these resources that we should be looking if we wish to develop our definitions and refine our understanding of LOs.

So if we jettison OOP theory, where does this leave us in terms of a definition of LOs? The definition we introduced at the outset is still useful:

A LO is a digital file (image, movie, etc.) intended to be used for pedagogical purposes, which includes, either internally or via associ-ation, suggestions on the appropriate context within which to use the object.

This definition is a starting point, though it is far from complete. As we have seen, LO users have considerable expectations about how LOs will perform. LOs are assumed to be providers of a host of fancy features that will make them useful pedagogically, economically and politically. In many of our estimations of LOs, an object is not an object – it is much more. But just how much more is a useful question that we need to explore in more detail. The map for that exploration can be easily laid. To estimate the potential of LOs, we need to ask several questions, including the following:

1. What is the point/purpose of LOs? Are they here to solve problems in the education system? Are they here to enhance current instruction? Do they really form part of a revolutionary front that will transform the provision of face-to-face or distance education?
2. What features of LOs will help realize educational objectives? Can simple image files function as objects or must these image files be enhanced in several ways to meet our objectives?
3. If files need to be enhanced, what technologies will be drawn upon to achieve educational objectives? The choice of technology will need to be guided by a clear set of objectives.
4. What role will standards play? A lot of work has been undertaken to develop standards for metadata. Given the purposes and features of LOs, will this work be relevant? Or can one get by with simpler notions of metadata?
5. How will LOs be evaluated from a practical and/or theoretical standpoint? Although this topic has not been broached at all, as a collective, educators have high expectations about how LOs will perform in the new economy. However, there is no way to evaluate the claims. Nor does it seem that anyone is ashamed to reduce themselves to polemical justifications (Downes, 2001). If LOs are to be taken seriously, evaluative mechanisms will be needed (see Chapters 11 and 21). Part of this will involve the development of theories of LOs in order to find the means to criticize, evaluate and evolve an understanding and use of LOs. Theories can be imported from, for example, instructional design, or modified and distilled from eclectic sources. However, these need appropriate theoretical underpinnings.

The process of answering these questions will be iterative. Educators will have to constantly move back and forth between theory, standards and actual implementations as they evolve their understanding of LOs and their applications. Theory must be grounded in implementation details and research on the pedagogical effectiveness of LOs. Through this basis, the implementation of theoretical notions of objects can be ensured. Then, the implementations will actually contribute something to the realm of educational theory and practice.

References

ASTD and SmartForce (2002) (accessed 5 January 2003) A field guide to learning objects, (Online) http://www.learningcircuits.org/fieldguides.html.

Baron, T. (2000) (accessed 1 March 2003) Learning object pioneers, *Learning Circuits*, (Online) http://www.learningcircuits.com/mar2000/barron.html.

Berard, E. (1993) *Essays on object-oriented software*, Prentice-Hall, New York.

CAREO (2000) (accessed 5 January 2003) Campus Alberta repository of educational objects, (Online) http://www.careo.org/.

Conway, D. (2000) *Object oriented PERL*, C. G. Manning, Greenwich, CT.

Downes, S. (2001) (accessed 12 April 2003) Learning objects: Resources for distance education worldwide, *International Review of Research in Open and Distance Education*, **2** (1), (Online) http://www.irrodl.org/content/v2.1/downes.html.

Friesen, N. (2001) (accessed 18 April 2003) What are educational objects?, *Interactive Learning Environments*, **9** (3): 219–30, (Online) http://www.careo.org/documents/objects.html.

Hathaway III, R. J. (2002) (accessed 28 April 2003) Object oriented FAQ, (Online) http://www.cyberdyne-object-sys.com/oofaq2/.

IEEE (1998) (accessed 29 April 2003) Learning Object Metadata (LOM): Draft document, *Learning Technology Standards Committee*, **2** (1), (Online) http://ltsc.ieee.org.

IMS (2001) IMS learning resource meta-data best practices and implementation guide, IMS Global Learning Consortium.

Ip, A. *et al.* (1997) Enabling reuseability of courseware components with Web-based virtual apparatus, in What works and why, ASCILITE '97, *Proceedings of the Australian Society for Computers in Learning in Tertiary Education Annual Conference*, ed. R. Kevill, R. Oliver and R. Phillips, pp. 286–91, Academic Computing Services, Curtin University of Technology, Perth.

Quinn, C. and Hobbs, S. (2000) (accessed 13 August 2002) Learning objects and instructional components, *Educational Technology and Society*, **3** (2), (Online) http://ifets.ieee.org/periodical/vol_2_2000/discuss_summary_0200.html.

Robson, R. (1999) (accessed 17 December 2002) Object-oriented instructional design and Web-based authoring, (Online) http://citeseer.nj.nec.com/327280.html.

Roschelle, J. *et al.* (1998) (accessed 28 April 2003) Scaleable integration of educational software: Exploring the promise of component architectures, *Journal of Interactive Media in Education*, **6**, (Online) http://www-jime.open.ac.uk/98/6/.

Notes

This chapter is based on an article, originally published as:

Sosteric, M. and Hesemeier, S. (accessed 1 December 2002) When is a learning object not an object: A first step towards a theory of learning objects, *International Review of Research in Open and Distance Learning*, **3** (2), (Online) http://www.irrodl.org/content/v3.2/index.html.

The image in Figure 2.1 is printed with permission from the CAREO Repository. It is available at http://aloha.netera.ca/uploads/crdc/unt5049b.jpg.

Chapter 3

Modelling units of learning from a pedagogical perspective

Rob Koper and René van Es

The title of this chapter could have been: Where is the *learning* in e-learning? The promise of e-learning, and the enabling learning technologies, is to make learning experiences in all types of settings more effective, efficient, attractive and accessible to the learners. In e-learning the Internet is used as the core medium for the delivery of information and the support of communication. Most people also think that the Internet, itself, is the key factor in the success of e-learning. However, a vast amount of research provides evidence for the proposition that it is not the medium (Internet), itself, which is accountable for the accomplishment of these promises, but the pedagogical design used in conjunction with the features of the medium (Clark, 1983, Clark and Sugrue, 1990; and Kozma, 1991).

The message is that we should concentrate on the quality of the pedagogical design and its relationship to the possibilities of the Internet if we want to accomplish the promises of e-learning. Another common belief is that learning is the same as knowledge transfer, meaning that it is enough to make knowledge available to learners according to some pedagogical structure. However, providing adequate knowledge is not enough: It has to be *learned*. This learning process is the focus when discussions concern instructional design or learning design. The question is: Where is the *learning* in e-learning? Moreover, much learning does not come from knowledge resources at all, but stems from the activities of learners solving problems, interacting with real course materials or devices, or with people in their social and work situations.

Recent research about learning suggests that learning does not come from the provision of knowledge. Learning occurs when learners interact with the learning environment. This does not mean that knowledge objects are unimportant in learning situations, but that they are not foremost in effective learning processes. This chapter will address the topic of the pedagogical design of learning events. Learning events are offered mostly in chunks, like courses. These chunks (in the next paragraph we abstract them to the concept of 'units of learning') are the major delivery units for e-learning. From a design perspective, the course is the aggregate containing all the necessary features to make learning successful. It is at this level of aggregation that educational modelling (or 'learning design') takes place, where the pedagogical models are implemented and where the quality of learning is determined.

Learning design is modelling 'units of learning'

In 1998, the Open University of the Netherlands (OUNL) initiated a research project with the goal of building a semantic notation for complete 'units of learning' to be used online. The concept of 'unit of learning' is fundamental. It is the smallest unit providing learning events for learners, enabling one or more interrelated learning objectives. This means that a unit of learning cannot be broken down to its component parts without losing its semantic and pragmatic meaning and its effectiveness in guiding learners towards the attainment of learning objectives. The unit of learning could be considered a Gestalt. In practice, there are units of learning of all types, sorts and sizes: a course, a study programme, a workshop, a practicum, a lesson. They could all be considered units of learning.

A unit of learning could be delivered through what is called:

- online learning (completely through the Web);
- blended learning (mix of online and face-to-face); or
- hybrid learning (mix of different media: paper, Web, e-books, etc.).

These units of learning can be annotated using an 'Educational Modelling Language' or EML (Koper, 2000). The EML specification has been further elaborated as an IMS specification, namely the current IMS Learning Design Specification (IMSLD, 2003). In this text we will refer to these specific implementations as EML/IMSLD.

The learning objects model

Learning objects (LOs) are generally smaller objects – smaller than courses – that can be reused in different courses. One of the underlying ideas is that courses in themselves can hardly be made reusable, because of all sorts of local factors (see Downes, Chapter 1). Few institutions accept full courses written by others, but many use the same content in LOs such as textbooks or maps. A common view of LOs is depicted in Figure 3.1.

There are several ways of viewing LOs. They are entities that may be referred to with metadata. The metadata are separate from the object they refer to. The metadata, and sometimes the LO itself, may be stored in a data-base. In principle, they have content (attributes and other LOs) and descrip-tions of the behaviour of the LO (operations). The major question from the perspective of use in real educational practice is: Does this model of LOs and

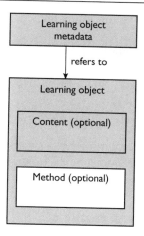

Figure 3.1 A common view of learning objects and metadata

packages provide us sufficient means to build complete, flexible and valid units of learning to be delivered through learning management systems?

The answer is 'No'. From an educational perspective, it is not enough to have LOs and metadata as such. Different types of LOs have different functions in the context of real education. A study task and a study text both have a different function in a unit of learning. Also, there are different constraints in the relations between different types of LOs. A study task (a type of LO), for example, almost always refers to resources (other types of LOs) needed to perform the task. So there is a structural relationship between tasks and resources within the context of a unit of learning.

The major problem with the LO model as it has been applied until now, is that LOs are not typed to their usage in the context of a unit of learning. The LO model expresses a common overall structure of objects within the context of a unit of learning, but does not provide a model to express the semantic relationship between the different types of objects in the context of use in an educational setting. As a result, the LO model also fails to provide for a model of the structure of the content of the different objects. The typing of objects also varies according to different peda-gogical stances, so there is a need for a meta-model to describe the relationships. The basic idea we have elaborated is to:

1. classify, or type, the LOs in a semantic network, derived from a peda-gogical meta-model;
2. build a containing framework expressing the relationships between the typed LOs; and
3. define the structure for the content and behaviour of the different types of LOs.

This approach has a lot of advantages, such as the following:

- It supports developers in building valid and high-quality units of learning, using and reusing smaller components.
- It supports builders of authoring and delivery tools by providing a common framework for valid units of learning.
- Learners and teachers can identify and search LOs, knowing their function within the framework of the course.
- It provides a semantic expression for the content of LOs, supporting reuse, interoperability and assembly of the components of units of learning into different units of learning.

Requirements for units of learning as a result of learning design

Actors in the learning process, dealing with units of learning, are typically learners and teachers as well as developers of units of learning, or the components this refers to such as study materials. Besides these direct users of the system, there are many other different actors in e-learning, namely different types of managers (system managers, human resource managers, etc.), vendors and publishers. The role of developer may be split among author, interaction designer, graphical designer, and so on.

The actors in e-learning have four principle needs: more effectiveness, more efficiency, more attractiveness and more accessibility. The different e-learning stakeholders approach these needs from their own perspectives. The general categorization of these needs can be expressed using an Educational Modelling Language, which describes a unit of learning. Such a language must meet the following general requirements:

1. The notational system must describe units of learning in a formal way, so that automatic processing is possible (*formalization*).
2. The notational system must be able to describe units of learning that are based on different theories and models of learning and instruction (*pedagogical flexibility*).
3. The notational system must explicitly express the semantic meaning of the different LOs within the context of a unit of learning. It must provide for a semantic structure of the content or functionality of the typed LOs within a unit of learning, alongside a reference possibility (*explicitly typed LOs*).
4. The notational system must be able to fully describe a unit of learning, including all the typed LOs, the relationship between the objects and the activities and the workflow of students and staff members with the LOs (*completeness*). And this regardless of whether these aspects are represented digitally or non-digitally.

5. The notational system must describe the units of learning so that repeated execution is possible (*reproducibility*).
6. The notational system must be able to describe personalization aspects within units of learning, so that the content and activities within units of learning can be adapted based on the preferences, prior knowledge, educational needs and situational circumstances of users. In addition, control must be able to be given, as desired, to the student, the teacher, a staff member, the computer, or the designer (*personalization*).
7. The notation of content components, where possible, must be media neutral, so that it can be used in different publication formats, including the Web, paper, e-books, mobile, and so on (*media neutrality*).
8. The description standards and interpretation technique must be separate. Through this, investments in educational development will become resistant to technical changes and conversion problems (*interoperability and sustainability*).
9. The notational system must fit in with available standards and specifications (*compatibility*).
10. The notational system must make it possible to identify, isolate, decontextualize and exchange useful LOs, and to reuse these in other contexts (*reusability*).
11. The notational system must make it possible to produce, mutate, preserve, distribute and archive units of learning and all of their contents including the LOs to which the unit refers (*life cycle*).

The pedagogical meta-model

A pedagogical meta-model is a model of pedagogical models. This means that specific pedagogical models, such as problem-based learning models or collaborative learning models, can be described (or derived) in terms of the meta-model. This is of importance when you want to express semantic relationships between pedagogical entities *and* want to be pedagogically neutral. Compare this, for instance, with a text editor such as MS Word. MS Word is neutral to the type of text one can edit with it. What great help it will be, when these types of tools become aware of the type of content being edited. Writers could expect much more support in the writing process than we are getting now. Text writing has so many varieties in practice that a real semantic framework for texts in general is not available at the moment, and may never be.

However, education is a more restricted domain with a great deal of common vocabulary and features. This is mainly due to the hard work done in research into learning and instruction. There are still many different stances when answering questions about learning, but there are also many commonalities. These commonalities are the focus of a meta-model. The differences are made by parameterization of the meta-model. This idea has led us to the work on the meta-model behind EML/IMSLD.

The main topics of the static structure of the pedagogical meta-model are expressed in UML diagrams here supplied by Booch *et al.* (1999). The pedagogical semantics of EML/IMSLD are designed according to this model. The model is based on educational research, specifically in the field of learning psychology and instructional design (De Block, 1982; Duffy and Cunningham, 1996; Duffy and Jonassen, 1991; Gagné, 1977; Gagné and Briggs, 1979; Jonassen, 1999; Mayer and Greeno, 1972; Merrill, 1983; Merrill, 1999; Reigeluth and Schwartz, 1989; Reigeluth, 1983; Reigeluth, 1999; Reigeluth and Stein, 1983; Van Merriënboer, 1997).

Most of these models in literature are expressed in natural language and ad hoc schemas. Like all models, this model abstracts reality. Course designs are something different from what actually happens when courses are instantiated and used in real practice. It is not the intention of course designs to abstract all the details of the course, but its major points.

Also, the UML diagrams are expressions of the pedagogical models underlying units of learning. It highlights the important points. In its details of implementation the models have more complexity. First the major packages in the pedagogical meta-model are shown in Figure 3.2.

There are four packages:

1. The learning model, which describes how learners learn, based on commonalities (consensus) in learning theories.
2. The unit of learning model, which describes how units of studies, which are applicable in real practice, are modelled, given the learning model and given the instruction model.
3. The domain model, which describes the type of content and the organization of that content. For example, the domain of economics, law, biology, and so on.

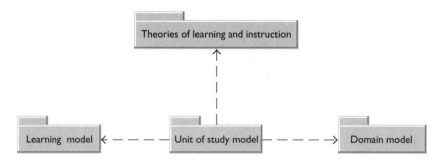

Figure 3.2 Packages in the meta-model

4.   Theories of learning and instruction, which describe the theories, principles and models of instruction as they are described in literature or
as they are conceived in the heads of practitioners.

The learning model

Figure 3.3 provides a summary of the learning model.
The learning model is based on the following axioms:

1.   A person learns by (inter-)acting in/with the external world.
2.   The real world could be considered to be composed of social and
personal situations, which provide the context for actions.
3.   A situation is composed of a collection of things and living beings in
a specific interrelationship.
4.   Communities of practice, or more specifically 'learning communities',
are a principal feature of any such situation.
5.   There are different types of learning. The one of interest to us is
learning invoked by instructional measures.
6.   Learning can be considered to be a change in the cognitive or metacognitive state. However, changes in conation and emotion can also
be considered as the result of learning. When a person has learned he
or she can (a) carry out new interactions or carry out interactions
better or faster in similar situations, or (b) carry out the same actions
in other situations (*transfer*).

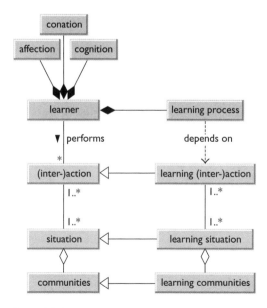

Figure 3.3 The learning model

7. A person can be urged to carry out specific interactions, if:
    – a person is willing to do so or stimulated to do so (conation/moti-
      vation factor);
    – a person is able to do so (*cognition factor*);
    – a person is in the mood to do so (*affection/emotional factor*); and
    – a person is in the right situation to do so (*situational factor*).
8. What has been set out here regarding persons is also valid for groups
    or organizations, so the criteria are not limited to individuals.

The model raises the following questions that should suggest no value
judgement in regard to the preceding axioms:

1. What does a person or group learn (knowledge, competencies, skills,
    insight, attitudes, intentional behaviour) and in what domain?
2. What kinds of activities must be carried out to learn? For example:
    observing, describing, analysing, experiencing, studying, problem-
    solving, experimenting, predicting, practising, exploring and answering
    questions.
3. How should a learning situation be arranged (context, what people,
    what objects) and what relationship does the situation have to the
    teaching–learning process?
4. To what extent are the components of the situation present externally
    and to what extent are they represented cognitively or internally?
5. How, precisely, do the learning and transfer processes occur?
6. How is motivation stimulated?
7. How is the learning result captured?
8. How should activities be stimulated?

The answers to precisely these questions determine the educational
philosophy, the instructional model and the more practical design of the
units of learning. The meta-model provides the semantic framework for
the units of learning's notational system, alongside the structure of learning
environments that was dealt with earlier.

In this vein, Duffy and Cunningham (1996), referring to Skinner, suggest
that there is general agreement that learning involves content with activities in a context. The traditional focus on information presentation and
processing is being challenged by constructivists who view learning as an
activity in a context or the entire learning situation or Gestalt.

The unit of learning model

Figure 3.4 describes the unit of learning model.

A model for a unit of learning is the result of a learning design process
in which a real product (the unit of learning) is the result. It must take
into account issues such as:

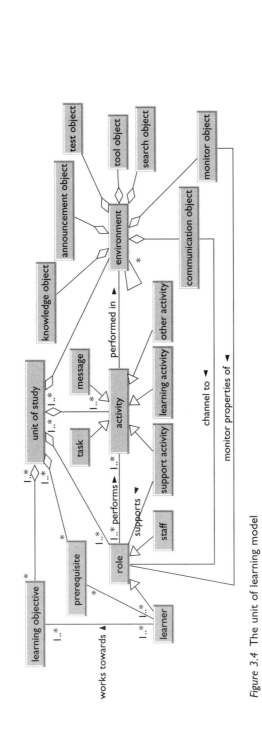

Figure 3.4 The unit of learning model

- the roles of staff and learners in the learning process;
- the learning objectives and target group;
- the prerequisites of the learners;
- other learner characteristics (learning styles, preferences, situational circumstances, etc.);
- the domain of learning (e.g. mathematics is different from cultural science);
- the context of learning (distance learning, blended learning, support structure available, library, etc.); and
- the assessment of learning.

In this model, the terms 'activity' and 'environment' are used as counterparts for 'action' and 'situation' in the learning model. However, in the unit of learning model, they refer to *planned* activities and environments. In essence this is the difference between the two models: the unit of learning model deals with the design of learning processes and the learning model deals with the way learning takes place in reality.

In EML/IMS LD these different information categories can be described in meaningful semantic terms so as they are open and not restrictive limiting developers to one particular methodology of teaching and learning.

The domain model

Pedagogical models must take into account the characteristics of the content domain. Content domains are, for example, mathematics, cultural science, economics, psychology, electrical engineering, law, and so on. Every content domain has its own structuring of knowledge, skills and competencies. There are different cultures and communities of practice. Often there are also specifically designed pedagogical models for particular domains such as history or mathematics teaching.

Theories of learning and instruction

Figure 3.5 provides a model of the generalization relationships between instruction models.

In educational technology, there are different streams in which the characteristics appear to have what Kuhn (1962) describes as scientific paradigms. Greeno, Collins and Resnick (1996) make – in a meta-analysis – a distinction between three major streams of instructional theories:

- Empiricist (behaviourist)
- Rationalist (cognitivist and constructivist)
- Pragmatist-sociohistoric (situationalist).

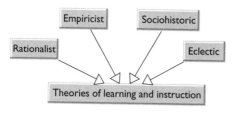

Figure 3.5 The model of the generalization of relationships between instruction models

Each theory proposes different views on topics such as knowledge, learning, transfer and motivation. Some of the differences are summarized shortly.

According to the *empirical approach*, as typified by Locke and Thorndike, all reliable knowledge is based on experience. Locke says: 'There is nothing in the mind that was not in the senses.' The assumption is that behaviour is predictable, given specific environmental conditions, and that processes can be analysed in isolation. Empiricists believe that learning can be influenced by events outside of its context and without knowledge of the internal learning processes.

In the *rationalist approach*, as typified by Descartes and Piaget, thinking is considered the only reliable source of knowledge. In this case, it is supposed that cognition mediates the relationship between a person and the environment. As there is the possibility of large individual differences in cognitive processing, for example, because of differences in prior knowledge (Dochy, 1992), meta-cognition (Flavell, 1979; Brown, 1980), motivation (Malone, 1981) and learning styles (Vermunt, 1996), the assumption of predictable behaviour falls away, and those involved must work with more open, authentic environments in which students themselves can build knowledge. The student is given a central, self-managing role in the educational process (Shuell, 1988; Schunk and Zimmerman, 1994).

The third approach is called the *pragmatic and cultural-historic* approach, as typified by James, Dewey and Vygotsky, and Leont'ev, or in educational theory as *social constructivism* (Simons, 1999). In this approach, the situation and the cultural-historical context that a learner is in are given primary attention (Lave and Wenger, 1991; Cole and Engestrom 1993). Knowledge is distributed among individuals, tools and communities, such as those of professional practitioners. The assumption is that there is collective as well as individual knowledge. Learning is considered as the adaptation of behaviour to the rules of the community.

Based on these stances there are – in literature – descriptions of hundreds of more theoretical or practical theories and models of learning and instruction. To name but a few: competency-based learning, project-based learning, mastery learning, problem-based learning, case-based learning, experiential learning, action learning, and so on (see literature such as Reigeluth, 1983, 1999; Merrill, 1983, 1999; Jonassen, 1999). Lots of more informal teaching plans are also available (see e.g. Eric's lesson plans at http://ericir.syr.edu/Virtual/Lessons/). Another approach is based in human resource management, mostly referred to as performance improvement (sometimes human performance technology, see Stolovitch and Keeps (1999) for an overview).

Most of these models were studied and analysed. The commonalities were mapped and the differences listed in order to derive the meta-model.

Also a fourth type of model was added: the eclectic model. These are instructional design models using principles from different stances, just for the practical occasion. These models can be explicitly formulated, but mostly they are implicit.

An integrated picture of the meta-model

The integrated picture of the meta-model could be drawn as in Figure 3.6. The focus in the model is also on the learner and not on the role of staff. It is drawn here to trace the dependencies within the model.

Implied elements

Not all pedagogical models address all elements in an explicit way. Sometimes these elements are kept *implicit*. For instance: there are learning management systems that don't provide activities to learners and/or staff. This can mean two things:

1. The activities 'read this book', 'solve this problem', 'answer the questions' are implied – the students have to find them out themselves. Mostly this is the case with classical forms of education with a lot of standard, quite evident, tasks, such as: 'read this book', 'solve this problem', 'answer the questions'.
2. The activities are not implied, but they are not part of the course offered through an LMS. The idea is that teachers will set the activities for students. This is the case in classroom situations. The LMS only serves some environment functions such as communication facilities and learning resources. In this case the LMS cannot support units of learning, only parts of it to be integrated by the teachers. The LMS isn't really a platform for all e-learning situations.

Conclusion

In this chapter the pedagogical meta-model behind EML/IMSLD is presented. In our analysis the current thinking about 'LOs' has some shortcomings. These were addressed and a containing framework for typed LOs was

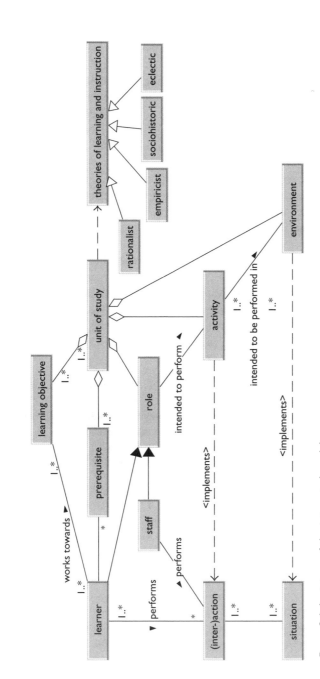

Figure 3.6 A picture of the integrated model

provided. This framework ensures that the structure of the units of learning used in e-learning is valid. However, this is in itself not the same as an effective, efficient and attractive pedagogical design; whether a design conforms to these criteria comes to a great extent from the theories and principles of learning and instruction. These theories form the basis for the design of the meta-model behind EML/IMSLD. On the other hand, the designs themselves are not enough to guarantee high-quality designs. They tend to be defined at too abstract a level, not providing enough details for the real structuring work that must be done when developing real units of learning.

EML/IMSLD makes the use of pedagogical models explicit. This is one of the factors needed to enhance the quality of a pedagogical design. So the combination of good design and good structuring of the design in a notation will bring us the quality of learning we are searching for. EML/IMSLD provides the framework to notate and communicate the designs in a complete form, to validate them on completeness in structure, and makes it possible to identify the functionality of LOs within the context of a unit of learning and provides means for real interoperability and reusability. Moreover, we think that EML/IMSLD can make the building of learning management systems easier (because the requirements are explicit) and can make learning management systems more effective, because the design of the systems can take advantage of the huge body of knowledge available in educational research, based on theories, empirical findings and the experience from practitioners.

References

Booch, G., Rumbaugh, J. and Jacobson, I. (eds) (1999) *The unified modeling language user guide*, Addison-Wesley, Reading.

Brown, A. L. (1980) Metacognitive development and reading, in *Theoretical issues in reading comprehension*, eds R. J. Spiro, B. C. Bruce and W. F. Brewer, pp. 453–81, Lawrence Erlbaum Associates, Hillsdale, NJ.

Clark, R. E. (1983) Reconsidering research on learning from media, *Review of Educational Research*, **53**: 445–59.

Clark, R. E. and Sugrue, B. M. (1990) North American disputes about research on learning from media, *International Journal of Education Research*, **14** (6): 507–20.

Cole, M. and Engestrom, Y. (1993) A cultural-historical approach to distributed cognition, in *Distributed cognitions*, ed. G. Salomon, pp. 1–46, Cambridge University Press, New York.

De Block, A. (1982) *Algemene didactiek*, Antwerpen: Standaard.

Dochy, F. J. R. C. (1992) *Assessment of prior knowledge as a determinant for future learning*, Open Universiteit, Heerlen.

Duffy, T. M. and Cunningham, D. J. (1996) Constructivism: Implications for the design and delivery of instruction, in *Handbook of research for educational communications and technology*, ed. D. H. Jonassen, pp. 170–98, Macmillan, New York.

Duffy, T. M. and Jonassen, D. H. (1991) Constructivism: New implications for instructional technology, *Educational Technology*, **31** (5): 7–12.

Flavell, J. H. (1979) Metacognition and cognitive monitoring: A new area of cognitive-developmental inquiry, *American Psychologist*, **34**: 906–11.

Gagné, R. M. (1977) *The conditions of learning*, Holt, Rinehart & Winston, New York.

Gagné, R. M. and Briggs, L. J. (1979) *Principles of instructional design*, Holt, Rinehart & Winston, New York.

Greeno, J. G., Collins, A. M. and Resnick, L. B. (1996) Cognition and learning, in *Handbook of educational psychology*, eds D. C. Berliner and R. C. Calfee, pp. 15–46, Macmillan, New York.

IMSLD (2003) (accessed 28 March 2003) *IMS Learning design information model*, (Online) http://imsglobal.org.

Jonassen, D. H. (1999) Designing constructivist learning environments, in *Instructional-design theories and models: A new paradigm of instructional theory*, ed. C. M. Reigeluth, pp. 215–40, Lawrence Erlbaum Associates, Mahwah.

Koper, R. (2000) (accessed 28 March 2003) *Educational modelling language reference manual*, Open University of the Netherlands, (Online) http://eml.ou.nl.

Kozma, R. B. (1991) Learning with media. Review of educational research, in *Self-regulation of learning and performance. Issues and educational applications*, eds D. H. Schunk and B. J. Zimmerman, pp. 179–211, Erlbaum, Hillsdale, NJ.

Kuhn, T. S. (1962) The structure of scientific revolutions, University of Chicago Press, Chicago.

Lave, J. and Wenger, E. (1991) *Situated learning*, Cambridge University Press, Cambridge.

Locke, J. (1609). (accessed 8 April 2004). An Essay Concerning Human Understanding (Electronic Version) http://enlightenment.supersaturated.com/johnlocke/book11chapter11.html

Malone, T. W. (1981) Toward a theory of intrinsically motivating instruction, *Cognitive Science*, **4**: 333–69.

Mayer, R. E. and Greeno, J. G. (1972) Structural differences between learning outcomes produced by different instructional methods, *Journal of Educational Psychology*, **63**: 165–73.

Merrill, M. D. (1983) Component display theory, in *Instructional design theories and models: An overview of their current status*, ed. C. M. Reigeluth, pp. 279–333, Lawrence Erlbaum Associates, Hillsdale, NJ.

Merrill, M. D. (1999) Instructional transaction theory (ITT): Instructional design based on knowledge objects, in *Instructional-design theories and models: A new paradigm of instructional theory*, ed. C. M. Reigeluth, pp. 397–424, Lawrence Erlbaum Associates, Mahwah.

Reigeluth, C. M. (1983) *Instructional design theories and models: An overview of their current status*, Lawrence Erlbaum Associates, Hillsdale, NJ.

Reigeluth, C. M. (1999) What is instructional-design theory and how is it changing?, in *Instructional-design theories and models: A new paradigm of instructional theory*, ed. C. M. Reigeluth, pp. 5–29, Lawrence Erlbaum Associates, Mahwah.

Reigeluth, C. and Schwartz, E. (1989) An instructional theory for the design of computer-based simulations, *Journal of Computer-Based Instruction*, **16** (1): 1–10.

Reigeluth, C. M. and Stein, F. S. (1983) The elaboration theory of instruction, in *Instructional design theories and models: An overview of their current status*, ed. C. M. Reigeluth, pp. 335–81, Lawrence Erlbaum Associates, Hillsdale, NJ.

Schunk, D. H. and Zimmerman, B. J. (1994) Social origins of self-regulatory competence, *Educational Psychologist*, **22**: 195–208.

Shuell, T. J. (1988) The role of the student in learning from instruction, *Contemporary Educational Psychology*, **13**: 276–95.

Simons, P. R. J. (1999) Competentiegerichte leeromgevingen in organisaties en hoger beroepsonderwijs, in *Competentiegerichte leeromgevingen*, eds K. Schlusmans *et al.*, pp. 31–46, Lemma, Utrecht.

Stolovitch, H. D. and Keeps, E. J. (1999) *Handbook of human performance technology*, Jossey-Bass Publishers, San Francisco.

Van Merriënboer, J. J. G. (1997) *Training complex cognitive skills: A four-component instructional design model for technical training*, Educational Technology Publications, Englewood Cliffs, NJ.

Vermunt, J. D. (1996) Metacognitive, cognitive and affective aspects of learning styles and strategies: A phenomenographic analysis, *Higher Education*, **31**: 25–50.

Chapter 4

Three objections to learning objects

Norm Friesen

As I write this chapter, governments around the world are spending tens of millions of dollars (and euros) on initiatives that promise the development of learning objects (LOs), LO metadata and LO repositories to store both these data and objects. In more plain language, LOs can be said to refer to digital educational resources; metadata refers to their systematic description to facilitate searching and administration; and repositories represent online, searchable collections of these resources. Examples of initiatives underway include the Curriculum Online project being undertaken for schools in the UK at a cost of approximately US$80 million, and the Australian Learning Federation, a project similar in emphasis with a US$30 million budget. Similar projects are also being currently undertaken in Canada (eduSource, 2003; SchoolNet, 2003) the USA (Heal, 2003; iLumina, 2003) and by regional and international consortia (The Universal Brokerage Platform, 2003).

Only recently has discourse in this area moved beyond broad generalizations, technical elaboration, or promotional précis. To my knowledge (and as claimed by Banks, 2001), there have been no in-depth studies of the pedagogical consequences of these systems and ways of thinking, and no examinations of their epistemological and ideological implications. Moreover, others have noted a general lack of adoption of these technologies by practitioners and vendors (e.g. Robson, Chapter 12; and Farance, 2003).

This chapter seeks to address these issues by summarizing a number of concerns that have already been raised in relation to LOs and associated technologies, and by outlining a number of further, outstanding issues related to the vision of LOs, e-learning standardization and the milieu from which it has arisen. It does so also from the perspective of someone who has been actively involved in these activities and this milieu for a number of years, and with a special emphasis on the interests and values of public education. It does so also in recognition of the fact that only through open discussion of both positive *and* negative aspects can the vision of sharing educational resources be made more relevant to the work of learning practitioners and to learners themselves.

What is a learning object?

The problems presented by LOs and related technologies begin with the definition of the term *learning object* itself. The particular meaning or meanings associated with this term have been the subject of much debate and discussion (see the Introduction). Often cited in these attempts is an early definition provided by the IEEE Learning Technology Standards Committee: 'Any entity, digital or non-digital, which can be used, re-used and referenced during technology-supported learning.' Such a definition – as the IEEE itself says – implies that LOs can include 'multimedia content, instructional content, instructional software and software tools [and] in a wider sense . . . learning objectives, persons, organizations, or events'. There are few things, in other words, that cannot be LOs. As Merrill puts it, 'No one seems to know what a learning object is in the first place. One of the absurd definitions I heard was, "as small as a drop, as wide as the ocean". In other words, if everything is a learning object, then nothing is a learning object' (Merrill cited in Welsch, 2002). The result of all of this, as Rehak and Mason describe it, is confusion:

> Different definitions abound, different uses are envisaged, and different sectors have particular reasons for pursuing their development. In this environment of uncertainty and disagreement, the various stakeholders are going off in all directions.
>
> (Rehak and Mason, 2003)

However, at the same time, the term *learning object* carries discernible indications of its origin and its own intrinsic characteristics. Polsani (2003) explained that 'the term was first popularized by Wayne Hodgins in 1994 when he named the CedMA [*sic*; Computer Education Management Association] working group "Learning Architectures, APIs and Learning Objects".'

CEdMA, in turn, describes its own purpose as providing a 'forum' for discussion of 'issues in computer training' (CEdMA, 2003). It would be strange indeed if the term didn't bear the imprint of this origin in the domain of computer technology and training. But more will be said about this connection later.

More important at this juncture is the fact that the term *object* in *learning object* has clear origins in 'object-oriented' programming, design, analysis and theory (Robson, 1999; Bratina, Hayes and Blumsack, 2002). This programming and design approach or 'paradigm' (Alhir, 1998) has been developed and consolidated in the area of software programming and design over the past thirty years. It started with the programming language SIMULA-67 around 1970, and 'became all-pervasive with the advent of C++, and later Java' (FOLDOC, 2002).

The form of design and analysis that goes by this name now also has considerable influence in the groups that are responsible for technical standards in e-learning. This influence is most clearly revealed in their adoption of formal description techniques based on object-oriented modelling, especially UML (Unified Modelling Language). Both this object-oriented description technique and object orientation generally, are based on 'such principles as abstraction, concurrency, encapsulation, hierarchy, persistence, polymorphism, and typing' (Microsoft Press, 1997).

It is at this point that this chapter's first objection to LOs emerges: namely, the fact that the term *learning object* juxtaposes two words that are in many ways incongruous and incommensurable. The first, 'object', is based thoroughly and very specifically on a technological paradigm (one whose basic principles are so specialized as to be difficult to express in everyday language). And the second, 'learning', is equally extreme in its vagueness, generality and broadly *non*-technical nature. It is this incongruity and incommensurability that can be seen as underlying the confusion and divergence in defining *learning objects*, and ultimately, as contributing significantly to their slow uptake by vendors and practitioners. The juxtaposition of disparate elements represented by the term *learning objects* will be discussed further as a part of the second objection presented in this chapter.

This collision of the technical and specific with the non-technical and general repeats a negative historical pattern that has recurred in different forms with previous innovations in educational technology. In this pattern, these innovations are introduced into educational contexts and practices clearly bearing the stamp of their technical origin. Instead of being presented in terms familiar and meaningful to educators, they bear connotations that appear unclear or even negative in these practical contexts. Next in this pattern is the appearance of various forms of resistance to these innovations on the part of practitioners. Finally, this is followed by teachers and other practitioners being blamed for their resistance and inflexibility in not adopting such innovations. Speaking specifically of research into school education, Larry Cuban describes this recurring pattern as follows:

> Since the mid nineteenth century the classroom has become home to a succession of technologies (e.g. textbook, chalkboard, radio, film, and television). . . . Yet the teacher has been singled out as inflexibly resistant to 'modern' technology, stubbornly engaging in a closed-door policy toward using new mechanical and automated instructional aids. . . . Seldom did investigators try to adopt a teacher's perspective or appreciate the duality of continuity and change that marked both schools and classrooms.
>
> (Cuban, 1986, pp. 2, 6)

Using a term that makes sense only in abstruse technical discussions, and that is opaque or even confusing to both experts and practitioners, does not make its potential benefits clear to teachers. Instead, it presents the potential of unproductively pitting those responsible for instruction against those advocating technological change. It is not that the innovation should not come from outside of education, or that it can come only from within. It is simply that innovations must be presented in terms that are meaningful for teaching practice.

A tradition of research into the spread or diffusion of innovations among populations underscores this point. This research shows that the rate of adoption increases significantly when innovations possess some of the following characteristics: (1) simplicity, (2) compatibility with existing methods and techniques, and (3) relative advantage in comparison with these established methods and techniques (Rogers, 1969).

Innovations such as e-mail or mobile phones provide good examples of technologies that meet these requirements. Although they are new and quite different from the technologies that they supersede, their very names provide a simple and direct comparison with these established technologies. Instead of suggesting the complexity of technological abstraction, the terms 'mobile phone' and 'e-mail' connote the relative advantage presented by these innovations: the mobility of cellular communication and the instantaneous nature of electronic telecommunications. The term 'learning object', on the other hand, suggests neither simplicity nor compatibility, nor any obvious relative advantage over existing technologies. In order for the positive potential of LOs to be realized in practice, they should be labelled and described in ways that make the simplicity, compatibility and advantages claimed for them readily apparent to teachers, trainers and other practitioners.

Where is the learning in e-learning standards?

National and international committees, consortia and other organizations have been busy developing standards and specifications for e-learning technologies at least since the late 1990s. They have been doing so with the understanding that the benefits of this standardization work will be manifold and variegated:

> Not only would the development and use of international standards [in e-learning] produce a direct cost savings, but the information technology systems could be used in a wider range of applications, and used more efficiently. Better, more efficient and interoperable systems, content, and components will produce better learning, education, and training – which has a positive effect upon all societies.
>
> (ISO Bulletin, 2002)

Organizations actively developing these standards and specifications include the IMS Global E-Learning Consortium, the IEEE Learning Technologies Standards Committee, and the ISO Subcommittee on 'Information Technology for Learning Education and Training'. Together, these groups are developing standards and specifications that, as McGraw (2001) explains, will provide 'the required components and functionality of learning'. 'Most e-learning', she explains, 'requires an open architecture, and must include standards for integrating existing elements, such as legacy learning, enterprise applications, online learning, and emerging tools.' E-learning standardization efforts, in other words, can be seen as attempting to lay the foundation for an infrastructure specifically to support learning, for example, a distributed network of LOs, metadata repositories and/or related services and resources (Downes, 2002).

One initiative that is making a major contribution to the realization of such visions goes by the name of 'SCORM' (Sharable Content Object Reference Model). SCORM is being developed by the Advanced Distributed Learning initiative (ADL), an effort sponsored by the US Department of Defence and the White House Office of Science and Technology Policy. The SCORM framework or reference model is intended to make a key contribution to the ADL's mission, 'to provide high quality instruction and decision aiding anytime, anywhere and tailored to each learner's needs' (ADL, 2001).

It seeks to do so by simplifying, combining and interrelating a number of specifications and standards for more ready implementation. The ADL itself describes the SCORM framework as representing 'a pedagogically neutral means for designers and implementers of instruction to aggregate learning resources for the purpose of delivering a desired learning experience' (ADL, 2001, pp. 2–3).

However, despite (or perhaps because of) these lofty claims, a number of those implementing or associated with SCORM have already been expressing misgivings specifically related to learning and issues of pedagogy. In contradistinction to SCORM's own claims to 'pedagogical neutrality', some of these experts have been asserting that SCORM is limited in its pedagogical scope, neutrality or relevance. Even worse, others have been warning that it will actually present a substantial *barrier* to accessible learning – rather than making it easily available in customized form, anytime, anywhere.

Rehak, one of the 'chief architects' behind SCORM, has stated that the pedagogical model implied in this framework (contrary to its own claims) is not suitable for some environments. 'SCORM', Rehak says, 'is essentially about a single-learner [whose learning is] self-paced and self-directed. This makes it inappropriate for use in [higher education] and K-12.' This was a report on what Rehak said in public, not based on something he wrote (Kraan and Wilson, 2002).

Anderson (a key contributor to many of the specifications incorporated into SCORM) has emphasized that the path that SCORM is taking must be modified in order for it to be instructionally useful and pedagogically relevant. Lanahas (cited in Maddocks, 2002), a senior systems engineer at Cisco Systems (a company that has invested heavily in educational object-based strategies for e-learning), is much more negative. He characterizes the experience of 'witnessing SCORM's evolution (as being) akin to "watching an impending train wreck".' The issue he foregrounds in his comments is the complexity of the specifications integrated into this framework. Lanahas (as cited in Welsch, 2002) further argued that SCORM's complexity will nullify the benefits that ISO and others identify as being promised by e-learning standardization: 'Instead of simplifying things and making content more affordable and accessible, SCORM is adding new layers of complexity that will drive up costs and completely hamstring the industry.'

Conflicting claims about educational scope, doubts about pedagogical relevance and neutrality, objections to unnecessary complexity: all of these problems necessarily arise, it can be argued, from the simultaneous claims to pedagogical value and pedagogical neutrality made by SCORM and also implied in many other e-learning standardization efforts. Like the definitional issues arising with the term *learning object*, these problems can be seen as the outcome of the collision of the technical and specific with the practical and general. *Specification* and *standardization* (as the words themselves suggest) presuppose that the matter at hand must be known and specified in great precision, reliability and detail. These terms or processes also presuppose a certain level of uniformity and homogeneity in their subject matter, and characteristics such as decomposability and modularity (Alhir, 1998; ISO Bulletin, 2002). As the Web and the Internet themselves palpably demonstrate, such characteristics can indeed be ascribed (at least on one level) to information and information interchange generically. The Internet and the Web are based on multiple layers of standardized protocols and specifications that can work across platforms and technological environments. One could also make the case that similarly specifiable characteristics might also be found in the processes and requirements associated with specific forms of education. For unlike the word *learning*, the term *education* readily implies or encompasses phenomena such as educational institutions, educational administration, educational certification or educational assessment. And each of these educational forms, as they appear within a particular domain, are indeed likely to display uniform, persistent and precise characteristics subject to specification and standardization. Examples of how such characteristics are being effectively exploited in specification development are even provided by the efforts of the Open Knowledge Initiative (OKI) and Schools Interoperability Framework (SIF). These initiatives are both working to create standard architectures for the effective interchange of data between existing systems in higher education (OKI) and school systems (SIF) (see OKI, 2003; SIF, 2003).

However, *learning*, especially as it might be understood generically, as extending 'neutrally' or 'agnostically' across contexts and practices, is quite a different matter. The incredibly wide variety of phenomena and entities to which this word can apply do not display the homogeneity, uniformity and modularity that is the necessary precondition for specification and standardization. *Learning*, as it is defined in the *Oxford English Dictionary* (Oxford University Press, 1987), is the 'action of acquiring knowledge' or 'a process which leads to the modification of behaviour or the acquisition of new abilities or responses'. Learning, in other words, is something that is not separable from the subjectivity of the learner. It is an action or process that the learner undertakes or experiences, and that is not intrinsic to any content or system. Learning could conceivably occur in an encounter with any kind of object, content, or system. As other chapters in this collection by Mason (Chapter 13), and Sosteric and Hesemeier (Chapter 2) indicate, learning is something that is highly dependent on 'intention', 'context' and other characteristics that are by definition difficult to embed with a modular, interchangeable object.

As such, learning itself cannot be simply decomposed and exchanged in the form of objects, or enumerated as a series of requirements and functionalities that can be supported in a generic learning 'infrastructure'. Consequently, it is not surprising that attempts to specify the characteristics and functionalities that might belong to LOs or to learning infrastructures have resulted in confusion, divergence and proliferating complexity. It seems that it would be more fruitful instead to deliberately focus on particular educational forms, practices and contexts in standardization and specification activities, and to explicitly acknowledge limits to the pedagogical value and applicability of such efforts.

Learning in a militarized zone

LOs and e-learning standardization bear the imprint of the ideology and culture of the American military-industrial complex, and of ways of thinking that are related either marginally or antithetically to the interests and values of education generally and public education in particular. In *The Classroom Arsenal*, Noble (1991) identifies the characteristics of what he calls the 'military worldview' that have shaped the US military's approach to training technology, and which in turn have had a significant influence on this technology in public education. Noble begins his study by emphasizing the preponderance of military educational research over its public counterpart in the United States:

> Within government agencies, the military spends seven dollars for every civilian dollar spent on educational technology research. Each year, for example, the military spends as much on educational technology research and development as the Department ... of Education has spent in a quarter century.
>
> (Noble, 1991, p. 2)

Using technical systems and weaponry of ever-increasing complexity, the US Department of Defence, as Noble explains, attempts to address its ever-growing training needs by employing the same approaches to education as are used in the development and deployment of weapons and command-and-control systems. Not surprisingly, characteristics of the military world-view in general reappear in its approaches to education in particular. Noble describes these characteristics and his own treatment of them as follows:

> The three principal ... characteristics of the 'worldview' ... of US military research and development to be addressed here are 1) technological innovation, 2) command and control, and 3) systems thinking. Subsidiary topics that are also discussed include the military research emphasis on speed, change, and efficiency; uniformity and standardization; task specificity; and simulation.
>
> (Noble, 1991, p. 5)

The characteristics of this worldview that are of special significance in this chapter are its emphasis on systems thinking and, of course, the prominence of uniformity and standardization.

As it has been understood in military contexts, systems thinking has generally been realized in the form of cybernetic, 'man-machine' weapons systems (the gender exclusivity of this last military phrase is deliberately retained). Indeed, cybernetics – 'the comparative study of automatic control systems' in biological and artificial entities (Merriam-Webster Dictionary, 2002) had its origin in military efforts to 'theorize humans as component parts of weapons systems' (Edwards cited in Noble, 1991, p. 27).

The end result of this approach is to understand training and the technologies that support it as a means of engineering and maximizing the performance of the human components of a larger system. The performance of these human components can be fine-tuned and optimized in a manner similar to the way their mechanical and electronic counterparts are maintained and refined. Edwards continued:

> Such training is considered within military training research to be a personnel corollary to advanced technological development; its principle objective is to fit human components – gun crews, computer operators, pilots, electronics technicians, equipment repairers, communications

specialists, clerical and managerial support, etc. – into complex man-machine weapons systems and information systems by the most efficient means possible. Therefore training is conceived in the military as a species of human engineering.

(Edwards cited in Noble, 1991, p. 48)

The understandings from which such an approach is derived are clearly emblematized in the diagram in Figure 4.1.

Through its depiction of varied content (screw-driver, soldier, teacher) being subjected to the machine processing of a 'Learning Management System', and being subsequently communicated to the relevant organ of the 'student', 'professional' or 'warfighter', this diagram depicts without apparent exaggeration a vision of e-learning and e-learning specification that the US military sees as attractive.

In this light, it is perhaps not surprising that many of the key participants in the e-learning specification cited above (Rehak, Hodgins and Lanahas, for example) are engineers themselves, or have close ties with engineering organizations (Hodgins, for example, is a 'Strategic Futurist' at Autodesk, makers of AutoCAD software for mechanical engineers).

Such an emphasis on the understandings and methods of engineering lead directly, as Noble himself explains, to a corresponding emphasis on technical standards and specifications as solutions to training challenges. If these challenges can be understood simply as deficiencies in engineering and design, then their solution lies in the development of rigorous technical standards, and the instantiation of these standards in strictly conforming systems and implementations:

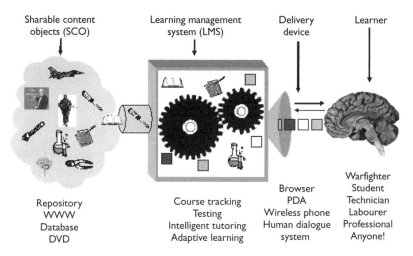

Sharable content objects (SCO)	Learning management system (LMS)	Delivery device	Learner
Repository	Course tracking	Browser	Warfighter
WWW	Testing	PDA	Student
Database	Intelligent tutoring	Wireless phone	Technician
DVD	Adaptive learning	Human dialogue	Labourer
		system	Professional
			Anyone!

Figure 4.1 ADL and the sharable content object reference model

Source: Slosser, S. (2001, 12 April)

> A system fulfills some purpose or intended use, and in order to do so a system must meet certain standards or criteria of operational effectiveness. This in turn, requires precise specificity of component design; the Department of Defense is notorious in industrial production for the rigor and idiosyncratic character of its 'military specifications' or 'milspecs.'
>
> (Noble, 1991, p. 34)

Education, despite its radically different funding levels and constitution, can be seen as having embarked on its own, idiosyncratic 'edspecs' enterprise. E-learning specifications, as well as the military and engineering connotations they carry with them, thus present an important challenge to public and other forms of education: namely, to carefully and accurately identify the limits of the relevance of these specifications and the efficacy of the general approach they embody.

For example, looking at the diagram in Figure 4.1, it is easy to realize that the vision it communicates is rather far afield from many of the practices, contexts and values that dominate public education, and that can also play a role in other educational forms. As Noble urges in the conclusion to his study, such an examination of the pedagogical relevance of technical specifications in public education, as an examination of any approaches engendered in a different context, must be undertaken with great care:

> While appearing to address problems in public education, [military educational technology] research actually participates in an entirely different enterprise, one with marginal and antithetical import for education. This is the design and engineering of man-machine systems.
>
> (Noble, 1991, p. 146)

The goals of public education, however they might be construed, are almost certain to be radically different.

Conclusion

For the full potential of e-learning standardization and infrastructure efforts to be realized, it is important that these efforts place significantly greater attention on existing educational practice, on issues of innovation adoption, and on the heterogeneity of educational activities and contexts in general. To deal properly with this divergence and complexity – and with issues also now emerging from training and other communities – it is necessary to look beyond systems engineering techniques and standardization processes. These techniques and processes may have worked well for more exclusively technical applications, but they are proving inadequate for dealing with the ambiguities implied in education and in the deceptively simple term 'learning'. They also bring with them a culture and set of connotations that are not entirely helpful in public education. Perhaps most importantly for e-learning content and standardization, it is important to recognize that objects and infrastructures for learning cannot simultaneously be *both* pedagogically neutral *and* pedagogically valuable. Developers and designers will have to recognize and choose relevant (and probably differing) pedagogical positions, or risk pedagogical irrelevance.

References

ADL (2001) (accessed 26 April 2003) Sharable content object reference model Version 1.2: The SCORM overview, (Online) http://www.adlnet.org/ADLDOCS/Documents/SCORM_1.2_Overview.pdf.

Alhir, S. S. (1998) *UML in a nutshell*, Sebastopol, CA.

Banks, B. (2001) (accessed 1 April 2003) Learning theory and learning objects, (Online) http://www.fdlearning.com/fdlearning/html/company/features/l-theory-l-objects.pdf.

Bratina, T. A., Hayes, D. and Blumsack, S. L. (2002) Preparing teachers to use learning objects, *The Technology Source*.

CEdMA (2003) (accessed 1 April 2003) Computer education management association, (Online) http://www.cedma.org/guestabout_cedma.html.

Cuban, L. (1986) *Teachers and machines the classroom use of technology since 1920*, Teachers College Press, New York.

Downes, S. (2002) (accessed 28 April 2003) Design and reusability of learning objects in an academic context: A new economy of education, (Online) http://www.downes.ca/files/milan.doc.

eduSource (2003) (accessed 28 March 2003) eduSource Canada, (Online) http://www.edusource.ca.

Farance, F. (2003) (accessed 18 April 2003) IEEE LOM standard not yet ready for prime time, *Learning Technology (Publication of the IEEE Computer Society Learning Technology Task Force)*, **5** (1), (Online) http://lttf.ieee.org/learn_tech/issues/january2003/index.html#8.

FOLDOC (2002) (accessed 23 April 2003) Free online dictionary of computing, (Online) http://wombat.doc.ic.ac.uk/foldoc/.

Heal (2003) (accessed 21 April 2003) Health education assets library: National multimedia repository, (Online) http://www.healcentral.org/index.htm.

IEEE (1998) (accessed 28 April 2003) Learning Objects Metadata (LOM): Draft document Learning Technology Standards Committee, 2 (1) (Online) http://itsc.ieee.org.

iLumina (2003) (accessed 20 March 2003) iLumina: Educational resources for science and mathematics (Online) http://turing.csc.uncwil.edu/ilumina/homePage.xml.

ISO Bulletin (2002) (accessed 12 June 2002) Information technology: Learning by IT, (Online) http://jtc1sc36.org/doc/36N0264.pdf.

Kraan, W. and Wilson, S. (2002) (accessed 28 April 2003) Dan Rehak: SCORM is not for everyone, (Online) http://www.cetis.ac.uk/content/20021002000737.

Maddocks, P. (2002) (accessed 24 April 2003) Case Study: Cisco Systems ventures into the land of reusability, *Learning Circuits: ASTD's Online Magazine All About E-Learning*, (Online) http://www.learningcircuits.org/2002/mar2002/maddocks. html.

McGraw, K. (2001) (accessed 1 May 2003) E-learning strategy equals infrastructure, *Learning Circuits*, (Online) http://www.learningcircuits.org/2001/jun2001/ mcgraw.html.

Merriam-Webster (2004) (accessed 8 April 2004) Merriam-Webster Online, (Online) http://www.m-w.com.

Microsoft Press (1997) *Microsoft press computer dictionary,* Microsoft Press, Redmond, WA.

Noble, D. D. (1991) *The classroom arsenal: Military research, information technology and public education*, Falmer Press, New York.

OED (1989) Oxford English Dictionary, Oxford University Press, Oxford.

OKI (2003) (accessed 20 March 2003) Open knowledge initiative, (Online) http://web.mit.edu/oki/.

Polsani, P. R. (2003) (accessed 28 April 2003) Use and abuse of reusable learning objects, *Journal of Digital Information*, **3** (4), (Online) http://jodi.ecs.soton.ac.uk/ Articles/v03/i04/Polsani/.

Rehak, D. and Mason, R. (2003) Keeping the learning in learning objects, in *Reusing online resources: A sustainable approach to e-learning*, ed. A. Littlejohn, pp. 20–34, Kogan, London.

Robson, R. (1999) (accessed 17 December 2002) Object-oriented instructional design and web-based authoring, (Online) http://citeseer.nj.nec.com/327280.html.

Rogers, E. M. (1969) *Diffusion of innovations,* The Free Press, New York.

SchoolNet (2003) (accessed 26 April 2003) Canada's SchoolNet, (Online) http:// www.schoolnet.ca/home/e/.

SIF (2003) (accessed 27 April 2003) Schools interoperability framework, (Online) http://www.sifinfo.org/.

Slosser, S. (2001) (accessed 1 December 2003) ADL and the sharable content object reference model, *Joint ADL Co-laboratory*, (Online) http://www.nectec.or.th/ courseware/pdf-documents/adl-scorm.pdf.

The Universal Brokerage Platform (2003) (accessed 1 April 2003) The Universal Brokerage platform for learning resources, (Online) http://www.educanext.org/ UNIVERSAL.

Welsch, E. (2002) (accessed 01 July 2002) SCORM: Clarity or calamity?, *Online Learning Magazine*, (Online) http://www.onlinelearningmag.com/training/search/ search_display.jsp?vnu_content_id=1526769.

Chapter 5

Learning objects revisited

Erik Duval and Wayne Hodgins

This chapter investigates advanced and innovative interpretations of the basic concepts underlying the learning object (LO) paradigm. We believe that it is necessary to start a new research cycle on more advanced models and methodologies for LOs. More specifically, we want to investigate:

- a taxonomy of LOs and their components;
- a component architecture for structuring composite LOs, and enabling their components to interact;
- the processes of aggregation and disassembly to produce new or repurpose existing LOs; and
- determinants for the efficiency and effectiveness of LO repurposing, and how these can be influenced by appropriate design methodologies.

Through this basic research, we want to enable large-scale share and reuse of multimedia content components, with a special emphasis on the deployment of such components in education and training.

In a very general sense, it has repeatedly been observed (Van Dam, 2002) that the actual impact of ICT on education and training is rather limited. As an illustration, the 'Grand Challenges' conference in 2002 identified A Teacher for every Learner: Scaleable Learner-Centered Education as one of the grand research challenges in computer science. The panel envisioned:

> building the technological infrastructure to support dynamic, ad-hoc communities of lifelong learners who interact within an environment of LOs through a creative blend of advanced computing technologies, high performance networks, authoring and collaboration tools.
>
> (York *et al.*, 2002)

It was estimated that a Manhattan project approach, with sustained major funding over a decade or longer, would be needed to finally realize this long-standing dream.

In recent years, much of the research in this area has focused on the notion of reusable multimedia content components, referred to as learning objects (LOs). Early pioneers in the domain recognize that this paradigm offers new opportunities and presents new challenges to realize their vision (Van Dam, 2002). The driving force stems from the notion that repurposing of such components can lead to important savings in time and money, and can enhance the quality of digital learning experiences. The end result would be faster, cheaper and better learning. Repurposing, or more generally, reuse, should be thought of in this context as the ability to use, without any (significant) changes, the same piece of content for a purpose significantly different from what it was originally intended for when created.

Early work in this area included the Educational Object Economy (Roschelle *et al.*, 1999) and ARIADNE (2002). Since then, and spurred by the development of the Learning Object Metadata standard by the IEEE Learning Technology Standards Committee (IEEE Learning Technologies Standardization Committee (LTSC), 2001) and IEEE LTSC LOM, numerous initiatives have been launched in academic and corporate contexts (Neven and Duval, 2002).

Relevant additional work on repositories of LOs includes CUBER (Lamminaho and Magerkurth, 2001), UNIVERSAL (Papatheodorou, Vassiliou and Simon, 2002), MERLOT (MERLOT, 2002) and SMETE (Dong and Agogino, 2001). Architectural aspects are the focus of work at the Learning Systems Architecture Laboratory at Carnegie Mellon University (Learning Systems Architecture Lab, 2002). The ADL initiative's SCORM includes the LOM standard (SCORM, 2003). Organizations such as IMS (IMS, 2003), Athabasca University with its CanCore (2003) profile and Singapore's E-learning Competency Centre with its SingCore (SingCORE, 2003) profile have developed guidelines to assist tool developers and end-users to adopt the new LO paradigm.

Recent developments in peer-to-peer infrastructures have also been explored in the context of LOs, with Edutella (Nejdl *et al.*, 2002) and SPLASH (see Richards, Hatala and McGreal, Chapter 18), as well as LOMster (Ternier, Duval and Vandepitte, June 2002). Finally, some of the researchers in the Adaptive Hypermedia Community are beginning to consider the implications of rich metadata that can be mapped against end-user requirements to dynamically generate meaningful and relevant learning experiences (Suthers, 2001; Conejo *et al.*, 2002).

However, we believe that much of this work is somewhat misguided, because of the too traditional and restricted view of what LOs are and how they can be put to use. The main objective of this chapter is to launch an investigation into advanced, innovative interpretations and generalizations of the basic concepts underlying the LO paradigm. There is a clear need for this kind of work, as many publications mention difficulties with the interpretation of some of these concepts. Indeed, recent 'guidelines' like CanCore and SingCORE (2003) were produced in response to this problem. However, they take a very traditional and restricted view of what LOs are and how they can be put to use.

The problem can be summarized as follows. Many actors in this research domain limit their vision of LOs to that of traditional documents or software applications (e.g. simulations). However, the current state of technology allows us to consider a much smaller level of granularity that enables more flexible and effective repurposing of content.

A useful analogy to consider is the building industry: it is reported that up to 85 per cent of construction work in the building industry rely on standardized components such as windows and doors. Earlier attempts to reuse complete kitchens, bathrooms, and so on failed because that larger level of granularity did not enable the flexible composition of tailor-made buildings. By analogy, we believe that the current document-based model in much of the LOs world will not realize the goal of 'share and reuse', but that a more innovative and flexible underlying model of 'doclets' or LO components is required. However, in order to put such an approach into effect, some basic research issues need to be addressed.

Overview

The following interrelated fundamental research issues are detailed in the sections below.

1. A LO taxonomy or a set of such taxonomies will be developed to identify different kinds of LOs and their components.
2. A component architecture or a set of such architectures for LOs will be developed, to enable structuring of composite LOs, as well as interactions between its components.
3. The processes of aggregation and disassembly, to produce composite LOs and to isolate their components, will be studied in detail, so as to better support these processes, and to exploit them for (semi-)automatic generation of metadata.
4. Methodological aspects that influence repurposing of LOs during the design phase will be investigated, so as to optimize the design for repurposing afterwards.

Research issue I – A learning object taxonomy

According to the LO Metadata (LOM) standard, a LO is 'any entity, digital or non-digital, that may be used for learning, education or training' (Duval and Hodgins, 2002). This definition allows for an extremely wide variety of granularities. This means that a LO could be a picture of the Mona Lisa, a document on the Mona Lisa (that includes the picture), a course module on da Vinci, a complete course on art history, or even a four-year master curriculum on Western culture. In one sense, this is appropriate, as there are a number of common themes to content components of all sizes. In another sense, though, this vagueness is problematic, because authoring, deployment and repurposing are affected by the granularity of the LO.

We have already developed a first starting point for such a taxonomy, in collaboration with the Learnativity Foundation. It is important to note that this taxonomy applies to multiple applications. The first two levels are application domain independent, and can, for instance, also be deployed in the field of technical documentation. Only the third and fourth levels are specific to the field of learning.

1. *Raw Media Elements* are the smallest level in this model: these elements reside at a pure data level. Examples include a single sentence or paragraph, illustration, animation, and so on. A further specialization of this level (or complementary taxonomy?) will need to take into account the different characteristics of time-based media (audio, video, animation) and static media (photo, text, etc.).

2. *Information Objects* are sets of raw media elements. Such objects could be based on the 'information block' model developed by Horn (Horn, 1998). While Horn's model refers to text and illustrations (as it is based on pioneering work in the mid-1960s!), the plan is to generalize the concepts to deal with more advanced and innovative content.

3. Based on a single objective, information objects are then selected and assembled into the third level of *Application-Specific Objects*. At this level reside LOs in a more restricted sense than the aforementioned definition of the LOM standard suggests.

4. The fourth level refers to *Aggregate Assemblies* that deal with larger (terminal) objectives. This level corresponds with lessons or chapters, which can in turn be assembled into larger collections, such as courses and whole curricula.

Clearly, information objects contain raw media elements. LOs contain information objects. Aggregate assemblies contain LOs and other aggregate assemblies.

The smaller level of granularity in this taxonomy is essential, as we believe that repurposing can only be accommodated by explicitly identifying the information objects and the raw media elements they contain.

Learning object component architecture

Structuring of learning objects

In order to realize the full potential of dynamic composition of LO components, it is necessary to develop a flexible architecture that enables the structuring of LOs and their components. An important general principle in hypermedia systems is the separation of content and structure from presentation. For structural aspects of aggregate LOs, starting points include the IMS Content Packaging specification (IMS, 2003), the Educational Modelling Language (EML) (Koper, 2001), the Synchronized Multimedia Integration Language (SMIL 2.0, 2001) and DocBook (Walsh and Muellner, 1999). All of these rather complementary initiatives have adopted an XML-based approach.

Innovative approaches to LO structuring should include dynamically generated components, based on some processing of (semi-)structured data. A simple example is a LO on weather forecasting that makes use of a set of current satellite images relevant to the location of the learner, accessing simple data about the learner and the time that the learning is to take place to retrieve a relevant set of images, so as to realize an authentic and thus an effective and efficient experience. This kind of context points to the need for structures that identify relevant components through search criteria, rather than just listing the identities of the components.

A more complex example would be to access information about the role of the learner in the organization, his or her personal goals and those of the organization, his or her agenda, and so on to generate a highly customized LO that would be relevant for the task at hand, and that would take into account the constraints (time, language, cost, location, etc.) that influence the particular context in which the learning is to take place. This approach to personalized learning is closely related to the field of adaptive (educational) hypermedia, intelligent tutoring systems, and so on (Conejo, Brusilovsky and De Bra, 2002). There are some successes in relatively constrained domains (Maddocks, 2002), but it is clear that much research is needed before generally applicable, large-scale implementations can be developed.

Learning object interactions

Enabling interactions between LOs and their components is important. The original approach focused on JavaBeans, where such interactions were based on a common API (Application Programming Interface) (Roschelle *et al.*, 1999). The use of JavaBeans or other component technologies aligns the concept of LOs much more with the equivalent notion of objects in the object-oriented programming paradigm.

Consequently, this kind of behaviour can be thought of as a specific application of general software engineering component-based approaches. In this specific context, there are many parallels between reuse of software artefacts in general, and LO reuse in particular. Even though this subject has a long research history in software engineering, large-scale applications in practice remain relatively few. Moreover, they are often constrained to particular domains or to particular technological approaches.

Indeed, not only has that approach not been adopted so widely in the context of LOs, but deeper interoperability also requires further considerations on interactions between, for instance, the models that underlie the behaviour of LOs. An example that illustrates this requirement is that of LOs that simulate different parts of the human body, and that need to exchange data between them (Van Dam, 2002).

Aggregation and disassembly

Aggregation and decomposition in LO authoring must be addressed. Traditionally, authoring tools mainly support the process of authoring from three points of departure:

- a blank document that needs to be 'filled' with content, where the structure of the LO is defined during the elaboration of that content;
- a template that needs to be instantiated, where the structure of the LO is defined a priori; and
- an existing LO that is edited and modified in the process of authoring, and then typically saved as a new LO.

Learning objects are created by selecting raw media elements and information objects from a repository, usually based on searches over metadata and profiles. These components can then be assembled into a new LO. This can be referred to as authoring-by-aggregation. The new LO, as it provides new context for the components, will need to provide 'glue' that takes the learner from one component to another.

A simple example of this kind of facility is the way that presentation tools (e.g. Microsoft PowerPoint or SliTeX) allow for existing slides to be included in new presentations and then automatically add 'next' and 'previous' transitions between those slides. More sophisticated 'glue' would enable the author of the aggregated content to include transitional material (e.g. 'In this chapter, we will illustrate the concept of relativity that was introduced in chapter V'), so as to give guidance to the learner on how the components fit together in the aggregate.

However, authors are typically not so comfortable with authoring really small content components or with structuring larger assemblies. The exception for the smaller LOs is that of photographers, who typically focus on authoring single pictures. In a more general sense, many authors find it difficult to produce small content units with a well defined, restricted scope. Therefore, methodologies and tools must be developed that allow authors to work on a level of granularity that they are comfortable with, and then decompose that object into components semi-automatically. In the case of video, for instance, scene cuts can be detected automatically, to suggest appropriate boundaries to separate components. Text segmentation tools support the transformation of text documents into pedagogical hypertext (Hill and Wentland, 1998). Another example would be to take an HTML file with embedded images and extract distinct components and the images.

The main point is that we need better support for authoring of LOs by aggregation and for automatic decomposition of LOs to extract the components of a LO that was originally produced as an aggregate. Moreover, this will have to be complemented by methodologies and techniques for a (semi-)automatic generation of metadata, as it will be impractical to describe all the components in detail manually. Several sources of metadata can be harvested with this intent:

- The *LO itself* can be processed for metadata. For instance, it is a relatively simple process to extract from an HTML LO the title, the language used, references to other LOs, the name of the author (often included in the metadata that is inserted by the authoring tool), and so on. Moreover, search engines such as Google illustrate that existing harvesting techniques can be quite powerful. More research on mapping the results of these techniques to the different metadata elements in structures such as LOM is needed.
- Further research is required on how metadata can propagate from one LO to a *related* one. The language of a textual component will most probably be the language of the composite to which it belongs. Likewise, if there are metadata available about the cost involved with component LOs, then it can be suggested that the cost involved with the composite is at least the aggregated cost of all the components involved. Also, existing techniques for document clustering and text mining need to be reconsidered in the context of explicit metadata, so that for instance the metadata of related and already described LOs can be used to generate metadata for new LOs.
- The *author(s)* of the LO is often the source of additional metadata, as authors typically produce LOs in one language only, or in one content domain, or for one kind of audience (say university level), and so on. Even for authors who produce more diverse LOs, the range of relevant values for many elements can be reduced significantly when characteristics of the author are taken into account.
- The more general *context* of LO authoring can also significantly reduce the number of relevant options. If the metadata authoring tool is launched within the context of a course, for instance, then metadata of the course can be suggested as starting values for the metadata of the LO.

In addition, *templates* of reusable metadata can be created, where many of the relevant fields can be pre-filled. Often, instantiating the template will involve little more than simple selection between a small number of relevant values for a few remaining fields. It is important to note that the 'psychological' effect of presenting an automatically generated metadata instance and then asking the end-user to verify that this description is correct. This is a much less intimidating proposal than being presented with an empty form that includes a large number of empty text boxes to be filled in, as well as many long lists of values to be selected from.

Design methodologies for content reuse

Authors should *avoid explicit references* to other components, as these other components may not be available in the context of reuse. Continuing the example from that section, a reference to 'chapter V' makes little sense if the context in which a component is reused doesn't include a 'chapter V'. We already mentioned that the aggregate LO should provide this kind of 'glue' information. This is one example of an issue that needs to be considered when content is designed to be reusable.

There are many more issues that need to be considered in this context:

- It should be easy to modify *mathematical symbols*. If one content component refers to an angle in a diagram as α, and another component is a visualization that refers to the same angle as θ, then the learner will have significant cognitive challenges to map α to θ. Whereas an expert in the domain may be expected to be able to do this kind of mapping without problems, the same cannot be expected of a learner. That is why content should be designed in such a way that it becomes easy to transform it from one symbolism to another.
- A related issue is that of *textual labels* in visual material. It should be simple to replace such labels with alternatives, for instance in a different language, or using an alternative vocabulary. This is a problem that has been studied in the context of multi-lingual user interfaces. There are some simple approaches that basically rely on separation of the labels from graphical material, but it remains quite difficult to deal with some of the more subtle issues, such as the differences in lengths of textual labels or the differences in reading direction (left-to-right versus right-to-left) in different languages. It should be noted that such labels can themselves be considered metadata that get 'added' to the actual content when the latter is visualized in a particular context.
- Generalizing further, methods need to be developed for adapting the *look and feel* of content. When different components are aggregated together, the result should not look like a collection of components from different origins. One could imagine aggregation tools that allow the author to apply a 'design template' to impose a specific look and feel on the resulting aggregate.

In a general sense, then, designing content to be reusable is largely a discipline of not including any more context than absolutely necessary in the content itself and instead adding in context at aggregation time. Alternatively, context can be provided through context-specific components, such as examples or exercises, which could reflect a very specific set of data, application, and so on.

Conclusion

We have outlined some of the research issues that need to be considered for advanced and innovative interpretations of the basic concepts underlying the LO paradigm. There are other issues that we have not considered here, that also need to be investigated if we want this new paradigm to realize its full potential. Those issues relate, for instance, to the use of social recommending and information visualization techniques for accessing relevant objects, and to the refinement of appropriate 'business models' for share and reuse of LOs. However, even if all of the other issues do get resolved in a satisfactory way, then much of the potential of this paradigm shift to LOs will remain unrealized if the issues discussed here are not dealt with in a satisfactory way.

References

ARIADNE (2002) (accessed January 2003) Home page, (Online) http://ariadne. unil.ch.

CanCore (2003) (accessed April 2003) Home page, (Online) http://www.cancore.ca.

Conejo, R., Brusilovsky, P. and De Bra, P. (eds) (2002) *Adaptive hypermedia and adaptive Web-based systems: 2nd International Conference AH 2002 Proceedings*, i–xiv, Springer-Verlag, Malaga, Spain.

Dong, A. and Agogino, A. M. (2001) (accessed 3 December 2003) Design principles for the information architecture of a SMET education digital library, University of California, Berkeley, (Online) http://www.smete.org/smete/public/about_smete/publications/JCDL-0601/dongagoginojcdl01–01.pdf.

Duval, E. and Hodgins, W. (2002) (accessed 23 April 2003) A LOM research agenda, (Online) http://www.cs.kuleuven.ac.be/~erikd/LOM/ResearchAgenda/ResearchAgenda.html#VanDam 2002.

Hill, S. and Wentland, M. (1998) Ophelia, object-oriented pedagogical hypertext editor for learning, instruction and authoring, *Hypermédia et Apprentissages*, 15–17 October, Observatoire des technologies pour l'éducation en Europe, Poitiers, France.

Horn, R. E. (1998) (accessed 3 February 2003) Structured writing as a paradigm, in *Instructional Development: State of the Art*, A. Romiszowski and C. Dills eds Englewood Cliffs, NJ, (Online) http://www.stanford.edu/~rhorn/HornStWrAsParadigm.html.

IEEE (2001) (accessed 29 April 2003) *Learning object metadata working group*, (Online) http://ltsc.ieee.org/wg12/s_p.html.

IEEE Learning Technologies Standardization Committee (LTSC) (2001) (accessed 23 November 2003) (Online) http://ltsc.ieee.org.

IMS (2003) (accessed April 2003) IMS Home page, (Online) http://www.ims project.org.

Koper, R. (2001) (accessed 28 June 2002) Modeling units of study from a pedagogical perspective: The pedagogical meta-model behind EML, Heerlen, Open University of the Netherlands, (Online) http://eml.ou.nl/introduction/docs/ped-metamodel.pdf.

Lamminaho, V. and Magerkurth, S. (2001) Unifying descriptions of higher education courses across Europe metadata specification in the Cuber project, in *20th World Conference on Open Learning and Distance Education*, International Council for Distance Education, Dusseldorf.

Learning Systems Architecture Lab (2002) (accessed 27 February 2003) Architecture for user-centric learning management systems, Carnegie Mellon University, (Online) http://www.lsal.cmu.edu.

Maddocks, P. (2002) (accessed 24 April 2003) Case Study: Cisco Systems ventures into the land of reusability, *Learning Circuits: ASTD's Online Magazine All About E-Learning*, (Online) http://www.learningcircuits.org/2002/mar2002/maddocks.html.

MERLOT (2002) (accessed 23 March 2003) *Multimedia educational resource for learning and online teaching*, (Online) www.merlot.org.

Nejdl, W., Wolf, B., Qu, C., Decker, S., Sintek, M., Naeve, A. *et al.* (2002) EDUTELLA: a P2P networking infrastructure based on RDF, Paper presented at *The 11th International Conference on World Wide Web, 2002*, ACM Press.

Neven, F. and Duval, E. (2002) Reusable LOs: A survey of lom-based repositories, *Proceedings of the ACM Multimedia Conference 2002*, pp. 291–94.

Papatheodorou, C., Vassiliou, A. and Simon, B. (2002) (accessed 1 December 2003) Discovery of ontologies for learning resources using word-based clustering, in *ED-MEDIA 2002 Conference*, August, Denver, (Online) http://www.wu-wien.ac.at/usr/wi/bsimon/publikationen/EDMEDIA2002.pdf.

Roschelle, J., DiGiano, D., Koutlis, M., Repenning, A., Phillips, J., Jackiw, N. *et al.* (1999) Developing educational software components, *IEEE Computer*, **32** (9): 50–58.

SCORM (2003) (accessed 21 February 2003) Advanced distributed learning initiative. Section on SCORM, *OASIS*, (Online) http://www.adlnet.org.

SingCORE (2003) (accessed April 2003) Home page, (Online) http://www.ecc.org.sg/eLearn/MetaData/SingCORE/index.jsp.

SMIL 2.0 (2001) (accessed August 2001) Synchronized multimedia integration language W3C Recommendation, (Online) http://www.w3.org/TR/smil20/.

Suthers, D. D. (2001) (accessed 3 December 2003) Evaluating the learning object metadata for K-12 educational resources, in *IEEE International Conference on Advanced Learning Technologies (ICALT 2001)*, 6–8 August, pp. 371–74, Madison, WI, (Online) http://lilt.ics.hawaii.edu/lilt/papers/2001/suthers-icalt-2001-lom.pdf.

Ternier, S., Duval, E. and Vandepitte, P. (2002) (accessed 3 December 2003) LOMster: Peer-to-peer LO metadata., *Dept. Computerwetenschappen, Katholieke Universiteit Leuven, Belgium*, (Online) http://www.cs.kuleuven.ac.be/~stefaan/LOMster/papers/LOMster_long.pdf.

Van Dam, A. (2001) (accessed 3 December 2003) Reflections on next-generation educational software, *Author*, (Online) http://www.cs.brown.edu/people/avd/Levrat.pdf.

Walsh, N. and Muellner, L. (1999) (accessed May 2003) DocBook: The Definitive Guide, (Online) http://www.oreilly.com/catalog/docbook/.

York, B. *et al.* (2002) (accessed 28 April 2003) A teacher for every learner, (Online) http://www.cra.org/Activities/grand.challenges/slides/education.pdf.

Part 2

Constructing and Creating Learning Objects

In this section, some different approaches to the construction and creation of LOs are introduced. These include both pedagogical and technical details. A unique conceptualization of LOs is followed by approaches to the reuse of LOs using chunks of information and educational modelling languages.

In Chapter 6, Ally recommends the learner-centred design of LOs, while ensuring proper tagging and adherence to standards for easy retrieval. He suggests that LOs can be designed using behaviourist, cognitivist, constructivist or other principles so long as they can stand alone and are reusable, revisable, customizable, scalable, linkable, interoperable, learnable and durable.

Ally insists that LOs should be tied to specific learning outcomes and the content and activities should result in their achievement. He refers to three components of LOs that make the learning meaningful for learners: pre-learning, presentation, and post-learning strategies. He also stresses the need for revising, retiring and finding the most suitable content, quality control and ownership.

Downes, in Chapter 7, suggests that the design of LOs is similar to the design of software objects in computer programming. In this chapter, he looks at some of the approaches and techniques employed in their construction and creation. This includes a simple description of how individual LOs are created and how courses are created from collections of LOs.

He explains how modern programmers use a methodology called RAD (Rapid Application Design) and how Object-Oriented Programming (OOP) is essential to RAD in the construction of online courses. He then points out that in modern programming, engineers reuse software components within the context of a CASE (Computer-Aided Software Engineering) environment.

In supporting the use of open standards in course construction, Downes describes three types of open standards: transport protocols, markup languages, and program interfaces. He follows this up with a description of some standards initiatives relevant to course construction. XML (Extensible Markup Language) is given as an example of the most useful markup language used for online course construction.

In Chapter 8, Polsani offers a conceptual definition that takes learning and reusability as the foundational principles for LOs. From these principles, he develops a model for creating and using LOs based semiotic theory. Polsani locates knowledge production at the intersection of computer networks, computer programming and interface design. He argues that where knowledge is stored, how it is managed, accessed, interacted with and used, have profound implications for how knowledge is conceptualized. He maintains that if LOs are to be created successfully and used appropriately, their creation should be a cooperative and closely aligned process.

In Chapter 9, Doorten, Giesbers, Janssen, Daniels and Koper of the OUNL address the question of how to deal with the reuse of existing course materials within the realm of a LO economy. This reuse is approached both on the level of individual subject experts and the broader organisational level. The authors stress the need for approved standards and compare the examples from the literature with the IMS Learning Design specification. After deriving recommendations and constraints regarding LO design, the authors describe the process of decomposing existing material in terms of checks and analyses that have to be made successively.

In Chapter 10, the OUNL's Peter B. Sloep discusses two approaches to the reuse of learning materials. The first approach is a familiar one. It uses chunks of content that are described through metadata. Although metadata should afford their reuse by detailing the conditions of their deployment, Sloep contends that this is not satisfactory and will ultimately fail to elicit actual reuse. The second approach is relatively new. It builds on recently developed pedagogical meta-languages with which the pedagogical inner structure of LOs may be described. Through the use of such languages, one of which is described in some detail, actual reuse may be brought about.

Sloep suggests that the information and education technological approaches both have something valuable to offer to support the flexible reuse of learning materials, but that each alone is not sufficient. Both, working in concert, are needed for actual reuse to flourish. He argues that this will delay any full-scale implementation of reusable LOs unless we can manage to embed reusable resources in reusable scenarios.

Nesbit and Belfer of Simon Fraser University Surrey, in Chapter 11 point out that the properties that distinguish LOs from other forms of educational applications have significant implications for evaluation. These properties include global accessibility, metadata standards, finer granularity and reusability. The authors propose a collaborative model for LO evaluation in which representatives from stakeholder groups converge towards more similar descriptions and ratings through a two-stage process supported by online tools.

The chapter reviews evaluation models that have been applied to educational software and media, considers models for gathering and meta-evaluating individual user reviews that have recently emerged on the Web, and analyses the peer review model adopted for the MERLOT repository. Their proposed convergent participation model is compared to other models and assessed with respect to its support for LO evaluation

Chapter 6

Designing effective learning objects

Mohamed Ally

The use of learning objects (LOs) in education and training has the potential to improve the way instruction is delivered. However, they must be developed using sound instructional design principles and learning theories. The LO definition proposed by this author is 'any digital resource that can be used and reused to achieve a specific learning outcome or outcomes'. The three key words in this definition are digital, reusable, and learning outcome. LOs must be in a digital format to facilitate storage in a digital repository that can be searched and retrieved electronically. They must be designed so that they can be reused in different lessons or courses and different instructional interventions or situations. And, a LO must be tied to a specific learning outcome so that appropriate content and assessment can be included, and the appropriate delivery medium can be identified. The overall goal is to promote learning and improve performance. Hence, it is important to know how students learn in order to design LOs that are effective and that are designed properly and efficiently with the learner in focus (Richards, 2002).

LOs are developed to teach specific learning outcomes in a discipline. LOs are then sequenced to form instructional events for lessons or learning sessions. Students will access and work through the activities in LOs so that they can improve their knowledge and skills and achieve learning outcomes. Students will also use LOs to develop personal meaning from the information presented and to apply the information in real life. Hence, LOs should be developed with the learner in focus, the purpose of LOs being to make people learn and apply what they learn in real-life settings and in creative ways. Instructors and/or learners will be able to build an instructional plan at any moment by selecting and assembling LOs from a repository (Gibbons, Nelson and Richards, 2002). Instant assembly of learning experiences would facilitate just-in-time learning and training. These are major benefits of using LOs; however, to realize these benefits the LOs must be designed using proven instructional design techniques and should be based on learning theories (Wiley, 2002b, 2002c).

Designing learning objects: Characteristics of learning objects and implications for design

Certain characteristics must be present in LOs to make them beneficial to education and training. They should be as follows:

Revisable

One should be able to revise LOs without affecting other objects (Wiley, 2002a). This requires that the LOs be independent and stand-alone. Discrete learning outcomes should be identified and the LOs should be based on the learning outcomes.

Reusable

Educators should be able to use LOs in multiple contexts and multiple lessons or courses. Wiley (2002a) suggests the use of Fundamental Information Objects, which are independent of context, resulting in a high level of reusability. They must be designed with multiple users in mind and must be tested with multiple users before they are placed in the repository. The readability level and language must be appropriate for different audiences and the presentation of the information and learning activities must be appropriate for different styles of learners. They should be usable in different delivery modes (Barritt, 2002). Users must be able to download them to use offline or copy to other electronic media for convenient access.

Customizable

Learners, educators, and trainers should be able to customize LOs to meet their individual needs. In addition, users should be able to customize lessons by selecting appropriate LOs, based on their needs and styles to build a personalized learning sequence.

Applicable

LOs should be applicable in different instructional settings. These include learning, remediation; just-in-time learning, job aids and enrichment. Learners should be able to access one or more LOs to achieve knowledge and skills outcomes for a discipline. If learners do not have the prerequisite knowledge and skills for a lesson, the learner should be able to access the appropriate LOs to achieve the required knowledge and skills. If a learner fails a lesson, the appropriate LOs should be available to facilitate the successful completion of the lesson. While working on a project or assignment, learners may need to acquire specific knowledge and skills to complete the project or assignment. For example, a learner working on a research project may have to do a correlation. If the learner has never done correlation before, LO (CAREO, 2002) on correlation can be accessed immediately to provide the just-in-time learning. A worker on the job may be assigned to complete a procedure but does not remember how to complete the procedure or the procedure has changed. The worker should be able to access the procedure from a LO repository to learn the procedure or to compare the procedure with an existing mental model. As learners complete a lesson, they may request enrichment activities. These enrichment activities can be developed as LOs for learners to access at anytime and from anywhere.

Stand-alone

A LO should be an independent segment of instruction. Chitwood and Bunnow (2002) refer to a LO as a small unit of learning. Before units are designed, thorough content and task analyses must be performed to identify the macro learning outcomes and the micro learning outcomes on which the LOs will be based. LOs must be tied to learning outcomes. After a learner completes the activities, he or she must feel a sense of completion and achieve a learning outcome.

Scalable

LOs should build on each other to form an instructional sequence. A basic LO can be developed initially, which could form the basis for higher-level LOs in the same discipline or other disciplines.

Linkable

Instructors should be able to customize lessons or courses by combining LOs for just-in-time development and delivery (Longmire, 2002). They must be able to combine LOs to build larger units of instruction, and linkable to form instructional events for a lesson or course. To make this possible, LOs should be tagged with the appropriate learning level, difficulty level, outcome and required prerequisites.

Durable

LOs must be designed so that they can be reused many times without becoming obsolete (Barritt, 2002). This requires that LOs be updated constantly as the content changes. As a guideline, content that changes frequently should not be developed as LOs since they cannot be reused and will need constant updating.

Learnable

Learners must be able to complete the LO and come away with a sense of accomplishment that learning has occurred. Sound design principles should be used when developing LOs to make sure students really do learn.

Interoperable

LOs should be accessible using different systems connected to the Internet (Hamel and Ryan-Jones, 2002). This will allow anyone from anywhere to access the LOs irrespective of the hardware or software system.

Cognitive psychology: Implications for design of learning objects

Cognitivists see learning as an internal process that involves memory, thinking, reflection, abstraction, motivation and meta-cognition. Cognitive psychology looks at learning from an information-processing point of view where the learner uses different types of memory during learning. Sensations are received through the senses into the sensory store before processing occurs. The duration of sensory store is less than one second (Kalat, 2002). If information is not transferred to working memory immediately, it is lost. The design of LOs should include strategies to allow learners to attend to the learning materials to facilitate transfer from the senses to sensory store and then to working memory, where the information is processed before entering long-term memory.

The amount of information transferred to working memory is dependent on the amount of attention that was paid to the incoming information and whether there are existing cognitive structures to make sense of the information. LOs must use effective interfaces to attract and maintain attention and provide activities that facilitate the recall of related existing cognitive structures to help process the new information. If the relevant cognitive structures are not present, pre-instructional LOs such as advance organizers should be included as part of the instructional event (Ausubel, 1974).

The duration in working memory is approximately twenty seconds and if information in working memory is not processed efficiently, it is lost and is not transferred to long-term memory for storage (Kalat, 2002). LOs must present the information and include strategies for learners to process the information in working memory. Since working memory has limited capacity, information in LOs should be organized or chunked in appropriate-sized pieces to facilitate processing. According to Miller (1956), since humans have limited short-term memory capacity, information should be grouped into meaningful sequences. He suggests that information should be chunked into seven plus or minus two meaningful units to compensate for the limited capacity of short-term memory.

After the information is processed in working memory, it is stored in long-term memory. The amount transferred to long-term memory is dependent on the quality and depth of processing in working memory. The deeper the processing, the more associations are formed in memory to the acquired new information. Information transferred from short-term memory to long-term memory is either assimilated or accommodated in long-term memory. During assimilation, the new information is changed to fit into existing cognitive structures. Accommodation occurs when existing cognitive structures are changed to incorporate the new information. LOs must include activities to allow learners to actively process the information to facilitate transfer to long-term memory.

Cognitive psychology postulates that information is stored in long-term memory in the form of networks. Information is stored in the form of nodes and the nodes are connected forming relationships between the nodes. Information maps that show the major concepts in a topic and the relationships between the concepts should be included in the learning materials. According to Stoyanova and Kommers (2002), information map generation requires critical reflection and is a method to externalize the cognitive structure of learners. For a lesson or topic there should be an information map to give learners the big picture before they start the lesson and presented at the end as a summary. To facilitate deeper processing, learners should be encouraged to generate their own information map objects, which could be stored in the LO repository as examples of information maps (Bonk and Reynolds, 1997).

Constructivism: Implications for design of learning objects

Constructivists see learners as being active rather than passive during the learning process. Knowledge is not received from the outside or from someone, but is created by the individual learner, processing what is received through the senses. Learners should be allowed to construct knowledge rather than being given the knowledge through instruction (Duffy and Cunningham, 1996). A major emphasis of constructivists is situated learning, which states that learning is contextual. Learning activities that allow learners to contextualize the information should be used when developing LOs. If the information has to be applied in many contexts, then learning strategies that promote multi-contextual learning should be used to make sure learners can apply the information in many contexts.

In the constructivist view of learning, learners use their own process to acquire personal knowledge rather than use someone else's process.

Learners are active in the learning process and could build their individual lessons, construct larger modules based on available LOs that are specifically chosen, or even modify them to meet their needs to personalize the information. Designers of LOs must be aware of the need of learners to adapt LOs to meet their needs and realize that learners may want to construct their own LOs based on the notes they make, their summary of lessons, and the research they conduct.

Bannan-Ritland *et al.* (2002) claim that the development of LOs from the perspective of the constructivist philosophy has not yet been considered. LOs must be based on the idea that learners construct knowledge. Instruction must provide the support to facilitate the construction of the knowledge. Learners should be allowed to modify LOs to meet their needs (Bannan-Ritland *et al.* 2002). The modified object should then be tagged as a student-generated LO and appropriate version control should be used. LOs should allow learners to elaborate on the knowledge to create personal meaning and knowledge structures.

According to Brown *et al.* (1989), knowledge should be acquired through enculturation, where learners make sense of knowledge based on how it is used in a practical sense. Enculturation can be promoted by encouraging learners to further develop their own personal LOs after interacting with the prescribed ones. These personalized LOs can be stored in the students' personal directory.

If designed and tagged properly, LOs have the potential to incorporate learner-centred, active, constructivist strategies in a viable system. Bannan-Ritland *et al.* (2002) have suggested a LO system based on constructivist theory. Their system starts at the micro level and then proceeds to the macro level. At the micro level, the LO will take the form of a fundamental LO where the content is context-independent. LOs at this level will be at a low level of granularity and would include items such as short video clips, photographs, graphics, concept maps and facts. At the macro level the objects will be learning activities that combine LOs from the micro level. Learners then will use the larger objects from the macro level to achieve the learning outcomes and to acquire personal meaning from the materials.

Learners should be allowed to generate their individual LOs to obtain personal meaning. During the generation of the lessons, learners process the information at a deep level facilitating transfer to memory and application (Craik and Lockhart, 1972). The LOs repository should have templates for learners to access to generate their own LOs as they go through the learning process. The learner-generated objects can be used by other learners to achieve similar learning outcomes. Learners may also want to generate LOs as a group in order to review, test and approve them. The LO system must be able to handle the learner-generated and group-generated LOs.

Behaviourism: Implications for designing learning objects

Behaviourists looks at overt behaviours that can be observed and measured as indicators of learning (Good and Brophy, 1990). When designing LOs, learners must be informed of what they will learn before they start the lesson. The purpose of the LO must be clear to the learner. This will allow learners to set expectations and to decide whether they have successfully learnt from the experience once they have completed the work assigned in the LO.

After completing a LO, the learner should be able to determine whether the session was successful. Learners need to be able to make this judgement. Therefore, the LO should include an assessment component or should link to another object that has the assessment items for the LO.

Proper sequencing methods should be used when assembling LOs to form an instructional sequence. Learners and instructors must be able to access LOs from a repository and to sequence the objects to meet their needs. The LOs must be tagged appropriately for learners and instructors to build their own sequence. The sequenced LOs then become a lesson with combined LOs for the learning process. As learners go through an instructional sequence, they should be provided with feedback on how they are doing and advised on what to do next. Feedback should be built into LOs, but activated only when required or there should be a feedback object to link back to a LO. The feedback object could give further information or could provide corrective information or action.

Tagging learning objects

LOs must be tagged properly to allow instructors, instructional designers and learners to access the LOs whenever they need them (McGreal and Roberts, 2001). The CanCore profiling system for tagging LOs consists of 8 main categories, 15 subcategories, and 36 elements (Friesen et al., 2002). The educational subcategory should be expanded and include elements to tag LOs to specific learning outcomes. This is consistent with Carey, Swallow and Oldfield (2002), who claim that LOs should form a cohesive unit of study to reflect domain knowledge within a subject. They have listed the names of different tags that can be used to mark learning activities within LOs. These should be developed to meet intended learning objectives. Learning outcomes are what drives the development of LOs, and therefore they should be tagged. When tagging LOs according to learning outcome, the appropriate learning level, delivery medium, and target audience should also be marked.

Model for developing learning objects

Programmes and courses of instruction need to be designed into smaller units in the form of LOs to make them flexible and reusable. Figure 6.1 illustrates a sample programme breakdown to facilitate development of LOs. Another method that can be used to identify LOs for development is to analyse multiple programmes, courses and modules and then identify the generic learning outcomes that are common across programmes (Figure 6.2). These generic learning outcomes across programmes and courses should be given high priority for developing LOs.

LOs must be developed and stored in a database to allow access anytime and from anywhere using different delivery media. There are no limits on the size of LOs. Instructors and developers are free to decide on their own sizes for LOs. There is a danger, however, in making a LO too large, as it may become too big to be reusable by others. Other developers may make LOs too small to make instructional sense to the learner. As the name suggests, LOs should result in students learning after interacting with the object. Hence, a LO should have at least three components (see Figure 6.1). The first component is a pre-learning strategy such as a learning outcome, pre-assessment, advance organizer, or overview. The second component is a presentation strategy, which includes the content, mate-

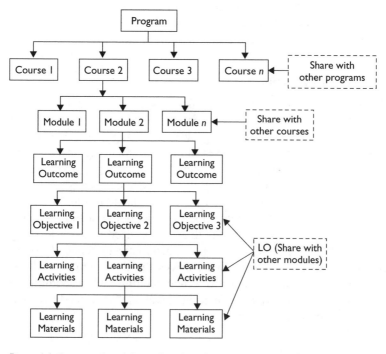

Figure 6.1 Program breakdown for identification of learning objects

rials and activities to achieve the outcome for the LO. The content includes facts, concepts, principles and procedures in the form of text, audio, graphics, pictures, video, simulations, or animation. Where appropriate, some of these activities could be learner-generated while others could be instructor-provided. The third component is a post-learning strategy in the form of a summary or a post-assessment to check for achievement of the learning outcome (see Table 6.1).

Table 6.1 Components of a learning object

Learning objects components	Micro-strategies
1. Pre-learning strategy	Learning outcome
	Advance organizer
	Overview
	Pre-assessment
2. Presentation strategy	Presentation of information
	Elaboration of information
	Embedded questions
	Demonstration
	Practice exercises with feedback
3. Post-learning strategy	Summary
	Post-assessment

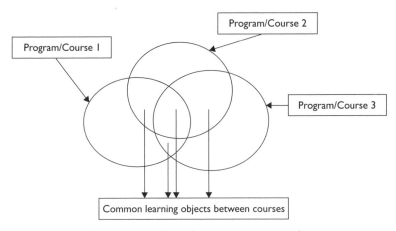

Figure 6.2 Identifying learning objects between programs and courses

Conclusion

The use of LOs in education and training has the potential to revolutionize the way instruction is delivered; however, this will be possible only if they are designed and tagged properly to promote learning and maximize their access. The design of LOs must keep the learner in focus and must be designed using sound instructional design principles. A major challenge is how to make LOs universal, since anyone may access the LOs from anywhere in the world. Some issues that still need to be explored are as follows:

- Who designs the learning objects?
- Who revises the learning objects once they are in the repository?
- Who makes the decision to retire a learning object?
- When should a learning object be retired?
- What content is most suitable for learning objects?
- Who is responsible for quality control and accuracy of the information in learning objects?
- Who owns the learning objects?

As the use of LOs increases and the field matures, intelligent agents should be developed within the LO system to match and adapt LOs to meet individual learner needs during the learning process (Richards, 2002).

References

Ausubel, D. P. (1974) *Educational psychology: A cognitive view*, Holt, Rinehart & Winston, New York.

Bannan-Ritland, B., Dabbagh, N. and Murphy, K. (2002) Learning object systems as constructivist learning environments: Related assumptions, theories, and application, in *The instructional use of learning objects*, ed. D. A. Wiley, pp. 1–41, Agency for Instructional Technology, Bloomington, IN.

Barritt, C. (2002) (accessed 12 April 2003) Learning objects and ISD, *Performance Improvement*, **41** (7), (Online) www.ispi.org/pdf/Barritt.pdf.

Bonk, C. J. and Reynolds, T. H. (1997) Learner-centered Web instruction for higher-order thinking, teamwork, and apprenticeship, in *Web-based instruction*, ed. B. Khan, pp. 67–178, Educational Technology Publications, Englewood Cliffs, NJ.

Brown, J. S., Collins, A. and Duguid, P. (1989) Situated cognition and the culture of learning, *Educational Researcher*, 32–42.

CAREO (2002) (accessed 5 January 2003) Campus Alberta repository of educational objects, (Online) http://www.careo.org/.

Carey, T., Swallow, J. and Oldfield, W. (2002) Educational rationale for learning objects, *Canadian Journal of Learning and Technology*, **3** (28): 55–71.

Chitwood, K. and Bunnow, D. (2002) Learning objects: Resources for learning, Paper presented at *18th Annual Conference on Distance Teaching and Learning*, Madison, Wisconsin, University of Wisconsin.

Craik, F. I. M. and Lockhart, R. S. (1972) Levels of processing: A framework for memory research, *Journal of Verbal Learning and Verbal Behavior*, **11**: 671–84.

Duffy, T. M. and Cunningham, D. J. (1996) Constructivism: Implications for the design and delivery of instruction, in *Handbook of research for educational communications and technology*, ed. D. H. Jonassen, pp. 170–98, Simon & Schuster Macmillan, New York.

Friesen, N., Roberts, A. and Fisher, S. (2002) CanCore: Metadata for learning objects, *Canadian Journal of Learning and Technology*, **28** (3): 43–53.

Gibbons, A. S., Nelson, J. and Richards, R. (2002) The nature and origin of instructional objects, in *The instructional use of objects*, ed. D. A. Wiley, Agency for Instructional Technology, Bloomington, IN.

Good, T. L. and Brophy, J. E. (1990) *Educational psychology: A realistic approach*, Longman, White Plains, NY.

Hamel, C. J. and Ryan-Jones, D. (2002) Designing instruction with learning objects, *International Journal of Educational Technology*, **1** (3).

Kalat, J. W. (2002) *Introduction to psychology*, Wadsworth-Thomson Learning, Pacific Grove, CA.

Longmire, W. (2002) (accessed 24 April 2003) A primer on learning objects, *Learning Circuits: ASTD's Online Magazine All About E-Learning*, (Online) http://www.learningcircuits.org/mar2000/primer.html.

McGreal, R. and Roberts, T. (2001) (accessed 1 May 2003) A primer on metadata for learning objects: Fostering an interoperable environment, *E-Learning*, **2** (10), (Online) http://elearningmag.com/ltimagazine/article/articleDetail.jsp.

Miller, G. A. (1956) The magical number seven, plus or minus two: Some limits on our capacity for processing information, *Psychological Review* **63**: 81–97.

Richards, G. (2002) The challenges of the learning object paradigm, *Canadian Journal of Learning and Technology*, **28** (3): 3–9.

Stoyanova, N. and Kommers, P. (2002) Concept mapping as a medium of shared cognition in computer-supported collaborative problem-solving, *Journal of Interactive Learning Research*, **13** (1): 111–33.

Wiley, D. (2002a) Learning object design and sequencing theory, Doctoral dissertation, Brigham Young University, Utah.

Wiley, D. (2002b) Connecting learning objects to instructional design theory: A definition, a metaphor, and a taxonomy, in *The Instructional Use of eLearning Objects*, pp. 1–35, Agency for Instructional Technology, Bloomington, IN.

Wiley, D. (2002c) eLearning objects need instructional design theory, in A. Rossett (ed.), *The ASTD E-Learning Handbook*, pp. 115–26, McGraw-Hill, New York, NY.

Chapter 7

Learning objects

Construction and creation

Stephen Downes

Today's online courses are like old computer programs. People typically think of an online course as being similar to a textbook, or at best, a classroom where a course is being delivered. But from the standpoint of course design, it makes more sense to think of an online course as being similar to a computer program. This is especially evident when the problems facing early computer programmers and computer users are compared to the problems facing today's online course designers. Early computer programs were written from scratch. They were expensive and time-consuming to create. Moreover, they didn't work with other programs: a document created by one program could not be read by another program.

Course construction and RAD

Modern programmers use a methodology called Rapid Application Design (RAD). Software engineers have long since learned that it is inefficient to design applications from scratch. Educators need to study design techniques learned by the software industry long ago. Specifically, they should consider using Rapid Application Design. RAD is a process which allows software engineers to develop products more quickly and of higher quality. It involves several components, including a greater emphasis on client consulting, prototyping and more informal communications.

Modern programmers use programming environments. In modern programming, the engineers reuse software components within the context of a CASE (Computer-Aided Software Engineering) environment. The idea of RAD for software development is that a designer can select and apply a set of predefined subroutines from a menu or selection within a programming environment. A good example of this sort of environment is Microsoft's Visual Basic, a programming environment that lets an engineer design a page or flow of logic by dragging program elements from a toolbox.

Analogies: the well-prepared chef and mechanic. Similar methodologies exist for a wide variety of creative or constructive tasks. A professional chef, for example, will carefully design a kitchen environment so that when he is called upon to create Crêpes Suzette, the essential ingredients – including pre-mixed recipe ingredients – are readily available. Auto mechanics also work in a dedicated environment and also have at hand every tool and component they may need to fix anything from a Lada to a Lamborghini.

RAD can be applied to course design. Online course developers, pressed for time and unable to sustain large development costs, will begin to employ similar methodologies. An online course, viewed as a piece of software, may be seen as a collection of reusable subroutines and applications. An online course, viewed as a collection of LOs, may be seen as a collection of reusable learning materials. The heart – and essence – of online course design is the merging of these concepts, of viewing reusable learning materials *as* reusable subroutines, applications and documents assembled by application specialists in a computer-assisted software environment.

RAD is being used in corporate learning already. Trainers in the corporate and software communities have known about this concept for some time. Wieseler (1999), an author working with Cisco Systems, wrote that reusable content stored in a database is the Holy Grail for e-learning.

Object-oriented design

Object-Oriented Programming (OOP) is essential to RAD. At the core of Rapid Application Design, and therefore central to the construction and organization of learning objects (LOs), is another concept from computer programming: object-oriented programming. The idea behind OOP is that bits of software common to many computer programs are designed as self-contained entities (or 'objects'), which are then used by different computer programs. It is these objects that are assembled by an application specialist.

Example: JavaScript alert box. In a similar manner, a person using JavaScript to design a web page application does not write detailed programming specifying the size, location and colour of the alert box that pops up on web pages. The JavaScript programmer simply writes a single line of code creating the alert box and giving it some text to display.

Example: the student object. The task bar and the alert box are examples of objects. In a similar manner, software objects can be used in online courses. Suppose, for example, a course designer wanted some educational text to refer to a student by name. When creating the document, the designer would first create a 'student' object. When created, the 'student' object automatically retrieves information about the student, for example, the student's name and address, and inserts it into the document text.

Objects are used by designers working within the programming environment. When a designer needs to refer to a student, the designer refers to the prototype and 'clones' a copy of the prototype in the computer's memory (it's actually called 'cloning' in computer science. In Perl the prototype is cloned and 'blessed' to reserve its place in memory). For example, the designer may click and drag the 'student' icon onto the page being designed. The newly cloned prototype is given a name, and then values or attributes are assigned to it by the program.

Objects interact with each other. Objects may interact, or more generally, be *related* to each other, in many ways. The most useful and common form of interaction is the *containing* interaction. Just as Fred may *contain* various other objects (such as a heart or a liver, most obviously, but also $4.95 in change, a six-inch ruler and a pager), one object may in general contain one or more other objects. A course may contain students, for example. Or a course may contain units or modules. A unit may contain a test. Each of these items is an object, defined from a prototype, which may interact with other objects in predefined ways. In a course that contained both a unit test and a grade book, for example, the unit test could interact with the grade book. What would happen is that Fred (the 'student' object) would interact with the test (the 'test' object), which in turn would interact with the grade book (a 'grade book' object).

Open standards

Open standards are like common languages. A third major concept drawn from the world of computing science – and especially from the recent emergence of Internet technologies – is the use of *open standards* in course construction. An open standard is like a language understood and used by everyone. Just as, for example, the meanings of such terms as 'Paris', 'the capital of France', and 'European' are understood by almost all speakers of English, so also in an open standard are the meanings of terms and definitions widely understood and shared.

Example: HTML. The open standard with which most online educators are familiar is Hypertext Markup Language, or HTML. This language is a shared vocabulary for all people wishing to read or write Internet documents. The term '<h1>' is commonly understood as a header tag; the term '<I>' denotes italics.

Open standards may be contrasted with *proprietary*, or *closed* standards. Consider a document written in an older version of MS Word, for example. This word-processing program used a special set of notation to define italics, bold face, and a wide variety of other features. Because other software manufacturers did not know these standards, only people using MS Word could read a document written in MS Word.

Open standards enable programs to interact with each other. The purpose of open standards is to allow engineers from various software or hardware companies to develop devices and programs that operate in harmony. A document saved in an open standard can be read, printed or transmitted by any number of programs and devices.

There are three major types of open standards. The *transport protocol* defines how digital material is transported over the Internet. The Internet is based on transport protocols such as HTTP (Hypertext Transfer Protocol) and FTP (File Transfer Protocol). The second major type of open standard is the *markup language*, which defines how parts of documents should be identified and displayed. HTML and XML are types of markup language. The third major type of standard is the *program interface*. The program interface defines what functions (or methods) can be called by one program in another. A web browser uses a program interface, for example, when it displays a plug-in such as a Flash animation or a Java program.

Learning objects require markup languages and program interfaces. Insofar as online learning is delivered using the Internet, it can use common transport protocols such as HTTP. However, the documents and programs used in online learning are unique to online learning, and therefore, there is no existing set of markup languages and program interfaces for LOs. Therefore, before we can use LOs, we need to define each of these. The next few sections will discuss efforts to establish common standards for online learning specifically.

A common markup language

Online learning uses XML. The common language adopted by online learning designers is XML (Extensible Markup Language), developed by the World Wide Web Consortium. It is being adopted by database programmers, librarians and designers around the world. XML represents documents according to their internal structure. Each element of the document structure is denoted with some standardized script, known as a 'tag'. For example, in a book, the chapters, chapter titles, and paragraphs would each be denoted with individual tags. The collection of tags used in a document is known as the document's 'markup'. More information about XML can be found at the W3 Consortium site < http://www.w3.org/XML/>.

Standards and standards-based initiatives

Standards initiatives define schemas and program interfaces. In order to enable the sharing of LOs, a variety of standards initiatives have been undertaken. These standards initiatives define the names of the XML tags, their allowable values and their meanings in online learning. Other standards define different tasks used by program interfaces. Not all standards initiatives define all of these elements, and some standards initiatives 'piggyback' on others, extending or more clearly 'defining' elements of the standards in question.

The purpose of standards initiatives is to enable interoperability. Initiatives such as the IMS Consortium promote the adoption of specifications allowing distributed learning environments and content from multiple authors to work together. These environments can be different sets of learning materials, authored in different programming languages using different programs and located on different computers around the world.

Interoperability amounts to programs being able to interact. This is an elusive goal. It amounts to enabling content produced using a learning management system such as Blackboard and stored on a computer in Istanbul (e.g. an interactive atlas) to be used in a course authored in WebCT and located in Long Island, New York. And by 'used', what is meant in this context is that the two elements, the atlas and the course, could *interact* with each other. The atlas, for example, might report to the course *how long* a given student spends studying cloud formations, and the course might instruct the atlas to display the appropriate university logo and links to discussion boards.

In order to interact, programs must use common definitions of objects. In order for this to work, the atlas in Turkey and the course in the United States must define similar objects in the same manner. For example, both programs must understand what was meant by 'course', or 'institution', or even 'logo'. Thus there is a need to obtain a common definition of the objects and properties used by the two separate systems. The core of the IMS specification involves the definition of prototype objects (or more accurately, descriptions of prototype objects, since they would be defined differently using different computer languages). The IMS Enterprise Information Model, for example, defines a 'Person Data Object', a 'Group Data Object', and a 'Membership Data Object'. In a similar manner, objects must interact with each other in predefined ways. If one program is expecting a grade as a digit and calls it 'grade', and the other sends it as a word and calls it 'score', then the two programs are unable to interact.

Conclusion

In this chapter, we have described some of the approaches and techniques employed in the construction and creation of learning objects. A simple description of how individual LOs are created and how courses are created from collections of LOs has been provided along with an introduction to the importance of standards.

Reference

Wieseler, W. (1999) (accessed 9 May 2000) RIO: A standards-based approach for reusable information objects, *Cisco Systems*, (Online) http://www.cisco.com/warp/public/779/ibs/solutions/publishing/whitepapers/.

Chapter 8

Signs and objects

Modelling learning objects on Peirce's theory of signs

Pithamber R. Polsani

The idea of the learning object (LO) emerged, was hyped and subsequently became a buzzword during the heyday of 'irrational exuberance in the dot.com world'. It was assumed that knowledge content organized as LOs would be traded freely like energy on commodity markets. However, the Real as Rational reasserted itself with force and the irrational dreams of speculative trading rapidly dissipated.

If the world is ruled by the Real now, are LOs relevant? Do they have any future? These questions, though seemingly strange in a chapter announcing creation of a model for LOs, are nevertheless highly relevant, since the responses will help determine the future of LOs. The success of LOs depends on what is posited as their objective. If we are striving to create an instant market for LOs then it will surely fail. If, however, our goal is to reorganize knowledge into machine and human readable form to take full advantage of the inherent flexibility, scalability and efficiency of information technology, then this goal can be achieved.

To reach this goal the efforts should be concentrated on organizations and domains of knowledge. In addition to a commitment to reorganizing knowledge, a useful model based on sound theoretical principles for creating meaningful LOs is also required. This chapter is aimed at offering such a model guided by enhanced learning and reusability as the fundamental principles.

Charles Sanders Peirce's (Hartshorne *et al.*, 1931–1958) theory of signs and his concept of information constitute the ideal model for LOs. In describing Peirce's theory and developing a LO model around it, this chapter will answer fundamental questions such as, What is the definition of a LO? What are its basic features? What are the principles of its architecture? What is the quantity of information contained in it? And how can they be used for instructional purposes?

One of Peirce's greatest achievements is the development of semiotics – a formal doctrine of signs. It systematically classifies signs, analyses their structure and relationships, and shows the ways in which signs grow and evolve. Semiosis is the process by which human beings recognize, interpret and communicate signs.

Learning is part of a general semiotic process wherein the learning materials function as signs that are interpreted in instructional situations. The principal goal of education is to create habits of thought and action. Habits can be defined as the process of recognizing, interpreting and connecting signs in a significant way and acting accordingly.

Peirce's theory of sign

Peirce defined the sign as a complex of interdependent triadic relations consisting of a sign (the technical term used by Peirce is *representamen*), an object and an interpretant. The term 'sign' should be understood in two senses: (1) sign as a complex of triadic relations and (2) sign as one of the elements of the triad as seen in Figure 8.1.

Sign

The sign in Peircean semiotics is a function, which represents an object, gives rise to an interpretant and establishes a relation between the two. A sign represents its object only in reference to an idea. For example, a footprint is a sign of a person, but from the footprint we cannot arrive at a complete knowledge of the person who made it (Parker, 1998). Similarly a paint chip represents the paint, but the relation between the paint chip and the actual paint is limited to colour (Castañares, 1994). Since the identity between a sign and the object that it represents is very tenuous, a sign that represents an object at one moment can represent another object at another moment. A wall-clock, for instance, represents the hours of the day, but the same clock could be a sign of workmanship of the artist who created it as well as a sign of the age of the building it is housed in. In each case, despite its differing objects, the sign exists as a 'cognizable' unit that is related to an object and gives rise to an interpretant. Cognition here involves, on the one hand, recognition of an object and, on the other, having 'meaning' to the interpreter's mind.

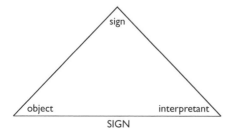

Figure 8.1 The elements of the triad

Object

While the sign is a function, the object is a position. The object-position comes to be filled by something because the sign represents it. As we saw in the preceding example of the clock, an object-position can be occupied by anything (time, workmanship, age, etc.).

Peirce divides the object into the immediate and the dynamic. The immediate object is that which is represented by a sign in a single signifying process and present in its totality. The dynamic object on the other hand lies outside a concrete act of semiosis. If we understand the paint chip as a sign, the immediate object would be the colour present on the chip and the actual paint its dynamic object.

Interpretant

For a sign to function as such, it must be related to a third element, the interpretant, which reveals to the sign reader something more about the dynamic object. Simply put, an interpretant is a sign produced by another sign, which has the same relation to the object as the sign that produced it. The interpretant of a sign is a 'more developed' form of an earlier sign because, through the interpretant, we have more information about the dynamic object.

Peirce divides the interpretant into three types: Immediate, Dynamic and Final.

1. *The immediate interpretant* is an 'impression,' or a sensation produced at first sight, for example the feeling we experience when we listen to Beethoven's Fifth Symphony or the immediate reaction or dislike we have when we look at a Cubist painting by Picasso.
2. *The dynamic interpretant* is 'the direct effect actually produced by a Sign upon an interpreter of it' (Hartshourne *et al.*, 4: 536). The reaction is the result of a sign exerting a certain force upon the semiotic agent and it could be either mental – provoking a thought in the interpreter – or physical, as when a policeman shouts 'Hey you!' and people on the street turn their heads.
3. *The final interpretant* is the proper meaning of the sign, and is most relevant for our purpose. The final interpretant can be defined as (1) the significance of the sign which is different from sense or action (immediate and dynamic interpretants), (2) the instrument with which the sign user connects or translates one sign into another, more developed sign and (3) the process of translating and connecting signs by which semiotic agents acquire habits of thought and action. Peirce himself offers an example to help understand the different features of

the final interpretant: the weathercock. When a weathercock is pointing in a northerly direction we interpret it to mean that the wind is blowing north. This would be the proper meaning of the weathercock in that instance of the signifying process, but we can interpret the weathercock in such a way because of our law-like behaviour, which states that the weathercock direction indicates the direction of the wind. Furthermore the habit of reading the weathercock accurately is a product of connecting different interpretants of the sign. Thus the final interpretant is the proper meaning of the sign in a particular instance, enabling us to connect the sign with other signs and develop rule-like or law-like habits of thought and action (see Figure 8.2).

As learning has been characterized as a semiotic process, the LOs can be identified as signs. In the LO-sign function there are two levels. On the first level it is a triadic sign containing a sign (*representamen*), an object and an interpretant. On the second level, that of instruction, the LO has the status of a single sign, with an object and an interpretant. The interpretant on the second level is related to the instructional process, which is on the one hand an interpretive process – the instructor interprets the materials of instructions – and on the other hand it is the very process of connecting different signs or translating signs into other signs. Through these two processes of instruction a learner acquires knowledge (the product of this process) and learns to analyse and connect signs.

What does it take to be a learning object?

As with signs, everything we encounter anywhere – any event, of writing, images, objects natural and manufactured, buildings – *could be* an LO, but every object *is not* a LO. Then, what does it take to be a LO? The following two examples respond to this question.

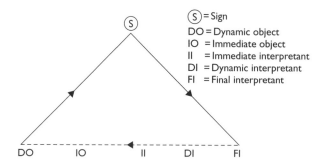

Figure 8.2 The learning object as a sign: Two levels

Example 1

A geology professor takes her students on an excursion into the surrounding mountains. During their journey the students encounter different types of rocks. Since the students can potentially learn from each one of them, current definitions would consider each rock to be a LO. But is a rock in itself a LO? Will a rock, however exotic it may appear, have any significance to the students who do not have sufficient knowledge of geology? According to the Peircean model the rock is a sign that represents geo-time and geo-event, but its *significant interpretant* is the professor's explanation, which explains the rock in the context of its origin, its place in the geological formation of the region and its importance among the differing rock formations on the earth. Only with this interpretant is the rock-sign brought into the learning process and thereby acquires purpose, direction and meaning, without which it would simply be a rock, one among many.

Example 2

Let us consider another example: a stock ticker, a LO according to David Wiley (2002). A stock ticker is a continuously scrolling event displaying symbols that represent companies and the value of their stock. When the ticker reads 'IBM 12¾', this symbol informs the viewers that the value of a stock of a company symbolized by the sign 'IBM' is '12¾' at this very moment of speculation on the stock market. The knowledge we gain about the dynamic object of the sign (IBM company) is limited to the information represented in the sign we perceive upon seeing the stock ticker. If this sign is to become meaningful and enable the learners to gain more knowledge of its dynamic object (IBM), it should be translated or connected with other signs such as the revenues and profits of the company, as well as the business direction and future potential of IBM. Hence, for the stock ticker to become a LO, it should contain an explanation about the symbol as well as demonstrate how to relate the information offered in the symbol with other pieces of relevant knowledge. Learning, as discussed earlier, consists not only in acquiring knowledge but also in learning to connect different pieces of information into a coherent whole, arriving at a reasonable conclusion and taking appropriate action.

From what has been said, we can respond to the earlier questions by concluding that (1) a LO requires three elements: a sign, an object and an interpretant; (2) the interpretant should be significant enough for the learner to gain more knowledge of the object; and (3) through the interpretant (which is knowledge as well as the process), a learner learns to recognize, connect and analyse.

Creating a learning object as a sign

Let us consider a step-by-step process of creating LOs by means of sign theory. According to many prevailing definitions, Figure 8.3 would be considered a LO. A learner who has not had previous knowledge of similar signs or of the event depicted in the figure would recognize it as a sign representing an actual or imagined event and interpret it as follows: 'A person standing on a tower or a tall building is dropping two balls, one large and the other small, to the ground.' This interpretation would be the immediate interpretant, which does not offer any information about the object other than what is represented in the sign. However, Figure 8.3 as it is presented cannot be a LO since it does not have an interpretant other than what is formed by the learners; the interpretant does not offer any meaning, explanation or information about the object represented and moreover it can exist without ever being interpreted like the aforementioned rock found by students in geology class. Figure 8.3 is potentially a LO but it has not become one.

Figure 8.3 Is it a learning object?

Suppose we attach an interpretant to this sign: 'Galileo's experiment about laws of bodies in motion.' This interpretant would cause a reaction in the learner (the sign reader), which consists of recognizing the sign as a representation of an experiment conducted by Galileo. The learner would recognize that the object represented is neither an imagined event nor is the person depicted fictitious. Rather, this is an actual event that took place in the life of a scientist called Galileo Galilee who lived in sixteenth-century Italy. Is Figure 8.3 together with a caption, a LO? The obvious answer is No, because the figure and the interpretant, as in the first instance, do not offer us any significant information about the dynamic object, Galileo's scientific experiment. It may only enable us to identify and acknowledge it as an experiment conducted by Galileo.

For Figure 8.3 to become a meaningful LO that offers significant information about the dynamic object it should answer these questions:

- When, where and how was the experiment conducted?
- What were the circumstances of the experiment?
- What was proved and disproved by the experiment?
- What was the significance of the experiment for the future of science?

The answers to these questions may lead us to other questions, which in turn lead to other questions, and all the questions and responses to the questions may eventually encompass the whole life and work of Galileo. Such an interpretant or the total information about the dynamic object Galileo, would be, according to Peirce, the final and logical interpretant through which we arrive at a perfect state of information. If the interpretant of Figure 8.3 is to encompass all the information about Galileo, then the modular feature of the LO and its reusability are defeated. Hence the challenge lies in determining the quantity of information that would provide significant knowledge about the object and at the same time retain the modularity and reusability of the LO for pedagogical purposes. In this regard we can avail ourselves of Peirce's theory of information to arrive at a model for determining the right quantity of information in a LO.

Peirce's theory of information

For Peirce, information/knowledge (he does not make a distinction between knowledge and information) is closely related to the interpretant of the sign. Information has two aspects: *depth* and *breadth*. The depth refers to the quantity of information conveyed by the interpretant of the sign and the breadth refers to all the objects the sign can be applied to. Therefore information is a product of depth and breadth of the sign and can be expressed as Depth × Breadth = Information. Peirce further divides breadth and depth into essential, informed and substantial.

The essential depth is the qualities or characteristics of the object the sign describes by way of the interpretant. The essential breadth is all the objects the sign refers to by virtue of the definition of the object offered through the interpretant. Strictly speaking the essential depth and breadth do not offer us much information other than what Peirce calls 'verbal knowledge'. In the first two iterations of Figure 8.3, what a semiotic agent learns through the interpretant and the objects it refers to is limited; hence it belongs to the category of essential depth and breadth.

The informed depth of the sign is the actual state of information and the informed breadth is all the actual objects the information can be applied to. The interpretant with informed depth provides the sign user concrete and verifiable knowledge, which can be applied to known objects. One can arrive at informed depth by reading a single sign or by aggregating or connecting various signs.

The substantial depth and breadth is the totality of knowledge and all the objects that information is applied to. In other words, it is the complete meaning ascribed to a sign. For example, if we take Galileo as a sign and its dynamic object as the Italian scientist of the sixteenth century, the substantial depth would be all the knowledge we possess about Galileo, his life, writings and contribution to the development of science and philosophy.

Determining the depth and breadth of a learning object

Peirce's division of information into essential, informed and substantial depth and breadth is a useful matrix for determining the quantity of knowledge a LO should contain (see Figure 8.4). As I have discussed earlier, the digital representation of images, stock tickers and other objects in the information sphere like a rock in the real world will evoke an immediate interpretant based on sensibility and offer only 'verbal knowledge'. These 'LOs' would have meaning only to those who possess relevant knowledge and the ability to connect them to other signs. However, a learner does not have such information nor is the learner capable of connecting them to arrive at a reasonable conclusion. The LO, as this minimal unit of the learning process, should be determined so that it be meaningful and be able to be connected with other LOs. Moreover it should be accessible for reuse in multiple knowledge and instructional contexts. Therefore *the depth of a LO is the quantity of information and the breadth is the reusability of the LO*. For creating LOs the crucial questions are how to determine an appropriate quantity of knowledge content and how to identify the contexts of reuse. The responses to these questions are mutually determinative. The most appropriate means of answering these questions is through a four-step process of demonstration by using Galileo as an example.

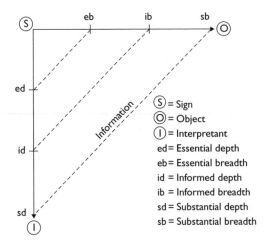

Figure 8.4 Determining the depth and breadth of a learning object

Step 1

In order to create LOs for a general field called Galileo we should begin by identifying all the domains of knowledge to which Galileo is relevant. Galileo's scientific discoveries and his writings are applicable in Mathematics, Mechanics, History of Science, History of Religion, Physics, Philosophy and Art as shown in Figure 8.5.

Step 2

Next we should group all the information we have about Galileo into different domains of knowledge and demarcate the sub-fields of each knowledge domain. Through this exercise we map the substantial and informed depth and breadth of Galileo. The substantial depth and breadth would be an aggregate of all knowledge and all the fields it is applied to. By studying all the material, complete knowledge about Galileo as a scientist and a person may be discerned. The informed depth and breadth would be all the knowledge about Galileo applicable in a particular domain. For example, Galileo's letter dated 26 June 1612 to artist Lodovico Cigoli, wherein he compares sculpture and painting, would belong to the Art domain since this informs us about Galileo's contributions to art criticism and his understanding of perspective, but not about his achievements in astronomy or mechanics.

Step 3

Then we draw lines of connection between the information that is common to two or more fields. For example, Galileo's discovery of Jupiter's four

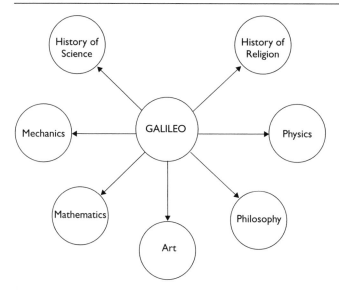

Figure 8.5 Galileo: Domains of knowledge

planets is relevant to astronomy as well as to the philosophy of science, since the discovery displaces Aristotle's doctrine of natural motion by demonstrating that there is more than one centre of motion in the universe. By drawing lines of connection between knowledge content pertaining to different fields, the informed depth is broken into fragments. Therefore the connecting lines establish the relationship between different fragments on the basis of the common characteristics that they share.

Step 4

Finally, we determine the exact quantity of information that the LOs should contain. The knowledge content of each fragment divided in Step 3 is reorganized with the aim of achieving maximum reusability. The guiding principle here is the reusability of the LO in different domains without modification. However, the reusability maxim should not override the learning principle – the quantity of information contained in a LO should be meaningful. It should provide us with more knowledge than represented in the sign and it should lend itself to be connected with other LOs. Therefore a digital image of Galileo, which can be reused in all the fields, cannot be considered a LO. This final step generates fragments of informed depth and breadth. As indicated earlier (Step 2) the informed depth and breadth refer to all knowledge applicable in a single knowledge field. A LO, as a fragment of informed depth and breadth, also has depth (the quantity of information) and breadth (reusability without modification). The depth and breadth of a LO can be referred to as intentional depth and breadth since the LO content has been purposefully organized for reuse in multiple knowledge contexts. The term 'informed depth and breadth' will be reserved for a collection of LOs employed for instructional objectives because, in instruction, LOs must be connected and interpreted, and can be combined with other digital assets and resources (see Figure 8.6).

In view of Peirce's theory of signs, a LO can therefore be defined as a form of organized knowledge content by means of triadic action involving learning purpose and reusable value. In the LO created with Figure 8.3, the image would function as the sign. However, the sign of a LO need not always be visual, instead it could be a title or a statement. The object is Galileo's experiment and the interpretant is the significant explanation that connects the sign with the object and informs the learner about it. It is through the interpretant that the LO acquires learning purpose, which can be characterized as the pedagogical orientation with the goal of offering the learner knowledge about the object. The value of the LO is derived from its optimal reuse in different knowledge domains.

In creating LOs we should ensure that the relation between LOs is not that of dependency since that would compromise the reusability principle. Although each LO contains a significant quantity of information, that in itself is not sufficient for generating instruction. As indicated earlier, the LO functions as a sign in the instructional situation with an object and interpretant. Therefore simply putting together a group of LOs would not fulfil educational needs nor will they contain informed depth and breadth. In order to employ LOs in a meaningful way, they must be connected and explicated and their significance be established. This responsibility lies with the instructor who employs the LOs for instructional needs.

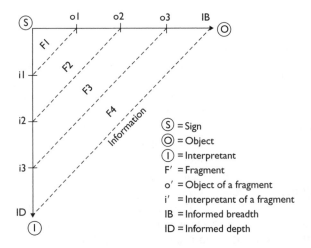

Figure 8.6 Informed depth and breadth

Conclusion

Traditionally knowledge production was conceived as the terrain of a solitary individual labouring alone to contribute to the body of knowledge. However, this territory is being transformed into an information space located at the intersection of computer networks, computer programming and interface design. Therefore, knowledge producers must now think anew about their labour, since where knowledge is stored, how it is managed, accessed, interacted with, and used have profound implications for how knowledge is conceptualized. If LOs are to be created successfully and used appropriately, their creation should be a cooperative and closely aligned process, wherein experts use each other's knowledge as a resource for originating ideas, turning them into LOs, making them visually compelling and facilitating their storage and retrieval mechanisms. Furthermore, as the nature and functional requirements of knowledge are ever-changing in the knowledge economy, no single academic or subject matter expert can generate the total knowledge adequate to the task.

References

Castañares, W. (1994) *De la interpretación a la lectura*, Iberediciones, Madrid.

Hartshorne, C., Weiss, P. and Burks, A. (eds) (1931–1958) *The collected papers of Charles Sanders Peirce*, Harvard University Press, Cambridge, MA.

Parker, K. A. (1998) *The continuity of Peirce's thought*, Vanderbilt University Press, Nashville, TN.

Wiley, D. A. (2002) (accessed 1 May 2003) The instructional use of learning objects, Agency for Instructional Technology and the Association for Educational Communications and Technology (Online) http://www.reusability.org/read/.

Chapter 9

Transforming existing content into reusable learning objects

*Monique Doorten, Bas Giesbers, José Janssen,
Jan Daniels and Rob Koper*

Although the debate on learning objects (LOs), their characteristics and (re)use in a LO economy is lively and relevant, so far little attention has been paid to the consequences of this shift towards object-oriented design and a LO economy for (the reuse of) existing course materials. Many institutions have developed a lot of material throughout the years and also see the economic and educational merits of (re)usable LOs. A process of decomposing existing ('non-object-oriented') learning material into smaller reusable objects is likely to take place (Downes, 2002; Wiley, 2000), but what will that process look like?

Since the success of the idea of a LO economy will highly rely on approved standards, and since the initial steps towards a learning design standard have now been taken, resulting in the IMS learning design (IMS Global Learning Consortium, 2003), we will further compare the examples from the literature with the IMS learning design, more specifically with respect to the smallest reusable objects defined in these approaches.

Having thus derived recommendations and constraints regarding LO design, the concluding section will describe the process of decomposing existing material in terms of checks and analyses that have to be made successively.

This chapter will address the question of how to deal with the reuse of existing course materials within the realm of a LO economy, both on the level of individual subject experts and the broader organizational level. We will first derive requirements of LOs from the literature in this area, concentrating not only on general principles of LO design but on some practical examples as well.

To the extent that the IMS LD can be understood as a pedagogically neutral set of building blocks, to flexibly design, store and deliver education, the higher-level sophistication of the learning design obviously places constraints and requirements on the lower-level LOs (not surprisingly similar to those generally found in the literature on LO design, stemming from the very purpose of reusability behind the logic of object-oriented design (modularity, transportability, etc.). Although the scope of this chapter is on reusable objects, rather than the question of how to aggregate them into a higher-level learning design, the investigation of IMS LD as compared to other object-oriented approaches in the educational field, leads to the opinion that although there is a common understanding of learning materials, broadly consisting of content, practice items and assessment items, the structure of IMS LD offers a more flexible approach for the reuse of different kinds of objects.

Problem description and guidelines

The increasing popularity of e-learning has brought into focus the desirability and in some cases the necessity of breaking up learning material into reusable parts called LOs. Perhaps the most important reason for doing so is economic (Koutlis, Roschelle and Reppening, 1999). One LO can be used in more than one lesson or course. This makes economic sense if a high number of people are willing to contribute, sharing the costs of the development and maintenance of a large LO repository, or more realistically network of repositories (see Downes, Chapter 1).

The economic benefit thus derives from resource sharing and increased flexibility. Another benefit that stems from increased flexibility is the support for more personalized delivery of educational materials (Longmire, 2000). A further benefit that may stem from sharing is the increase in collaboration within and between organizations. This way, it is possible to reuse high-quality material and by doing so improve the quality of education (South and Monson, 2000).

Two leading companies that are involved in e-learning, NETg and Cisco Systems, have adopted an object-oriented approach for the design of learning materials (L'Allier, 1997; Cisco Systems, 2001). Both companies felt a need for flexible reuse in order to shorten development cycles and so recognized that complete courses do not readily lend themselves for such reuse. They decided to compose lessons out of smaller reusable parts. The main differences between NETg and Cisco lies in how they defined and built their smaller reusable parts. This brings us to the question: What exactly do these smaller reusable parts look like?

Reusable learning objects: Requirements and constraints

In NETg's (2003) approach the smallest reusable object is called a 'topic', which consists of a single learning objective, a learning activity and an assessment. This means that it should teach 'something' (learning activity) towards an intended criterion-based result (learning objective) with a method to determine whether this result is met or not (assessment).

Comparable to NETg, Cisco Systems (2001) also has its own terminology to describe LOs. They developed a model in which the smallest reusable element is called a Reusable Information Object or RIO. One RIO consists of content items, practice items and assessment items all aimed at a single learning objective. The main subject that the LO deals with is determined by the content item. It merely provides information needed to perform the other elements of the RIO.

Cisco contends that a RIO is meant to let people learn something instead of merely presenting information. Practice items serve this purpose because they give the learner the opportunity to bring their knowledge and skills to practice. Assessment items consist of a question of a measurable activity used to determine if the learner has mastered the learning objective for the given RIO.

The design of the constructing elements of one RIO depends upon the learning objective that is to be served and the cognitive level that it is aimed at, as well as the type of RIO that is constructed. Five different types of RIOs are distinguished, classified as concerning a concept, a fact, a procedure, a process or a principle.

Taking the differences between NETg and Cisco into account, it is clear that there is no single 'right way' to create LOs. Several principles and guidelines are available in the literature that can be used to aid in the design process, but if the principle of reusing LOs is to be used on a greater scale, a unified process is desirable. In other words, it would be helpful to have a standard or at least some overall guidelines for the creation of LOs (Hamel and Ryan-Jones, 2002).

Several decisions have to be made and agreed upon before this is accomplished. One of the most important is the size or granularity of a LO and is not an easy question to answer. The granularity that South and Monson (2000) designed for Birmingham Young University may or may not be ideal for other situations. Small LOs can be used in many situations, but you must design a system of metadata so that each object can be easily found and identified (Quinn and Hobbs, 2000). Wiley (2002) argues that this choice should be based upon a comparison between the cost of decomposition including the adding of metadata to each object and the benefit you will gain from the reuse. Most likely, practice will show what the ideal granularity will be. As Jacobsen (2001) describes it: 'Object granularity will be largely solved as best practices emerge.'

The next question concerns the types of LOs that are to be constructed. An overall guideline for the construction of LOs would include a structure describing what elements are needed to construct a LO. The elements of which such a structure is built and the degrees of freedom one has when working with it are only two of many questions that have to be answered. Here too, a pragmatic view is applicable according to Downes (see Chapter 1). LOs can be defined by the problems that they solve.

Several problems are likely, such as the difficulty of locating LOs in the vast amount of learning material on the Internet and the impossibility of working with LOs that are in a different format (HTML, Java, etc.) at the same time. On the other hand, these problems point to a solution for their creation. By making an inventory of these problems, solutions become clearer too. Longmire (2000) has discerned some general aspects of LOs, which can be seen as requirements according to which they are to be developed:

- LOs are modular, free-standing and transportable among different learning environments;
- LOs are nonsequential;
- LOs are able to satisfy a single learning objective;
- LOs are accessible to a broad audience;
- LOs are coherent with predetermined schemas, so a limited amount of metadata can capture its essence; and
- LOs can be used in different visual schema without losing their essential meaning.

Of course there are still many questions to be answered that concern specific situations, but this is a good start.

Summarizing the findings from the literature and examining working examples, there seems to be a common understanding that a distinction can be made between three main elements in learning materials: learning activities, content and assessment. As to the more generally stated requirements of LOs, several authors in the field stress the importance of the issues granularity, accessibility and self-containedness, albeit in somewhat differing terms and with few specific guidelines.

Reusable objects in the IMS learning design

In recent years the Open University of the Netherlands has worked on a means to develop, store and deliver educational materials in ways that enhance flexibility in a number of respects:

- pedagogic neutrality;
- reusability;
- personalization; and
- medium neutrality.

The resulting Educational Modelling Language (EML), which is XML-based, so far has been used in the redesign of several existing courses and in the development of entirely new courses, mainly with a focus on reusability and/or personalization. It also has found further recognition in the fact that it was integrated into the IMS Learning Design (IMS LD), which is an important step towards standardization.

The basic principle underlying EML and IMS LD is quite simple – it distinguishes between activities and environments: people learn by doing (by performing learning activities) within a context that enables and/or supports them in performing these activities (established through the presence of proper environments and/or support activities). This chapter concentrates on those EML elements relating to the topic of reusable LOs: activities and environments. (It suffices to know that these and other main elements are labelled, contain metadata, and are provided with attributes like an ID, supporting reusability.)

There are two types of activities: learning activities (to be performed by the learner) and support activities (to be performed by a teacher or tutor). A learning activity can contain (several types of) learning objectives, and consists of at least an activity description and a completed statement, indicating when the activity is completed, which can be modelled to be left for the user to decide.

> The relationship between an activity and an environment can be derived from the linguistic description of the activities. Most nouns in the activity imply the availability of learning objects in the environment, references to other persons imply the availability of communication services, some verbs imply the availability of supportive services or tools. For instance the activity: 'read the problem and discuss solutions with your peers' refers to environment components: 'the problem' which must be available for reading; and 'peers' who must be available to communicate with (including communication means).
>
> (IMS Global Learning Consortium, 2003)

This means that the link between an activity and LOs and/or services is made by defining a learning environment containing LOs and/or services, within the activity. In this sense an environment is a so-called wrapper for LOs and/or services. LOs are defined here as any reproducible and addressable digital or non-digital resources used to perform learning activities or support activities. Examples are web pages, textbooks, productivity tools (text processors, editors, calculators, etc.), instruments (microscope, etc.), and test items.

Besides resources which can be defined at design time, numerous so-called 'service-facilities' are used during teaching and learning, such as chat, e-mail, monitoring, discussion forums, announcement channels, index-search, and so on. (These services can be declared at design time but have to be instantiated during run-time, because 'what is needed is an instance of the service that is unique to the run-time instance of a learning design and its assigned users' (IMS Global Learning Consortium).) This means that services can be 'replicated' as part of a design, rather than reused directly.

In short, environments are referenced from within the activity and can consist of either LOs or services. Figure 9.1 shows the different EML elements just described and the relationships between them.

Further investigating the implications of this model with regard to reuse, there are several points to make:

1. The term 'learning objects' holds a specific meaning within the IMS Learning Design and does not, for instance, include learning activities. Of course learning activities are reusable objects (elements, if you like), so the point that has to be made here is that, in order to avoid further confusion, we will from now on use the term reusable object, rather than reusable LO. Use of the term 'LO' will be restricted to the meaning it has within the IMS Learning Design: an object (text, tool, test-item) needed to perform an activity.
2. The terms 'activity' and 'environment' are pedagogically neutral.
3. The model in Figure 9.1 is a strong simplification in that it focuses on the level of a learning activity, whereas the IMS Learning Design shows that it is possible, for instance, to model activity structures with a single complete learning environment, available within every single activity within the structure. Although this obviously holds implications for reusability, this issue will not be addressed at great length here.
4. Figure 9.1 shows that the sole requirement of the element *learning activity* is that it contain an activity description; it does not necessarily contain a learning objective, nor environment references.
5. Both activities and LOs contain attributes, which make them retrievable and reusable independently.

This last point indicates an important difference from approaches such as NETg's and Cisco's, because the smallest reusable objects there consist of the 'composite' parts called a topic (NETg) or RIO (Cisco). These objects of course can be repurposed/adapted, but don't seem to allow, for instance, for a single content-item to be selected and reused, as Figure 9.2 illustrates:

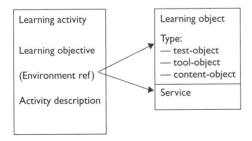

Figure 9.1 Learning activity

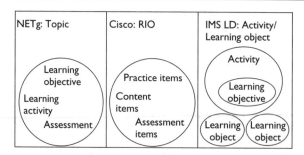

Figure 9.2 Smallest reusable objects in different object-oriented design approaches

Now bearing these different models in mind, let's return to the subject expert who once made a course, which he or she is now asked to revise in such a way that it will align with principles of object-oriented design. The next section will elaborate on the decision-making process that is likely to evolve.

Consequences for the reuse of existing course materials

Regarding the decomposition of existing course materials, the question is: What constituent parts can be distinguished and how can requirements for reusable object design be dealt with, especially when the materials concerned have been developed from a different perspective?

Some interesting differences have been explained between two working examples: NETg and Cisco. When breaking down existing courses into smaller reusable objects, these examples raise several questions, such as:

- Course materials quite often don't stand alone. They are embedded in services such as group tutoring, or individual tutoring. How does one deal with services like these when breaking down course materials into smaller chunks?
- In distance education (our home instructional mode), course materials are often developed with the aim of integrating content and practice (tasks, activities). How necessary and how easy is it to 'disentwine' these elements?
- Is it necessary to prescribe that a learning object should be built on a single learning objective? Is this not an undesirable and unnecessarily inflexible way to proceed?

These questions concern not only practical (efficiency) issues but touch on pedagogical issues as well. Besides efficiency- and pedagogy-related issues there is a third area on which questions arise regarding the transformation of existing course materials into smaller reusable objects relating to motivational/organizational factors.

Starting our investigation of possibilities to efficiently transform existing educational material into reusable learning objects, we formulated several premises:

1. Breaking educational materials down into smaller reusable chunks is a time-consuming endeavour requiring the cooperation of subject experts. It will be considered useful and sensible only to the extent that subject experts expect that they themselves or others might want to reuse (parts of) the existing material.
2. The term 'reuse' is often used in a broad sense, covering a wide range of possible actions. In our approach to the transformation of existing materials to reusable objects we expect to have to distinguish between several types of reuse: 'reuse as is', repurposing (reuse in a different context) and customization (reuse with adaptations made).
3. We expect reuse of existing materials at the Open University of the Netherlands to occur in respect to the development of new courses (including revised courses) and in the context of the development of courses for third parties.
4. Educational institutions favour the idea of object-oriented design as a principle to enhance reusability, ergo: the design of educational materials will increasingly follow an object-oriented approach and with that, parts of existing materials will be as it were 'automatically' integrated into new, reusable LOs.
5. Nevertheless, and most certainly within the setting of an educational institution, it will be necessary to adopt a model to guide the development of new materials along the principle of object-oriented design: What objects do we wish to design and how do we wish to (re)use (aggregate) them (Longmire, 2002)?
6. Taking the desire for reuse beyond the limits of a single institution there's a need to adhere to a standardised approach.

Against this background and in relation to the issues and premises stated above, the question we address further is: What recommendations can we draw from the IMS LD and the more general requirements referred to in this section, for an individual subject expert who is about to embark on the task of decomposing existing course materials into smaller reusable objects?

The process of decomposition: Checks, analyses and decisions

Earlier we have argued that teachers will decompose existing course material in a structured manner only if there is a balance between workload and future added value during the process of aggregation of new learning materials. Therefore, it is likely that institutions that aggregate according to a certain object-oriented instructional design will work systematically at the decomposition of existing materials. They will also be willing to put effort into slicing materials up into the most reusable form. We will describe the process of decomposition towards the smallest meaningful parts, preparing as many reusable objects as is conceivable, using as much of the existing material as possible. Our own situation at the Open University of the Netherlands will be the basis for this, while bearing in mind the findings from the literature as described earlier.

Let's assume that a certain faculty instructs its staff to decompose existing courses to reusable smaller parts. All parts in the existing courses can be determined as being either 'content', 'activities' (learning or support), 'assessment' or 'services'. Several checks, analyses and decisions will have to be made in this process, because not all existing course materials are instantly ready to be decomposed into digital objects. The course materials may not be available in electronic form, there might be problems with copyright restrictions or intellectual property rights. Is it, for instance, allowed to make changes in the original course material? Therefore, the process of decomposition starts with an investigation of the existing materials at hand and will involve the following steps:

1. Decide what course material is in demand for reuse and is likely to be part of newly developed courses/learning experiences. What materials would faculty or others want to reuse?
2. Check whether the material is available for reuse: copyright clearance, intellectual property rights. Bear in mind that copyright issues may differ along with the intended mode of delivery.
3. Check whether the course material is available in original format. For instance: a figure printed in a textbook might no longer be available separately, but only as an integrated part of a printing plate.
4. Check whether the original format matches the desired ('agreed upon'/'interoperable') format.

After the selection of available course material, the material has to be broken down into smaller reusable parts. All parts in the selected material have to be determined as either being 'content', an 'activity' (learning or support), an 'assessment item' or a 'service'. This is a relatively simple task. The hard work comes with the determination as to what parts are intrinsically meaningful and potentially reusable. The potential reusability of 'content' is expected to be generally high. Isolating content from existing material will mostly lead to a reusable object. But this is not the case for many activities in existing material. A large amount of activities are expected not to be intrinsically meaningful or potentially reusable if separated from the content. In that case the activity cannot be isolated and separated from the content without losing its semantic and pragmatic meaning and its effectiveness towards the attainment of the learning objective(s) (Koper, 2003). These learning activities are reusable only in combination with the prescribed content (environment), which make them not (or less) suitable for reuse in other contexts.

Another reason why the reusability of activities is more problematic, is that they might not stand on their own and might have side effects to the dossiers of learners – for instance, when a learner has to 'hand in' a copy of work done. As in the case of services, these kinds of activities might be reproduced but can't be simply reused.

In practice we expect to decompose into:

- content;
- learning activities free of content (more rarely found);
- learning activities with content (with prescribed learning environment); and
- test-objects.

So the next steps in the process of decomposition will be to:

5. Analyse the selected materials and decide what parts can be defined as being either content, an intertwined combination of activity and content, a learning activity free of content or a test object.
6. Check on possible side effects.

Having done so, it is still left to determine the smallest intrinsically meaningful parts. In order to do so we need to check whether the distinguished objects meet the requirements of being reusable in the sense that they appear to be self-contained and ideally non-sequential (Longmire, 2000), meaning that all concepts, principles, methods and so on are sufficiently explained within the object itself. Existing (non-object-oriented designed) course material will often contain references to other parts (e.g. chapters). These references need to be removed or adapted in order to make the objects free-standing. In practice objects will not always be 'non-sequential', or in order to be so they would become too large. Non-sequential therefore means that objects should be without any references to any presumed prerequisite prior knowledge, other than through the use of metadata.

Slicing existing course material therefore eventually requires that we:

7. Determine the beginning and end of each smallest intrinsically meaningful part (modularity) by determining the extent to which parts meet the requirement of being non-sequential and free-standing (self-contained).

This is what has to be done from the point of view of the subject expert. Although the process of decomposition is described here as a stepwise approach, in practice, of course, steps 1, 5 and 7 will appear to be inter-related.

Needless to say, reusability stretches further than this and presupposes that the subject expert will be offered appropriate tools such as an adequate content-management system and guidelines regarding formats/metadata and so on in order to make the objects addressable and available for others (sharing/repository). These issues are far from solved at this stage and include (re)defining tasks and responsibilities on an organisational level. The purpose of this chapter was to investigate the process of decomposing existing learning materials into reusable objects, against the background of current developments in the standardization of learning design.

Conclusion and discussion

A LO economy as envisioned by Downes (2000, 2002) is still far from being realized and requires for solutions on several levels: learning design, technology, standardization, economical principles, legislation (copyright) and organization. In this chapter we concentrated on the combined issues of learning design and standardization, by investigating IMS LD's structure and terminology as a tool/guideline for the decomposition of existing course material into smaller reusable objects.

Compared to other approaches towards object-oriented design in the field (NETg, Cisco), IMS LD offers a very flexible approach in terms of reuse of different objects and combinations of objects. However, the process of decomposing existing learning materials into reusable objects as described in this chapter appears to require minute attention to a variety of details from a subject expert. Furthermore the process as described earlier somewhat implies a 'shortest-route' approach in transforming current content into reusable objects, disregarding pedagogical issues and possible desires for transformations in this respect.

As to the creation of content objects, there might be little objection to such an approach. Rather, extra investments are likely to have to be taken into account with respect to the (re)design of learning activities. In this sense we expect the reuse of existing course materials and their transformation into reusable objects to remain largely confined to content objects.

Acknowledgement

The authors would like to thank Colin Tattersall for his useful comments on an earlier draft of this chapter.

References

Cisco Systems (2001) (accessed 18 May 2002) Reusable learning object strategy. Designing information and learning objects through concept, fact, procedure, process, and principle templates, (Online) http://www.cisco.com/warp/public/10/wwtraining/elearning/implement/rlo_strategy.pdf.

Downes, S. (2000) (accessed 28 April 2003) *The Need for and Nature of Learning Objects: Some Assumptions and a Premise*, 22 May, (Online) http://www.newstrolls.com/news/dev/downes/column000523_1.htm.

Downes, S. (2002) (accessed 13 August 2002) The learning object economy: Draft – August 5, 2002, (Online) http://www.downes.ca/files/Learning_Object_Economy.doc.

Hamel, C. J. and Ryan-Jones, D. (2002) (accessed 29 April 2003) Designing instruction with learning objects, *International Journal of Educational Technology*, **1** (3), (Online) http://www.outreach.uiuc.edu/ijet/v3n1/hamel/index.html.

IMS Global Learning Consortium. (2003) (accessed 21 March 2003) *IMS digital repositories interoperability specification*, (Online) http://www.imsglobal.org/digitalrepositories/index.cfm.

Jacobsen, P. (2001) (accessed 4 December 2001) Reusable learning objects – What does the fiuture hold?, *E-Learning Magazine*, (Online) http://www.ltimagazine.com/ltimagazine/article/articleDetail.jsp?id=5043.

Koper, R. (2003) Combining reusable learning resources and services with pedagogical purposeful units of learning, in *Reusing Online Resources*, ed. A. Littlejohn, pp. 46–59, Kogan Page, London.

Koutlis, M., Roschelle, J. and Reppening, A. (1999) Developing educational software components, *IEEE Computer*, **32**: 50–58.

L'Allier, J. J. (1997) (accessed 18 May 2002) Frame of reference: NETg's map to its products, their structures and core beliefs, *NETg*, (Online) http://www.netg.com/research/whitepapers/frameref.asp.

Longmire, W. (2000) (accessed 21 May 2000) A primer on learning objects: Excerpt from learning without limits, *Learning Circuits*, (Online) http://www.learningcircuits.org/mar2000/primer.html.

Longmire, W. (2002) (accessed 24 April 2003) A primer on learning objects, *Learning Circuits: ASTD's Online Magazine All About E-Learning*, 2003, (Online) http://www.learningcircuits.org/mar2000/primer.html.

NETg (2003) (accessed 21 February 2003) *NETg Home Page*, (Online) http://netg.com.

Quinn, C. and Hobbs, S. (2000) (accessed 13 August 2002) Learning objects and instructional components, *Educational Technology and Society*, **3** (2), (Online) http://ifets.ieee.org/periodical/vol_2_2000/discuss_summary_0200.html.

South, J. B. and Monson, D. W. (2000) A university-wide system for creating, capturing, and delivering learning objects, in *The instructional use of learning objects: Online version*, ed. D. A. Wiley, (Online) http://reusability.org/read/chapters/south.doc.

Wiley, D. A. (2000) (accessed 21 May 2002) Learning object design and sequencing theory. Academic dissertation, *Birmingham Young University* (Online) http://wiley.ed.usu.edu/docs/dissertation.pdf.

Wiley, D. A. (2002) (accessed 21 May 2002) Learning objects need instructional design theory, *2001/2002 ASTD Distance Learning Yearbook*, (Online) http://wiley.ed.usu.edu/docs/astd.pdf.

Chapter 10

Reuse, portability and interoperability of learning content

Or, why educational modelling languages?

Peter B. Sloep

Over the past few decades the demand for higher education has diversified considerably. The demand for initial higher education for adolescents is centuries old. However, since roughly the 1960s, we've witnessed a growing demand for higher education for adults. Initially, this demand was rather traditional in that its focus was on degree programmes. The knowledge economy has added to this, the demand for short programmes which primarily aim at fulfilling the students' educational needs. This type of education goes by such names as further education, continuous education, lifelong learning, and so on (Brown and Duguid, 2002; Westera and Sloep, 2001)).

In virtue of traditional education's orientation on academic curricula with fixed degree programmes, its programmes are rather homogeneous and mainly teacher-led. This contrasts strongly with the needs of further education with its emphasis on personalized arrangements offered in a setting of the student's own choice. The further education student has very particular needs in terms of the subject matter. He or she will want a highly specific slice of subject matter, one that exactly fits his or her needs at a particular time.

In addition, some students may prefer to be taught in a face-to-face setting, while others may go for the relaxed space and time constraints that distance learning affords. Some students may prefer to study individually, shunning contacts with their study-mates, while others might prefer collaborative work. Some students may want modern pedagogies such as problem-based, case-based, or simulation-based learning, while others may simply want to be told – orally or in print – what there is to know. All these preferences, in terms of both subject matter and pedagogy, are included in the mix. The upshot is that modern educational institutions that want to satisfy the needs of all students, are required to offer a veritable smorgasbord of options.

The crucial question now is: Can educational institutions meet the modern student's needs affordably? For, although *customized learning*, as one may call it, may strike us as the best solution, it comes at a price. Although traditional, cohort-based classroom teaching may offer little flexibility, it has proven to be affordable. Its development costs are typically low and so long as the staff-to-student ratio stays low, delivery costs can remain in tune with tuition.

If, however, one intends to meet the specific needs of each and every student, this argument loses its validity. There are no cohorts anymore, so classroom teaching, which is based on cohorts, becomes impossible. On the other hand, if groups of students with similar needs and schedules can be put together after all, the staff-to-student ratio will, in all likelihood, be very high. This increases costs, which can push up the price of tuition for students.

Traditional distance teaching has tried to overcome this problem by investing in the development of learning materials that are suitable for (guided) self-study and by offering only emergency tutoring. This does indeed meet the students' needs for flexibility in time, pace and place of study. It also meets the affordability criterion provided there are enough students, but it does not allow for customized content or customized pedagogies.

E-learning, roughly, the use of networked computers in support of education, has often been greeted as the solution to these problems. Particularly, the flexible reuse of educational materials 'content' or learning objects (LO) is a cornerstone of this argument. The slogan is: 'Write once, use many times.'

Although the development costs of LOs may be high, as in traditional distance teaching, through reuse, their cost per student can become low (Sloep and Schlusmans, 2001). Thus, the argument goes, tailored content, built out of a collection of LOs, may be developed quickly and efficiently; and consequently, e-learning lowers the costs to such an extent that the modern, further-education-seeking student's needs and wishes may be met in an affordable way.

In this chapter, I shall critically evaluate this line of reasoning. Under the heading 'the information technological approach' I shall discuss in some detail the current use of LOs and show it to be wanting. My argument will be that the use of LOs may, in principle, offer much flexibility in creating content, in practice it will not, particularly since it does not support pedagogical flexibility. Then I'll offer an alternative view, dubbed 'the education technological view'. This, I will show, is indeed capable of fulfilling all the needs of customized learning, both the need for custom content and the need for custom pedagogies. Some possible criticisms of my line of reasoning will conclude the chapter.

The information technological approach and why it will fail

What it is

This perspective, which is strongly espoused by the Advanced Distributed Learning initiative (ADL), holds that LOs should be durable across technological changes, interoperable across hardware and software platforms (e.g. web browsers), accessible when needed from remote locations, and reusable across applications and contexts. As the terminology reveals, it is very much a hardware and software orientated perspective. According to this view, LOs consist of (collections of) computer files: text, graphics, video and audio, and so on. An instructional designer may deploy these files as he or she sees fit. Typically, designers use authoring tools to create them. A Managed Learning Environment (MLE) or Learning Management System (LMS) will serve them to students in order to create actual educational experiences.

If everybody were to store their LOs in a simple, local file structure, the objects could hardly be reused by other systems or adapted by other designers. Local storage prevents access by non-local systems, and the simple file structure prevents the files from being discovered for anything but the smallest content collections. And of course, the benefits from flexible reuse become the more apparent, the larger the collection of objects. For this reason, digital LO repositories are now being established.

Examples of repositories include MERLOT <http://www.merlot.org>, the Scottish electronic Staff Development Library SeSDL <http://www.sesdl.scotcit.ac.uk> and the Universal Brokerage Platform for Learning Resources <http://www.ist-universal.org/>. They may provisionally be described as databases for educational materials. To add to the discoverability of the LOs in the database, the objects are described with the aid of their own metadata, which for the most part are based on the IEEE LOM metadata specification, which is now becoming accepted as an international standard for this purpose.

Furthermore, LOs preferably aren't uploaded as plain files but in the form of *content packages*. A content package contains not only the physical files themselves, but also their metadata descriptions, and an indication of the way the content coheres or is organized, for example like a book's table of contents. The IMS global consortium has put together a specification that details what content packages should look like. A content package thus is a compound LO, with metadata and an organizational description that speaks to its intended use.

Since these kinds of LOs are treated as computer files that happen to contain educational materials, they pose little challenge to the current state of information technology. The details have yet to be worked out as to how content packages may be swapped. Adequate software tools (repositories, metadata descriptors, content packagers, managed learning environments) have to be created. And the standards that these tools employ (such as content packaging and LO metadata) have to be worked out, and perhaps localized, and agreed upon.

Localizing is relevant for all specifications but particularly the LOM. It encompasses not just the translation to a local language of the labels used (e.g. 'author' to the Dutch 'auteur'), but also (and much more importantly) the creation of vocabularies and taxonomies (ontologies) for the fields' contents. For example, the American category 'K12' does not translate to any equivalent category in the Dutch educational system, and so on.

But this standardization and localization are a matter of time, not of technological innovation. To give an example, since the information technological approach pivots on swapping files, it does not make highly specific demands on the MLEs that have to serve up these files. Present generation MLEs or LMSs almost without exception use browser technologies on the client side and employ the help of standard plug-ins to render non-html file formats (rtf, ppt, flash, etc.). There is nothing of a specifically educational nature here.

From an educational point of view the information technological approach to the reuse of educational materials is one of changing a book- or paper-based 'LO' economy into a computer- and Internet-based economy. While the changes may be considerable and sometimes even hard to swallow for the educational establishment, they certainly aren't revolutionary.

So, the principles of file-based flexible reuse of content seem to be firmly in place. Content in the form of packaged LOs may be swapped between software systems. Hence, the interoperability of software systems seems to be assured. Or is it?

Why it will fail

The learning technology world is currently in the middle of the implementation of the information technological approach. Vendors of e-learning software abound. And bodies like IMS, CEN/ISSS, and so on, which draft specifications for learning technologies, thrive. So any judgement on the approach's true merits can only be provisional. It still has to show what it is really able to achieve. In my opinion, the signs aren't good.

Admittedly, the available empirical evidence is far from substantial. Little to no systematic research into actual reuse has been conducted. And how could it, in light of the fact that the entire approach is new and implementation projects have only just begun? Some early users of this approach include the Dutch Digital University <http://www.digiuni.nl>, and the Finnish Virtual University <http://www.virtuaaliyliopisto.fi/index.php?language=eng> (see also Werbach, 2000).

My evidence partly derives from ill-boding impressions personally communicated to me. In addition, it is based on my own inspection of available repositories. But apart from evidence-based arguments, there are other, a priori arguments as to why the information technological approach is unsatisfactory.

Content viewed the information technological way consists of mere chunks of information used in an educationally informed setting. But for their metadata description, there is nothing that intrinsically characterizes them as *educational* objects. In keeping with their true nature, they had perhaps better be called *information objects*. That term has actually been used, for instance, in a Cisco white paper on the reuse of learning materials (Wieseler, 1999; see also Barritt, Lewis and Wieseler, 1999; and Wiley, 2002). But since the term LO has stuck and is extensively used in the sense of a chunk of information, I will conform to this usage.

The important observation to make is that they can only acquire educational significance once they are hooked up in an educational context. This context is absent in digital repositories, except for the metadata description, which provides evidence for how the metadata author intended the LO to be used. This, however, does not suffice to start up an efficient and effective LO economy, as the following example will illustrate.

Martin Luther King's speech, held in Washington, 28 August 1963, in which he repeatedly uses the phrase 'I have a dream', may be used for educational purposes in many different ways. Obviously, it could serve as a resource in a modern history course on racial policies in the USA in the 1960s. Questions could be asked about what those policies were and what King's role was in changing them; or students could be asked to write a paper on King's ideas. Alternatively, the speech (i.e. the repeated use of the phrase 'I have a dream') could be used in a rhetoric class to illustrate a particular figure of speech. Students could be asked to name this figure, provide other cases, and so on. Or the speech could be used in a linguistics class to illustrate a version of Afro-American English.

The example shows that this LO, as that is what the speech is, may be used in many different ways for educational purposes. A metadata description would typically capture one or a few of them, but certainly not all. It is even logically impossible to capture all, as there is no limit to the imagination of the educational designer who might want to utilize it. Nevertheless, LOs may be stored, retrieved, changed and described, much the same way that information on the Internet at large is stored, retrieved, changed and described. Indeed, the Internet may be seen as one large digital repository of LOs (albeit, usually without the metadata descriptions). Nobody doubts that the Internet is a valuable repository; likewise repositories of LOs are valuable. The question is, however, whether it is rich enough to support the flexible reuse needed for customized learning. I do not believe it does, nor that it will be, given enough time. The approach is fundamentally at fault since it fails to address education-specific aspects. A digital repository of these kinds of LOs has little educational value, in spite of its name.

The education technological approach and why it may succeed

What it is

An educational approach to customized learning would examine what is required to generate full-fledged educational experiences. It would not stop at examining pieces of content and investigating what their ingredients are. Of course, an examination as meant here will reveal resources, such as books, collections of hyperlinks, graphics, video and audio files. These are the LOs of the information technological approach.

But, in addition to this, the investigation will focus on the education-ally relevant *structure* that the LOs are part of. This does not become apparent immediately. A thorough analysis is required. And even then one should be careful not to become enthralled by the particulars of the various possible pedagogical approaches, such as competency-based learning, problem-based learning, or case-based learning. That would lead to one set of descriptive categories for each approach investigated.

This is quite possible as examples of such approaches exist such as Targeteam <http://www11.in.tum.de/forschung/projekte/targeteam/>; LMML <http://daisy.fmi.uni-passau.de/db/literatur.php3?key=S00>; PALO <http://sensei.lsi.uned.es/palo/>; and TML/NetQuest <http://www.ilrt.bris.ac.uk/mru/netquest/tml/>. Still, this approach would not result in flexible reuse of LOs across pedagogies.

What is needed is a system of descriptive categories, a *pedagogical meta-language* that is general enough to capture all (most?) of the various pedagogical approaches and yet specific enough to remain educationally relevant. Various attempts at devising such a meta-language have been made in recent years. Some have been more successful than others in steering clear of the cliffs of pedagogical specificity and educational irrel-evance. The language that seems to fit the ideal best is the IMS Learning Design specification (IMS, 2003). It is based upon an earlier, field-tested attempt to create such a language: the Educational Modelling Language, EML, which was developed by the Open University of the Netherlands (Koper, 2000). Although EML and LD differ significantly in their details, from a conceptual point of view they are the same.

How does Learning Design (LD) succeed in being an adequate peda-gogical meta-language? LD succeeds by discerning such categories as 'activities', 'environments', 'roles', 'properties' and 'plays' (see Figure 10.1). *Activities* may be either learning activities or support activities,

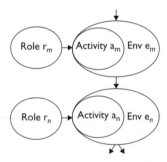

Figure 10.1 A schematic play with roles, activities, and environments

depending on whether they are carried out by students or by staff members. Learning activities guide students through their study; they may vary from 'read the accompanying paper and answer the following questions' to 'get together with your fellow students, discuss the accompanying problem, and jointly write a report on its solution'. Support activities can of course show a similar heterogeneity. These two examples also illustrate what the *environment* is. In the first case, it is the paper to be read, in the second the problem description that accompanies the activity. One may identify environments that are specific to some activity or that are common to any collection of activities. The environment really contains the learning *resources*, that is the LOs from the previous section. It may also contain *services*, such as, for instance, a collaborative learning environment, a simulation, or a chat facility.

The examples also illustrate the notion of a *role*. Two role types are standard: *learner* and *staff*. However, within each category, subcategories may be freely defined. In the collaborative problem-solving case, it might be a good idea to appoint a chair and a recorder. Either one would be a specific sub-role of the learner. There is little use in discerning roles if it wouldn't be possible somehow to keep track of what the persons in a role have been doing. This is achieved through the device of *properties*, which are variables that may be declared at will. Depending on the run-time system that 'plays' LD scenarios, particular properties may be built in already; examples would be 'time spent online', 'last time logged on', 'total session time', and so on.

Others are less generic and are specified by the designer. An example would be the score on a multiple-choice question or an entire questionnaire. If one needs the score to affect the flow of the learning experience, the questions or questionnaire need to be put together in such a way that it affects the values of a property. Such a property may be either local to a particular instantiation ('run') of a design or be carried along from course to course ('global'). In order to be able to set, update, monitor, etc., properties, some sort of container for them is needed. Not only the question or questionaire needs to be made available to the student, but he or she also needs to be able to interact with it ('click option A', 'review your answers'). The prime candidate for this type of interaction would of course be the IMS Question and Test Interoperability specification, but LD and QT&I have yet to be harmonized. (EML did contain such an interaction model.) Similarly, we need a specification in which a more general sense would allow one to structure content as needed. XHTML would be a suitable candidate for structuring the content of many learning objects. LD does not contain a specification for structured content, although the use of XHTML is recommended. (Again, EML did contain a whole suite of elements, based on the doc-book specification, for structuring content.)

Now we have activities, environments to support them, roles to carry them out, and properties to keep track of what goes on, but what we are still missing is a mechanism for describing the temporal sequence of activities. This is achieved by the *play* and a few similar devices, such as *acts*, *role parts* and *activity structures*. They allow a designer to couple any activity to a role, and to put activities (or groupings thereof) in a temporal order. When aided by conditions, the play also allows for conditional branching, so that various ordered subsets of activities can be identified and played out, depending on the teacher's choice, the students' preferences, or a particular set of property values. Although much more can be said, the present explanation suffices to grasp the essentials of LD.

Why it has a better chance to succeed

A pedagogical meta-language like LD allows one to put the LOs discussed earlier in environments and thus separate them from the didactic scenario in which they function. Crucially, one may edit the didactic scenario, i.e. the play, in isolation of the LOs. Thus the same objects may be used in various pedagogical scenarios. By taking the resources out of a particular play, one may even reuse the same pedagogical scenario with a different set of content items. Therefore not only LOs are reusable, so are the didactic scenarios. Obviously there are limits to the extent to which one may repurpose a particular didactic scenario. Or rather, a radically different implementation – say switching from a class-based, cohort-based course to a distance-taught course that employs collaborative learning – requires more effort than a marginal adjustment from a synchronous, teacher-led face-to-face course to an asynchronous, teacher-led distance-mode course. But in this respect the repurposing of resource materials fares little better.

The upshot is that now, for the first time, reusability has been extended to cover not only learning resources, but also didactic scenarios; not only static content, but also dynamic behaviour. This is a big step forward. Another benefit is that stored LOs can now be retrieved not only through their metadata descriptions but also through the actual educational experiences that they are a part of. This way, repositories do not become odd collections of chunks of content that, at best, someone has quite successfully used in some irreproducible way and at worst, the author wasn't determined enough to throw away. Repositories now (also, only) contain resources that have actually been *typed to their context of use*. So one may in fact inspect how they have been used. Obviously, this does not imply a commitment to reuse them in the same way. Rather, much like textbooks, one may become inspired by them and employ them however one sees fit. There is one big difference, though. A textbook contains an implicit pedagogy that cannot be changed easily since it is inextricably tied to the written material. One may skip paragraphs or even chapters, but the pedagogy stays in place. Through the use of a pedagogical metalanguage like LD, for the first time one may alter the pedagogy without necessarily altering the content. This is a genuine educational innovation and a substantial contribution to the flexible reuse of learning materials.

Conclusion

The information technological and the education technological approaches both have something valuable to offer to support the flexible reuse of learning materials. I believe, in contrast to the current consensus, that the information technological approach on its own falls short of the mark. Both, working in concert, are needed for actual reuse to flourish. This means that we have an even longer way to go to the full-scale implementation of a reusable LO economy. Current MLEs and LMSs cannot run instances of didactic scenarios described in LD. They may with some effort be able to process the LOs, but rendering the scenario instructions will take much more, as the scenario instructions will have to be interpreted and passed on to a user interface.

At first glance, this may seem a vice, but I suggest that it be viewed as a virtue. As argued, the information technological approach has little to offer in the way of innovative educational practices, if it is able to orchestrate actual reuse of educational materials at all. But if we manage to embed reusable resources in reusable scenarios, then we've made a significant step towards creating a flourishing LO economy.

This is a first step. It will certainly not suffice to guarantee success. It takes actual people, instructional designers, developers, and teachers, to get out and travel on the reuse road. People need incentives and rewards to get moving. They need to overcome their fears and anxieties. Organizations need to adapt. We've only just started to survey these social, economical, psychological and organizational issues, let alone solve them. There still is a long way to go.

Note

This chapter is based on a paper read at the 'Onderwijsresearchdagen (ORD) held in Antwerp, Belgium in June 2001.

References

Barritt, C., Lewis, D. and Wieseler, W. (1999) (accessed 23 April 2003) Cisco Systems – Reusable information strategy, (Online) http://www.cisco.com/warp/public/779/ibs/solutions/publishing/whitepapers/.

Brown, J. S. and Duguid, P. (2002) *The social life of information*, Harvard Business School Press, Boston, MA.

IMS (2003) (accessed 23 April 2003) IMS learning design specification, (Online) http://imsglobal.org/learningdesign/index.cfm.

Koper, R. (2000) *From change to renewal: Educational technology foundations of electronic learning environments*, Heerlen, Nederland.

Sloep, P. B. and Schlusmans, K. (2001) In *Thema, tijdschrift voor Hoger onderwijs & Management*, Vol. 4, pp. 15–21.

Werbach, K. (2000) (accessed 28 April 2003) Clicks and mortar meets cap and gown: Higher education goes online – Release 1.0, *Edventure.com*, **18** (8), (Online) http://www.edventure.com.

Westera, W. and Sloep, P. B. (2001) The future of education in cyberspace, in *Provocative and do-able futures for cybereducation: Leadership for the cutting edge*, eds L. R. Vandervert and L. V. Shavinina, pp. 115–37, Mary Ann Liebert Publishers, New York.

Wieseler, W. (1999) (accessed 9 May 2000) RIO: A standards-based approach for reusable information objects, *Cisco Systems*, (Online) http://www.cisco.com/warp/public/779/ibs/solutions/publishing/whitepapers/.

Wiley, D. (2002) Connecting learning objects to instructional design theory: A definition, a metaphor, and a taxonomy, in *The Instructional Use of E-learning Objects*, ed. D. Wiley, pp. 1–35, Agency for Instructional Technology, Bloomington, IN.

Chapter 11

Collaborative evaluation of learning objects

John C. Nesbit and Karen Belfer

When instructors and students search a repository to select a learning object (LO) for use, they have three questions in mind: Is it the right type? Is it the best I can find? How should I use it? Substantial effort has been spent in recent years building metadata standards and tools to assist users in answering the first question. Now, with repositories filling with thousands of objects, many dealing with similar subject matter and learning goals, greater attention and effort will turn to the second and third questions.

LO evaluation by third-party reviewers is a key element in promoting reusability because the availability of quality ratings can have an immediate and compelling effect on the outcome of repository searches. Quality ratings are already being used to order search results in MERLOT, a leading LO metadata repository for higher education. In MERLOT, highly rated LOs are returned ahead of objects that have lower ratings or have not been evaluated. The use of quality ratings in this way places significant responsibility on the e-learning research community to develop demonstrably valid evaluation methods because even minor variations in the method may have amplified effects on many thousands of users' selection decisions.

The challenge of developing effective evaluation systems is formidable because they must optimize on two opposing variables: the number of objects that can be evaluated versus the quality of the obtained evaluations. A costly model that returns highly accurate evaluations is of little use to the individual user if it can be applied to only a small fraction of a collection. Also, it is insufficient for reviews to return only numeric quality ratings. Reviews can most strongly benefit users by elaborating on pre-existing metadata to describe the situations and contexts in which the objects can be appropriately used.

Some definitions of LOs admit non-digital resources and cover a wide range of aggregation levels including whole courses and certificate programs (IEEE, 2002). But, because our goal is to facilitate reusability through quality evaluation, this chapter is primarily concerned with digital resources at the lower to middle levels of granularity, a scope that includes static images or text, animations, simulations, interactive lessons, tests, and so on.

We have identified eight interrelated reasons for developing effective LO evaluation systems:

1. Ratings and qualitative assessments aid individual users in searching and selecting objects.
2. Evaluations can provide guidance on how best to use an object.
3. Quality can be increased by formative evaluation throughout the design and development stages.
4. Evaluation standards can drive the practices of designers and developers.
5. Participation in evaluation activities can contribute to the professional development of those who work with LOs.
6. Evaluation activities can build and support communities of practice in relation to LOs.
7. Positive evaluations can promote social recognition of skilled designers and developers.
8. A trusted evaluation system is an essential step towards the development of a workable business model for the economic exchange of LOs.

Here we propose a convergent participation model that addresses all of the above goals. In the proposed model, evaluation is conducted by a panel drawn from different stakeholder groups. For example, in a college setting, learners, instructors, instructional designers and media developers might participate as panel members. There is a two-cycle process. During the first cycle the evaluators independently and asynchronously assess the object. During the second cycle, which may be conducted synchronously or asynchronously, the evaluators compare and explain their earlier assessments, adjusting their individual assessments as their judgement shifts in response to the panel's discussion.

During both cycles the evaluators use an assessment instrument that gathers numeric ratings and comments on a small number of dimensions. The process is managed by a moderator who guides discussion but does not directly assess the object. During the second cycle the moderator sequences the items under discussion to ensure that features about which there is greatest disagreement are discussed first.

In the convergent participation model, evaluators use online tools that enable fully distributed participation. The tools support the communication of individual assessments among group members and aggregation of individual assessments into collaborative reviews.

Evaluation of educational software and multimedia

In considering some of the alternative approaches to evaluating educational software and multimedia, we use the classification scheme of Worthen, Sanders and Fitzpatrick (1997) who distinguish between, among other things, consumer-oriented, expertise-oriented, objectives-oriented and participant-oriented evaluations.

Consumer-oriented evaluations of educational materials are conducted by governmental organizations and non-profit associations that train evaluators, often teachers, to apply standard criteria, checklists or rating scales, to examine the materials and produce reviews in a highly structured format. With costs in the same range as those for the production of basic LO metadata, consumer-oriented evaluation is one of the least expensive models, and for this reason alone is highly applicable to the problem of assessing large numbers of LOs. Containing over 7,000 reviews of K-12 materials, the EvaluTech repository (Southern Regional Education Board) is perhaps the best evidence of the cost-efficiency of a consumer-oriented model. The quantitative instruments often used in consumer-oriented evaluation provide a score for each object that enables repositories to order search results. Also, structured reporting formats have the advantage of facilitating comparison among objects.

The validity and descriptive power of consumer-oriented evaluations are limited by the same factors that make them cost-efficient. Evaluators typically work individually, unable to benefit from the specialized expertise of others. The depth of analysis, and the flexibility to deal with the special characteristics of objects, are restricted to whatever can be built into the instrument and procedure on which the evaluator is trained. In reviewing instruments for educational software evaluation, Gibbs, Graves and Bernas (2001) noted that the instruments have been subject to criticism for not being comprehensive, understandable and easy to use. There is evidence of low correlations among evaluators within the criteria that they use for evaluations, usually content, interface design and technical operation (Jolicoeur and Berger, 1986).

Expertise-oriented evaluations are conducted by recognized experts, either individually or in panels. In comparison with consumer-oriented approaches, they place less emphasis on structured formats, closed-response instruments and training, relying instead on the expert judgement of the evaluator. The MERLOT peer review process, described later, can be regarded as combining the expertise and consumer-oriented approaches because it brings expert evaluators together with standard scoring criteria and structured reports.

Expertise-oriented approaches have been criticized as being especially vulnerable to the subjective biases of the evaluators. And they often show low inter-evaluator consistency because individual expert evaluators tend to place greater importance on the specific factors that form the basis of their own expertise (McDougall and Squires, 1995; Reiser and Dick, 1990). As in the consumer-oriented model, there is no representation of stakeholders such as learners, and no testing of the object *in situ*. There may be representation from only a single expert community – perhaps only subject matter experts or only instructional design experts. Expertise-oriented approaches tend to be more costly than consumer-oriented approaches because they lack the efficiency advantages of a fixed procedure repeatedly applied by a trained evaluator.

Objectives-oriented approaches couple detailed analysis and definition of goals with empirical, quantitative studies using pre–post or comparative designs that test the extent to which the goals have been attained. Reiser and Dick (1990) developed a model for educational software evaluation that involved, in part:

- defining learning objectives through an analysis of the software and its documentation;
- developing test items and attitude questions based on the objectives;
- conducting an initial trial with three representative students; and
- conducting a similar trial with a larger group of students in the targeted learning environment.

Similar models have been used for demonstrating the efficacy of software for teaching skills such as spelling and fractions (Jolicoeur and Berger, 1988; Assink and van der Linden, 1993). A major drawback of objectives-oriented approaches is the cost associated with running an empirical study. Given our current systems, it is far more expensive to treat and test a group of students than to have a trained evaluator fill out a form. Another limitation of this approach is that in emphasizing goals and outcomes, objectives-oriented approaches tend to ignore the learning processes that occur as students interact with materials.

Unlike the consumer-, expertise-, and objectives-oriented approaches, participant-oriented approaches to educational evaluation explicitly acknowledge that learning is a social process dependent on social context. This implies that multimedia and software evaluation must account for interactions between the learners and those around them (Baumgartner and Payr, 1996). The methodology of participant-oriented evaluation is drawn from naturalistic and ethnographic research. Data is gathered by prolonged and persistent observation, informal interviews and document analysis, and reported as detailed descriptions or direct quotations (Neuman, 1989; Patton, 1980). There is often an emphasis on bringing stakeholders together in moderated discussion groups:

Participants in the group process become sensitized to the multiple perspectives that exist around any program. They are exposed to divergent views, multiple possibilities, and competing values. Their view is broadened, and they are exposed to the varying agendas of people with different stakes in the evaluation. This increases the possibility of conducting an evaluation that is responsive to different needs, interests, and values.

(Patton, 1982)

The recognition that programme evaluation reports are often underutilized or ignored has led to an interest in promoting organizational learning through the participant group process. Working within an activity theory framework in a university environment, Dobson and McCracken (2001) credited the success of an evaluation project that improved teaching and learning to a team-based approach in which academics and learning technology experts worked as equal partners in furthering innovation. Although the analysis is outside the scope of this chapter, activity theory (Nardi, 1996) offers a relevant perspective on all the evaluation approaches we describe. With its depiction of collective activity (e.g. collaborative evaluation) operating on an object to produce an outcome (e.g. a published review) through the use of mediating tools (e.g. an online evaluation instrument), it is especially consistent with the convergent participation model we are proposing.

Williams (2000) proposed two participant-oriented models that an organization can use to evaluate the LOs it creates. One model deals with externally contracted evaluations of larger instructional units that include LOs. It involves competitive requests for proposals, stakeholder interviews and the possible use of the Delphi technique to develop key questions to be addressed by the evaluation. This is followed by the formulation and execution of an evaluation plan. The second model deals with formative, internally conducted evaluations. It builds an evaluative component into every step of the ADDIE instructional design model (Assess needs, Design, Develop, Implement and Evaluate instruction). Both the internal and external models require meta-evaluation as a final stage.

There are features of most participant-oriented approaches that are incompatible with the requirements of LO evaluation. Often these approaches tailor the evaluation's guiding questions to situational demands to obtain an evaluative report with a unique format. This practice would make comparison of large numbers of LOs difficult. In participant-oriented approaches there are usually no quantitative ratings that can be used to sort search results, even though this is an extremely convenient feature that many users have already come to expect. Finally, extensive collection and analysis of detailed qualitative data is just too costly for use with large numbers of objects.

In the search for an efficient model that preserves many of the advantages of participant-oriented approaches, we were impressed with many of the interactive tools for communication and collaboration provided in online communities. By providing automated functions that facilitate voluntary contributions from users, these websites demonstrate the strengths of technology-mediated communities managed by their members.

Lessons from the Web

User ratings and comments have become much easier to gather with the establishment of the Internet. Increasingly sophisticated systems are emerging that address the problem of poor-quality contributions by classifying, filtering and sorting user comments on the basis of meta-evaluative ratings provided by other users. Featuring brief articles that may each be discussed by hundreds of comments posted by users, the Slashdot website <www.slashdot.org> led this trend by allowing certain community members to rate others' comments so that any reader could view only comments whose average rating fell above an adjustable threshold. By authoring highly rated comments, a member can acquire the prestigious 'karma points' that increase one's likelihood of being temporarily granted the privilege of rating others' comments. The whole system is extremely effective in ratcheting up the quality of user comments and bringing the most valued comments into the foreground.

The evaluation requirements of a LO repository are similar in several ways to those of an online book retailer. Amazon's user review and recommendation system offers significant insights into how object repositories might manage user reviews. Any Amazon user can submit a 1,000-word book review including a rating on a five-point scale. Other users can vote yes or no on the usefulness of the review, generating an approval rating that determines the order in which reviews are displayed. The user ratings of a book are combined with a customer's buying preferences and expressed interests to construct a personalized list of recommended books that are presented to the customer when entering the site.

Websites presenting consumer-authored reviews of items ranging from cameras to travel destinations further illustrate the design and operation of online evaluation communities. With over nine million unique visitors per month, and over a million published reviews, the Epinions website <www.epinions.com> is perhaps the best example of a venue in which producing and accessing reviews, not purchasing products, is the central transaction. Users can register in Epinions and create personal profiles including a photo, biography, link to homepage, favourite websites and links to reviews they have authored. Epinions supports meta-evaluation of both the review and reviewer. Reviews can be rated by any member on a five-point scale ranging from Very Helpful to Not Helpful. Of greater significance for community building, though, is the 'web of trust' linking member profiles. Members can choose to trust or block the authors of reviews they have read. Links to profiles of trusted others are presented on the member's own profile, forming a navigable network of shared interest and trust relationships. Epinions members can be promoted to Top Reviewer if they (a) frequently write reviews that consistently receive high ratings and (b) maintain trust links to other authors of other highly rated reviews. Members can be promoted to Advisor if they frequently contribute high-quality meta-evaluations. Aside from social recognition for high-quality contributions, the Top Reviewer and Advisor roles relate to the visibility and sort order of published reviews, for reviews authored by Top Reviewers, or highly rated by Advisors, are more prominently displayed.

Do Internet users pay attention to trust and reputation metrics? A study by Resnick and Zeckhauser (2002) on trust and reputation in the online auctions site eBay found both a high rate of transaction evaluation (> 52 per cent) and a low rate of negative or neutral evaluations (1 per cent). Items were more likely to be sold when the seller had a high reputation. When sellers were given a negative rating they often (29 per cent of the time) posted an explanation in an attempt to avoid reputation damage. Especially in review websites, trust and reputation take on differing functions that go beyond the role of predicting honest behaviour. Trust can indicate interpersonally shared interests and attitudes. The 'web of trust' is really a sub-network of members with similar beliefs and goals. Reputation, on the other hand, tends to signal community-wide norms and standards. A 'Top Reviewer' models the attitudes and review style valued by the majority, and thereby carries the ability to shift community values in new directions.

Noticeably lacking from existing review websites is the opportunity for dialogue among reviewers and other users, or for collaborative reviews. For reasons we present in this chapter, we believe that, in the case of LO evaluation, promoting relevant discussion and engaging members in review panels will lead to higher-quality reviews and stronger incentive for community participation.

The individual user reviews made possible by the Internet offer huge cost advantages over the more formal evaluation approaches we have discussed, and they seem essential for any comprehensive system of LO evaluation. But the effectiveness of meta-evaluation mechanisms like those that control quality of user contributions on Slashdot, Amazon and Epinions has been demonstrated only on high traffic sites, and for objects that attract many reviewers and meta-evaluators. LO review sites, that we presume would serve a smaller market, might need higher levels of community participation to benefit from these same meta-evaluation mechanisms. Perhaps a key to designing whole LO evaluation systems is to find ways for user reviews and formal reviews to interoperate in a complementary fashion. For example, a member who completed a sufficient number of highly rated individual reviews might be invited to participate in formal panel reviews. Formal panel reviews might resolve cases where an object received strongly conflicting individual user reviews. Formal reviews might also be expected to set standards emulated by individual reviewers.

MERLOT

In contrast to other large metadata repositories, MERLOT <www.merlot. org> has established a set of relatively mature evaluation practices and tools. Emphasizing disciplinary expertise, the approach to LO evaluation in MERLOT is largely modelled on the academic peer review process for scholarly research and publication familiar to a university faculty. The MERLOT website currently supports 14 discipline-specific communities, each with an editorial board that guides peer review policies and practices.

Anyone can self-enrol to become a member of MERLOT and submit individual member comments on materials registered with the repository. Peer reviews, on the other hand, are conducted by members of a discipline community, usually two university faculty with relevant content expertise. After the reviewers prepare ratings and comments individually, one of them combines the individual assessments and averages the ratings to create an integrated review that may be edited by the other reviewer and discipline co-leaders.

The discipline communities usually select higher-quality objects for peer review. Of the 8,157 objects listed in MERLOT at the time of this writing, 22 per cent had at least one member comment and 9 per cent had a peer review. For both member comments and peer reviews, a large majority of evaluated objects were rated at level 4 or 5. We conjecture that large sampling bias in favour of higher-quality objects will be found in almost all systems of LO evaluation. Although effort might be invested in culling obsolete or low-quality objects on the basis of prima-facie judgement, a practice that has been adopted within some MERLOT discipline communities, there is little benefit from allocating significant resources to evaluating low-quality items. The MERLOT peer review system was designed to encourage adoption within the academic culture of university faculty. The MERLOT organization's careful attention to the values of that culture, such as professional volunteerism and respect for disciplinary knowledge, seems to have worked well in sustaining growth of the collection, the membership and the discipline communities. However, in our view, the MERLOT peer review process needs to be extended to match the conditions under which LOs are developed and used, and to better meet the needs of students. Unlike journal articles written by and for academic researchers, high-quality LOs are very often created by teams that include faculty, instructional designers, media developers or programmers;

and they are used by instructors and students. As we have discussed earlier, assessment models that include representative participation from all stakeholder groups are more likely to result in valid evaluations that will be used by practitioners.

Repositories like MERLOT that emphasize community building and evaluation features would do well to implement meta-evaluation and trust systems similar to those we described earlier in this chapter. We believe that filtering out lower-quality reviews and highlighting reviews that receive top ratings increases members' motivation to submit thoughtful reviews and boosts the value of the service for all users. In addition to governance structures such as editorial boards, true communities are rooted in the interpersonal relationships of their members. Community websites can strengthen these relationships by explicitly representing them as hyperlink networks connecting members with shared interests and beliefs. For more information on MERLOT in this book, see Chapter 21.

Convergent participation

The convergent participation model with the Learning Object Rating Instrument (LORI), depicted in Figure 11.1, is a panel evaluation process designed to obtain better outcomes than the peer review model without resorting to expensive field studies. When applied to the evaluation of LOs, it is presumed to exist in an online community, similar to that of MERLOT, in which users post individual member reviews that include comments and ratings. Panel reviews are organized by a moderator who selects one or more objects for review according to criteria established by the community. The moderator also selects and invites panel participants who represent different stakeholder groups, some of whom may have already posted individual member reviews of the object(s) to be evaluated by the panel.

In both cycles of this two-cycle model, the reviewers use an evaluation instrument capable of gathering ratings and comments specific to several different features of LOs. In the first cycle, through an asynchronous process lasting several days, the participants examine the object and submit an individual review no different from those they might post outside the panel evaluation process. Those who had already submitted a review might edit their existing review or simply revisit it to recall the reasoning behind their judgement.

In the second cycle, the reviews from all participants are exposed in an integrated format, and the moderator leads a discussion focusing on the points of greatest divergence among the participants. The moderator's role is to keep the discussion on track without revealing views he or she may have about the object or otherwise biasing the judgement of the participants. A critical characteristic of the model is that the reviews produced in the first cycle are used by the moderator to sequence the discourse so that features of the LO about which there is least agreement are discussed first. As the second cycle proceeds, the participants may edit their individual reviews using tools that immediately update the integrated view available to the entire panel. When the time allocated for the second cycle expires, the moderator brings the discussion to a close and asks all participants to approve the publication of the panel review consisting of the integrated ratings and comments. Integrated reviews show the range and central tendency of individual ratings with comments concatenated within different evaluative categories. Only data from participants who approve publication are included in published review.

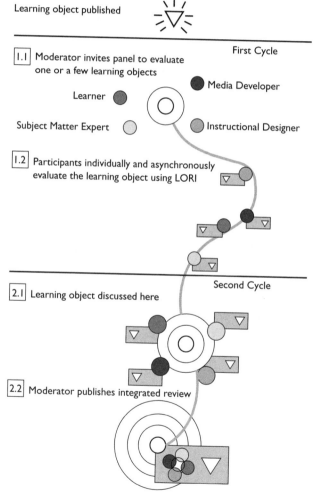

Learning object published

First Cycle

1.1 Moderator invites panel to evaluate
one or a few learning objects

Learner

Media Developer

Subject Matter Expert

Instructional Designer

1.2 Participants individually and asynchronously
evaluate the learning object using LORI

Second Cycle

2.1 Learning object discussed here

2.2 Moderator publishes integrated review

Figure 11.1 Convergent participation with LORI

Several features of the model have been left undetermined: some because they seem situation dependent, and others because we have insufficient experience with the model to make a well-founded recommendation. Our preference is to conduct the second cycle as a real-time meeting supported by synchronous communication tools, but there may be conditions under which asynchronous discussion would be more suitable. Anonymity of the participants, both among themselves and in relation to the larger community, is a potentially important element that invites further investigation.

In a recent study we tested a prototype of the convergent participation model with 12 participants divided into three internationally distributed panels (Vargo *et al.*, 2003). The participants included instructional designers, university faculty and media developers. Each participant evaluated eight LOs: four objects were individually evaluated and four were evaluated through convergent participation. The participants used an early version of the LORI. LORI (version 1.4) presents a five-point scale for each of the nine items shown in the list below (Nesbit *et al.*, 2002).

- Content Quality: Veracity, accuracy, balanced presentation of ideas and appropriate level of detail;
- Learning Goal Alignment: Alignment among learning goals, activities, assessments and learner characteristics;
- Feedback and Adaptation: Adaptive content or feedback driven by differential learner input or learner modelling;
- Motivation: Ability to motivate, and stimulate the interest or curiosity of, an identified population of learners;
- Presentation Design: Design of visual and auditory information for enhanced learning and efficient mental processing;
- Interaction Usability: Ease of navigation, predictability of the user interface and the quality of UI help features;
- Accessibility: Support for learners with disabilities;
- Reusability: Ability to port between different courses or learning contexts without modification;
- Standards Compliance: Adherence to international standards and specifications.

Inter-rater reliability was measured by separate intraclass correlations for first-cycle and second-cycle evaluations (Shrout and Fleiss, 1979). The results showed more consistent convergence (i.e. increased inter-rater reliability) for the collaboratively evaluated objects than the individually evaluated objects. Some participants spontaneously commented that the process was an excellent way to develop their knowledge about LOs. Participant comments also established that training on some of the dimensions of LORI is a requirement for effective use of the instrument.

There are points of similarity between the convergent participation model and the practice of focus groups as described by Krueger (1994). As with focus groups, the moderator's role is to facilitate a conversation among the participants, not to conduct a series of interviews with individual participants. In addition to pacing the discussion and maintaining focus, the moderator must establish an environment where participants feel comfortable to express differing views and to support their views through argumentation.

Although there is evidence that participants, in both the proposed model and in focus groups, do converge in their views as a result of discussion (Krueger, 1994), the emergence of consensus is not a required or even desired outcome of either approach. In using the convergent participation model, one hopes that participants will come to a common understanding of the instrument and how it applies to the LO, but it is expected that reviews will often be published that show disagreement among the reviewers.

One might question why the whole panel is expected to judge dimensions on which only some participants have professional expertise. Although in principle participants can select a 'don't know' option, the moderator does encourage all participants to contribute a rating for each dimension. This practice invites any expert on the dimension under consideration to explain the rationale behind his or her ratings and comments so that others are persuaded to rate in a similar way. When two experts disagree, the other ratings will sway to the side that can most persuasively communicate its argument to the panel.

Support for the goals of LO evaluation

In the introduction to this chapter we offered the claim that the convergent participation model addresses eight goals for LO evaluation. We are now in a position to discuss the extent of support it provides for each of these goals, relative to support provided by other models.

Aid for searching and selecting

Like the peer review model, the convergent participation model is likely to be too costly to fully cover a large repository containing many thousands of LOs. We believe that it can complement individual user reviews and consumer-oriented reviews by offering better quality evaluations in high-demand areas and for objects that for any reason require greater attention and analysis. We hope that, by drawing a broader cross-section of participants into the collaborative review process, a larger base of trained reviewers can be established to carry out high-quality individual reviews. The model seems well suited to comparative reviews that evaluate a few objects occupying overlapping curricular space, although it has yet to be extended or tested for that application.

Guidance for use

The extent to which a convergent participation review suggests ideas to instructors and learners about how best to use an object depends on the nature of the instrument that structures the discussion. We would argue, though, that a discussion on lesson planning or assignment design that includes instructional designers, learners, subject matter experts and instructors will offer greater insight than one in which only one of these roles is represented.

Formative evaluation

Convergent participation reviews can certainly reveal strengths and weaknesses in an early version of an object in a format that would be very useful for a development team. On the other hand, in its current form the model does not offer the continuous monitoring that is regarded as optimal for formative evaluation. The model could be extended to work within an instructional design or project planning model, perhaps by substituting different instruments as appropriate at different project milestones. We caution that, as an evaluation model, convergent participation cannot substitute for the range of functions carried out by an instructional designer.

Influence on design practices

Regardless of whether one is considering curricular, instructional, or media design, an evaluation standard will tend to drive design practices if it represents the values of the community of designers and developers. When one community determines the standards used to evaluate the work of other communities, tensions arise between communities, evaluations are under-utilized, and individual design practices are unaffected. Convergent participation is a boundary-crossing activity that should assist in establishing common evaluation standards that are accepted across represented communities and are capable of influencing individual practice within each community.

Professional development and student learning

When communicating across the boundaries of disciplinary expertise, it is often necessary to expose tacit assumptions and press implicit knowledge into explicit language. In our view this has great educative value for all concerned and forms ideal conditions for professional development. Further, if the instrument adopted with the model is derived from research, the participants are naturally led into an increased familiarity and critical understanding of the underlying research base. Under some conditions, it seems justifiable to assign course credit or professional development release time for work on convergent participation review panels. This issue is developed further by Kestner in Chapter 21).

Community building

The work of evaluating LOs in an intensely collaborative setting both expends and creates, in greater measure, what Putnam (2000) calls social capital, the pro-social motive normally generated in any matrix of active interpersonal relationships. Social capital is community-building glue that can drive community members to act in the common interest, perhaps contributing unpaid hours to observe learners interacting with a new user interface, or spending a portion of sabbatical time on redesigning a curriculum. Because the activity of developing high-quality LOs requires the cooperation of different professional groups, it is important that social capital generated in the evaluation activity be spread across those groups to form an inclusive community.

Social recognition

Although many different evaluation systems can inform the granting of professional awards, these surely carry greater social recognition value when established in a social context wider than the specialized professional guild to which the recipient belongs. A media development award will garner more respect among professors when professors are represented in the evaluative process that granted it.

Evaluation for economic exchange

The quality of evaluative information is very often a deciding factor in the purchase of any commodity. The availability of higher-quality evaluations may reduce licensing costs by eliminating the need for the purchaser to carry out in-house evaluations. We argue that evaluation from any single disciplinary perspective, whether that be content, instructional design, or media design, is insufficient; and further that those who buy LOs to assemble commercially offered courses are most interested in the views of the end-user, the learner.

Conclusion

To summarize, the strengths of the convergent participation model are that it brings together representatives of stakeholder groups, efficiently focuses their attention on the points that may be in greatest need of resolution, and produces a review that concisely presents areas of agreement and dissent among the evaluators. Advancement of the model requires more study of how converging participants interact, along with the development of tools to support that interaction.

Note

This chapter is based on work published in:

Nesbit, J. C., Belfer, K. and Vargo, J. (2002) A convergent participation model for evaluation of LOs, *Canadian Journal of Learning and Technology*, **28** (3): 105–120.

References

Assink, E. and van der Linden, J. (1993) Computer controlled spelling instruction: A case study in courseware design, *Journal of Educational Computing Research*, **9** (1): 17–28.

Baumgartner, P. and Payr, S. (1996) (accessed 27 April 2002) Learning as action: A social science approach to the evaluation of interactive media. Conference on Educational Multimedia and Hypermedia, Association for the Advancement of Computing in Education, (Online) http://www.webcom.com/journal/baumgart. html.

Dobson, M. and McCracken, J. (2001) Evaluating technology-supported teaching and learning: A catalyst to organizational change, *Interactive Learning Environments*, **9** (2): 143–70.

Gibbs, W., Graves, P. R. and Bernas, R. S. (2001) Evaluation guidelines for multimedia courseware, *Journal of Research on Technology in Education*, **34** (1): 2–17.

IEEE (2002) (accessed 16 March 2003) Draft standard for Learning Object Metadata (LOM), Learning Technology Standards Committee (LTSC), (Online) http://ltsc.ieee.org/doc/wg12/LOM_WD6_4.pdf.

Jolicoeur, K. and Berger, D. E. (1986) Do we really know what makes educational software effective? A call for empirical research on effectiveness, *Educational Technology*, **26** (12): 7–11.

Jolicoeur, K. and Berger, D. E. (1988) Implementing educational software and evaluating its academic effectiveness: Part I, *Educational Technology*, **28** (9): 7–13.

Krueger, R. A. (1994) *Focus groups: A practical guide for applied research*, Sage, London.

McDougall, A. and Squires, D. (1995) A critical examination of the checklist approach in software selection, *Journal of Educational Computing Research*, **12** (3): 263–74.

Nardi, B. (1996) *Context and consciousness: Activity theory and human-computer interaction*, MIT Press, Cambridge, MA.

Nesbit, J. *et al.* (2002) Communities for learning object evaluation, Paper presented at the Presentation to the Educational Technology User Group Fall Workshop, 21 November, Richmond, BC, ETUG.

Neuman, D. (1989) Naturalistic inquiry and computer-based instruction: Rationale, procedures, and potential, *Educational Technology, Research & Development*, **37** (3): 39–51.

Patton, M. Q. (1980) *Qualitative evaluation methods*, Sage, Beverly Hills.

Patton, M. Q. (1982) *Practical evaluation*, Sage, Beverly Hills.

Putnam, R. (2000) *Bowling alone: The collapse and revival of American community*, Simon & Schuster, New York.

Reiser, R. A. and Dick, W. (1990) Evaluating instructional software, *Educational Technology, Research and Development*, **38** (3): 43–50.

Resnick, P. and Zeckhauser, R. (2002) Trust among strangers in Internet transactions: Empirical analysis of eBay's reputation system. The economics of the Internet and e-commerce, in *Advances in applied microeconomics II*, ed. M. R. Baye, Elsevier Science, Amsterdam.

Shrout, P. E. and Fleiss, J. L. (1979) Intraclass correlations, *Psychological Bulletin*, **86**: 420–28.

Vargo, J. *et al.* (2003) LO evaluation: Computer mediated collaboration and inter-rater reliability, *International Journal of Computers and Application*, **25** (5).

Williams, D. D. (2000) (accessed 18 April 2002) Evaluation of learning objects and instruction using learning objects, (Online) http://reusability.org/read/chapters/williams.doc.

Worthen, B. R., Sanders, J. R. and Fitzpatrick, J. L. (1997) *Program evaluation: Alternative approaches and practical guidelines*, Longman, New York.

Part 3

Contextualization and Standardization of Learning Objects

This section introduces the concept of contextualization as well as explaining standardization in the LO context. The problems of contextualization when designing LOs for reuse are presented. The relationship between context and metadata schema and standards is discussed, followed by a description of a tool that aids in the contextualization of learning. The benefits of a reference architecture are suggested, followed by a discussion of the issues related to the management of learning object metadata and describing a Learning Object Metadata Management System (LOMMS).

Robson, in Chapter 12, points out that although the ability to reuse and repurpose LOs is seen as being their major benefit, to date little reuse is actually taking place. He argues that the higher contextual component of learning objects and the associated cost of contextualization are inhibiting reuse and repurposing. He suggests that standards and specifications such as LO Metadata (LOM) and the Sharable Content Object Reference Model (SCORM) serve to reduce that cost and thereby promote the reuse of LOs while preserving their pedagogic impact.

He suggests that context is the 'culprit'. The highly contextual nature of LOs adds significant cost to reuse, but must be preserved as they are handed off from person to person and system to system. This preservation of context made possible through the use of international standards and specifications is what makes reuse possible. By looking at heuristic value curves, Robson argues that standards and emerging technologies can make it possible to reuse LOs with higher contextual components making reuse even more attractive.

In Chapter 13, Mason highlights the issue of context in determining what might best inform the next generation of metadata schema that will in turn best support learning, education and training. He considers context to be the critical component in a value-chain that renders data and information into knowledge. In proposing a way forward, he identifies *context* as a candidate for independent modelling from content – as either 'context objects' or rules that might be applied when triggered by certain events.

Such an approach, he contends, may provide a high value-added feature to the development, access and application of online educational resources.

He further explains that the data models developed by the Dublin Core Metadata Initiative (DCMI), the IEEE Learning Technology Standards Committee (IEEE LTSC), and the IMS Global Learning Consortium (IMS) have provided critical foundations for the growing infrastructure that supports e-learning. The author believes that knowledge sharing based on these standards and specifications will depend on the development of complex adaptive systems that are sensitive to context.

Allert, Richter, Dhraief and Nejdl from the Lower Saxony Learning Laboratory describe their Open Learning Repository 3 (OLR3) in Chapter 14. Their tool enables learners as well as teachers to choose a preferred learning concept. The design of the OLR3 was guided by a scenario-based design approach made up of a domain model, an instructional model and a structural model. Using OLR3, students and student groups are enabled to identify their topics of interest and choose their favourite experts in order to ask them for support and consult them and their work. Students then form instances of expertise-trails in order to share their work and learning progress. They search for LOs on the Web, collect and provide LOs themselves, write reports and present their own ideas and strategies. Online experts communicate with students.

The authors point out that several different experts were asked to draft their strategies and provide LOs within the OLR3. This allowed students to compare different strategies, procedures and routines within different scientific communities. Students then chose their favourite experts and consulted them. From this, expertise-trails were created so that their work could be shared.

In Chapter 15 Luis Anido of the Universidade de Vigo, Spain identifies common services for e-learning that are supported by a reference architecture. This architecture is composed of reusable software components with open and clearly identified interfaces. All interfaces in the architecture define their externally visible properties to facilitate the development of distributed, interoperable and standards-driven online learning environments. This chapter presents a contribution to e-learning standardization defining a reference architecture and particular interface specifications for the business logic tier of a distributed online education environment.

The reference architecture that Anido proposes is conceptual and implementation independent, and may be instantiated for different technological infrastructures. It is composed of a set of reusable sub-systems that provide fundamental services to build final applications. Defined services are the consequence of the strict application of a systematic methodology to obtain service architectures. Components defined can be easily identified by those agents involved in the e-learning standardization process, as they encapsulate different standardized information models in separate sub-systems.

Anido describes Common Object Request Broker Architecture (CORBA) as a specific implementation environment. CORBA is an object-based distributed architecture that allows distributed and heterogeneous applications to interoperate on a network. The CORBA community defines high-level services, clearly oriented to particular domains. One such domain, CORBAlearn, includes the definition of data structures encapsulating outcomes, exceptions and service interfaces.

Anido further distinguishes between Educational Content Providers (ECPs) who are responsible for developing learning objects (publishers) and Educational Service Providers (ESPs) (schools, universities, other academic institutions). ESPs use ECPs to access, sometimes for a fee, online courses using a broker.

In Chapter 16, Sampson and Karampiperis, of the Informatics and Telematics Institute (ITI), Greece discuss issues related to the management of learning object metadata, identifying the design and functional considerations of a Learning Object Metadata Management System (LOMMS). LOMMSs are environments for accessing learning object repositories, providing services such as indexing, storing, searching and reusing LO metadata.

The authors propose reasons why learning object metadata is essential in e-learning environments. It describes the main design considerations that should be satisfied to provide an effective LOMMS. These features include the creation and modification of LOM files, structural and semantic validation, support of emerging XML technologies and mapping between different metadata schemas.

Chapter 12

Context and the role of standards in increasing the value of learning objects

Robby Robson

Learning Objects (LOs) promise to take learning to new levels of personalization and relevancy. They promise to offer an environment for individualized learning that is easily accessible and enabled by the use of reusable components over networks (Shepherd, 2001). Yet anecdotal evidence and informed opinion indicate that relatively little reuse is taking place as of yet. If one believes informed opinion, much less of the promised reuse and repurposing is taking place than is desired (Hartnett, 2002; Dodani, 2002).

This causes us to ask whether there is something inherent in LOs that makes them more expensive or less feasible to reuse and repurpose than it does, for example, to reuse and repurpose news reports, website components and other similar content that also derives its value from its ability to bring about a sustained change in memory, behaviour or effect. It is hypothesized that high contextual content and an associated high cost of contextualization is what is inhibiting reuse and repurposing of LOs.

At a basic level, LOs contain information. Wilson (1984) defines information as *data plus context*. This might also be expressed as *data put into a context*. How one quantifies context is not clear, but it is clear that the size of the data is not the only thing that matters when determining the value of a LO. In terms of bytes, the entire text in the *Encyclopedia Britannica* is comparable in size to a fifteen-minute film clip of a professional wrestling match, but the encyclopedia contains far more informational value, unless you are interested specifically in professional wrestling. Context plays a very important role in the value of information!

The cost of context

When analysing the economies and advantages of creating content using LOs, we must take into account all possible cost and quality factors, *including the preservation of context*. If information-based content is to be reused and if the creation and processing of informational content is to be carried out by people playing different roles in different places, then the content must be transported from place to place and person to person as it goes through the production process. This has a cost, analogous to the cost of transporting goods for industrial processes. Cairncross (2001) argues that the cost of transporting information has become negligible and insensitive to distance. This is true in as much as broadcast media, telephony and the Internet allow huge quantities of data to be transmitted with little or no loss and at little or no cost. But information depends on context to maximize its meaning, and context may not be explicitly represented in a data stream. A message out of context may be completely meaningless even if all of the data are faithfully preserved.

Losing context not only has an impact on the quality of an LO but can also introduce costs required for contextualization. For example, not much is to be gained by reusing an instructional module describing a product if the designer must update all the terminology to conform to new marketing approaches while also rewriting the set of recommended practices to take advantage of new functionality. The context may well have changed sufficiently to make the cost of contextualization too high.

As another example, suppose that several authors are asked to contribute to an educational website. If they can simply add their text to a template, then there is almost no cost to distributing the writing effort. If an editor is required to harmonize the authors' writing styles, then a higher cost is incurred. If an editor is required to merge the authors' writing and in the process must go back and forth with the authors about what they meant and what common terminology to use, then the cost becomes significant. If the authors' perspectives are too contradictory and if the assumptions made about the readers are too diverse, then contextual incompatibilities may make it impractical to proceed.

Context also affects reusability. Dependence on context diminishes opportunities for reuse, which acts as a disincentive to produce reusable objects in the first place. The degree of this diminution is a function of both the depth of dependence on context and the narrowness of the context. An exercise in the back of a computer science graduate textbook on data structures will have less opportunity for reuse than a news report on an earthquake in China or footage of the winning goal in a World Cup football match. If the data structures exercise is in addition based on a series of four preceding exercises and explicitly refers to examples and notation from the book, the chances of reuse are even smaller, and repurposing the exercise for use in a class or on a test requires the additional work of building up the context in which it makes sense. A LO that makes sense only in a narrow context has less potential market size.

As indicated by examples like the ones above, it is reasonable to hypothesize that there are inherent differences in the contextual complexity of general content and the contextual complexity of LOs. LOs typically have deeper dependence on more restrictive contexts. This is why news reports are more easily and widely reused and repurposed than LOs.

The value of context

The conclusion to be drawn is that much observed behaviour, including the lack of widespread reuse and repurposing of LOs, is a reaction to the highly contextualized nature of information used for education and training. The cost of preserving this context, which is an integral part of an information object, is simply too high.

On the other hand, there is a great value to context. The value of an LO is measured by its effect on users, and that depends in part on contextual phenomena. Much learning literature is devoted to learning styles, 'teachable moments', role models and other issues of a contextual nature. The better the contextual match between a LO and the learner, the more effective it is likely to be.

It is therefore important not to simply give up on the notion of reuse and repurposing LOs. Instead, it makes sense to find ways to preserve context, thereby lowering the cost of contextualization and preserving value at the same time.

Learning object metadata

Other chapters in this book discuss the mechanics and format of LO metadata (see Introduction and Chapter 17). Metadata apply to information objects in general, and are often portrayed as ways of describing the properties of objects. A more accurate view may be that their role is to capture context. Thus, when a LO is defined as a resource plus metadata, it could equally well be defined as data plus context.

Some examples can illustrate how metadata enable contextualization, in other words, how metadata can make it easier to introduce a LO into a larger framework such as a course or training module. As a first example, consider (as we did earlier) an exercise from a graduate school text that is based on a series of preceding exercises and that explicitly refers to examples and notation from the text. A LO metadata record can log the level of difficulty of the exercise, the subject matter of the exercise and its relationship to other exercises and the text. This allows the exercise to be properly catalogued and to be accessed by metadata-enabled search engines. If an instructor finds the exercise using such an engine, then the instructor will know that the exercise matches the level, language, subject area, format and other essential criteria that must be met in order to effectively use the exercise. The search results can display additional information (for example the relationship to other exercises) that might nonetheless make it clear that the exercise cannot be used or that might provide the bonus of revealing further useful resources. If the exercise depends on other exercises, a good system can automatically provide links to them or, as we will see below, make them available as part of the package. These capabilities may still be a long way from automating the process of discovering and reusing highly specialized educational content, but they may save enough time to make reuse not only feasible but desirable.

SCORM

In the production of learning content, it is important that as much context be captured as is possible. Although the IEEE LOM metadata standard addresses some aspects of the context of a LO, it does not address all of them. When LOs are assembled, one needs to include or reference all of the other objects (for example, multimedia files) on which a given object depends. It is also important to know the order in which components are (or should be) delivered to the learner and how their presentation might be affected by elements such as the technical capabilities of the delivery device and the profile of the learner. Interactions between the learner and LOs need to be managed and recorded. All of these factors belong to the context associated with a LO, and all of these are addressed by specifications and standards that are now part of the Sharable Content Object Reference Model (SCORM, 2003) that is being disseminated by the Advanced Distributed Learning initiative.

SCORM is not a single standard. Technically, it isn't a standard at all. SCORM is a collection of specifications and standards collaboratively developed by organizations including the IEEE Learning Technology Standards Committee, the Aviation Industry CBT Consortium, and the IMS Global Learning Consortium (MASIE, 2002; Robson, 2001). SCORM lives as a collection of related documents, each of which addresses a specific kind of functionality. As time goes on, the number of documents in the collection is projected to grow, but as of this writing SCORM includes three basic pieces with a fourth about to be added.

The first part of SCORM features LO metadata. As previously noted, LO metadata provides objective and subjective descriptors that identify and differentiate information objects from each other. Every type and granularity of content object within SCORM can carry metadata.

The second part of SCORM describes a method that learning platforms can use to communicate with web-based content. The information that can be exchanged includes but is not limited to the student's name, the time a student has spent interacting with content, the results of individual quiz questions, overall scores, and pass/fail information on both the content as a whole and on individual learning objectives.

The third part of SCORM presents a packaging format (also called an aggregation model) that supports the assembly, transport and disassembly of collections of digital LOs and learning resources. A SCORM package includes control data called a *manifest* whose primary function is simply to name what is in the package and attach metadata to the components.

But the manifest also contains information about how the contents of a SCORM package can be organized into a coherent learning experience.

The fourth part of SCORM, which as of this writing is still in the process of development, is a specification that tells a delivery platform how and in what order to deliver the content within a SCORM package. The order can depend on what previous content a student has completed, on how many times a student has interacted with a LO, and on what learning objectives have been met.

Using SCORM, smaller LOs can be assembled into modules and courses, imported into a learning platform and delivered in a moderately adaptive fashion. Or, to put it another way, SCORM allows the creation of LOs, large and small, that carry the contextual information needed to make them a meaningful part of a digital learning experience.

SCORM has given a tangible meaning to the notion of a LO. In SCORM, there are units called *sharable content objects*, or simply SCOs, which must meet well-defined technological criteria, as well as smaller objects called *assets* and larger objects called *packages* that have just been described. In practice these are the objects that can be produced by authoring environments and delivered by learning systems and therefore are LOs from a down-to-earth operational perspective. SCORM can already be reasonably called a de facto standard, and having attained that status, it paves the way for reuse, disaggregation of roles and distribution of labour. By offering a consistent, commonly agreed upon framework within which LOs *can* be assembled, context and all, SCORM enables genuine gains by creating repositories of LOs for reuse and repurposing.

Is an 'educational object economy' based on SCORM growing where others have failed to take root? Organizations involved in learning content development are gearing up to produce SCORM content because of its 'write once run anywhere' characteristics (Jacobsen, 2001). Large government projects are banking on SCORM (Hill, 2002; ITSC, 2003). Consortia are investing in SCORM (COLIS, 2002; EduSpecs, 2003; OASIS, 2003) and various projects are experimenting with metadata-enabled repositories of SCORM content (OASIS, 2003).

Perhaps even more significant is a trend towards distributed SCORM content production. In this process the development of training content is carried out by organizations completely separate from those responsible for designing the content. This indicates that the cost of contextualization is lower than the savings that can be realized from disaggregating and distributing the production process for learning content.

The value of learning objects

Having discussed the costs of creating LOs, we must also consider the benefits. What determines the value of a LO? It is reasonable to posit that the value of a LO is determined by the number of times it can be (re)used and the impact it has in each use. Although it is illogical to imagine that an information object has the same impact every time it is used, a rough estimate of its potential impact can be given by its contextual content. In other words, if we think of information as 'data plus context', then it is the contextual component that determines its potency.

To illustrate this, suppose your task is to design an interactive online course. If you are lucky enough to find an existing two-hour module that you can drop into your course 'as is', you have saved yourself a lot of effort. The same amount of effort might also be saved by finding a Java applet that can be dropped into your course that provides a simulated computing environment and an entire series of relevant exercises. From the perspective of the task at hand, they have the same value. However, if the Java applet is constructed so that it can generate exercises appropriate for other courses, then it can be reused more often, and its overall value is higher, at least to someone such as a publisher who is selling the applet, or to a librarian who is creating an institutional repository of LOs with the intent of saving time and money by avoiding duplication.

In practice, LOs with lower contextual value can be reused more. This has led a number of authors to observe that there is an inverse relationship between the 'size' of a LO and its potential for reuse (see Chapter 5; Elliott, 2003; Hodgins and Conner, 2000; Wagner, 2002) This applies to any information-based content. For example, a stock photo can be used in many editions of many newspapers, a single story can be used in a single edition of many newspapers, and an entire edition of a newspaper can be used in its entirety exactly once. But it is not 'size' that matters. The real issue is context. Information objects with larger contextual components are generally less reusable.

The value curve

There is a tension between reusability and context, but both contribute positively to the value of an object. Figure 12.1 represents a coordinate system with context as the x-axis and reuse as the y-axis. This is meant to be a heuristic based on a conceptual representation; we don't claim to have reasonable quantitative measures of context or reuse at the current time, although anecdotal evidence suggests the value of further exploration. To each point in the x–y plane we can assign the value of an information (or learning) object with that degree of reuse and context. This means that the classes of objects with the highest worth are those represented by points in the fourth quadrant of Figure 12.1.

The curve on Figure 12.1 represents the inverse relationship between reuse and context. Again, we have no real idea of the shape of these curves, and the diagram is meant to be heuristic only. However, we believe them to be passable representations of the situation in which we find ourselves.

Under appropriate conditions, an interesting consequence of the existence of an inverse relationship between reuse and context, plus the positive dependence of value on both variables, is that there are points along any one of the curves where maximum value can be obtained. The curve labelled 'Without metadata' on Figure 12.1 does not pass through the area of the x–y plane where value is highest. This, we feel, represents the situation in the absence of metadata. LOs without sufficient metadata are sufficiently expensive to contextualize that even the optimal value that can be derived from a LO is less than desirable. The ones that are rich in context are too hard to reuse and the ones that are easy to reuse do not carry enough context to make them truly valuable.

The addition of metadata and SCORM to LOs does not alter the relationship between reuse and context but changes the shape of the value curve. This pushes it up a bit, moving the maximum closer to the high-value area. The right type of technology can push the curve even higher, as diagrammed in Figure 12.1. This is what we see being done by some learning content management systems that integrate learner profiles and roles directly into the structure of LOs.

Conclusion

At the start of this chapter it was suggested that LOs may not be as reusable as one would hope for. Context has been identified as being the culprit. The highly contextual nature of LOs adds significant cost to reuse. In this chapter we point out that standards like LO metadata and specifications like those found in SCORM have the effect of preserving the

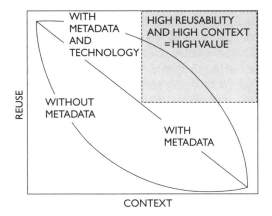

Figure 12.1 The relationship between reuse, context and value

context of a LO as it is handed off from person to person and system to system. This makes reuse more feasible. By looking at heuristic value curves, we can imagine that standards and emerging technologies can make it possible to reuse objects with higher contextual components than has hitherto been possible. This makes reuse even more attractive and at the same time increases the inherent value of LOs. With standards in place, along with appropriate practice built around the standards, predictions of educational object economies as in EOE (2003) and other similar visions may well end up being correct.

Acknowledgements

The author would like to thank Dr Ellen D. Wagner and Geoff Collier for valuable discussions while writing this chapter.

References

Cairncross, F. (2001) *The death of distance*, Harvard Business School Press, Boston.
COLIS (2002) (accessed 10 January 2003) Colis project press release, (Online) http://www.colis.mq.edu.au/projects/demo_pr_jul02.pdf.
Dodani, M. (2002) (accessed 14 March 2003) The dark side of object learning: Learning objects, *Journal of Object Technology*, **1** (5), (Online) http://www.jot.fm/issues/issue_2002_11/column3.
EduSpecs (2003) (accessed 10 January 2003) EduSpecs, (Online) http://tomcat-dev.iinet.ca/eduspecs/index.html.
Elliott, S. (2003) A context model for reusability, Paper presented at the Content Management Strategies Workshop, Center for Information-Development Management, Washington DC, 30 April, (Online) http://www.cm-strategies.com/program.htm.
EOE (accessed 21 February 2003) Educational object economy foundation, *EOE*, (Online) http://www.eoe.org.
Hartnett, J. (2002) (accessed 24 April 2003) Where have all the Legos gone?, *Online Learning Magazine* (21 February), (Online) http://www.onlinelearningmag.com/training/search/search_display.jsp?vnu_content_id=1278802.
Hill, D. (2002) (accessed 21 February 2003) *eLearning scaleable implementation?* (Online) http://www.imsglobal.org/otf/IMSeUbackground.pdf.
Hodgins, W. and Conner, M. (2000) (accessed 17 April 2003) Everything you wanted to know about learning objects but were afraid to ask, *LineZine* (Fall), (Online) http://www.linezine.com/2.1/features/wheyewtkls.htm.
ITSC (2003) (accessed 21 February 2003) *Specification for an e-learning framework*, (Online) http://www.itsc.org.sg/sg_it_stds/abstract_ss496_1.html.
Jacobsen, P. (2001) (accessed 14 March 2003) Reusable learning objects, *eLearning Magazine*, (Online) http://www.elearningmag.com/elearning/article/articleDetail.jsp?id=5043.
MASIE (2002) (accessed 21 February 2003) Making sense of specifications and standards. An industry report, (Online) http://www.masie.com/standards/S3_Guide.pdf.

OASIS (2003) (accessed 21 February 2003) Sharable Content Object Reference Model initiative (SCORM), (Online) http://xml.coverpages.org/scorm.html.

Robson, R. (2001) (accessed 14 March 2003) SCORM steps up, *eLearning Magazine*, (Online) http://www.elearningmag.com/elearning/article/articleDetail.jsp?id=32340.

SCORM (2003) (accessed 21 February 2003) Advanced distributed learning initiative. Section on SCORM, *OASIS*, (Online) http://www.adlnet.org.

Shepherd, C. (2001) (accessed 21 February 2003) Objects of interest, (Online) http://www.fastrak-consulting.co.uk/tactix/features/objects/objects.htm.

Wagner, E. D. (2002) (accessed 21 February 2003) Steps for creating a content strategy, *eLearning Developers Journal*, (Online) http://www.elearningguild.com/pdf/2/102902MGT-H.pdf.

Wilson, B. (1984) *Systems: Concepts, methodologies and applications*, John Wiley and Sons, Chichester, UK.

Wiley, D. (accessed 21 February 2003) Learning objects need instructional design theory, (Online) http://wiley.ed.usu.edu/docs/astd.pdf.

Chapter 13

Context and metadata for learning, education and training

Jon Mason

Historical perspective is useful in that it provides some sense of time and place, of circumstances and progression, of the dynamics of society and technology. In a word, historical perspective provides *context* for understanding current developments.

'What do we know that we didn't know ten years ago? That learning and knowledge are the result of multiple, intertwining forces: *content, context, and community*' (Seely Brown, cited in Ruggles and Holtshouse, 1999, p. ix).

It is hardly overstating things, to muse that in just a few short years the World Wide Web has assumed a pivotal role for an ever-increasing number of stakeholders actively involved in learning, education or training. There are many factors that have contributed to this situation, including: research and development of key technologies that promote interoperability of content and applications (such as XML); increased capacity of telecommunications infrastructure; the 'rise of the network society' (Castells, 1996); and an international effort aimed at developing technical standards and protocols to facilitate e-learning.

Of course, it is also somewhat sobering to consider that in those few short years we have also witnessed the bursting of the expectations bubble that drove the dotcom investment boom of the late twentieth century. Among the casualties were some well-resourced institutions and consortia focused on being first-to-market in delivering innovative e-learning products and services (Ryan and Stedman, 2001). Such boom and bust scenarios have always characterized the dynamics of the stock market. However, we should guard against making premature assessments as to the emerging e-learning industry itself based upon such data and events. Why? Because if the development of standards is understood to be an indicator of market maturity and stakeholder commitment (as it conventionally is), then we can safely say that in this initial boom and bust no such standards were yet developed!

While there existed earlier efforts (e.g. initiated by the Aviation Industry Computer-based-training Committee), standardization in the area of (online) learning technology began to seriously move forward from around 1997, through the IEEE Learning Technology Standards Committee (IEEE LTSC). Arguably, one of the most significant developments to take place since this time has been the standardization by the IEEE of Learning Object Metadata (IEEE, 2002). It has been significant because it is a foundation from which other e-learning industry specifications are forming. It has also been significant because it represents the first signs of maturation of e-learning standardization. And it is no accident that this standard is concerned with metadata, for metadata are a key feature of structured information.

Librarians and archivists have been routinely concerned with metadata almost from the day their industries began – through tasks such as classification, indexing, record-keeping, and information management enabling information retrieval and resource discovery. With the birth of the Web, it is no surprise that the Dublin Core Metadata Initiative soon got underway. Its major contribution, pre-dating the IEEE LOM by only a few years, has been the development of a simple data model that distills the main metadata requirements of librarians and archivists and is designed to facilitate networked information discovery and retrieval at a generic, cross-domain level. Within this background context, the following discussion considers issues concerning aspects of structured information, the modelling of context and how context might be better used through metadata in learning, education and training.

Organizing information

Information can be organized in a multiplicity of ways:

* hierarchically structured, based upon authoritative classifications and taxonomies (such as the Library of Congress Subject Headings or Dewey Decimal Codes);
* in enterprise databases (such as a contacts listing);
* associatively (via hyperlinks on the Web); or even
* in a pile of papers chaotically assembled on an office desktop or floor.

While some methods may be more persistent over time than others (such as structured library catalogues), in each case *relationships* can be imputed to exist between discrete information resources. Structure and relation can therefore be seen as two sides of the one coin and are key organizing principles for making sense from information. The 'entity-relationship' model has thus become an important conceptual foundation for the W3C-led initiative on RDF (Resource Description Framework) (Miller, 1998). It may yet prove to be even more profound as further coalescence between heterogeneous networks (social, technical, informational) evolves.

In the development of technical specifications, it has become standard practice – certainly within organizations such as the IMS Global Learning Consortium – to begin with articulating use-cases in the requirements gathering phase. Such use-cases convey both a sense of flow and a sense of context. Once a suite of requirements is gathered, then the next step is to develop an *information model* or *data model*. Without such modelling, technical specifications for the design of information systems or systems that support learning are of dubious value.

As Heimbürger (2002) suggests: 'Modelling is needed to understand, explain, organise, predict, and reason on information. It also helps to master the role and functions of components of information systems.'

From an entirely different perspective based upon a 'sense-making' methodology that also contests the 'innocence' or 'neutrality' of information, Dervin (1998) introduces the notion of the early twenty-first century as a 'dialogic era'. A dialogic era is a time (and place) configured more as an interplay of coincident polarities, an era that has moved beyond the struggle of modernity versus post-modernity. In developing this idea, she suggests that the 'innocence' of information is humbled if some basic premises regarding its formation and veracity are considered:

> One of these premises is that human beings make and unmake information in times and spaces, in dialogue. The second is that information is made despite and at the same time in human fallibilities. The third is that information can capture at best only a portion of reality for there is inherent discontinuity in reality itself. The combination of these three ideas suggests that all knowledge is inherently fallible and must be humbled to the time and place and procedurings of its origins.
>
> (Dervin, 2001)

A complex state of affairs, especially for knowledge workers! Of course, when Dervin's analysis is applied back on her own conceptual frameworks then the *discontinuities* inherent in reality must also coincide with the *continuities*. A metaphor for this situation is that much of the digital information we process, we also typically experience as analogue and continuous. Analyses such as Dervin's are important in achieving authenticity of our information models and compare well with Wenger's (1998) notion of 'duality' that is used to describe the interplay of explicit and implicit knowledge.

Such an abstraction may at first reading seem philosophical, but when considered further it can be seen as strongly pragmatic. We live in a world (or worlds) of relativity – there is not one classification system or one analysis that we all subscribe to. As Shabajee (2002) suggests: 'Any object, physical or virtual, could be described and discussed in possibly limitless ways.' It is no wonder, then, that we are confronted with the problem of having to develop sophisticated communications systems that can facilitate the interoperation of different schema.

Why metadata?

So how do metadata help? In terms of organizing digital information, there are arguably three main kinds of metadata that can be pragmatically applied: descriptive, administrative and structural – particularly if one is primarily concerned with describing and managing *content*. Depending on the classification scheme, many more specific functions of metadata can be discerned, although it is debatable whether these functions can be regarded as unique high-level categories in themselves. Examples would include metadata that carry information about technical aspects, intellectual property, or preservation aspects of a resource, or domain-specific metadata such as those which carry educational information.

Given the proliferation and wide-ranging functions of metadata schema, the Digital Library Federation released in 2002 a specification for encoding metadata that would facilitate interoperability between digital objects and libraries. Known as METS, the Metadata Encoding Transmission Standard presents a five-layer schema that includes descriptive, administrative and structural metadata together with two other key layers: 'file groups' (all the sub-files that might comprise a digital object), and 'behaviours' (information concerning run-time behaviours that might be associated with particular content) (METS, 2002). This model has many structural similarities to the IMS *Content Packaging* specification (IMS, 2002).

Many of us may be quite familiar with descriptive (e.g. 'subject' and 'keywords') and administrative (e.g. 'last updated') metadata, but it is likely that structural metadata require some further explanation. This is summarized well in the METS documentation:

> The metadata necessary for successful management and use of digital objects is both more extensive than and different from the metadata used for managing collections of printed works and other physical materials. While a library may record descriptive metadata regarding a book in its collection, the book will not dissolve into a series of unconnected pages if the library fails to record structural metadata regarding the book's organization, nor will scholars be able to evaluate the book's worth if the library fails to note that the book was produced using a Ryobi offset press. The same cannot be said for a digital version of the same book. Without structural metadata, the page image or text files comprising the digital work are of little use . . .
>
> (METS, 2002)

The IMS Content Packaging specification provides this kind of information within a specific context: the exchange of e-learning content between applications such as Learning Management Systems where the content is typically an aggregation of learning objects. But a 'content package' is not complete if it has no metadata. In this sense, metadata can be understood as providing context (such as relations between learning objects in the package to each other or rules that might specify when a file must be launched).

It follows, then, that most metadata arguably provide some sense of context about the data or information they describe. This is true even for minimalist (proposed) metadata formats or 'kernels' such as the Electronic Resource Citation (ERC) where compactness and ease are aimed for in four simple statements describing 'who', what', 'when' and 'where' (Kunze, 2001). As the discussion later in this chapter argues, each of these four information placeholders provides contextual perspective.

Content for some – Metadata for others

In modelling the functional components that were needed to develop the IMS Global Learning Consortium's Digital Repository Interoperability specification (IMS, 2002) it proved to be pragmatic to identify 'digital assets' or 'content' as one entity and 'metadata' (that describe those assets) as another. However, while such models help to identify systems inter-actions, it is also true that such models can mask deeper complexity. For example, in the case of a repository designed to broker resource discovery, the 'assets' it gathers into a collection might only be metadata records. Thus, *one person's (or service's) metadata may be another's content*. The complexity of this relationship is summarized in Figure 13.1, which is a representation of relationships in the digital domain, where there is always recursive potential between data, information and knowledge.

In a similar way it can be argued that while content and context can be modelled as separate entities and are commonly understood as sepa-

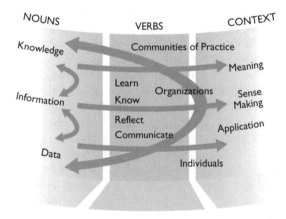

Figure 13.1 Relationships of the digital domain

rate, they are often experienced as fused, or as having ambiguous boundaries. Moreover, where context is encoded as a discrete information resource, it therefore assumes an operational function in much the same way as content. One person's context may be another's content. And one person's knowledge will likely be another's information. Of course, this does not mean that ambiguous models are needed. On the contrary, it may be that through a disciplined separation of content and context, as advocated by Naeve (2001) and his colleagues (Nilsson, Palmér and Naeve, 2002), interesting innovations in online interaction will take place. The development of their *Concept Browser*, a tool designed to navigate their *Knowledge Manifold*, includes:

> a strict separation of *context* and *content*, contextual descriptions in terms of a collection of semantically visual context maps, which can be navigated by moving through *contextual neighborhoods*, presentation of the content components through context-dependent *aspect-filters*, and *contextualization* of content components that are themselves context maps.
>
> (Naeve, 2001)

Such issues as the separation of content and context in information modelling can be seen as important, not only for managing educational resources for learning and training, but also for managing workflow within knowledge management systems. But, before delving further into that topic, let's take a step back and consider context in more detail.

What is context?

Like beauty, context is discovered through the eye of the beholder – a user's perspective is what ultimately counts when defining context. With this caveat in mind, the following discussion is aimed at examining how context might impact the development of metadata schema and other tools designed to support learning, education and training.

McCarthy (2000) notes: 'Contextual information is that extra, associated, related, assumed and perhaps *a priori* information or knowledge that is required to meaningfully interpret the content of any given information source.' His definition comes from an archival or cultural informatics perspective where issues of provenance (origins) of a resource are pre-eminent. As such, descriptions of the person or creator of a resource are as important, if not more so, than the 'resource' itself. This emphasis can be seen as an attempt to apply rigour to the processes of constructing meaning from documents and objects through the assignment of cultural (time and place) context. And again, implicit in such a perspective is the role of relationship – information in relation to other information, data, knowledge, or understanding.

Thus, for archivists, a primary function is the documentation and preservation of 'records in context' (McCarthy, 2000). But why should just the archivists be concerned by such matters? Surely these issues must be of importance to any educator concerned with authentic enquiry and an appreciation for human history. Such perspective should also be of concern for those interested in information infrastructure that persists over medium- to long-term time horizons. If such issues are not attended to, then it may yet prove to be a grand irony that while the Internet may survive a nuclear holocaust it may not survive the revolutions in information technology. For example, many scenarios may flourish where public trust loses ground to suspicion, and quality-assured information is challenged by new forms of disruptive corporate espionage or media norms (O'Neill, 2002).

In responding to this challenge, the cultural informatics community is developing Encoded Archival Context (EAC, 2002) as an archival standard (in XML) through an international collaboration. EAC extends the current capability of Encoded Archival Description (EAD) and will enable encoding of discrete records that carry information about the creators of archival materials (such as biographical details and agency histories) (Pitti, 2001). The CIDOC Documentation Standards Group is also pursuing work in this area through development of a common conceptual reference model for documentation (CIDOC, 2003).

But for archivists and non-archivists alike, context also helps establish things such as authenticity, quality, authority and credibility. A book published by MIT Press, for example, will typically be recognized as having more credibility than, say, the British tabloid press.

Related to this function of context is the notion of 'truth'. 'Truth' is not a necessary requirement in sense-making because the patterns within data sets and information help establish meaning and narrative through interpretation. In determining the truth or otherwise of assertions, statements, or documents, it is sometimes crucial that the context in which such things were made is also known. To illustrate this with an educational example, we may be tempted to accept as true the geometric assertion that the aggregate angles of a triangle will always equal 180°. However, while this is true for two-dimensional plane geometry it's not necessarily true in other geometries, such as the surface of a sphere or hyperbolic geometry. Following this last point it is important to emphasize that 'objectivity' in metadata creation is probably unattainable because a cataloguer still makes indexing *choices*, even if they are informed.

Context and learning

When considering how context is important – and *what it is* – in learning, education and training, added to McCarthy's definition given earlier should also be information about *how*, *when*, *where*, and even *if* the information might be *applied*. Knowledge can be characterized as having a dynamic dimension that is not intrinsic to information alone. This sets it apart from information. Another way of saying this is that *know-how*, *know-when*, *know-where* and *know-if* are possible applications of educational resources (Norris, Mason and Lefrere, 2003). Indeed, such facets of knowing are prime candidates for encoding as educational resources.

Application is a keyword here. When 'information resources' are indexed or catalogued they may be assigned a range of contextual information (such as the simply conceived ERC format of who, what, where, when) but it is typically the case that the metadata that are applied are largely concerned with 'aboutness', or *know-what*. Thus, in its inaugural meeting in 1999 the DCMI DC-Education Working Group clearly identified *teaching methods* and *learning activities* as important information that could be used to enhance the descriptiveness and utility of online educational resources. However, due to a range of factors such as the complexity involved in producing a schema DC-Education has not yet produced substantive work in this area (DC-Ed, 2003).

Learning and knowing

Figure 13.1 is also intended to convey the complexity of the relationships between entities (such as data, information and knowledge) in the context of learning, education and training. The METS standard clearly identifies *behaviour* as an aspect of a resource, either intrinsic or potential. The IMS *Simple Sequencing* specification also deals with such information – although, to the uninitiated, the specification could hardly be regarded as 'simple' (IMS SS, 2003). The key point here is that many complex issues need to be addressed, when data models and information models (and, for the argument's completeness, knowledge models) are developed to be applicable in learning, educational and training contexts. For example, while an interaction in the digital domain can be logged and subject to systems analysis, certain judgement calls are made if such interactions are modelled as components of learning and knowing. Not only are *learn*, *know*, *reflect* verbs, but such actions are always shaped by context. Thus, in harnessing the capabilities of the Internet in the pursuit of learning and knowledge sharing, it seems there is a fundamental requirement to model learning, educating and training as complex adaptive systems (Jaworsky, 1996).

When Lave and Wenger (1991) coined the term 'communities of practice' they argued that learning and knowledge sharing are typically informal and highly conditional upon context. Their views have since had a significant impact upon learning theory – in particular, constructivism (Jaworsky, 1996). More recently, Wenger (1998) has defined *learning* as 'the engine of practice, and practice is the history of that learning'. Such a recursive description has important implications for the design of online systems that are intended to support e-learning as well as knowledge management. How will such systems facilitate the reflective learning required in coming to grips with 'histories of learning'?

In teaching and learning, context plays an important role in developing critical thinking and discernment skills. Constructivism, as an important pedagogical theory, emphasizes the construction of meaning through *sense-making* as pivotal in the learning process. Thus, as Barbara Jaworsky distils it:

> knowing is an action participated in by the learner. Knowledge is not received from an external source. Learning is a process of comparing new experience with knowledge constructed from previous experience, resulting in the reinforcing or adaptation of that knowledge.
>
> (Jaworsky, 1996, p. 7)

Describing educational resources

From another perspective Shabajee (2002) describes a 'fundamental dilemma' that confronts developers of educational resource repositories and online resource discovery services. In the politics and confusion of early adoption, however, various stakeholder groups have sometimes missed the significance of this dilemma. So what is it? In simple terms, it has to do with a tension between *generality* and *specificity* of description, and it arises from the parallel standardization efforts of various metadata initiatives – such as IEEE LOM and DCMI. While both initiatives have explicitly pursued standardization of data models that promote interoperability, their purposes have been differently conceived. For the IEEE LOM the interest has always been in providing a richly conceived model that can express specific, granular descriptions of resources (learning objects) that have been purposely designed for learning (as 'learning objects'). Such specific metadata are also defined to enable the run-time management of learning objects within applications.

For DCMI, the main purpose has always been facilitating cross-domain resource discovery – that is, discovery of information on the Web that has not necessarily been purposely designed for learning. Thus, while it is true that a generally described resource may be discoverable and then purposely designed for learning, a specifically described resource is typically discoverable only within applications that are similarly specified. Conversely, a resource that is described for a precise purpose is likely to be better suited to that purpose than one that is closely related (Ip *et al.*, 2000). In other words, metadata can derive their utility from both ambiguity and precision.

An instance of the dilemma can be seen in the assignment of 'audience' information as an attribute of a resource. For example, while a resource might be developed specifically for teachers, tagging it so that *only* teachers can discover it may not yield the full usefulness of that resource. In Shabajee's words:

> developers are unlikely to want (or be able) to restrictively specify who their users should be and, in particular, how they *should* use individual assets in their particular educational contexts . . . [however] they must make decisions about what metadata terms to choose to describe their assets.
>
> (Shabajee, 2002)

The issue of 'audience' has historically been the subject of many debates within the DCMI. On the one side are advocates of a 'sixteenth' element being added to the core element set. On the other side are advocates of a strict dividing line between descriptions concerning 'aboutness' of a resource and descriptions of 'usage' (how the resource might be used) or 'audience' (who might use it).

In late 1999 the DCMI formed its first domain-specific working group, the DC Education Working Group, with an initial scope of work broadly defined to make recommendations about extensions and/or 'qualifiers' that would assist in describing educational resources. It became clear very soon that for stakeholders in educational settings some facets of audience (such as user level) can be important and even intrinsic attributes of an educational resource (Sutton and Mason, 2001).

Context and LOM

Having established the conceptual framework of this discussion, it is now worthwhile to consider the *one* industry standard that has been developed to support metadata application to educational resources, the IEEE LOM.

> The purpose of this Standard is to facilitate search, evaluation, acquisition, and use of learning objects, for instance by learners or instructors or automated software processes. The purpose is also to facilitate the sharing and exchange of learning objects, by enabling the development of catalogs and inventories *while taking into account the diversity of cultural and lingual contexts* in which the learning objects and their metadata will be exploited.
>
> (IEEE, 2002, p. 5, my emphasis)

1. Within the LOM data model, 'context' has two main semantic usages: Context is used in an explanatory way – for example, within

data element 5.3: Educational Interactivity Level – 'The degree of interactivity characterizing this learning object. Interactivity in this context refers to the degree to which the learner can influence the aspect or behavior of the learning object. NOTE 1: Inherently, this scale is meaningful within the context of a community of practice.'

(IEEE 2002, p. 25)

2. As data element 5.6: Educational Context – 'The principal environment within which the learning and use of this learning object is intended to take place' (IEEE 2002, p. 28). And thus, the permitted values include 'school, higher education, training, other'.

Again, historical perspective is useful in considering this standard – it took close to five years of collaborative effort to formalize. However, its origins were at a time when 'content' was considered 'king' and object models were in the ascendancy. While the LOM data model attempts to do justice to context issues – and in many ways LOM is designed to enable the versatile application of learning objects in a range of different contexts – an argument can be sustained that it is still a content-centric model, or perhaps a *content view on context*. After all, consider the morphology of the term 'learning object': *object* is a noun and *learning* an adjective. Systems, such as learning management systems, that utilize these objects may be configured to support *activities* such as learning processes but ultimately the learning objects are managed as *content*. And systems that are designed to manage learning objects are commonly referred to as learning content management systems.

There follows, then, another argument that the extraction of context from content together with independent modelling and development of context information may provide a high added-value to the development, access and application of online educational resources. These may be represented as either 'context objects' or rules that might apply when triggered by certain events.

W3C technologies

The preceding discussion is, of course, largely theoretical. Where the real acid test takes place – after the refinement of information models – is in the development of technology that not only works but triggers stakeholder adoption. Within the wide scope of the research and development conducted by the World Wide Web Consortium there are two key technologies that have succeeded in gaining widespread attention: XML (Extensible Markup Language) and RDF (Resource Description Framework). Of course, it is the former that has succeeded in the marketplace, while the latter remains very much in the realm of a 'promising technology', it being the foundation for the Semantic Web initiative. It is promising, because it provides a means for the machine parsing of structured metadata that carry 'meaning', the parsing of semantics, not just syntax. RDF-based encoding thus provides a method involving not just connected *documents* but also connected *statements*. From an RDF perspective, hierarchical taxonomies are tempered by relational ontologies. In other words, RDF explicitly models the relativity of all semantics while providing a framework for closer meshing of related semantics – and sense-making from semantics are ultimately revealed.

In responding to the kinds of challenges that arise when context is considered as having potential for independent modelling, some innovative research and development has been undertaken by Mikael Nilsson and his colleagues at the Swedish Royal Institute of Technology. Through exploring the potential application of RDF in peer-to-peer applications, their work may yield new practical ways to develop and manage metadata for educational resources while accommodating a richer application of context than current tools allow (Nilsson *et al.*, 2002). Certainly, in the development of an RDF binding to the LOM data model, Nilsson's work has revealed a number of interesting issues (Nilsson, 2003).

Conclusion

A range of methods can be currently discerned where the development of metadata for educational resources is concerned. These range from the application of metadata to resources that have been purposely designed for learning, to the application of educational contexts, to information resources that were not necessarily originally designed for learning. The standardization of the IEEE LOM can be regarded as a significant milestone in an ongoing effort to make educational resources accessible.

In proposing a way forward, *context* has been identified as a candidate for independent modelling from content – as either 'context objects' or rules that might apply when triggered by certain events. Such an approach may provide a high added-value to the development, access and application of online educational resources.

References

Castells, M. (1996) *The rise of the network society. The information age – economy, society and culture*, Blackwell, Oxford.

CIDOC (2003) (accessed 21 March 2003) Scope definition of the CIDOC conceptual reference model, Conceptual Reference Model, (Online) http://cidoc.ics.forth. gr/scope.html.

DC-Ed (2003) (accessed 23 March 2003) Dublin Core Education Working Group, (Online) http://dublincore.org/groups/education/.

Dervin, B. (1998) (accessed 7 April 2004) Sense-making theory and practice: An overview of user interests in knowledge seeking and use, *Journal of Knowledge*

Management, **2** (2): 36–46, (Online) http://communication.sbs.ohio-state.edu/sense-making/art/artabsdervin98km.html.

Dervin, B. (2001) Clear . . . unclear? Accurate . . . inaccurate? Objective . . . subjective? Research . . . practice? Why polarities impede the research, practice, and design of information systems and how sense-making methodology attempts to bridge the gaps (Lazerow Lecture), Florida State University.

EAC (2002) (accessed 23 March 2003) Encoded archival context – work in progress, (Online) http://www.library.yale.edu/eac.

Heimbürger, A. (2002) (accessed 24 March 2003) Context, metadata, ontologies and time – key issues in information modelling, (Online) http://www.nordinfo.helsinki.fi/publications/nordnytt/nnytt2–3_02/heimburger.htm.

IEEE (2002) (accessed 16 March 2003) Draft standard for Learning Object Metadata (LOM), Learning Technology Standards Committee (LTSC), (Online) http://ltsc.ieee.org/doc/wg12/LOM_WD6_4.pdf.

IMS (2002) (accessed 24 March 2003) IMS Global Learning Consortium – Content packaging Specification, IMS CP, (Online) http://www.imsglobal.org/content/packaging/index.cfm.

IMS SS (2003) (accessed 3 May 2003) *IMS simple sequencing XML binding: Version 1.0 final specification*, 3 March, (Online) http://www.imsproject.org/simplesequencing/ssv1p0/imsss_bindv1p0.html.

Ip, A. *et al.* (2000) (accessed 28 April 2003) Managing online resources for teaching and learning, in *AusWeb 2000*, (Online) http://ausweb.scu.edu.au/aw2k/papers/ip/paper.html.

Jaworsky, B. (1996) (accessed 23 March 2003) Constructivism and teaching – the socio-cultural context, (Online) http://www.grout.demon.co.uk/Barbara/chreods.htm.

Kunze, J. (2001) (accessed 24 March 2003) A metadata kernel for electronic permanence, in *International Conference on Dublin Core and Metadata Applications*, (Online) http://www.nii.ac.jp/dc2001/proceedings/product/paper-27.pdf.

Lave, J. and Wenger, E. (1991) *Situated learning. Legitimate peripheral participation*, Cambridge University Press, Cambridge.

McCarthy, G. (2000) (accessed 24 April 2003) The structuring of context: New possibilities in an XML enabled World Wide Web, *Journal of the Association for History and Computing*, **3** (1), (Online) http://mcel.pacificu.edu/JAHC/JAHCIII1/ARTICLES/McCarthy/index.html.

METS (2002) (accessed 26 March 2003) Metadata encoding transmission standard – Overview, (Online) http://www.loc.gov/standards/mets/METSOverview.html.

Miller, E. (1998) (accessed 24 April 2003) An introduction to the resource description framework, *D-Lib Magazine*, (Online) http://www.dlib.org/dlib/may98/miller/05miller.html.

Naeve, A. (2001) (accessed 4 June 2003) The knowledge manifold – an educational architecture that supports inquiry-based customizable forms of e-learning, in *2nd European Web-based Learning Environment Conference (WBLE 2001)*, 24–26 October, Lund, Sweden, (Online) http://kmr.nada.kth.se/papers/KnowledgeManifolds/KnowledgeManifold.pdf.

Nilsson, M. (2003) (accessed 21 January 2003) *Semantic issues with the LOM RDF binding*, (Online) http://kmr.nada.kth.se/el/ims/md-lom-semantics.html.

Nilsson, M., Palmér, M. and Naeve, A. (2002) (accessed 30 January 2003) Semantic Web metadata for e-learning – some architectural guidelines, in *11th International World Wide Web conference*, Honolulu, (Online) http://kmr.nada.kth.se/papers/SemanticWeb/p744-nilsson.pdf.

Norris, D., Mason, J. and Lefrere, P. (2003) (accessed 24 March 2003) Transforming e-knowledge, Society for College and University Planning, (Online) http://www.transformingeknowledge.info/.

O'Neill, O. (2002) (accessed 20 March 2003) A question of trust, (Online) http://www.bbc.co.uk/radio4/reith2002/.

Pitti, D. V. (2001) (accessed 24 May 2003) Creator description: Encoded archival context, in *Computing Arts 2001: Digital Resources for Research in the Humanities*, University of Sydney, 24 May, (Online) http://setis.library.usyd.edu.au/drrh2001/papers/pitti.pdf.

Ruggles, R. and Holtshouse, D. (eds) (1999) *14 visionaries speak on leveraging knowledge for marketplace success*, Capstone, Dover, NH.

Ryan, Y. and Stedman, L. (2001) (accessed 27 April 2003) The business of borderless education – 2001 update, Department of Education, Science, and Training, (Online) http://www.dest.gov.au/highered/eippubs/eip02_1/eip02_1.pdf.

Shabajee, P. (2002) (accessed 26 April 2003) Primary multimedia objects and 'educational metadata' – A fundamental dilemma for developers of multimedia archives, *D-Lib Magazine*, **8** (6), (Online) http://www.dlib.org/dlib/june02/shabajee/06shabajee.html.

Sutton, S. and Mason, J. (2001) (accessed 23 April 2003) The Dublin Core and metadata for educational resources, International Conference on Dublin Core and Metadata Applications, (Online) http://www.nii.ac.jp/dc2001/proceedings/product/paper-04.pdf.

Wenger, E. (1998) *Communities of practice: Learning, meaning and identity*, Cambridge University Press, Cambridge, UK.

Chapter 14

Contextualized models and metadata for learning repositories

Heidrun Allert, Christoph Richter,
Hadhami Dhraief and Wolfgang Nejdl

Open Learning Repositories (OLRs) are metadata-based course portals that structure and connect modularized course materials distributed all over the Web. The modular content is integrated by explicit metadata information in order to build courses and connected sets of learning materials. Modular content can be reused for other courses and in other contexts, leading to a course portal, which integrates LOs from different sources and authors. The system houses a relational database to store all metadata. The database does not store content, but references it by Uniform Resource Locator (URLs). The OLR system at the time of writing houses two courses, one in Artificial Intelligence and one in Software Engineering.

The focus in the first and second generation of Open Learning Repositories (Dhraief *et al.*, 2001) was the technical infrastructure. The main questions were, how to store the metadata, whether to use O-Telos (Mylopoulos *et al.*, 1990), XML (World Wide Web Consortium, 1999) or other applications and languages. However, there was a lack of pedagogical background in the first and second generation of OLRs. Therefore, we decided to design and implement a new generation of OLR, which was designated as 'OLR3'. This learning repository is open to different pedagogical approaches, which can be implemented explicitly. This means that different views on LOs and different learning strategies, guided by instructional as well as situated approaches, can be implemented. The system extended the LO Metadata Standard LOM (IEEE Learning Technology Standards Committee, 2002) to incorporate a strong focus on pedagogical approaches.

The results of an evaluation of the second generation of the Open Learning Repository revealed that the system did not meet the students' needs. Therefore in the design of OLR3 the investigators addressed the entire educational setting, which is supported by technology instead of focusing on the technology in an isolated way. For this, a scenario-based approach was developed to guide the design process of OLR3 in order to address the technology as well as the educational setting. The design of the educational setting influences the use of an e-learning system. The multi-disciplinarity of the project team required a medium for communication that allows the communication of ideas and theories beyond the different areas of expertise. The scenario-based approach explained by Carroll (2000) helped to handle this task.

Different views on learning objects: Models in the OLR3

Within the OLR3, users, such as lifelong learners, can choose their preferred learning strategy. The OLR3 contextualizes learning objects (LOs), offering several contexts to the user rather than just one. Each context is designed according to a specific pedagogical approach. From a pedagogical point of view these approaches can be very diverse. They can be derived from different learning paradigms and principles, such as situated learning, based on theories of situated cognition and instructional models, based on information processing theories. While some models focus on distributing domain-specific knowledge to individual users, others focus on co-construction of knowledge by learning communities. Some models focus on developing competencies, such as coordinating teamwork, managing projects or conducting scientific work. Each of these learning models is based on different approaches, but with several choices, learners, teachers or tutors might be able to choose the most suitable learning model and learning/teaching strategy for their particular needs.

In a lifelong learning context, learners should be able to decide on learning needs themselves and should be given a choice of their preferred way of learning. This requires reflection on one's own strategies for learning and teaching. Rautenstrauch (2001) explains:

> Life-long learning will be a learner's own decision . . . the learner is mature . . . he [sic] will identify and define his own needs and preferred ways of learning . . . he [sic] will learn to learn self-organized, self-determined, and independent from predetermined curricula and institutional forms of organization.
>
> (p. 6)

Metadata models

Therefore the Open Learning Repository (OLR3) was designed to be open to different learning and teaching strategies. Specifying different metadata models in the OLR3 is a means of representing different views on LOs. In the OLR3 there are three models to specify different aspects/views: *Domain Model*, *Instructional Model* and *Structural Model* as shown in Table 14.1. These different models can be structured by various experts in the different fields. For example, experts in the subject domain may structure the Domain Model, whereas instructional designers may extend the Instructional Model.

Domain Model

In the Domain Model, domain and subject-specific ontologies are specified, both hierarchical and associative (Meder, 2000). This knowledge space includes the conceptualization of subject-specific knowledge, skills and competencies.

Instructional Model

As mentioned earlier, pedagogical models are diverse. Nevertheless most of these models have one thing in common: they structure learning processes in phases. Within the OLR3 these phases form guiding sequences – learners are guided through learning processes or processes of cooperation.

There is no unique ontology for learning, but different views, approaches, theories and models. In the Instructional Model, learning phases and learning processes are specified. They are derived from different learning models and learning theories, such as Problem-Based Learning, Case-Based Learning, Expository Learning, Communities of Practice, and so on. As the investigators tried to represent these aspects in LO metadata, it was realized that existing metadata standards do not address learning processes (Allert, Dhraief and Nejdl, 2002). This issue is also adressed by Meder (2000), who stresses that LOs should be defined in six dimen-

Table 14.1 Domain model, instructional model and structural model

Domain model	*Instructional model*	*Structural model*
Domain specific ontologies (Matter of Fact Relations, Meder, 2000). Structuring subject specific knowledge, skills, and competencies.	Instructional relations derived from different pedagogical approaches and learning models. Structuring learning processes and processes of cooperation in phases to guide learners and learning groups, and to support different learning strategies.	Relations (e.g. theory is generalizing example) are derived from different learning theories (cognitive science). The ontology of knowledge types is taken from Meder (2000). Within OLR3 relations (called 'turn-offs') support exploration.

sions, where one of these dimensions defines the position of an LO within the process of knowledge acquisition:

> A LO must be defined in the dimension of logic-operative modes of processes, i.e. there are methods which determine the process of acquisition of knowledge. [Ein didaktisches Objekt muss bestimmt sein . . . in der Dimension logisch-operativer Verlaufsformen, d.h. es gibt Methoden – im definierten Sinne – die den Verlauf der Aneignung von Wissen bestimmen können.]
>
> (Meder, 2000)

The Instructional Model defines learning phases and presents them as guiding structures (learning sequence) to the learners. Here are exemplified two different models, which have been implemented so far:

1. Expository Learning (Ausubel, 1968);
2. A process-oriented model called 'Trails of Competence'. The design of this model was guided by the principles of situated learning and the concept of Communities of Practice. Next to subject-specific learning objectives, learners also study how to conduct scientific work or how to manage a project. The phases are structured according to activity theory (Oesterreich, 1981; Volpert, 1999) as in Table 14.2.

These different sequences, specified in the Instructional Model, serve as navigational threads and address the problem of linking de-contextualized objects to stringent learning sequences and coherent structures. The defined structures work as guidance to authors presenting learning material as well as to students navigating through the material. The process-oriented model also facilitates students in coordinating their project and their cooperation with peers.

Structural Model

By separating the Instructional Model from the Structural Model, one can model guiding as well as explorative structures. Whereas in the Instructional Model learning processes are specified in order to support guidance, in the Structural Model knowledge types and relations are specified in order to support exploration and elaboration. Course authors may also use the relations to integrate further material and LOs, beyond the guiding sequence. Here are some examples of knowledge types and relations (also, see Table 14.3):

- theory generalizes example;
- exercise applies theory;
- is similar to;
- is different from;
- is prerequisite for.

Table 14.2 Phases modelled in OLR3

Phases modelled along the model of expository learning by Ausubel (1968)	Phases modelled along the activity theory (Oesterreich, 1981; Volpert, 1999)
Orientation (advance organizer) Conceptualization (progressive differentiation) Practice Integrating and connecting	Ask questions Plan proceeding Apply plan Analyse Interpret and discuss

Table 14.3 Methodical relations specified in the structural model

Entity	Relation	Entity
LO (theory)	generalizes	LO (example)
LO (exercise)	applies	LO (theory)
LO	is similar to	LO
LO	is different from	LO
LO	is prerequisite for	LO

In order to model these relations, each LO must be categorized with regard to its knowledge-type. The ontology of knowledge-types is taken from Meder (2000). Based on these models the interface of the OLR3 looks as shown in Figure 14.1.

Contextualizing learning objects: Diverse learning models

The use of LOs within the OLR3 depends on the learning model, which guides the design of the learning sequence. A LO can fill various roles within different learning sequences. For instance, a text or video-file can be used in the phase called 'Advance Organizer' (Expository Learning) as well as in the phase 'Apply Plan' (Trails of Competence). The concept of Role-Based Metadata, which specifies static as well as dynamic meta-data was proposed (Allert et al., 2002).

Expository learning in OLR3

According to the model of Expository Learning by Ausubel (1968), learning proceeds through four phases. Within the OLR3 LOs that serve the specific instructional purpose of a phase are presented to the user as shown in Table 14.4.

This learning theory concentrates on distributing knowledge in a struc-tured way. To guide learners, the phases form a path-like navigation

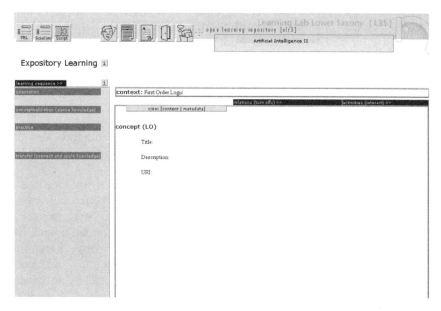

Figure 14.1 Screenshot: interface: 'Expository learning'

Table 14.4 Phases of expository teaching according to Ausubel

Phase	Instructional purpose
Orientation (Advance Organizer)	Prepare for integration of new knowledge. Subsuming bridge between new learning material and existing related ideas. Present introductory material that helps students relate new information to existing knowledge schemes. New ideas and concepts must be 'potentially meaningful' to the learner. Help to relate new ideas to existing scheme. Ask questions such as: What do you want to find out? What operations do you need to perform to get there? What do you already know?
Conceptualization (Progressive Differentiation)	The most general ideas of a subject should be presented first and then progressively differentiated in terms of detail and specifics. Organize new material by subordination, superordination and coordination.
Practice	Practice and apply.
Integration and Connection	Integrate and link new knowledge to other fields of knowledge and context areas as well as to the Advance Organizer. Instructional materials should attempt to integrate new material with previously presented information through comparisons and cross-referencing of new and old ideas.

Source: Ausubel, 1968.

structure on the interface. To support exploration, related LOs are presented via links called '*turn-offs*'. According to Ausubel (1968) relations such as 'is similar to' and 'is different from' support learning. Furthermore, the interface provides functions such as 'add comment', 'add bookmark', 'add keyword to metadata'.

Trails of competence

This process-oriented model focuses on competencies. The core idea of this model is well described by Seufert, Lechner and Stanoevska (2002):

> The goal in education is to teach knowledge not additively, but inter-linked by means of questions arising from business practice and scientific research. Only such inter-linked knowledge can be consciously disposed of in concrete situations. The quantity of information and the speed information gets outdated demands that formative, open-up knowledge be taught which enables learners to apply knowledge creatively to problem-solving, and gives them the opportunity to create new knowledge (Nanoka and Takeuchi, 1995). The linkage of factual knowledge and creative problem solving techniques may constitute such formative open-up knowledge.
>
> (p. 44)

Investigators identified two major competencies:

- the competence to manage and coordinate project-oriented teamwork;
- the competence to plan and conduct scientific work.

Both of these competencies are relevant to students' further academic as well as professional careers. Phases were identified, which are relevant in both scientific work and project management. From the point of view of psychology, both of these processes can be characterized as intentional and goal-oriented activities. Therefore these activities were then structured according to activity theory (Miller, Galanter and Pribram 1960; Oesterreich, 1981) and organized into phases. The phases are meant to provide orientation, structure student activities, and guide navigation.

Reflecting the author's concept, we realized that universally valid concepts of scientific work cannot be discerned. At this point investigators decided on the principle of Communities of Practice, that both research methods and scientific communities are diverse (heuristic, empiric as well as hermeneutic among others). There are communities focusing on multi-disciplinary topics such as technology and education. For example, there are communities such as Semantic Web, Digital Libraries, Peer to Peer, Robotics, Adaptive Hypermedia, Media Education (a very local community within Germany), Molecular Bioinformatics, Paleo Anthropology, and so on. Any of these communities share different routines, rules and procedures such as where and how (and how often, within months or years) to publish results and share ideas (conferences, scientific magazines, or books); where and how to meet and communicate (at local workshops or at international conferences).

Boettcher (2001) views learning as situated activity. Its central characteristic is a process called *legitimate peripheral participation*. Learning means to allow students to move from peripheral participation to full membership. Scientists, for example, are full members or participants of the core group within a specific scientific community. Therefore, within the OLR3, members of specific communities (experts) explain their strategies of scientific work: how they describe the state of the art and identify relevant research questions; how they conduct research; and how they publish. They give examples of their own research work, point out relevant conferences, mailing lists and papers. Within each phase, experts also provide LOs that are relevant to understanding the research topic. To support reflection on learning, experts are also asked to state criteria of what they think is 'a good research question' and so on.

As several experts were asked to draft their strategies and provide LOs within the OLR3, students may compare different strategies, procedures and routines within different scientific communities. Students and student groups are enabled to identify their topics of interest and choose their favourite experts in order to ask them for support and consult them and their work. Students then form instances of expertise-trails in order to share their work and learning progress. They search for LOs on the Web, collect and provide LOs themselves, write reports and present their own ideas and strategies. Experts (full members of communities) communicate with students. For the project-based expert-trails, investigators consulted experts, who actually manage projects. These competence-based trails are called ScieCom: *Introduction to Scientific Communities* <http://www. learninglab.de/~allert/olr/studie4/site/index.htm> as shown in Figure 14.2.

The finished system is planned to provide a library, which will provide collections of expert-trails and students' finished work. Creating a new course means sampling relevant trails and entities. A group of students used the 'Trails of Competence' OLR3 in the summer semester of 2003. They were asked to affirm the state of the art and identify relevant research questions. They shared their work, provided documents and described their strategies.

At first, the focus of this research was on designing, using and evaluating the 'Trails of Competence' as soon as possible. Therefore, the complete metadata-based architecture was not implemented, but a functional mock-up was built. This prototype, which is able to simulate the intended functionality, allowed investigators to rapidly use and evaluate the 'Trails of

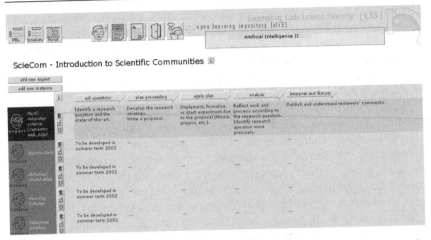

Figure 14.2 Screenshot: 'Trails of competence' (Introduction to Scientific Communities)

Competence'. Use-cases were drafted and UML (Unified Modelling Language) diagrams were prepared. The interface was designed, and HTML pages were built and integrated with a basic workspace (BSCW, 1995–2001) in order to enable and support cooperative activities. Currently, this learning concept has been integrated into the metadata-based architecture.

Architecture and technology

The third generation of the Open Learning Repository, OLR3, is implemented in Java and works as a JavaServlet, running on an open source Enhydra Application Server (Madl, 2002). It is connected to an Oracle Database via JDBC, which is used to store the metadata entered by course authors and students. There are two types of metadata: structured metadata and annotated metadata. The structured metadata represent information about the structure of a given course or course unit, the navigation path within this course or course unit, and the relations between different LOs. Annotated metadata represent the information about the content itself. A subset of the LOM metadata standard has been implemented to annotate the LOs. All metadata are represented in RDF and RDFS (World Wide Web Consortium, 2002). The RDF schemes, needed for either the annotation or the structure of learning, can reside anywhere on the Web, as do the LOs. The database holds only the metadata, and assembles courses from these records (see Figure 14.3).

The system works on a 'StatementPool' which holds all metadata known to the system at run-time, relevant for a given course. When an author starts working on a course, the pool is filled with the already existing data about that course from the database, and all statements from the used RDF

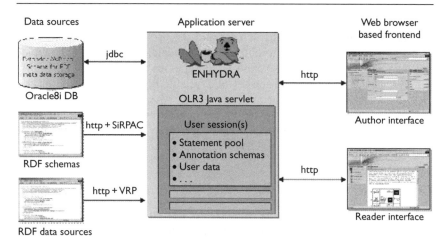

Data sources   Application server   Web browser
                                                  based frontend

Figure 14.3 OLR architecture

schemes. Any referenced RDF schema will be parsed using the SiRPAC
RDF parser (Melnik, 2001), whereas imported RDF files are parsed by a
VRP RDF parser (Tolle, 2001), which provides semantic checks against
given RDF schema rules.

Web interface

OLR3 provides a web-browser-based metadata editor/viewer and two major
user interfaces <http://130.75.152.218:8080>, loginName: *guest*, login
Password: *guest*). The first one is used for readers preferring a more graphically oriented view and only minor functions for manipulation of the
underlying metadata. The second one is designed for authors to provide
a schema-driven and browser-based metadata editor with flexible binding
to different RDF schemes.

The Learner Web Interface

A specific engine prepares and filters the content, and displays it based
on a stored layout. The reader interface also offers the reader the possibility of making minor additions to the metadata of a selected course
element by providing functions such as 'add comment', 'add bookmark',
'add keyword to metadata', and so on. All those additions can be made
private or public to other course readers.

The Author Web Interface

The second interface provides the actual metadata editor, which is intended
for course authors, who can navigate through the structure tree of a course

and select any sub-element. All existing editable metadata for this element are shown in the centre of the screen, and the user can choose from a set of existing RDF properties, to add to the metadata, or to modify the existing data. The author can also bind RDF schemes (e.g. DC, DCQ, LOM) stored on the Web to extend the set of available properties for annotation, or unbind RDF schemes that are not needed anymore. A 'toolbar' holds those bound RDF schemes and offers the possibility of navigating through their structure by displaying an expandable tree view of any available property.

Conclusion

Computer-Supported Learning intends to design an entire educational setting, which is supported by technology. Lifelong learners have to reflect their own learning needs in both form and content. Within OLR3, learners as well as teachers can choose a preferred learning concept. The design of the OLR3 was guided by a scenario-based design approach and the evaluation of a former version of OLR (OLR2). Designers and implementers were asked to write 'scenarios of *intended* use' whereas students were asked to write 'scenarios of *actual* use' at the end of Winter semester 2002. In comparing these scenarios, the design team realized that some functionalities provided by OLR2 (such as 'add public comment', 'add URL') have not been used by students. An analysis of the entire educational setting revealed that cooperation among students, which is enabled by technology, did not take place as the educational setting itself did not support cooperation.

Therefore, in the Summer semester of 2002 the entire educational setting of the course was redesigned and supported by OLR3. Learning objectives of the course comprised domain-specific knowledge as well as the competencies of scientific work.

Diverse metadata schemes and ontologies have been developed within different projects. The German Institute of Standardization (DIN), Working group DIN-EBN Didactics, compares and integrates different approaches taking into account both national and international concepts, standards and specifications. Projects may not reinvent the wheel but use existing ontologies. In the further development of OLR3, designers and implementers will also take into account existing ontologies and concepts.

References

Allert, H., Dhraief, H. and Nejdl, W. (2002) Meta-level category, 'role' in metadata standards for e-learning: Instructional roles and instructional qualities of learning objects, *The 2nd International Conference on Computational Semiotics for Games and New Media*, July, CCSGN, Augsburg, Germany.

Ausubel, D. P. (1968) *Educational psychology: A cognitive view*, Holt, Rinehart and Winston, New York.

Boettcher, J. (2001) (accessed 5 July 2001) The spirit of invention: Edging our way to 21st century teaching, *Syllabus Magazine*, (Online) http://www.syllabus.com/syllabusmagazine/article.asp?id=3687.

BSCW (1995–2001) (accessed 23 March 2003) Basic support for cooperative work, *FIT and OrbiTeam Software GmbH*, (Online) http://bscw.gmd.de/.

Carroll, J. M. (2000) *Making use: scenario-based design of human-computer interactions*, MIT Press, Cambridge.

Dhraief, H. *et al.* (2001) Open learning repositories and metadata modeling, *International Semantic Web Working Symposium (SWWS)*, Stanford University, California.

IEEE Learning Technology Standards Committee (2002) (accessed 28 April 2003) Draft standard for learning object metadata, (Online) http://ltsc.ieee.org/doc/wg12/LOM_WD6_4.pdf.

Madl, A. (2002) (accessed 20 March 2003) Enhydra open source Java/XML application server, (Online) http://enhydra.enhydra.org.

Meder, N. (2000) Didaktische ontologien, in *Globalisierung und Wissensorganisation: Neue aspekte für Wissen, Wissenschaft und informationssysteme*, eds H. P. Ohly, G. Rahmstorf and A. Sigel, Ergon Verlag, Würzburg.

Melnik, S. (2001) (accessed 21 April 2003) SiRPAC RDF parser, (Online) http://www-db.stanford.edu/~melnik/rdf/api.html.

Miller, G. A., Galanter, E. and Pribram, K. H. (1960) *Plans and the structure of behavior*, Holt, New York.

Mylopoulos, J. *et al.* (1990) Telos: A language for representing knowledge about information systems, *ACM Transaction on Information Systems*, **8** (4).

Nanoka, I. and Takeuchi, H. (1995) *The knowledge creating company*, Oxford University Press, New York.

Oesterreich, R. (1981) *Handlungsregulation und kontrolle*, Urban & Schwarzenberg, München.

Rautenstrauch, C. (2001) *Tele-Tutoren – Qualifizierungsmerkmale einer neu entstehenden profession*, Norbert Meder, Bielefeld Hrsg.

Seufert, S., Lechner, U. and Stanoevska, K. (2002) A reference model for online learning communities, *International Journal on E-Learning*, **1** (1): 43–54.

Tolle, K. (2001) (accessed 28 April 2003) VRP RDF parser – High-level scalable tools for the Semantic Web, *Forth ICS*, (Online) http://www.ics.forth.gr/proj/isst/RDF.

Volpert, W. (1999) Wie wir handeln – was wir können: Ein Disput als Einführung in die Handlungspsychologie, *überarb. u. akt. Aufl. – Sottrum*, **2**.

World Wide Web Consortium (W3C) (1999) (accessed 28 April 2003) Resource Description Framework (RDF) Model and syntax specification, (Online) http://www.w3c.org/RDF.

World Wide Web Consortium (W3C) (2002) (accessed 10 April 2003) RDF vocabulary description language 1.0: RDF Schema, *World Wide Web Consortium (W3C)*, (online) http://www.w3c.org/RDF.

Chapter 15

Moving further in e-learning standardization

Towards a reference architecture

Luis Anido

Many institutions take advantage of advances in multimedia, networking and software engineering to offer training products and services at all levels. Educational systems and resources proliferate, and a need for standardization becomes apparent. As in other standard-driven initiatives, standardization applied to learning technologies will enable reuse and interoperation among systems.

The e-learning standardization process is an active, continuously evolving process that will last for years to come, until a clear, precise and generally accepted set of standards for educational-related systems is developed. Among the main contributors to this effort let us mention the IEEE Learning Technologies Standardization Committee (LTSC); the IMS Global Learning Consortium (2002); the Aviation Industry Computer Based Training Committee (AICC, 2004); the US Department of Defense's Advanced Distributed Learning, 2001 (Advanced Distributed Learning, 2002) initiative; and projects Alliance of Remote Instructional Authoring and Distribution Networks for Europe (ARIADNE, 2002); Getting Educational Systems Talking Across Leading-edge Technologies (GESTALT; FD Group, 2001); and the European Committee for Standardization through its Learning Technologies Workshop (CEN/ISSS/LT, 2002).

The IEEE's LTSC is the institution that is actually gathering recommendations and proposals from other learning standardization institutions and projects. Specifications that have been approved by the IEEE go through a more rigorous process to become ANSI or ISO standards. In fact, an ISO/IEC JTC1 Standards Committee for Learning Technologies, SC36 (International Standardization Organization, 2001), was approved in November 1999.

Outcomes from the e-learning standardization process can be divided into two levels:

I. Specification of the information models involved

Several proposals have been produced to specify the format, syntax and semantics of data to be transferred among heterogeneous platforms. Among the relevant areas of interest we can mention Learning Object Metadata (LOM), the first IEEE standard. Learner Records and Profiles provide the information that characterizes learners. The two most relevant specifications in this area come from IEEE LTSC and the IMS consortium. Educational Modelling Languages (EML) support interoperable definitions for learning object structures and learning processes. The IMS, ADL, the AICC and the Open University of the Netherlands are the most relevant contributors in this field. The IMS consortium also leads in other standardization areas such as Content Packaging and Question and Test Interoperability.

2. Specifications of the architectures, software components and provided interfaces

At the second level, standards define the expected behaviour of software components responsible for managing learning objects in online environments. Software interfaces for educational components would allow us to build new online learning systems without needing to develop them from scratch. The standards also facilitate interoperability among heterogeneous systems at run-time. So far, viable standards have been scarce. These include conceptual models, such as IEEE LTSC's Learning Technology Systems Architecture (LTSA), which defines five refinement layers as shown in Figure 15.1. Other implementations include software interfaces such as the ADL SCORM specification that includes interface definitions for the components responsible for delivering learning objects to students and tracking their progress. IMS has also identified the needed interfaces for digital repositories.

The GESTALT project identified a system architecture for online learning platforms, which was based on integrating architectures developed in previous projects. Unfortunately, important information concerning the interfaces among components (even those coming from the same project) have not been published, whereas those that are documented may be considered to be underspecified.

Additionally, there are other relevant proposals that are more pedagogically driven, which, in this aspect, complement my position. In the Open Knowledge Initiative (OKI), Stanford University proposes an API-based infrastructure for educational application development and support that is learner-centered in conception (Open Knowledge Initiative, Massachusetts Institute of Technology). Moreover, the Learning Systems Architecture Lab in Carnegie Mellon (Learning Systems Architecture Lab, 2002) advocates an architecture for user-centric learning management systems, for use in a virtual university. Further information on e-learning standardization is available from Santos et al. (2002) and from the websites of these institutions.

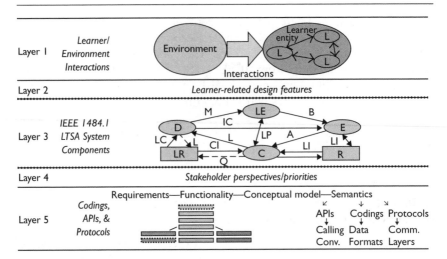

Figure 15.1 IEEE P1484.1 LTSA architecture

Contributing to the second level of standardization

From the previous section, we can conclude that the first level of standardization has already produced mature specifications, and some proposals are considered *de facto* standards (e.g. LOM metadata specification). However, specifications at the second level have been scarce so far and a complete proposal does not exist. There is still considerable work to be done to provide suitable standards for the business logic tier.

This chapter presents a contribution to a discussion about this second level of standardization by identifying common services for e-learning that will be supported by a reference architecture. This architecture will be composed of reusable software components with open and clearly identified interfaces. All interfaces in the architecture define their externally visible properties to facilitate the development of distributed, interoperable and standards-driven online learning environments.

The reference architecture will be designed for a specific implementation environment. The selected technology is CORBA (Object Management Group, 2001), an object-based distributed architecture that allows distributed and heterogeneous applications to interoperate on a network. Today, one of the key activities in the CORBA community is the definition of high-level services, clearly oriented to a particular business domain. Already available domain facilities are targeted to domains such as Telecommunications, Manufacturing, Finance or Healthcare. At the time of this writing there is no domain facility for e-learning. Our reference architecture will be put into practice through the proposal of a new domain CORBA facility for e-learning: CORBAlearn.

Some notes on the development methodology

Services supported by the reference architecture and eventually provided by CORBAlearn are the consequence of the application of an appropriate design methodology. This methodology (Anido *et al.*, 2002) is devoted to the definition of service architectures for a particular business domain starting from user requirements. The proposed methodology includes a reference model as an initial stage and defines a reference architecture as an intermediate stage. The overall process is illustrated in Figure 15.2. It was developed by Anido (2001).

Reference model

The reference model is obtained from an analysis of the domain and previous authors' experiences. Three elements have been identified (see Figure 15.3). *Educational Content Providers* (ECPs) are responsible for developing learning objects. They are equivalent to publishers in conventional education. *Educational Service Providers* (ESPs) are the schools, universities, or academic institutions in these virtual environments. ESPs use ECPs to access, maybe under payment, online courses to be offered at their institutions. This could be done directly or indirectly, using a *Broker*, which is the third party involved. Brokers are responsible for helping both learners and ESPs to find suitable learning resources: learners use broker services to find and locate those institutions (ESPs) that offer courses they are interested in; ESPs will use broker services to find learning resources offered by the ECPs to enrich their catalogues.

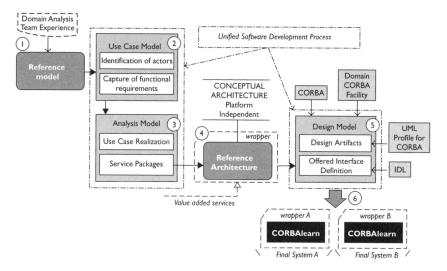

Figure 15.2 Software development methodology

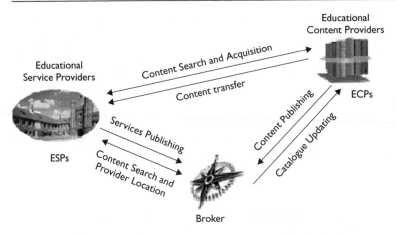

Figure 15.3 Reference model

Reference architecture

The reference architecture is a decomposition of the reference model, reflecting all components implementing the functionality of the proposed methodology, together with the corresponding data flows. Basic functional requirements are fulfilled by the reference architecture, whereas others, qualified as 'value-added services', are assigned to the wrapper as shown in Figure 15.2. The reference architecture is obtained from a detailed analysis of the functional requirements, and includes further specific requirements identified through this analytic process. Elements in the reference architecture are identified from loosely coupled service analysis class packages, which, in turn, are composed of tightly coupled objects. The basic properties of this reference architecture are:

- *Service architecture based on reusable sub-systems.* Architecture sub-systems correspond to reusable service packages embedding fundamental services within the e-learning domain. The only additional elements for basic e-learning systems are boundary classes representing user interfaces and logic control for other sub-systems in the architecture.
- *Standard-driven architecture.* Sub-systems in the architecture correspond to components implementing business logic for the information models identified by standardization bodies and institutions.
- *Scalability.* Construction of systems can be completed in an incremental process through the successive assembling of new elements from the architecture. These sub-systems are loosely coupled, and dependencies are directed from more complex to more basic components.
- *Adaptability.* It is possible to replace specific sub-systems by functionally equivalent ones.

- *Oriented to local changes*. Different functional requirements or standardized information models are handled by different sub-systems in the architecture.
- *Interoperability among heterogeneous systems*. Open software interfaces and a common reference architecture will support interoperation, provided final systems conform to the architecture. Added-value features are then implemented through the elaboration of wrapper classes.

Figure 15.4 outlines the proposed reference architecture, including the reference model decomposition into reference architecture elements and the analysis package each service package belongs to.

ESP reference architecture elements

Six sub-systems for the ESP reference architecture were identified:

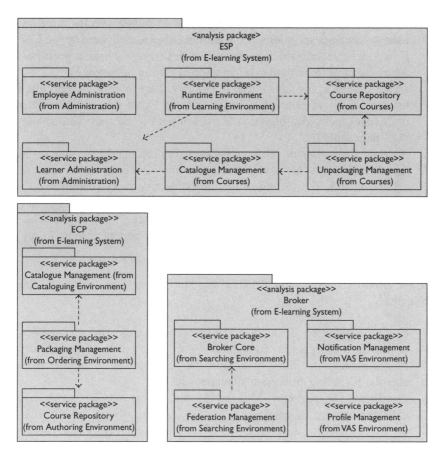

Figure 15.4 Reference architecture

- *Learners Administration*. It offers services to develop management systems for administrative information concerning *Learners*. Implementations of this sub-system should offer introspection mechanisms to identify supported profile data models. This sub-system also provides the business logic for Learner registration and enrolment.
- *Employee Administration*. This sub-system deals with administrative data for other actors: *Tutors*, *Teachers* and *Reviewers*. No standard specifications are available at this time to define the underlying data formats. However, models from other domains can be used (e.g. vCard).
- *Course Repository*. It supports the development of repositories at ESPs responsible for course management and storage. Specifications for course structures and EMLs are used in this sub-system to facilitate its use by Runtime Environments (see below).
- *Catalogue Management*. Developers of ESPs would use this sub-system to build cataloguing and searching tools. Metadata specifications are used to handle descriptions of the learning objects delivered by the ESP. It includes customizable searching services using Learner's profiles to adapt searches to particular learning/presentation preferences.
- *Unpackaging Management*. Services offered by this sub-system allow the unpacking of courses transferred from ECPs using encapsulated units (packages), compliant with a given packaging specification (e.g. IMS packaging).
- *Runtime Environment*. This sub-system is responsible for supporting the development of new delivery/runtime environments. Services offered include scheduling of learning object delivery (using both the static and dynamic views of a course structure, etc.), Learner tracking, or adaptation of contents to student preferences. It is directly based on the LTSA proposal, where both processes and persistent storage have been included.

In the proposed architecture, ECPs are built from three different subsystems:

- *Course Repository*. It handles the creation, storage and management of learning objects. In comparison with ESP's Course Repository, ECP's includes facilities to support the development of new learning objects, including fine-grain management.
- *Catalogue Management*. This sub-system offers services to support the development of catalogues for the learning objects provided by the ECP, including searching services, both external (to locate courses to be transferred to ESPs) and internal (to locate those learning objects that can be reused to build new content).

- *Packaging Management.* Developers of ECPs use this sub-system to create applications to transfer all the resources related to a course. As for its counterpart in the ESP, specifications for content packaging are used to create packages.

Broker reference architecture elements

Brokers that intermediate between ECPs and ESPs or between ESPs and Learners are developed from basic services offered by four sub-systems:

- *Broker Core.* This is the fundamental sub-system that provides basic services to implement searching, publication and retrieval of educational resources. Services correspond to basic features needed to handle broker catalogues, which include both resource descriptions and descriptions of the services offered on these resources by providers. Metadata specifications are also handled by this element.
- *Profile Management.* Using the services offered by this element, the wrapper is able to customize searches and notifications to the particular characteristics of each user. Profile data models and metadata specifications were considered here, including support for translations from profile records to metadata specifications.
- *Notification Management.* An asynchronous notification facility can be built over the services provided by this sub-system. Subscribers to the notification service would be reported whenever a new learning object that fits their requirements is published through the Broker.
- *Federation Management.* Brokerage capabilities will be clearly improved if intermediation is performed by the collaboration of a group of Brokers. The Federation Management sub-system supports the management of federation topologies and the use of federated searchers whose results may come from different sources (i.e. federated Brokers). Apart from metadata describing learning objects, this element also deals with the use of Quality of Service (QoS) recommendations.

A short overview of the design model

The elements defined in the design model are the design counterparts of the more conceptual elements defined in the analysis model, in the sense that the former are adapted to the implementation environment, whereas the latter (analysis) elements are not. From the reference architecture elements, we derive a set of design service sub-systems (cf. Figure 15.5). Reference architecture sub-systems have been assigned with specific responsibilities. Along design, service sub-systems will materialize these responsibilities in a concrete programming language or, as in our case, interface definition language.

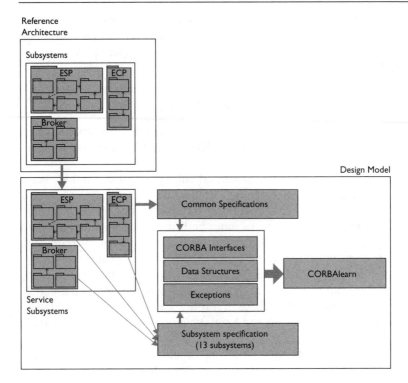

Figure 15.5 From a reference architecture to a specific design model

At this stage, we selected CORBA and the framework provided by the CORBA domain facilities as the implementation environment. Each service sub-system is defined using a separate specification where service interfaces, data structures and exceptions are included. There is also a set of common specifications, horizontal to the whole domain facility. Together, they form the proposal (Anido, 2001) for a new CORBA domain facility for e-learning: CORBAlearn. The whole set of specifications (for the three elements in the reference model) includes 69 service interfaces and a total of 888 method definitions. Let us recall here that, as our aim is to propose a domain facility, we focused on interface definition. Products from different vendors may provide different performances, but their functionality must be the same if they claim to be compliant with the interface.

As an example, Figure 15.6 includes what the method definitions look like. CORBAlearn specifications are composed of UML class diagrams (see Figure 15.7 as an example) to model the static view of the defined interfaces and UML sequence, collaboration and state diagrams as shown in Figure 15.8 to model the dynamics for products compliant with them.

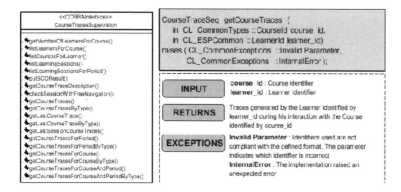

Figure 15.6 CORBAlearn method specification

Summary

While the first level of standardization, which deals with specifications for information models, is mature enough with some *de facto* standards available, the second level, which deals with definition of architectures and software interfaces, is still in its infancy and there is a lot of work to do. In this line, this chapter presents a contribution to the e-learning standardization at the second level, defining a reference architecture and particular interface specifications for the business logic tier of a distributed online education environment.

The reference architecture proposed is conceptual and implementation independent, and may be instantiated for different technological infrastructures. It is composed of a set of reusable sub-systems that provide fundamental services to build final applications. Defined services are the consequence of the strict application of a systematic methodology to obtain service architectures. Components defined can be easily identified by those agents involved in the e-learning standardization process, as they encapsulate different standardized information models in separate sub-systems. This property, together with the separation of functional requirements, makes our architecture oriented to local changes, and able to support the development of new systems in a scalable way.

Concrete software interfaces are defined as a proposal for a new domain CORBA facility for e-learning: CORBAlearn. CORBAlearn includes the definition of data structures to encapsulate outcomes from the first level of standardization, exceptions and service interfaces, which are distributed among 13 different specifications that cover the whole spectrum of functionalities included in full-fledged e-learning environments. Open publication of these interfaces will assure interoperability among products developed by different vendors, provided they are built over CORBAlearn-compliant products. Also, software reuse is promoted as new systems can

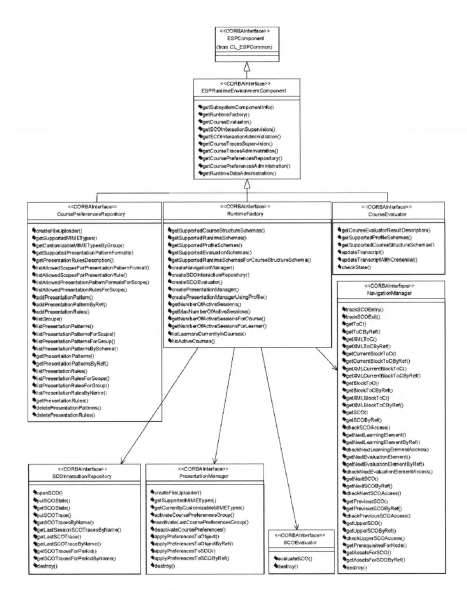

Figure 15.7 Partial view of CORBAlearn runtime environment interfaces

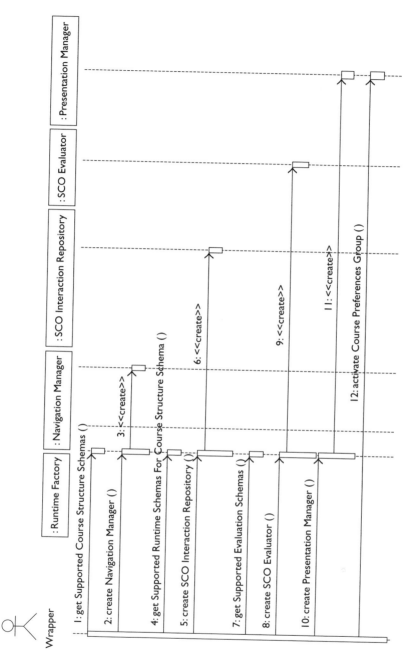

Figure 15.8 Steps to activate objects involved in a learning session

be built over components offering the basic and fundamental services defined by the CORBAlearn specifications.

References

Advanced Distributed Learning (2002) (accessed 26 November 2002) Home page, (Online) http://www.adlnet.org.

Anido, L. (2001) Contribución a la Definición de Arquitecturas Distribuidas para Sistemas de Aprendizaje Basados CORBA, PhD Thesis, Ordenador utilizando, Departamento de Ingeniería Telemática, Universidad de Vigo.

Anido, L. *et al.* (2002) The Unified Modeling Language. Lecture notes in computer science – Applying MDA concepts to develop a domain, *CORBA Facility for E-learning*, **2460**: 321–35.

AICC (2004) (accessed 28 April 2003) Aviation Industry Computer Based Training Committee, (Online) http://www.aicc.org

ARIADNE (2002) (accessed 12 January 2003) Home Page, (Online) http://ariadne.unil.ch.

Aviation Industry Computer Based Training Committee (accessed 23 November 2001) (Online) http://www.aicc.org.

CEN/ISSS (2002) (accessed 17 April 2003) Information Society Standardization System – Learning technologies workshop, (online) http://www.cwnorm.be/isss/workshop/it.

CEN/ISSS/LT (2002) (accessed 23 November 2002) Home Page, (Online) http://www.cenorm.be/isss/Workshop/lt/.

FD Group (2001) (accessed 28 April 2003) GESTALT: Getting Educational Systems Talking Across Leading-Edge Technologies, (Online) http://www.fdgroup.co.uk/gestalt.

GESTALT (accessed 23 November 2001) (Online) http://www.fdgroup.co.uk/gestalt.

IEEE Learning Technologies Standardization Committee (accessed 23 November 2003) (Online) http://ltsc.ieee.org.

IMS Consortium (2002) (accessed 23 November 2002) Home Page, (Online) http://www.imsproject.org.

International Standardization Organization (2001) (accessed 23 November 2002) *Institute Electrotechnical Commission Committee for Learning Technologies (ISO/IEC JTC1 SC36)*, (Online) http://www.jtc1sc36.org.

Learning Systems Architecture Lab (2002) (accessed 27 February 2003) Architecture for user-centric learning management systems, *Carnegie Mellon University* (Online) http://www.lsal.cmu.edu.

Object Management Group (2001) (accessed 23 November 2002) Architecture and specification. Revision 2.5 OMG, *Common Object Request Broker*, (Online) http://www.omg.org/cgi-bin/doc?formal/01-09-34.

Open Knowledge Initiative (2002) (accessed 23 February 2003) Home Page, Massachusetts Institute of Technology, (Online) http://web.mit.edu/oki.

Santos, J. *et al.* (2002) Standardization in TelE-learning. A critical analysis. TelE-LEARNING: The challenge for the third millennium in *17th IFIP World Computer Congress*, Montreal, Canada, 25–30 August.

Chapter 16

Reusable learning objects

Designing metadata management systems supporting interoperable learning object repositories

Demetrios G. Sampson and
Pythagoras Karampiperis

Worldwide, a vast amount of educational content is constantly being produced, in order to support learning and teaching, in a wide range of contexts such as school, academic, training or lifelong learning. The rapid increase in the quantity of available learning objects makes it difficult to search or reuse them by adopting or integrating them into new educational contexts. This problem can be handled efficiently by using learning object metadata. With consistent descriptions of the learning objects characteristics, *searching* becomes more specific and in-depth; *managing* becomes simpler and uniform; and *sharing* becomes more efficient and accurate.

The evolving need for introducing learning object metadata for the description of learning objects has grown to become a requirement when designing and developing metadata management systems. Such systems can be generally identified with the term *Learning Object Metadata Management Systems* (LOMMSs) and can be described as environments that can access, maintain and support learning object repositories in such a way that they provide all the necessary services required for efficient indexing, storing, searching and reuse of the stored metadata information.

Currently, there are many LOMMSs that are designed to collect, share and reuse distributed learning objects, presenting the end-user with a uniform interface to search, access and evaluate the resources, such as the ARIADNE Knowledge Pool System (Duval and Forte, 2001), the CAREO (Campus Alberta Repository of Educational Objects, 2002) <http://www.careo.org>, the US-based Science, Mathematics, Engineering and Technology Education Digital Library <http://www.smete.org>, the Educational Network Australia <http://www.edna.edu.au>, the Gateway to Educational Materials (GEM) digital library <http://www.geminfo.org>, the Scottish electronic Staff Development Library (SeSDL) <www.sesdl.scotcit.ac.uk>, the LearnAlberta Portal <www.learnalberta.ca>, the COLIS <www.edna.edu.au/go/browse/0>, the SMETE <www.smete.org>, the Multimedia Educational Resource for Learning and Online Teaching (MERLOT) <www.merlot.org>, the TeleCampus <http://telecampus.edu>, the Universal Brokerage Platform for Learning Resources <www.educa next.org>, the World Lecture Hall <www.utexas.edu/world/lecture/>, the Globewide Network Academy <www.gnacademy.org>, the McGraw-Hill Learning Network (MHLN) <www.mhln.com> and others.

The main goal when designing a LOMMS is to achieve interoperability between similar systems, so as to be able to reuse the stored and managed information, both at a lower representation level (*physical level*) and at the level of description and organization (*logical level*). The first goal can be achieved using standard interchange technologies such as XML (Extensible Markup Language). The second goal can be achieved by adopting commonly agreed learning technology specifications. Although today a generally accepted international standard for describing educational material exists, namely the IEEE Learning Object Metadata standard (IEEE, 2002), many LOMMSs are still using other metadata models for describing learning objects (ARIADNE, 2003; Dublin Core, 2003; Sutton, 1999), or previous versions of the IEEE LOM standard, e.g. the Campus Alberta Repository of Educational Objects (CAREO) is using the IMS Metadata version 1.2.2.

Furthermore, the internationalization of each specification defined by the CEN/ISSS Learning Technologies Workshop (CEN/ISSS, 2002) as the sum of processes whose purpose is to facilitate search, evaluation, reusability and processing of learning objects within a multicultural and multilingual scenario, leads to the existence of multiple translations of each specification, providing evidence that two systems may not be able to interact, even when they use the same learning object metadata specification.

A possible solution to this problem is to define mapping specifications between different metadata schemas or different translations of a specific one, but this implies extra effort and extra cost. Another less costly approach is to make use of methodologies that are capable of transforming the metadata schemas used for the description of learning objects, mini- mizing human intervention. Several such approaches are currently being applied in other fields (Popa *et al.*, 2002) with impressive results. However, even if simulations results over a wide range of learning objects prove the efficiency of such solutions (Karampiperis *et al.*, 2003), there are few LOM management systems incorporating such techniques.

This chapter discusses issues related to the management of learning object metadata, identifying the design and functional considerations of a Learning Object Metadata Management System, encapsulating modules such as efficient mapping algorithms.

Learning object metadata

Today, the web community has embraced the collection and use of meta- data to characterize and index learning objects. This has the potential to support a semantically more accurate retrieval of information. In general, metadata are information about data. The four aspects of metadata usage are shown in Figure 16.1. The aspect '*search, browse, retrieve*' is driven by the human user's need to answer questions about the usefulness of the retrieved information or the effectiveness of the browsing process. The aspect '*ingest, assure quality, reprocess*', is driven by the need to acquire high-quality information with a precisely defined data dictionary, ensuring the logical integrity of the stored metadata information. The aspect '*application to application transfer*' is driven by the need to transfer, without human intervention, information from one repository to another on different platforms using different metadata schema. The aspect '*store, archive*' is driven by the need for efficient implementation of search and retrieval within an overall goal of total cost minimization, including both infrastructure and human resources.

With the recent approval of the Learning Object Metadata (LOM) specification as a standard by the IEEE, learning object metadata models have achieved a stable common reference that provides implementers and developers with a solid foundation for creating metadata infrastructures to meet the needs of educators and learners. Given the necessarily abstract nature of this standard, the task of adapting it to meet the specific and concrete needs of these stakeholders, requires interpretation, elaboration, extension, and in some cases, the specialization of both the syntax and semantics. Such processes lead to multiple elaborations and/or representations of the same standard, depending on the application (*application profiling*). These

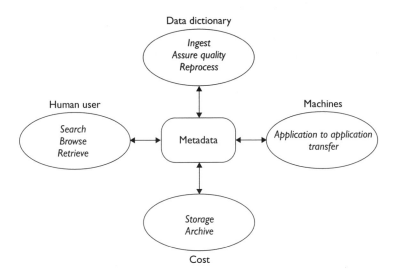

Figure 16.1 Aspects of metadata usage

differences can affect interoperability between learning object repositories, and the reusability of the stored learning objects. Hence, it identifies the need for learning object metadata (LOM) management infrastructures and environment that can support the twin goals of interoperability and reusability with the minimum human interference. The CanCore metadata application profile is one attempt to address this problem (see Chapter 17).

Both from the higher information abstract level, that is knowledge sharing, and from the lower level, that is data sharing, the need identified is to manage and facilitate the ability to share learning objects from one repository to another, with different management engines and without human intervention.

Metadata management systems needs and requirements

Metadata authoring and management tools

The need for creating and managing metadata has led to the development of numerous software tools addressing the needs of metadata authoring and management. These tools can be roughly classified into two major categories:

Generic XML tools

This category includes tools for the creation of XML files. XML is the most commonly used format for metadata of all types and is not restricted to educational uses. These tools usually support a number of functionalities, including the mapping of XML documents to other metadata formats, updating, structural validating, searching and manipulating XML documents, and so on. These tools are not specifically developed for educational purposes, but they can be used for the creation of LOM files, if the user imports the corresponding learning object metadata XML schema. This, however, requires substantial expertise in metadata technologies.

Learning object metadata tools

This category includes tools that have been specifically developed for educational purposes. They usually facilitate (through user-friendly interfaces) the creation of learning object metadata files that are based on a specific learning object metadata model. However, these tools usually do not support the management of metadata files or the validation of both the structure and the semantics. Even if such tools are designed for the management of LOM files, they support only one LOM model, which makes it almost impossible to integrate data from other sources.

Limitations

Metadata tools can provide functionalities for meeting specific requirements; however, some limitations are encountered when applying them in the education field. They are not always oriented to educational needs, or they require the editor to be an expert having prior knowledge of at least XML or educational metadata standards. The educational community has not yet exploited the full potential of learning object metadata, since many learning objects are available on the WWW without metadata description. Furthermore, for those learning objects that are described through LOM files, their description can be based on different metadata models (e.g. IEEE LOM, IMS Metadata, Dublin Core). Even when LOM files are based on the same metadata model, they can still differ if they are developed through different metadata tools, due to the fact that different tools use different XML bindings.

Standardization and conversion

The basic function that underlies systems intercommunication is the exchange of information. The major barrier that prevents system intercommunication, limiting the interoperability between metadata management systems, is the use of different specifications that define the structure of the exchanged information (*standardization diversity*). However, assuming that two systems use the same standardization format, interoperability cannot be ensured if this common format is described in different natural languages (*internationalization problem*). In both cases, there are two possible ways to achieve interoperability between LOM management systems: either the use of a neutral, standardized format or a conversion between varying formats (either different specifications or different translations of the same specification) (Critchlow *et al.*, 1998; Wustner *et al.*, 2002).

Figure 16.2 shows the overall standardization and conversion costs depending on the standardization level. Standardization costs contain all the costs that are necessary to implement a standard (Weitzel *et al.*, 1999), for example software costs, hardware costs and personnel costs. Obviously standardization costs are proportional to the level of standardization. The graph of overall conversion costs is reversed, since with high standardization hardly any conversion is necessary, whereas precise conversions between multitudes of specifications and guidelines cause comparatively high costs.

The overall conversion costs, as schematized in Figure 16.2, are the sum of:

- *Costs for generating the converter*: These accrue through developing the necessary software and through acquiring a thorough knowledge

Costs

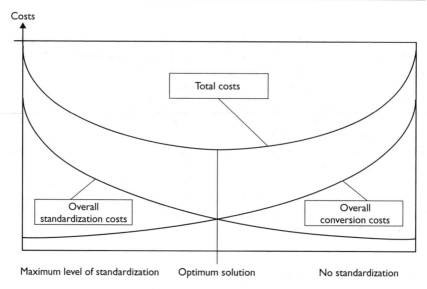

Figure 16.2 Trade-off between standardization costs and conversion costs

of the data that has to be converted. The process of acquiring this kind of knowledge is mentioned by CEN/ISSS, which addresses the problem of internationalization in the case of the IEEE LOM standard.

- *Costs resulting from an insufficient conversion result*: These costs can occur if the conversion instrument is error-prone or information loss could not be avoided. The probability of information loss obviously increases with the heterogeneity of the metadata schemas used. Costs resulting from insufficient results include expenses for manual post-editing of the conversion result.

Apparently there is a trade-off between the overall costs of standardization and overall conversion costs. The optimum solution lies at the point where the sum of standardization and conversion costs is minimal. We make the assumption that the use of mapping algorithms implicates a right-shift of the overall conversion cost, as illustrated in Figure 16.3. This right-shifting is due to the fact that the conversion costs have been reduced, since less need is required for the user to interfere in the conversion process, thus reducing the cost of acquiring knowledge of the data that need to be converted. On the other hand, this right-shifting also implies a further reduction of the needed standardization costs. This does not mean that no standardization is needed, but that fewer efforts are required to support the exchange of information in the context of internationalization.

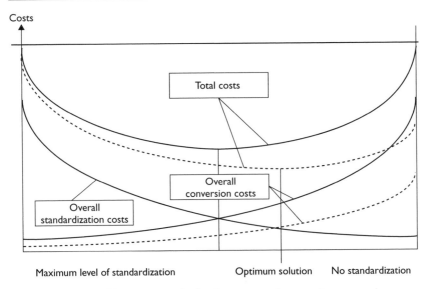

Costs

Total costs

Overall
conversion costs

Overall
standardization costs

Maximum level of standardization   Optimum solution   No standardization

Figure 16.3 Trade-off between standardization costs and conversion costs when a
schema-mapping algorithm is applied

Improving the interoperability between LOMMSs

The basis of many systems that integrate data from multiple sources is a
set of correspondences between source and target schema. Correspondences
express a relationship between sets of source attributes, possibly from
multiple sources, and a set of target attributes. In real-life scenarios it is
very difficult to identify the correspondences since the metadata schemas
are very complex and in most cases the attributes are related with each
other not with a 'one-to-one' relationship. Mapping mechanisms relieves
users of that problem, by suggesting correspondences between source and
target attributes almost automatically (Karampiperis *et al.*, 2003).

These mapping mechanisms can be roughly classified into two major
categories: *attribute-driven*, when the mapping process is based on the
names of the attributes and not on the values that they hold; and *data-
driven*, when the mapping process is based on the similarity of the data
values that the attributes hold.

The data-driven mechanisms have better performance since the corresponding transformation maps can be the result of comparing more than
one example. This property does not exist in attribute-driven mechanisms,
which produce the mapping only by comparing the name of the attributes
between the two given schemas. The two categories of methods have
comparable performance when only one input example is used by a data-
driven mechanism.

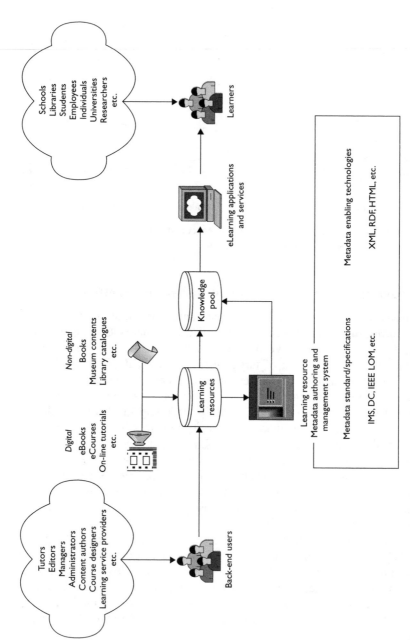

Figure 16.4 Dimensions of a learning object metadata environment

Requirements for learning object metadata (LOM) management

The main requirements for learning object metadata management can be derived from Figure 16.4, where the different actors, technologies, tools, and so on, involved in metadata management are shown (Sampson *et al.*, 2002). As shown in this figure, metadata management towards a collective and harmonized LOM repository requires the support of most common LOM standards/specifications; the creation of new and the modification of existing LOM files; the validation of metadata information; the support of most common metadata technologies, and so on. The design considerations of a LOM management system supporting these requirements are briefly elaborated in Figure 16.5.

Support of most common learning object metadata models

LOM management should support the creation of LOM files based on most common LOM standards/specifications. Moreover, a LOM management system should support the definition of new LOM models in order to support many application profiles over a specific metadata model.

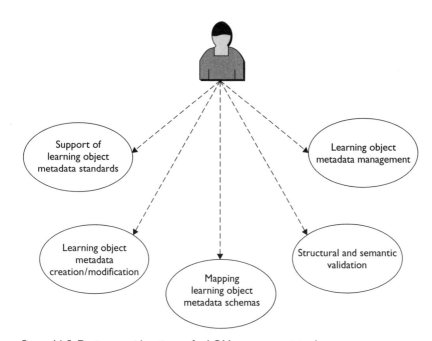

Figure 16.5 Design considerations of a LOM management tool

Creation/modification of learning object metadata files

This is the most basic function in LOM management. The user should have the option to define a new or modify an existing LOM file according to any of the supported LOM standards and/or specifications (e.g. create an IEEE LOM). Moreover, since this function is mainly targeted to educational content authors, who are not necessarily experts in metadata technologies, it should be supported through a user-friendly interface (e.g. through wizards), providing help concerning the information that needs to be inserted into each LOM field.

Mapping of learning object metadata models

The LOM files can be created according to a number of LOM models or different bindings. Therefore, a LOM management system should be able to map LOM files that are based on a specific LOM model or binding to another, in order to create a homogeneous and harmonized metadata repository.

Validation of learning object metadata

One of the main problems with LOM files is that they may contain inaccurate information. Therefore, a LOM management system should facilitate the validation of the information in LOM files, when this is possible. The user should be informed if the entries in the fields are unacceptable (e.g. when text is inserted in fields where a number is expected). In addition, LOM management should facilitate the validation of the structure of LOM files, concerning their conformity with the selected learning object metadata model.

Metadata document management

A LOMMS should provide the functional framework in order to support repository managers in finding, updating, deleting, sorting and grouping any set of LOM files through multiple document selections, multiple editing in LOM files, through a graphical interface that supports user-friendly features such as 'drag & drop'.

In terms of non-functional requirements, the system should meet the following principles (Singh, 2002):

- *Modularity*: The system should consist of several independent modules.
- *Portability*: The system should be able to run in any platform.
- *Extensibility*: The system should be extendable (e.g. metadata specifications should be kept in a metadata schema repository and not be hard coded to allow import of new metadata specifications and allow translation of the interface language to other languages).

LOMMS architectural design

Figure 16.6 presents the architectural diagram of a LOM management system showing the structural components of the system and their inter-connection paths. Interconnection between components is modelled by associations (directed arrows). The direction of each association shows which component initiates communication. These associations can represent direct connections or they can also be used to abstract away details of more complex connection and communication patterns (e.g. indirect communication based on events). Interfaces are shown by the oval interface symbols and by adding dependency arrows between the interfaces and the components using them. The components of this architecture can be grouped into two different layers.

- Interface layer: A layer visible by the users of the LOMMS. It contains all the components of the user interface. These are the XML editor/wizard, the management interface, the publishing interface and the map generator.
- A layer non-visible by the users of the LOMMS. It contains all the repositories involved and the operations that are performed. The repositories involved are the learning object metadata repository, the XML schema repository and the XML transformation maps repository and the operations are validation and mapping.

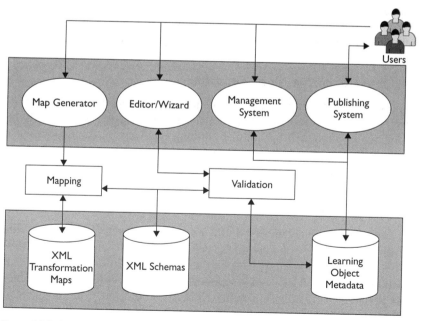

Figure 16.6 Architecture diagram of a LOMMS

Repositories

Every XML metadata file is accompanied by an XML schema. The purpose of an XML schema is to define the legal building blocks of an XML document. It defines the document structure with a list of legal elements and additional information such as the type of the elements. An XML schema file can be declared in the XML document, or as an external reference. To store both the learning objects metadata and the corresponding schemas, a LOMMS has to use three different repositories:

XML schemas repository

This repository is a system directory containing all the XML schema files for the corresponding learning object metadata standards/specifications that the LOMMS supports.

Learning object metadata repository

This repository stores the metadata description of the learning objects. This repository is an XML-based database, whose information structure is inherited from the corresponding XML schema. The best practice is to use internally only one database and transform the metadata structure if desired, through the mapping procedure, to every supported metadata schema, instead of maintaining one database per standard/specification, since then the number of required resources is dramatically increasing each time a new XML schema needs to be imported.

XML Transformation Maps Repository

As previously mentioned, a LOMMS should allow mapping of XML files between learning object metadata models. Transformation maps should be automatically generated by a corresponding mechanism, by associating a number of elements of one metadata schema to a number of elements of another schema.

Validation process

The validation mechanism of a LOM management system should provide two different types of validation: structural validation and semantic validation. Structural validation checks if the XML files conform to the element structure and hierarchy of the associated XML Schema files. On the other hand, semantic validation checks if XML files conform to the associated XML Schema in terms of data types and/or vocabularies defined (see Figure 16.7).

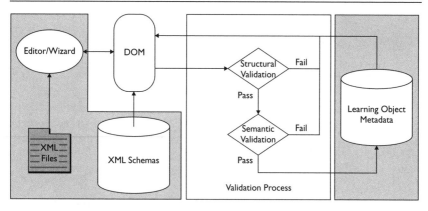

Figure 16.7 Validation process flow chart

Mapping process

Before a user can convert LOM from one metadata schema to another, the relationship between the nodes of the source metadata schema and the nodes of the corresponding destination metadata schema must be defined. A description of this relationship is stored in a special XML document called a transformation file or map. Each transformation file contains two things: the mapping between the nodes of the source schema and the nodes of the destination schema, and a skeletal XML document that represents the structure for the results of the transformation. A transformation is a one-way mapping: from an XML schema or document to another XML schema or document. Once the user has created a transformation file that indicates how to transform an XML document based on a specific schema into another schema, he can create XML documents based on the desired schema for any XML document that conforms to the original schema used in the transformation. In Figure 16.8, the general diagram of the mapping procedure is shown.

Conclusion

It is widely accepted that the use of metadata can improve the efficiency and effectiveness of information retrieval. In addition, it can provide the means for customized retrieval, based on user knowledge and preferences. This chapter outlined a number of reasons that make the use of learning object metadata essential in e-learning environments. It described the main design considerations that should be satisfied to provide an effective LOM management system that offers features such as the creation and modification of LOM files, structural and semantic validation, support of emerging XML technologies and support of any learning object metadata model through the mapping between different metadata schemas.

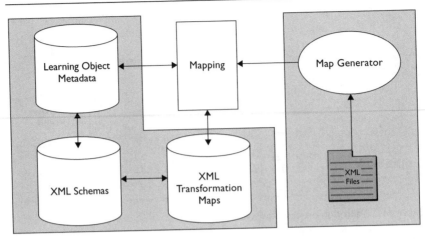

Figure 16.8 Mapping process of educational metadata schemas (a data-driven approach)

References

ARIADNE project (2003) (accessed 5 January 2003) Home Page, (Online) http://ariadne.unil.ch.

CAREO (2002) (accessed 5 January 2003) Campus Alberta Repository of Educational Objects, (Online) http://www.careo.org/.

CEN/ISSS (2002) (accessed 5 January 2003) Information Society Standardization System – Learning technologies workshop, (Online) http://www.cwnorm.be/isss/Workshop/lt/.

Critchlow, T., Ganesh, M. and Musick, R. (1998) (accessed 24 February 2003) Meta-data based mediator generation, in *3rd IFCIS Conference on Cooperative Information Systems*, January 2003, (Online) http://citeseer.nj.nec.com/critchlow98 metadata.html.

Dublin Core (2003) (accessed 10 January 2003) Dublin Core Metadata for Resource Discovery, (Online) http://www.ietf.org/rfc/rfc2413.txt.

Duval, E. and Forte, E. (2001) The Ariadne knowledge pool system, *Communications of the ACM*, **44** (5).

IEEE (2002) (accessed 16 March 2003) Draft standard for Learning Object Metadata (LOM), Learning Technology Standards Committee (LTSC), (Online) http://ltsc.ieee.org/doc/wg12/LOM_WD6_4.pdf.

Karampiperis, P., Kastradas, K. and Sampson, D. (2003) A schema-mapping algorithm for educational metadata interoperability, in *15th World Conference on Educational Multimedia, Hypermedia and Telecommunications ED-MEDIA*, Honolulu, Hawaii.

Popa, L. *et al.* (2002) (accessed 3 December 2003) Mapping XML and relational schemas with CLIO, Almaden Research Center, (Online) http://www.almaden.ibm.com/cs/clio/papers/icde02demo.pdf.

Sampson, D., Papaioannou, V. and Karadimitriou, P. (2002) EM2: An environment for editing and management of educational metadata, *Educational Technology & Society*, **5** (4).

Singh, H. (2000) (accessed 2 May 2003) Achieving interoperability in e-learning, *Learning Circuits*, (Online) www.learningcircuits.org/mar2000/singh.html.

Sutton, S. (1999) Conceptual design and deployment of a metadata framework for educational resources on the Internet, *Journal of the American Society for Information Science*, **50** (13): 1182–92.

Weitzel, W. *et al.* (1999) (accessed 3 December 2003) The standardization problem in networks – A general framework, Institute of Information Systems, J. W. Goethe University, (Online) http://www.wiwi.uni-frankfurt.de/%7Ewestarp/publ/frame/frame.pdf.

Wustner, E., Hotzel, T. and Buxmann, P. (2002) (accessed 3 December 2003) Converting business documents: A classification of problems and solutions using XML/XSLT, Freiburg University of Technology, (Online) http://www.wiwi.tu-freiberg.de/wi/publications/rp/converting_business_documents.pdf.

Part 4

Learning Object Profiles, Applications and Models

This section introduces metadata application profiles, as well as some applications and models used for the implementation and distribution of LOs. The CanCore profile is becoming widely accepted internationally. The two peer-to-peer applications POOL and EduTella illustrate a selection of tools that can be used for accessing and distributing LOs, while Explor@2 is presented as an example of a Learning Content Management System (LCMS).

In Chapter 17 Friesen, Hesemeier and Roberts describe the CanCore metadata application profile. They explain that CanCore seeks to simplify, interpret and refine the IEEE LOM standard to aid implementers. CanCore identifies a subset of the many elements in the LOM and provides recommendations for the semantics and syntax of all of the LOM elements.

The authors describe Learning Object Metadata generally, and CanCore's role as an application profile for this metadata standard specifically. They then explain the understandings and rationale informing CanCore's Guidelines document, concluding by addressing a number of common misconceptions regarding the implementation of the Learning Object Metadata standard

In Chapter 18, Richards, Hatala and McGreal introduce the Portal for Online Objects in Learning (POOL) project. POOL was a consortium project of the TeleLearning NCE to build a LO repository scalable to the national level. The authors describe two focal technologies: a distributed architecture for a network of LO repositories titled 'POOL, POND and SPLASH', and 'SPLASH', a peer-to-peer desktop repository application. They elaborate on the evolution in the technology that can be expected as user communities form, protocols emerge for the functional linking of these structures, and the underlying technology becomes less visible.

In Chapter 19 Nilsson introduce Naeve and Palmér the Edutella project. They consider the pedagogical consequences of the design of the technical frameworks to be essential. Edutella, they claim, is part of an e-learning infrastructure with a decentralized vision that encourages sharing among small-scale content repositories and where anyone can participate in the exchange and annotation of e-learning resources.

They point out that Edutella is a Peer-to-Peer (P2P) network for exchanging information about learning objects and not for exchanging content. It is built with semantic web technology applying the latest P2P research. They discuss the technologies that make Edutella possible, explaining the vision and importance of the project, and how applications can use it.

In Chapter 20 Paquette, Lundgren-Cayrol, Miara and Guérette introduce the Explor@2 third-generation LCMS system, providing an overview of its management functions. Its application of the IMS-CanCore metadata referencing for learning objects is described along with the bilingual meta-tagging interface. The resource aggregation environment is also shown along with the extensions presently being built for the eduSource project.

The authors present Explor@2 as a suite of tools that among other things serves to cover the identification–referencing–search–use cycle in LO repositories. Explor@2 can be used to identify LOs on the Internet or on a Local Area Network and publish or reference them in a standardized metadata repository. Services to access, structure, annotate and search such a repository are described along with three types of editors used to combine LOs into a larger LO, to integrate them in an actor's environment, and to build instructional structures or scenarios integrating activities, roles and LOs. The Explor@2 system, the authors explain, is not just a distance learning platform or even an integrated, generic software or an authoring system. Rather, it is a specialized operating system or Learning Content Management System (LCMS).

Kestner's chapter rounds out this section with a proposal to use the MERLOT learning object repository as a model for creating a professional evaluation system that will promote the scholarship of teaching among university professors. This model can be developed from evaluation systems already put in place by the MERLOT participants. He comments on the generation of promotion guidelines that will properly document and give credit for non-paper (usually electronic) materials in the typical university tenure package.

Chapter 17

CanCore

Guidelines for learning object metadata

Norm Friesen, Susan Hesemeier and Anthony Roberts

The IEEE LOM (Institute of Electrical and Electronics Engineers (1990) Learning Object Metadata) standard is both complex and general in character, containing a broad range of elements, and leaving open many possibilities for interpretation. CanCore seeks to simplify, interpret and refine this standard to aid implementers. CanCore began this task by identifying a subset of the many elements in the LOM – selecting them on the basis of their simplicity and their utility for resource discovery and sharing. CanCore's Guidelines for Learning Object Metadata provide recommendations for the semantics and syntax of all of the LOM elements. These recommendations and refinements are based on best practices in classification and metadata communities.

This chapter begins by describing Learning Object Metadata generally, and CanCore's role as an application profile for this metadata standard specifically. It then explains the understandings and rationale informing CanCore's Guidelines document, and concludes by addressing a number of common misconceptions regarding the implementation of the Learning Object Metadata standard.

Metadata definition

Metadata, or data about data, act similarly to cards or records in a library catalogue, providing controlled and structured descriptions for resources through searchable 'access points' such as title, author, date, location, description and subject. And like a typical library catalogue record, a metadata record can be located separately from the resource it describes, or packaged or embedded with that resource.

CanCore explains and interprets a particular metadata standard developed specifically for the description of learning objects (Institute of Electrical and Electronics Engineers) or reusable digital educational resources. This metadata standard, officially known as 'IEEE 1484.12.1 – 2002', is functionally equivalent to the IMS metadata specification, or IMS 'Learning Resource Meta-Data'. CanCore's Guidelines document considers implementation issues on a level of detail that is much greater than the normative information provided in the LOM, but in no cases does CanCore seek to diverge from the general, normative framework provided by the LOM.

The LOM standard is comprised of a multiplicity of parts: a data model, which defines the metadata elements and their general characteristics; and a number of bindings, which indicate how these elements are to be encoded in XML and other formats.

CanCore history

The CanCore initiative was established in November 2000 to address common concerns regarding information management and resource discovery within a number of Canadian public and private sector e-learning projects. These include the Broadband Enabled Lifelong Learning Environment (BELLE) and Portal for Online Objects in Learning (POOL) projects, sponsored by CANARIE (Canadian Network for Advanced Research for Industry and Education) and Industry Canada, a department of the Canadian federal government. These projects also include CAREO (Campus Alberta Repository of Educational Objects), the LearnAlberta.ca Portal and TeleCampus, sponsored by provincial educational ministries. All of these projects, together with TeleEducation NB and the Electronic Text Centre at the University of New Brunswick, were the founding partners in CanCore. Their key concern in forming CanCore was to synthesize efforts with respect to metadata creation and sharing. This collaboration is continuing with the pan-Canadian eduSource project <http://www.edusource.ca> (see also Richards and Hatala, Chapter 24).

Before and during the development of this guidelines document, the CanCore team had:

- devised a workable subset of the IEEE Learning Object Meta-data Information Model, known as the CanCore Element Set <http://www.cancore.ca/elementset.html>;
- become a participant in the IMS Global Learning Consortium, Inc. through the sponsorship of Industry Canada;
- become a participant in the IEEE LTSC (Institute of Electrical and Electronics Engineers, Inc. Learning Technology Standards Committee) through the sponsorship of Athabasca University;
- become a part of the Canadian Delegation to the International Standards Organization (ISO) International Electrotechnical Commission Joint Technical Committee 1 (ISO/IEC JTC1/SC36, the committee that is reviewing the possibility of making the LOM an ISO standard);
- developed informal ties with the Dublin Core Metadata Initiative; and
- co-chaired the IEEE LTSC study group on digital rights expression languages, co-writing the IEEE White Paper, 'Towards a Digital Rights

Expression Language Standard for Learning Technology' <http://xml.
coverpages.org/DREL-DraftREL.pdf>.

CanCore's approach to metadata

CanCore's understanding of metadata is directly informed by conventional
and emerging practices and techniques in library and information sciences.
CanCore believes that much can be gained by incorporating the practices
and solutions developed by librarians, cataloguers, and indexers that
address long-standing information management problems.

One metadata standard (other than the LOM itself) that has been especially significant for CanCore is the Dublin Core Metadata Element Set
(DCMES). This element set 'was created to provide a core set of elements
that could be shared across disciplines or within any type of organization
needing to organize and classify information' (DCMI, 2002). The CanCore
guidelines make significant reference to normative statements, recommendations and documents issued by DCMI (Dublin Core Metadata
Initiative) and members of the Dublin Core community in general.

CanCore's element subset was defined in keeping with Dublin Core's
minimalist approach. According to this approach, minimizing the variety
and complexity of metadata elements is seen as ultimately benefiting metadata creation and implementation, and as assisting in resource discovery.
CanCore sees this as applying to LOM metadata as well, and understands
a law of diminishing returns as governing metadata use and creation. Like
any other data management processes, the creation of metadata requires
an investment of resources. However, the relationship between investment
in metadata creation and the resulting level of resource discoverability is
not linear. The more elements from a metadata set that are implemented,
the greater the investment of resources that is required, and the greater
the chances for error and divergence between record creators and implementations. CanCore's work proceeds from the assumption that a few
well-chosen and well-implemented metadata elements will enhance
resource discovery in a cost-effective manner. However, for those wishing
to implement the full LOM the CanCore minimalist set is being expanded
to include all of the LOM fields.

CanCore as an application profile

In choosing a subset of elements from the Learning Object Metadata standard, and in explicating the meaning of all of the LOM elements, CanCore
is developing a 'Metadata Application Profile'. In a document written
jointly by representatives of the Learning Object Metadata and Dublin
Core communities, an application profile is defined as 'an assemblage of

metadata elements selected from one or more metadata schemas and combined in a compound schema' (Duval *et al.*, 2002). In the case of CanCore, these elements have been chosen from only one metadata schema.

However, CanCore has done much more than select elements. CanCore provides a great deal of fine-grained information about each element in the LOM (information that takes the form of recommendations, examples and references to other interpretations). In this sense, CanCore represents an application profile that is perhaps more accurately captured by the commonly accepted definition provided by Clifford Lynch: 'customizations of [a] standard to meet the needs of particular communities of implementers with common applications requirements' (Lynch, 1997). However, CanCore and its guidelines emphasize refinement and explication rather than customization or modification; CanCore has intentionally developed its application profile to meet the needs of a broad range of communities.

The CanCore element subset, as well as its best practice guidelines, has been created through close consultation with a wide and varied community of educational participants involved in a variety of public projects and organizations. These have included both Anglophone and Francophone universities, school-level organizations, and public sector entities.

This predominantly public sector participation does not imply that many of the indexing and data management best practices incorporated into the CanCore Guidelines are not relevant to other sectors and applications. Nor does it mean that the subset of elements identified by CanCore might not also be useful for business and training applications of Learning Object Metadata. In fact, the 'Metadata Principles and Practicalities' paper cited earlier argues that precisely such profiling and decision-making need to be undertaken by those involved in implementation and application generally (Duval *et al.*, 2002). While users in these and other sectors might decide to depart from some of CanCore's recommendations and choices, their decisions would benefit by referencing the rationale and interpretations explicated and disseminated in the CanCore Guidelines (see Friesen, Mason and Ward, 2002).

Semantic interoperability

Another way of understanding CanCore's approach to metadata is to consider it from the perspective of interoperability. For metadata to be shared and used, both within and between communities of practice, at least two aspects of interoperability need to be supported:

1. The syntax and the protocols used to encode and transmit metadata records have to be specified in an unambiguous and consistent manner across systems.

2. Within the semantic context of the metadata record itself, ambiguity needs to be minimized, and common ways of using and describing learning resources need to be established and formalized.

Much work has been done in the area of syntactic and protocol inter-operability. Prominent examples of this include IMS work in developing and maintaining bindings for Learning Object Metadata (IMS, 2001), and the Metadata Harvesting Protocol of the Open Archives Initiative <http://www.openarchives.org/documents/FAQ.html>. Less has been done to develop a consensus and refine understandings regarding LOM semantics. There are precise ways of specifying the XML tags that make up a LOM record, but few precise ways of specifying the values that should go in between many of these tags.

Because semantic interoperability relies on human languages, which are by their very nature ambiguous, inexact and incomplete, such interoperability can be achieved only by degrees. The way it is achieved, moreover, is quite different from the ways in which syntactic and protocol interoperability are attained. Common understandings of terms and meanings must be negotiated and made explicit within communities of practice. The CanCore Guidelines document is the product of an initial process of consultation and explication in the public education community of practice within Canada. This process is ongoing as the guidelines and documents, and the interpretations they contain, are updated and validated both inside and outside Canada. These guidelines also provide a basis for the further development of this consultation. It is only by establishing shared meanings where possible (and by acknowledging the limits of common semantic ground where consensus is not possible) that semantic interoperability can be optimized.

Besides serving as a guide for implementation and decision-making, the CanCore guidelines can serve as a straw-man for teasing out differences and ambiguities in understanding, definition and use between different communities and user/implementer groups (Friesen, 2002).

Guidelines document

The CanCore Guidelines have developed through two phases: in the first phase, a draft was produced in June 2002 based on the IMS version 1.2.1 Learning Resource Meta-data specification. In the second phase, this draft was updated to reflect the version of Learning Object Metadata that has been approved as a standard by the IEEE (note that the IMS specification will be revised and made identical with the IEEE standard).

The guidelines provided in this document include for each element and element group:

• explication and interpretation of element definitions and descriptions;
• recommendations based on best practice;

- recommendations for vocabulary (or 'value space') values and definitions;
- multilingual plain language examples;
- XML-binding examples; and
- technical implementation notes.

CanCore users

The intended audience for the CanCore Guidelines is diverse. System administrators, metadata managers and individual indexers will all benefit by making use of the guidelines.

Scenarios in which these guidelines would be put to effective use, each derived from real-life implementation and support requests, appear as follows:

1. A group of French language or immersion schools are developing a LO collection for internal use. As a part of this process, they are surveying standards-based tools and the support available. They are particularly interested in integrating a complex hierarchical set of learning outcomes set by their department of education, and want to ensure that these learning outcomes are appropriately accommodated in the LOM. General documentation available on the CanCore website can assist them in their survey of tools and other supports. The CanCore Guidelines provide them with recommendations and guidelines for creating standards-based educational metadata for their collection. These guidelines also provide specific recommendations and examples derived from work in other jurisdictions related to the integration of hierarchically ordered learning objectives into the 'Classification' element group in the LOM.

2. An existing, national database wishes to align itself with e-learning standards. However, in doing so, those responsible for its maintenance are wondering about the data normalization, element title and vocabulary translation and other crosswalking issues that may be involved but are not addressed in detail by standards documents. The CanCore Guidelines provide these implementers with interpretations of element titles and meanings, and with detailed definitions of vocabulary terms used in the LOM. These guidelines also provide recommendations regarding the formatting and other characteristics of element values. In this way, reference to CanCore is able to maximize the potential for the creation of interoperable metadata through the crosswalking process.

3. A private firm with existing e-learning systems and content wishes to become compliant with SCORM (Sharable Content Object Reference Model). The technical management at the firm has acquired a SCORM

test suite, but is looking to provide in-depth support for the creation and maintenance of metadata. Because the CanCore Guidelines provide recommendations for all of the metadata elements defined as mandatory for SCORM content, CanCore Guidelines provide substantial assistance in this. The firm decides to develop and integrate a well-documented, semi-automated interface for metadata creation with their company's systems. The firm is able to adapt CanCore's descriptions of the purpose and application of various metadata elements for use in its documentation, and refers to CanCore's recommendations to provide appropriate defaults and data-checking features for the interface.

The need for CanCore best practice guidelines

An indispensable part of standards implementation, the CanCore Guidelines are generic and can be effectively utilized by a wide variety of different educational communities. Similar or complementary guidelines have been created for other communities implementing different metadata specifications. Examples include:

*   the Dublin Core Usage Guide titled 'Using Dublin Core;' <http://www. dublincore.org/documents/usageguide/>;
*   the 'CIMI Guide to best practice: Dublin Core' <http://www.cimi. org/public_docs/meta_bestprac_v1_1_210400.pdf>; and
*   the 'Online Archive of California Best Practice Guidelines' <http:// www.cdlib.org/about/publications/oacbpg2001-08-23.pdf>.

In all of these documents, an explication of the data model at hand is followed by descriptions, interpretations and examples provided on an element-by-element basis.

The complexity of the LOM, as well as its widespread adoption among educational institutions, underscores the need for similar guidelines in the e-learning community. The apparent lack of a publicly available, normative interpretation and explication of LOM elements represented a conspicuous gap that the CanCore Guidelines were designed to address.

Interoperable metadata creation vs. exchange

The way that the normative import of the CanCore element subset is understood should be dependent on the context to which it is being applied. This subset is used in clearly different ways in the context of record creation versus the context of metadata record storage and sharing.

In the context of creating or populating metadata records, the CanCore element subset does not represent a set of 'mandatory' or 'required' elements, which must be filled out or supplied for each metadata record created. Any number of elements can be provided or omitted in the meta-data creation process (this last recommendation may change as a body of best practices related specifically to CanCore and the LOM develops). At the same time, the CanCore element subset has not been developed with the intention of limiting the kinds or number of elements that can be used in the metadata creation process. Indexers or implementers are certainly welcome to include elements outside of the CanCore subset when creating metadata records. These elements could be other LOM elements, exten-sions to the LOM element set, or from other metadata specifications or requirements. The CanCore element subset has been developed to simplify LOM implementation, with each element being selected on the basis of its utility for resource discovery and sharing.

For metadata storage and sharing, the CanCore subset is not intended as an acceptable minimal element set for systems that support the storage and sharing of metadata. These systems should be able to process, store and share all of the elements in the LOM, not just the elements identi-fied in the CanCore subset. This will help to ensure that systems supporting CanCore will be able to interoperate with systems that support the LOM in general. Data elements not included in the CanCore subset will not be lost when LOM records are transmitted from one system to another. To maintain this type of interoperability, and to ensure that all the LOM data elements are included in implementations, CanCore has deliberately not made available any binding document or schema that just incorporates those elements in the CanCore subset.

Common metadata misconceptions

Perhaps because of its novelty, and the changing communities and tech-nologies to which it is applied, metadata in general and Learning Object Metadata in particular have been subject to a number of misconceptions. These misconceptions are addressed by focusing on tools developed for metadata record creation, and on a number of areas that are 'out of scope' for the LOM standard.

Relation of guidelines to creation tools

CanCore sees the development of tools to support the creation of high-quality learning object metadata as indispensable to the successful imple-mentation of the LOM standard. However, the creation of such tools must be focused not on the needs of LOM users as a single homogenous group. Instead, these tools must be developed in such a way that they directly address (or can be adapted to address) the requirements of particular user groups and local implementations. This need arises from the complexity, flexibility and specialization of many LOM structures, and associated encodings. An example of a metadata creation tool that addresses the needs of a particular project and set of users is provided by CUBER (personalised CUrriculum BuildER in the federated virtual university of the Europe of Regions; see <http://www.cuber.net/Test-Prototyp/ai/guide_start.jsp>). Examples of tools that present the complexity, flexibility and specialization of the LOM structures and encodings directly to end-users are numerous (see <http://www.cancore.org/lomsurvey.html> for examples of these).

As a result of this need for adaptation and simplification, these guidelines are themselves not intended as a generic set of rules and recommendations for end-users generally. They are instead intended to inform the development of metadata creation and management tools, and to serve as the basis for documents and supports that would be used in their implementation.

Automated metadata creation

New technologies are even now being developed or implemented that may change the way metadata are created in practice. For example, artificial intelligence technologies may be able to populate a number of the fields of a LOM record. Additionally, semi-automated metadata components already integrated into content creation tools may also be able to supply values for certain LOM elements (for example, it may be possible to derive some LOM elements from 'document properties' information that is already automatically generated by some popular word processing programs).

However, these types of solutions for the present are either not readily available in educational communities, or are not designed or used specifically for the purposes of LOM record creation. This guidelines document seeks to address present needs and requirements of public institutions, projects and educators. Consequently, the understanding of metadata that informs it is one that emphasizes human agency and interpretation, and existing classification practices, rather than mechanisms of automation or calculation. Others involved in metadata have advocated a similar understanding or approach (Milstead and Feldman, 1999).

Should the creation of LOM records eventually be automated or otherwise greatly simplified, it is hoped that CanCore's Guidelines might be useful in the application of such automation or simplification procedures. These guidelines might also facilitate the evaluation of the semantics and syntax that such tools might generate.

Metadata is not to be directly exposed to end-users

Of the concerns that are out of scope for Learning Object Metadata, perhaps the most important is that many of its terms and structures are not to be directly exposed to end-users. These terms and structures include metadata element titles, the hierarchical structure in which they are embedded, and the encoding required for a number of element values. Tools for creating Learning Object Metadata often seem to suggest that presenting users with an expandable, hierarchical listing of LOM element titles with text boxes and other form elements is acceptable in practice. However, a brief consideration of one or two LOM elements reveals this to be unadvisable – except for the most highly trained end-users. To enter something as simple as an author or creator of a learning object, while referring only to the terms and structures associated with the LOM, requires the following:

1. Recognizing 'Lifecycle.Contribute.Entity' as the correct element for this information.
2. Ensuring that Author is the most appropriate value for element 'Lifecycle.Contribute.Role' from a list that includes values such as script writer, subject matter expert, and publisher – none of which are unambiguously defined or differentiated from 'Author'.
3. Entering specialized vCard markup required for this element. This may involve:
   1) locating an existing vCard record;
   2) using a separate vCard creation tool (whose output would then have to be coordinated with the LOM tool); or
   3) entering vCard markup and values manually.
   In the latter two cases, the user would be required to decide which of the dozens of vCard elements are appropriate for the record.

CanCore is not for version or rights management

Learning Object Metadata does not provide a means for the management or enforcement of digital rights associated with a learning object or for version tracking and control. Although Learning Object Metadata does provide elements that address some of these concerns very generally, these elements do not do so in a way that is sufficient for the requirements of many projects. This is most conspicuous in the case of rights management, for which Learning Object Metadata provides only four elements, none of which provides the possibility of inserting a machine-readable linkage to a rights management service or expression document. The emerging vision for managing these types of information is one involving distributed, specialized, modular metadata records and lookup services.

CanCore is not a content model

Learning Object Metadata does not encapsulate or otherwise imply a specific model for learning object content. It does not provide a detailed account, for example, of the way that this content is aggregated (into lessons, units, courses, etc.) or of the particular ways that learners can interact with this content. As in the case of rights management, Learning Object Metadata provides elements that address such concerns on a very general level. However, these elements do not address these issues on the level of specificity that is available through other specifications and forms of expression. (Examples of content models that provide this level of detail include Educational Modelling Language and IMS's Learning Design specification).

Conclusion

Careful and coordinated implementation of the LOM standard is the linch-pin of many of the visions of discoverable, accessible and reusable educational objects. The CanCore Guidelines present an important contribution to what can sometimes be a difficult implementation and interpretation process. If the recommendations provided by the CanCore Guidelines are used to inform this work generally, the potential for interoperability between implementations will be greatly increased.

References

DCMI (2002) (accessed 12 March 2003) DCMI Frequently Asked Questions (FAQ), *Web Page*, (Online) http://www.dublincore.org/resources/faq.

Duval, E. *et al.* (2002) (accessed 18 April 2003) Metadata principles and practicalities, *D-Lib Magazine*, **8** (4), (Online) http://www.dlib.org/dlib/april02/weibel/04weibel.html.

Friesen, N. (2002) (accessed 12 May 2003) Semantic interoperability and communities of practice, in *Global Summit of Online Learning Networks*, ed. J. Mason, Adelaide, pp. 104–07, (Online) http://www.educationau.edu.au/globalsummit/papers/nfriesen.htm.

Friesen, N., Mason, J. and Ward, N. (2002) (accessed 23 February 2003) Building educational metadata application profiles, in *Dublin Core and Metadata for e-Communities: Supporting Diversity and Convergence*, 13–17 October, Florence, (Online) http://www.bncf.net/dc2002/program/ft/paper7.pdf.

IMS (2001) (accessed 12 March 2003) IMS learning resource meta-data XML binding specification, (Online) http://www.imsglobal.org/metadata/imsmdv1p2p1/imsmd_bindv1p2p1.html.

Institute of Electrical and Electronics Engineers (1990) *IEEE Standard computer glossaries: A compilation of IEEE standard computer glossaries*, New York.

Lynch, C. A. (1997) (accessed 12 March 2003) The Z39.50 information retrieval standard. Part I: A strategic view of its past, present and future, *D-Lib Magazine*, (Online) http://www.dlib.org/dlib/april97/04lynch.html.

Milstead, J. and Feldman, S. (1999) (accessed 11 March 2003) Metadata: Cataloging by any other name, (Online) http://www.onlinemag.net/OL1999/milstead1.html.

Chapter 18

POOL, POND and SPLASH

Portals for online objects for learning

*Griff Richards, Marek Hatala and
Rory McGreal*

Digital repositories are built on database technology, but seek to go beyond simple warehousing to provide mechanisms to encourage the discovery, exchange and reuse of learning objects (LOs). This chapter describes the evolution of POOL (Portal for Online Objects in Learning), a consortium project of the TeleLearning Research Network National Centre of Excellence, and chronicles the lessons learned in our efforts to build a LO repository scalable to the national level. Funded in part by the CANARIE Learning Program, POOL has contributed to the development of two enabling technologies: 'POOL, POND and SPLASH', a distributed architecture for a peer-to-peer network of variously sized LO repositories.

Learning objects: The building blocks of e-learning

The promise of digital LOs lies in reusability. If constructed appropriately, warehoused wisely and catalogued accurately, then a LO might find usage beyond its original audience and instructional context. Given the relatively high cost of developing good LOs, the promise of reusability receives considerable attention from administrators and publishers trying to amortize the cost of production and maximize the potential return for each of these digital investments. Reuse and wider use may also bring greater recognition for the author.

For educators, the promise of reusability goes beyond the economic argument to encompass notions of quality (Bowden and Marton, 1998) and the reuse of exemplary teaching strategies in other contexts. CAREO <www.careo.org> and MERLOT <www.merlot.org> are web portals founded partly on the premise that academic peer review of LOs can improve their quality and enhance the quality of online education. LOs are posted not just to advertise their availability, but also so others can observe the way they are crafted to suit the needs of the learners, see how they can be adapted to new instructional settings, or how the instructional strategies might serve as models for other content areas.

Early references to LOs often oversimplified the notion of their being the 'building blocks' of e-learning to be combined in many creative ways to suit the needs of the learners. While this attractive analogy implies that standardization is the key to interoperability, like real building blocks, we can expect LOs to come in many shapes and sizes. For reasons of functionality, sophistication and competitive marketing, LOs will probably not all be compatible and interlocking. Fortunately, learners, like children, will be oblivious to this fact and will integrate them into their learning experiences and use them in ways unimagined by the original designers and creators.

Learning object repositories: More than digital storehouses for learning objects

Repositories may be simply viewed as places to put digital objects. A central repository would be one that aggregates a collection of objects for a defined community or organization and stores them in a single locality. As objects can vary in number, size and file type, it is unlikely that a single central repository would be able to collect or even physically hold and effectively serve all of the available LOs in any given field (Hamilton, 2001). As with libraries, organizations or communities may have something about everything or everything about something, but having everything about everything is unlikely. Thus, a decentralized or 'distributed' model that links a variety of LO repositories is a likely scenario, where the actual storage of objects is scattered around a number of places that are linked with Internet technology.

Using the common web browser approach, the physical distribution of the objects need not be apparent to the user because in an ideal setting they would interface with the collection through a single access point or *portal*. If a number of different organizations are involved, inevitably there will be some technical differences in the computer systems employed. However, a portal serves as a consistent access point to find online information. Thus, the key to a successful LO repository strategy lies in its ability to promote the sharing of information and exchange of records, and in its ability to facilitate access to the objects themselves.

Repositories might hold collections of LOs as a book warehouse might store books, or they could hold collections of information about LOs as a library catalogue might hold descriptions about books. The catalogue descriptions are referred to as the 'metadata' – data about the data contained in the elements. Continuing the analogy, just as a book's dust jacket contains metadata about the book, its title, and its intended audience, this 'information about the information' can become part of a LO's metadata.

Some repositories may specialize in the type of information they carry, for example the Australian AVIRE repository (Shannon, Roberts and

Woodbury, 2001) contains only architectural objects, and the metadata are specialized to describe the needs of the architectural community. TeleCampus <http://telecampus.edu> houses only metadata linking to full courses or lessons. CAREO has a more open approach and welcomes information about LOs in a wide range of content areas. MERLOT holds descriptions of LOs, peer reviews, lesson plans or assignments, and in a growing number of cases, marketing information about availability, price and conditions of sale. Any given repository may offer a wide variety of services based upon the service it seeks to give its supporting user community.

Because not all repositories store the actual object files, a key function of repositories is to identify the storage location of the objects, and provide an indexing system that enables the efficient search and discovery of the objects. The way in which repositories accomplish the first is a function of their architecture; the latter is a function of their catalogue information or 'metadata'.

The architecture of POOL, POND and SPLASH

'POOL, POND and SPLASH' evolved as a catch-phrase to explain a distributed architecture that could flexibly meet the needs of many groups. Designed to support the individual instructor or learner, SPLASH is conceived of as a small single-user repository that would be made freely available for download from the Internet. SPLASH combines a database program and a peer-to-peer search engine with a CanCore metatagging interface. Built on Sun Microsystems JXTA platform <www.jxta.org>, each SPLASH site holds those objects of immediate importance to the owner, and has the ability to search other SPLASH peers and exchange LOs or metadata with other members of the network.

SPLASH development is partly driven by the notion that the most important place to hold a LO is close to the developer and close to the user. SPLASH enables instructors, developers and learners to become consumers of, and contributors to, a network of LO repositories. SPLASH enables individuals to collect and manage LOs, perhaps creating portfolios of their personal learning experiences to reduce the transience of the e-learning experience. At the community level the main success of SPLASH may simply be its proliferation of desktop tools that encourage and assist the learning community to metatag their objects and create a large virtual pool of otherwise undiscoverable LOs. Subsequent testing of SPLASH led to the replacement of JXTA with a smaller, custom peering application more capable of crossing firewalls.

Communities and organizations are a reality of the world of education and training. Ministries of Education, universities, school boards, schools and employers are typical of organizations that will have an interest in providing their constituents with access to specific collections of LOs. (They may also have interest in denying access to other 'unauthorized' LOs.) These organizations will also have special needs to govern the access, workflow and life-cycle management of their LOs. They may have access to financial and technical resources that will support them in building specialized and robust databases such as the initial POOL prototype developed by IBM Canada, or the CAREO repository developed in the Province of Alberta. While serving the defined needs of their communities, these sites also have the potential to become 'PONDs' in our network architecture – community sites that primarily serve the interests of their clients, but through their interoperability with the POOL network provide those outside of the community with access to POND resources.

Finally, a third level of aggregation, POOL Central, was devised to replicate search requests in topological regions of the repository network, and overcome the horizon effects that arise in decentralized peer-to-peer networks such as Gnutella. The designation of a number of 'super nodes' could facilitate a faster and more exhaustive search of all of the member repositories via a high-speed and high-bandwidth connection to the CA*Net 3 optical highway. The network architecture can be visualized in Figure 18.1.

The significance of POOL, POND and SPLASH is that it defines not so much a repository structure, as a method of linking repositories. Any repository of any size can be cross-searched simply by adding on the

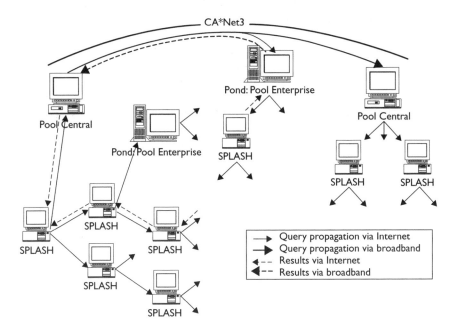

Figure 18.1 POOL network architecture

SPLASH search mechanism as long as it adheres to the IEEE LOM standard or the SCORM metadata protocol. Of course it must also open its database to the network.

Real-world trials of the POOL applications and CanCore (see Friesen *et al.*, Chapter 17) are being conducted using the TeleCampus <http://tele campus.edu> and other online repositories. The TeleCampus houses metadata with links to more than 55,000 online programmes, courses, modules, or lessons (McGreal, 2002). It is being adapted as a specialized node of POOL to gather LO metadata from SPLASH sites. As such, it is presently implementing CanCore into its LOM compatible database structure.

The evolution of learning repositories

Although conceptually elegant, POOL, POND and SPLASH are just entering their test phase. To be declared a success, POOL must use this infrastructure to unite a community of users with useful content. Much like the fire triangle of fuel, heat and oxygen, the absence of any one element will extinguish the flame. We know there are users and they have content, but only through a program of iterative evaluation and simplification of the tool set can we lower the learning curve to the point where everyone can join the pool.

A significant hurdle lies in the current complexity of metatagging. Indeed, explicit metatagging has recently been described as an overly complex activity (Doctorow, 2001). A number of methods for simplifying the schemas and automating the tasks with visual interfaces are under examination (Bray, 2001). Developers of metadata application profiles – the specification of metadata fields and proscribed vocabulary for a particular collection of LOs – are caught between the horns of a dilemma as they try to determine the degree of effort that should be allocated to global issues of discovery versus local issues of detailed descriptions such as AVIRE's *fenestration*. This ongoing battle will continue as each community of practice defines itself through its shared vocabulary, ethics and practices.

SPLASH and POOL are designed with flexibility to accommodate these needs; however, they are conceived of as generic tools. It may be necessary to develop multi-level strategies for managing LOs – perhaps a global search that returns not only probable hits, but identifies the specialized node and the native metadata schema necessary for a thorough localized search. It may be necessary for SPLASH to flexibly accommodate a number of interchangeable metadata schemas while keeping this complexity hidden from the user (Hatala and Richards, 2002). Natural language is also a barrier, but POOL is collaborating with another CANARIE project, SavoirNet (Paquette, 2002) to develop French language versions of the interface and the CanCore application profile.

Security is an issue that will require much attention in a network of LO repositories. Security impacts on the willingness of content creators to see their wares exchanged on the network. POOL does not have an inherent rights management system, but it could work with a third-party system where encrypted files can be located and distributed in POOL with the distribution of decryption keys handled by a secure broker using whatever business model it feels is appropriate.

Persistence and integrity are two other issues of great interest to the repository community. Persistence implies that the object will actually be retrievable upon demand, and while this is often used by proponents of centralized servers to criticize peer-to-peer systems, the reality is that every instructional delivery system must grapple with this issue, and short of local caching of the file, there is no foolproof way to guarantee persistence on any networked system. Indeed, centralized services are prone to failure when demands for service exceed capacity, while peer-to-peer systems actually increase their capacity to serve data each time a new copy is made of a file.

A final concern of the authors is that while LO repositories may provide a better means of discovering and distributing LOs, repositories do not in themselves address issues of pedagogy. To those educators who pose the question of quality assurance for LO repositories, our response is to look to the communities of use for self-regulation of these issues. For example, SPLASH provides user-defined specifications to enable restriction of searches to particular lists of nodes. Thus a self-defining community need only maintain its own list of adherents to their community norms, and advertise those norms just as it might post its metadata schema and defined vocabulary.

Nesbit, Belfer and Vargo (2002) have proposed a LO Rating Instrument (LORI) to enable the creation of consumer reviews (see also Nesbit and Belfer, Chapter 11). A test implementation of this strategy is now being developed for SPLASH. User reviews not only add value for all members of the community, but as they also encourage the metatagging of content by the consumer, they increase the number of objects that are tagged in the network. Nesbit *et al.* (2002) also see the process of collaborative community review of LOs as a mechanism for professional development for educators and a way of establishing and sharing design heuristics and benchmarks that will enhance the overall quality of the LOs. In a similar vein, Kestner (see Kestner, Chapter 21) recommends the use of peer reviews of LOs for tenure and promotion evaluations in universities.

These issues are only the tip of the iceberg when it comes to LO repositories. As we move forward and the user community and content base expand, we hope to have created in POOL and SPLASH a sufficiently flexible base and an open-enough mindset that these and other issues yet to come may be easily addressed. Indeed, one deliverable of the POOL project has been an examination of the community governance structure to ensure the long life and usefulness of the tools developed.

Conclusion

POOL is but one of many international efforts to create LO repositories. Others, such as MERLOT and CAREO, have been created to meet specific community efforts, and there is a growing abundance of LCMS (Learning Content Management Systems) in the commercial e-learning market (Washburn, 1999).

CANARIE, which has sponsored POOL and other repository initiatives through its Learning Program, also recognizes the need for convergence of effort, and is supporting a new pan-Canadian project called eduSource (see Chapter 24), which regroups the various Canadian repository projects into a single effort seeding a national strategy for the advancement of LO repositories (MacLeod, 2001).

Canada is not alone in these efforts to build repository tools. The UK, Australia, Singapore, Spain, Sweden, Greece and Holland, among others, are also moving rapidly in repository research and development. Indeed, the POOL team is in ongoing correspondence with a European group building Edutella <http://edutella.jxta.org/> – a peer-to-peer model that is being built using the same JXTA platform as SPLASH (see Nilsson, Chapter 19). We would hope to see convergence of these international efforts so that a universal repository model can emerge.

LO repositories are the libraries of the e-learning era. They will be the fundamental first step in knowledge discovery and object exchange. They will provide the foundation for future learning and commerce in the knowledge market. They will fuel e-learning as the stock exchanges fuelled the industrial era. This is why they are of priority interest.

Note

This chapter is based on work presented at the IS2002, Informing Science + IT Education Conference, June 2002, Cork, Ireland. It is published with the permission of the IS2002 organization (IS2002, 2003).

References

Bowden, J. and Marton, F. (1998) *The university of learning: Beyond quality and competence in higher education*, Kogan Page, London.

Bray, T. (2001) (accessed 10 December 2002) Antarcti.ca visual interface for navigating through metadata, (Online) www.antarcti.ca.

Doctorow, C. (2001) (accessed 7 April 2003) Metacrap: Putting the torch to seven straw-men of the meta-utopia, (Online) http://www.well.com/~doctorow/metacrap. htm.

Hamilton, C. (2001) (accessed 24 March 2003) Software combinations for learning object repositories, in *Canarie E-Learning Workshop*, 3 October, Toronto, Ontario, (Online) http://www.canarie.ca/funding/learning/workshop_2000/meeting/Hamilton.ppt.

Hatala, M. and Richards, G. (2002) Global vs. community metadata standards: Empowering users for knowledge exchange, in *International Semantic Web Conference 2002*, eds I. Horrocks and J. Hendler, pp. 292–306, Springer, LNCS 2342.

IS2002 (2003) *IS2002, Informing Science + IT Education Conference, June, 2002*, eds E. Cohen and E. Boyd, Cork, Ireland.

McGreal, R. (2002) Téléapprentissage et mondialisation de l'enseignement, *Éducation*, **42** (1): 8–11.

MacLeod, D. (2001) *eduSource report*, CANARIE Learning Program Senior Steering Committee, Canadian Repository Action Group, Ottawa.

Nesbit, J. C., Belfer, K. and Vargo, J. (2002) A convergent participation model for evaluation of learning objects, *Canadian Journal of Learning and Technology*, **28** (3): 105–20.

Paquette, G. (2002) (accessed 4 June 2003) The Explor@-II system for learning resource management, in *Second Canadian National E-Learning Workshop*, 25–26 February, Montreal, (Online) www.canarie.ca/funding/learning/workshop_2002/presentations/paquette_explora.ppt.

Shannon, S. J., Roberts, I. W. and Woodbury, R. F. (2001) vGallery: Scaffolding reflection-in-action for students and teachers, in 18th Conf. of the Australasian Society for Computers in Learning in Tertiary Education, 9–12 December.

Washburn, C. (1999) Evaluating integrated course management products, *NAWeb 99*, Fredericton, NB.

Chapter 19

The Edutella P2P network

Supporting democratic e-learning and communities of practice

Mikael Nilsson, Ambjörn Naeve and Matthias Palmér

The infrastructures we use for developing, finding and combining learning objects influence the usage of the material – inflexible frameworks will not support flexible learning. For this reason, it is essential to consider the pedagogical consequences of the design of the technical frameworks that are used in e-learning systems. Much of the current work in e-learning technology targets learning objects stored in LMS (Learning Management System) applications and/or in other centralized servers, often of very large scale. Even though standards such as IEEE LOM increase the interoperability of such systems, they are still mostly information islands. Cross-searching of repositories is not a reality. It has even been said that the Web is still in the 'hunter-gatherer phase' with respect to searching. This is certainly true for learning objects. We have not yet reached the goal of a global e-learning society. In addition, many institutions are reluctant to give up control over their learning resources. This is problematic for many central-server-based methods of learning resource sharing, (e.g. e-learning 'portals'). Such portals are costly and difficult to maintain.

Edutella takes a different approach. It is one piece in an e-learning infrastructure with a decentralized vision. By encouraging sharing among small-scale content repositories, anyone can participate in the exchange and annotation of e-learning resources. By allowing anyone to participate, the learners are given more control over their learning process, leading us one step closer to the dream of a learner-centric educational architecture.

Edutella is a peer-to-peer (P2P) network for exchanging information about learning objects (and not for exchanging content). It is built with semantic web technology applying the latest P2P research. This chapter will discuss the technologies that make Edutella possible, explaining the vision and importance of the project, and how applications can use it.

The Edutella project is being developed by a number of institutions – among others, the Learning Lab Lower Saxony (2003); the KMR Group (2002) at KTH; the Uppsala Database Laboratory (2003); Stanford Infolab, (2003); and the UNIVERSAL project (2003) – and it is still expanding. The latest developments can be found at <http://edutella.jxta.org>.

Edutella technology

By using a distributed technology, Edutella enables institutions and individuals to actively participate in a global information network, without losing control over their learning resources. Edutella connects highly heterogeneous peers (heterogeneous in uptime, performance, storage size, functionality, number of users, etc.). The goal of the Edutella project is to make the distributed nature of Edutella services (e.g. repository search) completely transparent to Edutella clients.

The first building block of Edutella is an open-source peer-to-peer technology called JXTA Organization (2002) initiated by Sun Microsystems. JXTA is a generic P2P protocol, designed to be used in many diverse kinds of P2P applications, focused on interoperability, platform independence and ubiquity.

The second building block of Edutella is Resource Description Framework (RDF, 2003), which is a framework for representing information in the Web. It has been developed by the World Wide Web Consortium (W3C). The RDF specifications provide a highly sophisticated, lightweight framework for exchanging ontology-based knowledge, containing facilities for combining resource descriptions using different vocabularies and from different sources. It will be seen shortly how the decentralized nature of the RDF metadata descriptions plays a central role in the Edutella platform.

Figure 19.1 shows the kinds of queries Edutella manages, constructed in the Conzilla concept browser. In Figure 19.1, X represents the resource that is searched for. The arcs are properties of that resource. In plain English, the Edutella query asks for (counter-clockwise) scientific works on the subject of politics, having Lebanon as subject or keyword, with a title (Y), written in English, German or French, created or contributed to by a Person (Z), employed at a University, and created after 1980.

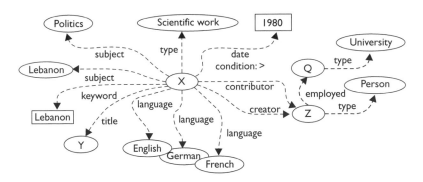

Figure 19.1 Edutella query in Conzilla

(There are several occurrences of 'or' in this transcription. However, this information is not explicit in the figure, but is represented separately. See <http://www.conzilla.org>.)

Edutella takes queries of the above complexity, distributes them to peers capable of answering the query, collects the answers and returns them to the originator. It is possible that parts of the answers are located on different peers. In the example, the university employee information is perhaps not located on the same server as the resource metadata. Edutella will be able to handle these kinds of situations transparently.

Edutella deals with metadata about content, not with content itself. Access to educational content is not always as simple as downloading a file – it might include logging in to a web service, or starting a certain application with specific parameters. As Edutella uses RDF, each resource must have a URI (Uniform Resource Identifier). The route from that URI to the resource itself is not determined by Edutella. It may be an HTTP URL, so that your Edutella-aware application can point your browser in the right direction. Or it might just be a URN (Uniform Resource Name), uniquely naming the resource but not locating it, and you must go through some sort of lookup service to find it.

Nodes in an Edutella network

Edutella adds a search service to the JXTA platform, so that any node, or peer, that carries metadata about some resources, can announce an Edutella search service to the network. When looking for information on Edutella, your question will be routed to peers that can answer your query, and they will return matching results to you.

There are actually three types of roles to fill in an Edutella network: provider (provides a query service), consumer (asks questions) and hub (manages query routing in the network). An Edutella network will contain many types of peers which may combine several of the roles.

Hubs are typically set up to increase performance in the network. Most providers will not need to care about hubs at all, as they operate transparently in the Edutella network. Examples of providers, exposing data to the Edutella network, could be:

- a traditional LMS system at an educational institution;
- a modern RDF-based repository such as UNIVERSAL, OLR or SCAM;
- a metadata harvester that collects information from legacy archives, such as OAI archives or Z39.50 sources; and
- a mediator database such as AMOS, that searches a number of databases in combination, while only exposing one query service to Edutella; or
- any other kind of database containing learning object metadata.

Many other kinds of metadata providers can be imagined. To be a provider, all that is required is that you are able to answer questions formulated in the Edutella query language. Any kind of information source can be given an Edutella interface. Examples of consumers that use Edutella to find information could be:

- the 'search' tool in a LMS system that uses Edutella to get answers;
- a generic self-contained search tool, such as Conzilla, or a domain-specific search tool such as the SWEBOK example application;
- an end-user applications that uses Edutella to enhance the user experience with metadata information (such as 'related material');
- an augmented-reality system that displays and uses metadata for objects in three-dimensional space (real or virtual);
- a web portal that includes an Edutella search interface;
- a mobile device (PDA, cell phone, etc.) that gathers information from Edutella to enhance your stay in Rome;
- a smart software agent that gathers relevant information from Edutella to help construct a learning environment; and
- a crawler or push-based system such as CourseWare Watchdog, that uses Edutella as an additional information source.

It should be evident from this list that Edutella support can be added to many kinds of software. And as Edutella supports any kind of metadata expressed in RDF, all kinds of information can be distributed, and not only the pure learning object metadata.

The vision behind Edutella

Edutella is driven by a vision of a global Democratic Information Network – democratic in the sense that anyone is allowed to say anything about anything. This kind of vision is not new. The Internet has been designed as a peer-to-peer network where anyone can connect to anyone, and that is one of the main reasons for its success. In the same way, the success of the WWW through leveraging hypertext is fundamentally dependent on a peer-to-peer model, where anything may link to anything. This creates a global democratic Web, where there is no single point of control, no middle man in control of the network.

However, the Web has developed into a predominantly client-server-based system, which mainly relies on centralized information handling, something that is at odds with basic Internet technology. This trend is even more evident in the case of e-learning systems, where large-scale databases of learning objects are becoming the standard. Peer-to-peer networks can be a way out of that trap. Edutella makes it possible for anyone, even with very limited technical and financial resources, to participate in the exchange and annotation of learning resources.

For Edutella, this vision means that anyone must be able to attach any metadata to any learning object. What makes this such an important feature? We will now look into the design goals of Edutella that enable a different kind of e-learning infrastructure.

Design goal 1: Subjectivity in metadata

Many metadata-aware systems contain only indisputable information such as title, author, identifier, and so on (most Dublin Core elements are of this kind). Learning objects also need many other kinds of metadata, such as an indication of the granularity of objects, pedagogical purpose, assessments and learning objectives. However, many implementers are skeptical about using such metadata.

One of the reasons for this skepticism is the fact that properties of that kind do not represent factual data about a resource, but rather represent interpretations of a resource. When metadata are treated as authoritative information about a resource, adding descriptions of subjective features becomes not only counter-productive, since it excludes alternative interpretations, but may also be dishonest or authoritarian, forcing a subjective interpretation on the user. This creates unnecessary conflicts of interest and is unfortunately hindering the adoption of metadata technologies.

Edutella takes the position that this problem is partly due to lack of technological support for a different model. When metadata descriptions are instead properly annotated with their source, creating metadata is no longer a question of finding the authoritative description of a resource. Multiple, even conflicting, descriptions can co-exist. This amounts to a realization that metadata descriptions are just as subjective as any verbal description. We must allow people and institutions to express different views on learning objects.

It is a fact of life that consensus on these matters will likely never be reached, and the technology must support diversity in opinion, not hinder it. Meta-metadata (information about metadata) and subjective metadata are thus of fundamental importance for a metadata architecture. In a democratic network, 'objectivity' is defined by consensus, not by authority. Metadata needs to be a part of that consensus-building process.

Naturally, the problem of supporting this fundamental subjectivity is not trivial. By designing Edutella on top of the Semantic Web framework, the built-in support in RDF for meta-metadata will make this task surmountable. Imagine, as a simple example, adding a link called 'Who said this?' to each search result. Another possibility is to add functionality to search using only trusted sources. This example emphasizes the need for networks of trust and digital signatures of metadata, in order to ensure the sources of both metadata and meta-metadata. Supporting webs of trust will be a fundamental part of the Semantic Web infrastructure, and thus of Edutella.

Design goal 2: A metadata ecosystem

Implementing metadata as authoritative, objective information about a resource, consisting of facts that do not change, also has the effect of efficiently hindering context-dependent metadata. How do you describe a resource if you don't know what its intended use is? For example, a single piece of media such as a photograph can have different meaning when used in a History context from when it is used in a Photography context. These contexts may very well not be known when the resource is published, and new uses of resources may arise long after publication. So the choice is to fix a context at the outset, or not describe any context-specific information at all.

Many resources that are useful in learning (such as the material in libraries) are not even designed to be learning objects. Forcing the creator to annotate them using learning object metadata descriptions is unreasonable and often unrealistic.

In Edutella, metadata can be handled as a distributed work in progress, where updating and modifying descriptions is a natural part of the metadata publishing process. There is no central repository where your metadata changes need to be pushed – all metadata are stored at the provider, and there can be several providers supplying information around a single resource.

Treating metadata as work in progress and allowing subjective metadata leads to a new view of metadata. Metadata is information that evolves, constantly subject to updates and modifications. Competition between descriptions is encouraged, and thanks to RDF, different kinds and layers of context-specific metadata can always be added by others when the need arises. Any piece of RDF metadata forms part of the global network of information, where anyone has the capability of adding metadata to any resource. Edutella then handles combining resource metadata using different vocabularies and coming from different sources.

In this scenario, metadata for one resource need not be contained in a single RDF document. Translations might be administered separately, and different categories of metadata might be separated. Additional information might be contributed by others.

Consensus-building then becomes a natural part of metadata management, and metadata can form part of an ongoing didactic discourse. The result is a global metadata ecosystem, a place where metadata can flourish and cross-fertilize, where it can evolve and be reused in new and unanticipated contexts, and where everyone is allowed to participate. In this way, Edutella provides support for a bottom-up conceptual calibration process, which builds consensus within communities of practice.

Design goal 3: Extensible syntax and semantics

In developing and applying metadata standards for learning objects, important considerations include interoperability and extensibility. Interoperability in this context means that different systems are able to exchange information about learning objects without requiring complex translation tools, while extensibility means that they are able to incorporate other metadata elements and vocabularies than those explicitly specified in the standard. Both issues are very important for Edutella, as interoperability enables cross-searching of repositories, and advanced extensibility is needed to support domain- and application-specific additions to the metadata.

Edutella uses RDF for metadata expressions in order to be maximally compatible with these two principles. It makes interoperability simple, as RDF provides a single framework for expressing any kind of metadata, while leaving the flexibility for defining a custom vocabulary. RDF also includes powerful facilities for extensions. These extensions come in two kinds:

1. Structural extensions. This includes adding completely new metadata elements to resources. This is built into RDF itself, and can be done in the same metadata document ('model' in RDF terms) or in a separate one.
2. Semantic extensions. This includes refining existing elements and vocabulary terms, the way 'abstract' refines 'description' in Dublin Core, or the way 'Digital Text' is a kind of 'Text' in the case of a learning resource type. Expressing this in RDF is done in the RDF Vocabulary Description Language (also known as RDF Schema).

The need for extensions will explode with the number of domain- and application-specific standards that are developed. Most deployments will have a need for extensions of many kinds, both domain-specific and application-specific. The problems with mixing metadata vocabularies can therefore be expected to increase. However, current metadata standards in wide use in the e-learning domain, notably XML versions of Dublin Core and IEEE LOM, do not support a common model for extensions.

Edutella avoids many parts of this problem by relying on the built-in mechanisms of RDF and RDF Schema. Supporting mix-and-match vocabularies and supporting semantic extensions are design goals at the very core of Edutella.

The vocabularies most frequently used (separately and in combination) within Edutella, at the time of writing are:

*   Simple Dublin Core;
*   Dublin Core Qualifiers;
*   Vcard;
*   IEEE LOM;
*   IMS Content Packaging;

as well as a number of locally developed taxonomies, vocabularies, refinements and element sets.

Using Edutella

Some of what Edutella wants to accomplish has now been shown, along with the technologies that are used to implement the Edutella visions. It remains to understand how Edutella is supposed to be used, and how it can support practical work in e-learning. The following scenario highlights some of the possibilities. While it is not realistic in every detail, it is hoped that it will demonstrate the different ways in which Edutella-enhanced tools can enrich the learning experience. The readers are also encouraged to add their own visions to this picture – Edutella is an infrastructure on top of which many kinds of functionality can be added.

A story about an Edutella user

You are studying Taylor expansions in mathematics. Your teacher has not provided the relevant links to the concept in your concept browser, Conzilla, so you first enter 'Taylor expansions' in the search form. The result list shows that Taylor expansions occurs in several contexts of mathematics, and you decide to have a look at Taylor expansions in an approximation context, which seems most appropriate for your current studies.

After having studied the background material on the different kinds of approximations for a few hours, you decide that you want to see if there are any appropriate learning resources. Simply listing the associated resources turns out to return too many, so you quickly enter a query for 'mathematical resources in Swedish that are related to Taylor expansions, and are on the university level and part of a course in calculus at a Swedish university'. Finding too many resources again, you add the requirement that an older student at your university must have given a good review of the resource. You find some interesting animations provided as part of a similar course at a different university, which has been annotated in the portfolio of a student at your university, and start out with a great animation of three-dimensional Taylor expansions. The animation program notes that you have a red-green colour blindness and adjusts the animation according to a specification of the colour properties of the movie, which was found together with the other descriptions of the movie.

After a while you are getting curious. What, more precisely, are the mechanisms underlying these curves and surfaces? You decide you need to more interactively manipulate the expansions. So you take your animation, and drag it to your graphing calculator program, which retrieves the relevant semantic context from Conzilla via the application framework, and goes into Edutella looking for mathematical descriptions of the animation. The university, it turns out, never provided the MathML formulas describing the animations, but the program finds formulas describing a related Taylor expansion at an MIT OCW course site. So it retrieves the formulas, opens an interactive manipulation window, and lets you experiment.

Your questions concerning Taylor expansions multiply, and you feel the need for some deeper answers that the computer cannot give you. Asking Edutella for knowledge sources at your own university that have declared interest in helping out with advanced calculus matters, you find a fellow student and a few maths teachers. Deciding that you want some input from the student before talking to the teachers, you send her some questions and order your calendaring agent to make an appointment with one of the teachers in a few days.

A week later you feel confident enough to change the learning objective status for Taylor expansions in your portfolio from 'active, questions pending' to 'on hold, but not fully explored'. You add your exploration sequence, the conceptual overviews you produced in discussion with the student, and some annotations, to the public area of your portfolio. You conclude by registering yourself as a resource on the level 'beginner' with a scope restricting the visibility to students at your university only. This way, your knowledge is made available both as annotations to Edutella, and as a real-life contact.

This scenario is not a complete fantasy. Tools to enable this kind of learning experience via Edutella are being designed right now, and research is underway to make them even better. Some of the important features of Edutella can be seen being used in this scenario:

- distributed material and distributed searches; mixtures of metadata schemes (for example, personal information and content descriptions) being searched in combination;
- machine-understandable semantics of metadata (calendaring information, animation parameters, finding the right kind of resources):
  - human-understandable semantics of metadata (contexts, persons, classifications);
  - tool interoperability – any tool can use the technology;
  - distributed annotation of any resource by anyone, using digital portfolios;
  - personalization of tools, queries and interfaces, affecting the experience in several ways; and
- competency declarations and discovery for personal contacts.

Conclusion

Learning, just as other human activities, cannot and will not be confined within rigidly defined boundaries such as course systems. There is a strong need for more decentralized structures. Moreover, a learning environment has to support trust-building and rich forms of communication between teachers and learners as well as between learners. In order to be powerful, the environment must be inspiring and trigger curiosity for the learning task. Semantic Web technologies form a basis for realizing a multitude of fascinating e-learning visions, by giving software access to the semantics of your material. Edutella is a way to support the introduction of such technologies in e-learning systems.

Although much of the present development within e-learning is driven by the so-called knowledge economy, there are more fundamentally important issues for the future, namely, how to provide access to knowledge for people who cannot afford to pay. The Edutella project is driven by the overall vision of a global knowledge community, where relevant information and efficient support for the knowledge construction process is freely available for all. For more information, see the website of the KMR group at <http://kmr.nada.kth.se>.

References

AIFB Home Page (2003) (accessed 23 January 2003) University of Karlsruhe, (Online) http://www.aifb.uni-karlsruhe.de.

JXTA Organization (2002) (accessed 7 May 2003) JXTA Home Page, (Online) http://www.jxta.org.

KMR (2002) (accessed 23 April 2003) Knowledge Management Research group, (Online) http://kmr.nada.kth.se.

Learning Lab Lower Saxony (2003) (accessed 7 May 2003) Home Page, (Online) http://www.learninglab.de/.

RDF (2003) (accessed 7 May 2003) Resource Description Framework Information, (Online) http://www.w3.org/RDF.

Stanford Infolab (2003) (accessed 21 May 2003) InfoLab Home Page, (Online) http://www-db.stanford.edu.

UNIVERSAL project (2003) (accessed 7 May 2003) Home Page, (Online) http://nm.wu-wien.ac.at/research.

Uppsala Database Laboratory (2003) (accessed 7 May 2003) Home Page, (Online) http://www.dis.uu.se/~udbl.

Chapter 20

The Explor@2 Learning Object Manager

*Gilbert Paquette, Karin Lundgren-Cayrol,
Alexis Miara and Louis Guérette*

Explor@2 is the result of a long process that started a decade ago at Télé-université's research centre LICEF. The initial research efforts (Paquette, 1995) focused on a Virtual Learning Center (VLC) model, architecture and prototypes. To build the VLC model, object-oriented modelling techniques were applied, for example Jacobson's use cases methodology (Jacobson, 1993) and object models (Rumbaugh *et al.*, 1991). These were used to identify sets of actions that different actors would do while interacting within a virtual campus. Five theoretical actors were identified within a VLC: the learner, the trainer, the content expert (informer), designer, and manager. Sixty-three roles were defined for the various actors.

Right from the beginning the ambition was to build a distance learning operating system capable of supporting a variety of roles within a variety of delivery models, such as the ones presented in Table 20.1 adapted from Paquette (2002). From 1995 to 1999, we have conducted ambitious research and development efforts, supported by the Quebec Information Highway Fund and the Telelearning Network of Centers of Excellence (TL-NCE), leading to the implementation of the VLC architecture using web-based technology. In 1999, the Explor@1 implementation of our VLC model was achieved and distance learning courses were developed and delivered via Explor@1, mainly at Télé-université, but also in pilot applications at Hydro-Quebec and in professional corporations.

The Explor@1 system had a set of features that were innovative at that time and still are, when compared with many commercial platforms:

- In divergence from the general authoring system paradigm, Explor@1 focused, from the beginning, on a resource management orientation, making it possible to assemble a set of teaching support tools and learning objects (LOs) to be shared across all the organization's programmes, courses or activities.
- The system had more flexibility beyond the now traditional learner–trainer–manager trio and even our initial five-actor VLC model,

Table 20.1 Some of the actors' roles in five typical delivery models

	Learner	Content expert/Informer	Trainer	Manager	Designer
High-tech distributed classroom	Getting presentations, doing exercise	Teacher presenting information	Teacher giving assistance	Teacher preparing environment	Teacher designing plan and materials
Web/MM self-training	Navigating through MM	Sites and MM content materials	Help components, FAQs	Manager organizing events and support	Team designing websites or MM
Online training	Interacting in a forum, getting information	Teacher referring to learning material	Animating forums	Manager organizing events and support	Teacher designing activities
Community of practice	Exchanging expertise and know-how	The learners and some documents	Group animator	Manager organizing events and support	Designing process-based scenarios
Performance support	Solving situated real-life problems	Organization's data, documents	Intelligent help	Manager supervises systems learners	Designing process-based scenarios

enabling the combination of any set of actors. Each course could also be designed following different models using a variety of proprietary or third-party tools made available not only to learners but also to course designers and other learning facilitators, such as instructors, content experts (informers), training programme administrators, and so on.

- The Explor@1 system was also designed to support the integration of existing web courses without changing their format, thus enabling an organization to transform its training methods progressively.

- Finally, the open structure of the system made it possible to significantly reduce design time, speeding up implementation and periodic updates by the design team. Overall environment maintenance also became much easier. Once the first course was implemented, each additional course integrated into Explor@ could be limited to a few web pages along with hyperlinks to existing documents (most of the LOs being already available for integration).

From 1999 to the Autumn of 2002, we conducted a third major effort within Technologies Cogigraph, a spin-off from Téléuniversité's research centre, to improve the Explor@1 system. The Explor@2 system was developed and two implementations were performed, one at Télé-université, and the other at Canal Savoir, which was building its SavoirNet delivery infrastructure and services to the universities in Quebec. Canal Savoir (Knowledge Channel) is a non-profit organization that operates an educational television station in Quebec and French Canada, together with a set of educational web-based services. It groups most of the universities and some colleges in Quebec.

Figure 20.1 presents a high-level view of the core architecture of the Explora@2 system. Explor@2 deals with four types of objects: actors (or roles), LOs (or resources), knowledge and competency (or content), and structures of operations (or functions). Actors operate functions composed of operations (or activities) where LOs are used or produced. Knowledge and competencies describe the information owned or processed by actors, processed in operations or contained in LOs. Four corresponding managers store and retrieve information in a database, construct information structures and display information to users.

In the rest of the chapter, we will concentrate on the resource manager, which is used to build aggregated LOs, the actor's environment or the operational structures. Figure 20.2 presents the main components of the Explor@2 resource manager and their relationships. The two upper components, *LO Aggregator* and *LO Launcher*, operate on the LOs themselves

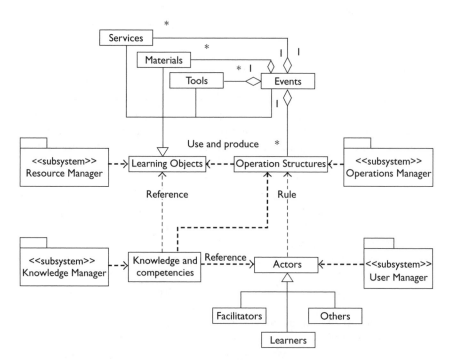

Figure 20.1 High-level architecture of the Explor@2 System

found in one or more repositories, located on servers somewhere on the Web. We will discuss these components later in this chapter.

The six other components all relate to a central metadata repository, a set of files in a relational/XML database, that describe a LO Model. There is only one LO Model for each LO or resource in the metadata repository.

A central component is the *Metadata Editor*. The Metadata Editor provides forms to describe all the IEEE/IMS/Cancore metadata for any LO that has a LO Model entry, and stores the metadata file in the Explor@2 permanent relational/XML database.

The five other components are specific user services of a metadata repository. They will be described later in the chapter.

*   *The Metadata Repository Builder* helps find the location of interesting LOs on the Web or on a Local Area Network and creates a LOM entry for each LO or resource. Sometimes, to make a LO more widely available, this component will transport the LO on some predefined server location.

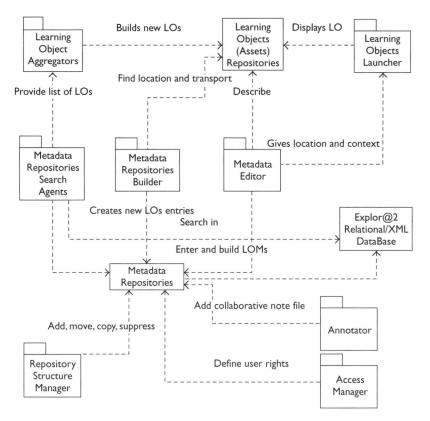

Figure 20.2 Main components of the Explor@2 learning object manager

- *The Repository Structure Manager* selects a folder or grouping where a LOM record will be found. It can move a Metadata record from one folder to the other, copy an alias in another folder, suppress a record or a folder, and duplicate a record to speed up the metatagging of a similar LO.

- *The Repository Search Agents* apply user-defined constraints involving Metadata attributes to find and display a set of the corresponding metadata records. Presently, Explor@2 provides only one such agent, but others are being planned.

- *The Access Manager* helps define a user's profile, access rights to folders, metadata files, and LOs described by the metadata file. Rights include viewing, adding, modifying, deleting and assigning rights to other users.

- *The Collaborative Annotator* manages a local user group forum where users can exchange messages about a LO. It is integrated into the LO repository. These messages are also stored in the Explor@2 database.

Metadata referencing

The increased need for the reuse of LOs and the interoperability of e-learning systems have led to a vast movement towards international standards for LOs. Duval and Robson (2001) presented a review of the evolution of standards and specifications starting with the Dublin Core metadata initiative in 1995. The IEEE Learning Technologies Standardization Committee (IEEE LTSC, 2002a), and its joint work with organizations including ARIADNE and IMS, has finally produced, in June 2002, a metadata standard for Learning Object Metadata (IEEE LTSC, 2002b).

At the beginning of 2002, while developing the Explor@2 system, we joined the group developing the Canadian Core Learning Object Metadata Application Profile (CanCore). CanCore is explained in Chapter 17. Table 20.2 shows which CanCore/IEEE LOM metadata are included in the Explor@2 system and where they appear in the Metadata Editor Tabs. Of these metadata, format, language and title are obligatory entries. A demonstration version can be found at <http://explora2.licef.teluq.uquebec.ca/demo/>.

Figure 20.3 shows the Explor@2 Metadata Editor with the Classification Tab and the Resource (LO) type classification active. We have supplemented the metadata Classification Tab with our own LO typology in order to maximize search and discovery using the extensive LO taxonomy work developed by the instructional design team for the MISA (méthode d'ingénierie d'un système d'apprentissage [Learning Systems Engineering Method]) (Paquette, 2002). In this Resource taxonomy, part of the 17 classifications of LOs that have been produced for MISA have been

Table 20.2 Metadata elements used in the Explor@2 system

Metadata editor Element group	Element names	Comments
General 1. General 4.3. Technical/ location 3. Meta-metadata	Catalogue entry, Title, Location, Description, Language of the Resource, Author of the metadata, Date, etc.	Location is from the Technical group but logically appears in the general group. The system captures the location automatically. The meta-metadata is captured automatically.
Technical information 4. Technical	Format, Size, Required Software, Duration, Required Hardware and Installation rules	The LO format is captured automatically in most cases. MIME specification is used.
Classification 9. Classification	LO type, Skill Type, Dewey's content classification	This Tab can receive any number of classification schemes, thus it can vary according to the needs of the organization. The Explor@2 Repository has 2 proprietary classification schemes: LO and skills taxonomy.
Educational 4. Educational 7. Relations	Period, Duration, Target Audience, Complementary LOs	The complementary LOs are linked to the referenced LO by using the relations statement; for example the components of a course can be directly linked to the course or versions of the same LO can be linked.
Context 2. Life cycle 6. Rights	Version, Version Date, Author(s), Role, Owner, Price/Cost, Access rights	These metadata help search for LOs according to version, date, price and cost of a LO as well as by authoring roles.

integrated into 4 major classes, Material/Document, Tool/Application, Service Providers and Course/Events.

- *The Material/Document* class allows the user to categorize the LO according to the type of information, the type of media elements it contains, the type of media support, usage context and/or aggregation mode. Each of these categories has its set of subcategories.
- *The Tool/Application* class classifies these LOs into navigation, communication, production/design, assistance, research, or management tools or applications.
- *The Service Providers* aim to classify human resources that provide service to other actors or towards other types of LOs. Classes are organized according to whether the actor provides technological, informational, organizational, student support, public relation, or training location support in a classroom, a laboratory, a virtual library or an outside ground.

- *The Course/Events* class is subdivided according to the type of *instructional structure*: course, activity, workshop, etc.; the type of the *delivery model*: technological class, web self-learning, community of practice, etc.; the type of instructional method: presentation and exercise, case study, problem-based instruction, etc.; the type of functional model: knowledge management, resource management, learning evaluation, self-managed learning.

Our classification scheme, containing a total of 187 subcategories, is a very large superset of the IEEE LOM. The LOM proposes the following LO vocabulary: exercise, simulation, questionnaire, diagram, figure, graph, index, slide, table, narrative text, exam, experiment, problem statement, self-assessment and lecture. This set of keywords mixes activity types (experiment, problem, lecture) and low-level types of information (diagram, figure and table). Furthermore, compared to the above IEEE LO definition, this vocabulary leaves aside many types of LOs such as media types, tool categories, and actors' services classification even though these are also LOs that require a metadata description. More extensive classification schemes are necessary for any metadata editor. Field studies ought to be conducted to investigate whether our proposed vocabulary can be easily applied by most users.

The actual IEEE LOM standard seems more adapted for materials and documents than for the description of the other LO categories. The improvement should not come from restricting the official IEEE learning object definition, as proposed for example by Wiley (2002). Even though a LOM can and should be used to describe any LO and hence enable LOs to be

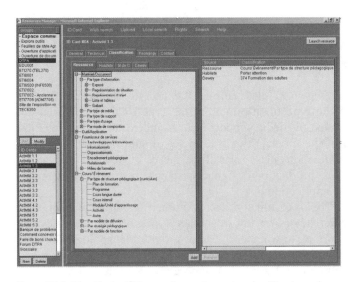

Figure 20.3 The Explor@2 metadata editor, the classification tab

used effectively, the already large set of metadata elements should not be extended to make it impracticable. A possible solution is to distinguish metadata attributes taking into account the granularity of a LO. Hodgins (2002) proposes a five-level content hierarchy to classify LOs, where each level has it own metadata (see also Duval and Hodgins, Chapter 5). At the lowest level, one finds raw data and media elements, qualified as the 'most' reusable, and at the upper level, we find courses and collections that are the least reusable. The taxonomy also proposes different levels of LOs, the course/event classes being aggregates of the other three categories.

Instead of extending the number of LOM attributes, a better approach would be to make optional or compulsory different metadata entries depending on the category of the LO, adding, if necessary, metadata elements that are not actually considered, but that are useful to the description of certain categories. These new metadata elements and classification schemes should rely on a declarable ontology specifying a LO's context, content and structure (Staab *et al.*, 2001). Metadata records in LO repositories should make some semantic description available to computer search agents. Such semantics, according to the W3C Semantic Web proposal (Berners-Lee, Hendler and Lassila, 2001), are expressed using XML files structured within the Resource Description Framework (RDF), in the form of subject–attribute–value triples.

Another important international problem, especially acute in Canada and Europe, concerns *bilingual and multilingual metadata editing*. Due to the global distribution of LOs on the Internet, it is indispensable to provide translation possibilities by providing multilingual vocabularies for all vocabulary-based metadata. As put forth by Trigari (2001) there should be effective control of the indexing language, covering selected concepts and inter-language equivalence among descriptors. Controlled multilingual vocabularies will increase discoverability and interoperability by enabling terms that are 'understood' the same way.

Actually, the Explor@2 Metadata Editor has a quick translation interface for the title and description entry available in French, English and Spanish. Our future research and development aims at increasing these functionalities to include the automatic translation of all controlled vocabularies, increasing the possibility to make the multilingual Semantic Web closer to becoming a reality. Many initiatives in Europe (The European SchoolNet, CEN/ISS), and Canada (CanCore) are working on standardizing the translations of the IMS vocabularies. However, so far no standard is readily available and collaboration is needed between groups and developers.

Metadata repository services

The Explor@2 Metadata Repository Services are comprised of agents that can assist in and carry out the following roles: adding a LO record, grouping and annotating LOs, assigning access rights and searching the repository. Before using the Metadata Editor, LOs need to be identified on the Web or on a Local Area Network (LAN). A metadata description of such a resource can be added to a metadata repository in three different manners, namely by:

- searching the Web and creating a LOM entry;
- searching the LAN and creating a LOM entry; and
- uploading a LO from a LAN to a server and publishing its LOM.

Figure 20.4 shows the LO Manager Web search interface. This service lets the user search the Web by choosing a search engine, Google in this example (left window in the figure). The user executes a search, views a website (centre window in the figure) and then decides whether or not to add a metadata ID card into the repository by clicking on the Group button. The LO remains where it is, but the agent creates a new LOM entry with the URL and the meta-metadata automatically filled in.

There are two ways to add a LO from a LAN client, labelled on the interface in Figure 20.4 as 'Local search' and 'Upload'. Both options open a dialogue window enabling the user to browse the local disks and select a LO for which a LOM entry will be produced. The Local Search service enables designers to reuse LOs, for example on CD/DVD drives, and still be able to record it as LOM from which it can be launched in its actual location. The Upload service begins the same way, but it enables the designer to transport a LO from a LAN to a web server from which it will be launched, and then to produce a corresponding LOM entry. Figure 20.5 shows this Upload service. The Display button lets the user launch the LO to decide if it will be entered or not.

Figure 20.4 The Web search interface

On the left side of Figure 20.4, we see the metadata repository's LO 'Groups'. Groups can be created according to any criteria. In this version, there is a group of LOs available to all, another group contains the core Explor@ tools. Two groups of widely used commercial tools and documents are followed by user-defined groups of LOs intended for use in specific projects.

Functionalities are available to duplicate a metadata ID card, to transfer or copy a metadata record (ID card) from one group to another, or to suppress a metadata record in a group or from all groups. An annotation function (right window in Figure 20.4) enables authorized users to associate a message to a metadata record and to answer previous messages about the same record, in a local newsgroup fashion.

The administrator of the Explor@ system can assign a user to act as a manager for each group. This person has the right to delegate rights to other users. There are different levels of rights: to annotate, to consult, to modify the LOs of that group or to delegate rights to it. By default, users who create a group are that grouping's manager. Besides rights on groups, rights can be given on individual LOs or its metadata ID card. Figure 20.6 (right screen) shows the rights assignment interface.

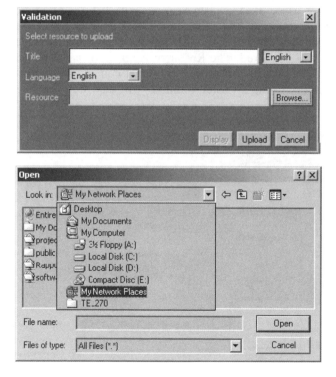

Figure 20.5 The LAN publishing service

Figure 20.6 (left window) presents the Search interface. The actual search method is based on the attributes in a Metadata record compliant with CanCore guidelines. Using the Search interface, a user can constrain a search using metadata attributes and their values, combined with Boolean AND/OR operators. The search will display the corresponding metadata records in a table presenting the attributes selected in the 'Display' section of the interface. The search results in a record set from which a user can select a record, display the metadata content and launch the corresponding LOs. The aggregation tools presented next also use this search function.

Learning object aggregation and launching

The preceding sections have presented the main functionalities of the metadata repository and its functions. This section will present the three LO aggregation tools and then consider briefly how different kinds of LOs can be launched and displayed to the users.

First, we can combine LOs into a larger LO aggregate, accessible through a web page without using a HTML editor such as FrontPage or DreamWeaver. The *Resource Aggregator*, itself a LO referenced in a metadata repository, builds a hierarchy of LOs selected by browsing the Metadata groupings or using the Metadata Search agent. It helps integrate titles, text descriptions, anchors and separators and a presentation style sheet to the web page. The designer can select a group where the Metadata of the resulting LO will be stored. The Resource Aggregator can be used to build Webographies or to list all of the LOs in a course, subdivided by modules and authors as in a poster room. It can also help build a

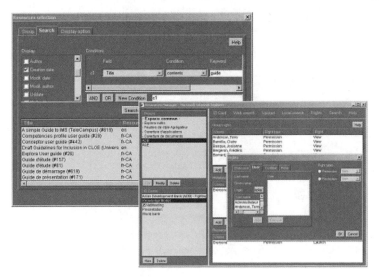

Figure 20.6 Search agent and access right definition

Frequently Asked Question (FAQ) web page, describe activity assignments or provide a list of resource persons.

The second aggregation tool is the *Role Environment Editor* aggregating LOs according to the roles of an actor. Figure 20.7 presents such a tool (upper left window) and the corresponding resulting learner environment (lower left). Using this Editor, a designer identifies the different roles an actor is to play in a course or a learning event and defines it indirectly by listing spaces grouping resources this actor will use. Figure 20.7 shows three LOs launched respectively from the Self-management, Library and Communication menus.

The third aggregation tool is an *Instructional Structure Editor*. It enables a designer to import or build a learning environment describing a learning event or course scenario, grouping activities and LOs used or produced in the scenario's activities. Figure 20.8 presents the Instructional Structure Editor results displayed in a learner's progression tool. This course structure is, in this case, subdivided in modules, and then into learning activities. Below each activity are the resources to be consulted, used or produced within the activity. Figure 20.8 displays an assignment page associating 2 with activity 2.1, a conference in a video streaming page and a discussion forum. These LOs were selected using the Metadata browser and search services.

LO launching occurs in an aggregate collection produced using one of the above aggregation editors, or directly, within the LO Metadata manager. Considering one by one the four main categories of LOs, tools can be launched based on their extension, their Windows name or a path on a server or a client, which is stored in the Metadata record.

Materials and documents can be launched as summarized in Table 20.3. Depending on their type, documents can be opened remotely or downloaded locally with their associated application; opened remotely using Internet Explorer; or opened on DVD/CD-ROM or a local disk. Courses

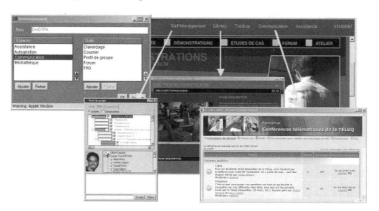

Figure 20.7 Building an actor's environment

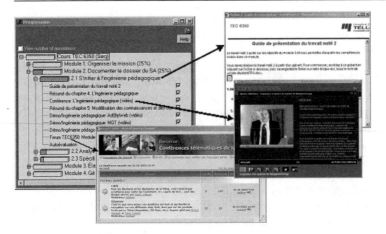

Figure 20.8 Building instructional structures

Table 20.3 Types of document launching

Type of document launching	Office (DOC, XLS, PPT)	PDF	ZIP Archive	XML file	Image (GIF, JPG...)	MOT Model	Web-site (HTML, ASP...)	ASCII Text
Opened remotely with its associated application	X	X						
Downloaded locally with its associated application	X	X	X	X	X	X		X
Opened with Internet Explorer	X	X		X	X		X	
Opened on a CD-ROM or a local disk	X	X	X	X	X	X	X	X

and events, group materials, tools, and service providers, bundled in a website are all launched using their URLs. Service providers are users referenced in the Explor@ system where their e-mail address or URI can be found. They can also be described in a metadata record where this access information and other information, such as the user's roles and competencies, can be found.

Conclusion

The Explor@ system is sometimes labelled as a distance learning platform, but it is more akin to a specialized operating system than an integrated, generic software or an authoring system. We would describe it as a 'third-generation' Learning Content Management System (LCMS), a term used in relation to the evolution of generic software. At the beginning, text editors wouldn't communicate information easily to spreadsheets or database software. The first generation required programming efforts to overcome these interoperation difficulties. Then, the so-called 'integrated software' was built. This second generation made transfer from one tool to the other very easy as long as you stayed inside the integrated software. The third generation tools of today allow integration at the operating system level, so you can use one tool from one vendor and interoperate it with a tool from another vendor or one you have built that respects the same standards.

The same evolution is happening in distance learning delivery systems. The first distance learning courses that were built before 1997 required important programming efforts. We built one in 1992 called the 'HyperGuide' for a Télé-université course using HyperCard and Toolbook on a client station linked to e-mail, file transfer and forum services. Today, the majority of platforms qualify as second-generation. Analysing a review of distance learning platforms (Harmbrech, 2001), we have noticed that the current platforms are designed for predefined actors, usually providing a fixed set of tools and resources for a designer, a learner and, sometimes, a trainer. The international LO standards project is of course a way to move towards inter-platform interoperability.

Explor@ has been built from the beginning with a third-generation LCMS in mind. It allows building environments for any set of actors without predefining the functions or roles. It allows the implementation of interactions between actors using LOs dynamically related to the operations the actors perform in the system. Hence, within the same system, by aggregating LOs and functions, it is possible to build quite different distributed learning systems such as Electronic Performance Support Systems (EPSS) integrated in a workplace activity, communities of practice or, at the other end of the continuum, distributed classroom activities.

We are currently upgrading the Explor@ system, so that a multi-actor interface facilitates the actors' interactions and coordination at run-time. This is a more general and dynamic alternative to the actual hierarchical structures used in Explor@2 and in most LCMSs. This new version will display a graphic interface for each function of the learning system. It will inform the actors about the context of the operations they perform in different functions; give access to the latest version of the LOs produced by other actors; and provide access to update the LOs they provide to others. In addition, communication and notification, metadata referencing, group annotation and assistance facilities will be accessible from the graphic object representing any operation.

We believe this approach will resolve many of the coordination difficulties encountered in distributed learning systems. Especially in contexts where the actors and LOs change regularly, the learners will benefit from constantly knowing where a specific LO or information can be found and which actors they can communicate with.

The main challenge for the interoperability of LOs lies in advances in instructional design models rather than the metadata standardization initiatives that have motivated their initial development. We believe that instructional engineering is the key to offer sound and practical solutions to the aggregation and interoperability of LOs. We hope that the ideas presented in this chapter will contribute to efficient and significant solutions to build more meaningful and useful distributed learning systems.

References

Berners-Lee, T., Hendler, J. and Lassila, O. (2001) The Semantic Web, *Scientific American*, May.

CEN/ISSS (2002) (accessed 23 January 2003) Information Society Standardization System – Learning technologies workshop, (Online) http://www.cwnorm.be/isss/Workshop/lt/.

Duval, E. and Robson, R. (2001) Guest editorial on metadata, *Interactive Learning Environments: Special issue: Metadata*, **9–3**: 201–06.

EUN (2002) (accessed 20 April 2003) European SchoolNet, (Online) http://www.en.eun.org/eun.org2/eun/en/etb/sub_area.cfm?sa=441&row=1.

Harmbrech, W. R. (2001) *Corporate e-learning: Exploring new frontiers*, W. R. Harmbrech & Co.

Hodgins, H. W. (2002) The future of learning objects. E-Technologies in engineering education, in *A United Engineering Foundation Conference*, Davos, Switzerland.

IEEE LTSC (2002a) (accessed 23 November 2002) IEEE Learning Technologies Standardization Committee, (Online) http://ltsc.ieee.org.

IEEE LTSC (2002b) (accessed 28 April 2003) Draft standard for learning object metadata, (Online) http://ltsc.ieee.org/doc/wg12/LOM_WD6_4.pdf.

IMS (2002) (accessed 23 January 2003) IMS specifications, (Online) http://www.imsglobal.org/specificationdownload.cfm.

Jacobson, I. (1993) *Le génie logiciel orienté objet*, Addison-Wesley, Paris.

Paquette, G. (1995) Modeling the virtual campus, in *Innovating Adult Learning with Innovative Technologies*, eds B. Collis and G. Davies, Elsevier Science, Amsterdam.

Paquette, G. (2002) Modeling and delivering distributed learning environments, in *World Conference on Computers in Education*, Montreal.

Rumbaugh, J. *et al.* (1991) *Object-oriented modelling and design*, Prentice Hall, Englewood Cliffs, NJ.

Staab, S. *et al.* (2001) Knowledge processes and ontologies, *IEEE Intelligent Systems*, 26–34.

Trigari, M. (2001) (accessed 4 April 2003) Multilingual Thesaurus, why?, (Online) http://www.en.eun.org/eun.org2/eun/en/etb/content.cfm?lang=en&ov=3813.

Wiley, D. A. (2002) Connecting learning objects to instructional design theory: A definition, a metaphor, and a taxonomy, in *The instructional use of learning objects: Online version*, ed. D. A. Wiley, (Online) http://www.reusability.org/read/chapters/wiley.doc.

Chapter 21

The MERLOT model and the scholarship of teaching

Neil R. Kestner

Creating Learning Objects takes a lot of time and effort. However, faculty are increasingly concerned about the recognition they will get for all their effort. Such concern are really part of a more general anxiety, namely faculty recognition for teaching activities and, in particular, electronic and multimedia projects. In recent years more attention has been given to instructional activities as part of the promotion and tenure guidelines even at the Doctoral/Research Universities. In addition, there are a number of groups who are now generating promotion guidelines that will properly document and give credit for non-paper (usually electronic) materials in the tenure package (among them are the Association of Research Libraries, Conference on College Composition and Communication of NCTE, and the University of Michigan under the direction of Carl Berger).

In contrast, there is a also a very sizeable group of faculty who express concerns that the new emphasis on teaching is, in some way, diluting the role of research and allowing routine teaching to be overcounted. Those faculty members have a legitimate concern and one way to prevent the misapplication of the new guidelines is by better-defined criteria for excellence in teaching.

Ernest Boyer and others have argued that to really advance the status of teaching requires us to develop a scholarship of teaching. This view is supported by the Carnegie Academy for the Scholarship of Teaching and Learning (CASTL) <http://www.carnegiefoundation.org/CASTL/>, as well as by many other groups, such as those at the American Association for Higher Education and the Center for New Designs in Learning and Scholarship (CNDLS) <http://cndls.georgetown.edu/> at Georgetown.

In order to develop instruction as scholarship we need to apply review criteria to teaching activities of similar exactness to those we use in evaluating our research activities. One rationale for the many reasons teaching has been so underemphasized is that quality of teaching is so hard to measure. At most universities most of the evaluation is done by a simple student evaluation of teaching. Years of academic experience suggest that these have some use and may define the very best and the very worst, but otherwise they do not provide administrators or other faculty much guidance for judging the vast majority of our faculty. Many schools are now using a multitude of measures to try to get a better picture of a person's teaching accomplishments, but still that is largely based on their classroom behaviours as measured against local standards.

When we judge a person's research, which seems easier than judging teaching, what we do is something rather different. True, we judge how that person presents seminars and interacts with her/his peers, but the real merit of a person is what new discoveries that person has made and how that person has promoted or published that work. In research, if a person does not *publish* the work it is useless to society and we do not reward that faculty member. Furthermore, that research will not be published unless it meets the *standards* of the profession *as judged by his/her peers*.

To judge the quality of instructional materials scholarship including learning objects, especially when those materials are used in online instruction, we need to be able to judge the scholarship of the teaching as well as we now demonstrate the research activities of our faculty for promotion and tenure decisions. To do this we need a new set of tools and some collectively agreed upon standards of quality. We now consider one aspect of this problem, namely standards and a mechanism for evaluating the quality of online materials.

One aspect that is often downplayed is the amount of work necessary to develop quality materials. That time represents a major commitment on the part of the faculty to the profession and as such, needs to be shared extensively. Also, since the development requires so much work, one needs to share the workload and make the results public, much as we do routinely with research results. But there are real problems in just sharing one's work. Granted, there are some discipline-specific databases and websites as well as some commercial sites that are appropriate for certain disciplines and in some cases, even well-advertised, but in most cases the faculty member's work is sought out by word of mouth or a lucky hit from a search engine. Too often the only choice is for the author to give out his material with little recognition in return. In addition, while most faculty want their courses to be individualized by being able to pick and choose what items to include, commercial sites, at least most of those currently available, want the user to buy all of the content or none – and at a price.

According to Shulman (1998, p. 6), 'A scholarship of teaching will entail a public account of some or all of the full act of teaching – vision, design, enactment, outcomes, and analysis – in a manner susceptible to critical review by the teacher's professional peers and amenable to productive employment in future work by members of that same community'. Notice the key words *public, analysis, review,* and *community.*

One organization that has begun to deal with this issue in a comprehensive way is MERLOT (Multimedia Educational Resource for Learning

and Online Teaching) <http://www.merlot.org>. The MERLOT organization is a joint project of 22 major educational organizations, many being
state boards of higher education, and the National Science Foundation
Digital Library project. It provides a location for the faculty to display
their work in instructional technology, usually learning objects. It contains
a faculty-driven database of online educational applets or learning objects
for anyone to use freely (in all senses of the word). MERLOT is an attempt
to increase the dissemination of learning objects for faculty across many
disciplines, improving the instruction for all while developing a real
community of online material producers and users, while at the same time
recognizing the nature and proper authorship of the material.

MERLOT is a large collection of links to online learning objects in 14
disciplines (over 6,000 items with 2,800 user comments and 620 reviews
as of September 2002) with over 10,000 registered as members. However
MERLOT is different from most collections. These items are reviewed
and commented on by experts and users of the materials. The reviewers
also use well-defined criteria. So what is not fully appreciated by many
is that MERLOT is above all a process as much as or more than a searchable database of quality materials. It is that process that is most important
in the present context.

MERLOT has to be understood at several levels, all of which relate to
the scholarship of teaching. There are users, authors, members and non-
members, reviewers and the editorial boards, all interacting communities.
We start with a small educational applet URL submitted to site. Any
member or the author can submit it. It is automatically indexed, the author
is notified, and the item is made available to everyone via a very extensive search engine.

Three things happen next. First, users can begin using these applets by
going to the author's website. Those users are also invited to join the
MERLOT community (it's free) and submit comments on their use of this
item. Second, the review committee (or two people, specifically, in the
case of chemistry) will first triage the item based on their quick review
and initial guess as to quality and importance (ranking them from 'review
immediately' to 'remove' on a five-point scale). Third, the editorial board
assigns or the reviewers individually decide what items to review. Those
reviews are performed according to published standards agreed upon within
the discipline and consistent with the MERLOT general criteria. It is very
important that there be such discipline-specific guidelines.

As an example, the chemistry discipline team drafted its criteria and
review process after a very extensive period of discussion. There are three
general categories of evaluation standards within MERLOT-Chemistry:

1. Quality of content;
2. Effectiveness as a teaching-learning tool; and
3. Ease of use.

These three categories are interdependent to some degree, but separate ratings are given for each. Specific evaluation criteria are applied within each category (see details in the Appendix to this chapter or at the website <http://taste.merlot.org/disciplines/eval_criteria/chemcriteria.html>. Some criteria are applicable to several categories. The reviewers pay a lot of attention to the learning outcomes and good pedagogy in their reviews. It is the duty of the reviewers to make sure that the items are rated on their use and interactivity, and their learning potential, even more than on the content and ease of use. Most of those details are not published but form the basis of the two reviewers' final rating and final composite review. The judgements of the reviewers, especially on effectiveness, are also different depending on the intended use of the materials as indicated by the author (e.g. Lecture/Demo, Tutorial, Homework, Lab – group or individual learning or other use).

The authors are fully informed that a review is underway and at the end of the review process they are notified, just as in the case of a peer-reviewed article in any respected journal. There then develops an ongoing dialogue with the authors about the review. The authors can make further comments to the reviewers, just as in the case of a journal article. The reviews are briefly summarized by a star system (five stars is exceptionally good), but most important are the details in the written comments. Those reviews are posted for all to see. One of the many other advantages of our reviews is that they alert the user to any special issues involved in their use: maybe a plug-in is needed, maybe it works only with certain browsers, maybe there are some obvious improvements that could be made, and so on. We also encourage the authors or any member user to add online learning assignments for each item so that others may see how these items are specifically used in the course. In some cases entire midterm exams or homework worksheets are available based on some item in the collection. It is a very *public* process.

At the end of the process, authors with items rated as high-quality items have the option of having MERLOT inform their superiors of these reviews and in many cases these have played major roles in the promotion of faculty members. So MERLOT is not only of interest to the users (faculty and students) but to administrators who see the value of its reviews as illustrating the quality of the author's activities and thus his or her scholarship in educational activities. Since it is the collective view of many experts and users in the discipline, it has much more validity than other measures often used. These comments are also external to the university, which gives it national and even international validity. Furthermore, MERLOT is now adding a section for each member to construct an electronic portfolio of objects they have developed along with other assignments and materials created so their collective contributions can be displayed.

So what is MERLOT accomplishing by its actions? First of all, it is making the instructional process more public. It is developing a community of instructors dedicated to the scholarship of teaching, especially those involving technological applications. It is generating a set of defensible discipline-specific standards by which items are judged by one's peers. In short, it is trying to model the peer review process so familiar to us in evaluating research activities. MERLOT or any similar database cannot judge the complete merits of any instructor nor even begin to address how well the learning process occurs, but it does judge the merits of one of the products of that educational activity.

We also suggest that the well-defined discipline-specific peer review process by external experts used by MERLOT could also be adapted to one's own institution and to other collections. While the final reviews that MERLOT posts provide strong supporting evidence in tenure and promotion decisions and for various teaching awards, the process is even more important. It is hoped that institutions and individuals will join with MERLOT and adopt similar standards and processes that can be used in tenure and promotions considerations. Some have even suggested that MERLOT or another agency could provide teams that could review instructional materials for promotion considerations.

We have made progress. We are getting many testimonials from faculty members who use the MERLOT reviews in their promotion and tenure packages (Young, 2002). Many like the fact that their work is being shared and also that they can use the products of others and not spend time doing everything themselves as in the 'Lone Ranger' approach. The anonymous reviews by experts are highly rated in many promotion and tenure packages. However, the bottom line is that ultimately a tenure decision is made by a group of faculty sitting in a small room. Universities need well-defined rules for how to judge electronic materials following the lead of the University of Michigan. For a collection model, MERLOT is on the right track in setting standards for others to follow.

References

Shulman, L. (1998) (accessed 3 December 2003) Course anatomy: The dissection and analysis of knowledge through teaching, in *The course portfolio: How faculty can examine their teaching to advance practice and improve student learning*, ed. P. Hutchings, pp. 5–12, American Association for Higher Education, Washington, DC, (Online) http://frontpage.uwsuper.edu/scholars/SchulCA.pdf.

Young, J. (2002) Ever so slowly, colleges start to count work with technology in tenure decisions, *Chronicle of Higher Education*, 22 February.

Appendix to Chapter 21

EVALUATION STANDARDS FOR CHEMISTRY DISCIPLINE MERLOT, 2002

The following information is provided for users and authors of MERLOT-Chemistry materials to help them better understand both the criteria used to evaluate items in the database and the Peer Reviews. The goal for MERLOT-Chemistry Peer Reviews is to provide information for users on the best material in the Chemistry database and the requirements for author development of premium materials for MERLOT. The following information is also provided to new reviewers to advise them of the evaluation standards to be used in the MERLOT Peer Review process of chemistry materials.

There are three general categories of evaluation standards within MERLOT-Chemistry:

1. Quality of Content.
2. Effectiveness as a Teaching-Learning Tool.
3. Ease of Use.

These three categories are interdependent to some degree, but separate ratings are given for each. Specific evaluation criteria are applied within each category. Some criteria are applicable to several categories. Such criteria appear in the one most relevant category to avoid replication of ratings across categories.

Quality of Content

1. Does the content present valid (correct) concepts, models, and results?

a) For qualitative content, are the trends correct (e.g., doubling an input doubles an output for a linear relation)?
b) For quantitative content, are the numerical results correct and in agreement with graphics or figures?
c) Is the textual content accurate and current?

2. Is the target model or concept significant and presented effectively?

a) Does the content stay on target?
b) Is the model or concept difficult to teach and/or learn?
c) Is the model or concept a pre-requisite for more advanced material?

3. Can the content be readily integrated into the chemistry curriculum?

a) Does the content fit into standard presentations of chemistry?
b) Can the content be used with standard textbooks or problems?
c) Can the content be used in a nontraditional manner?

4. Is the content flexible?

a) Can the content be used to explore a range of different physical situations (e.g., it is NOT applicable to only one of a few physical systems)?
b) Is there control over the initial state of the system?
c) Is there control over the important physical parameters in a problem?
d) Is the content modular so that it can be used in different ways?

Potential Effectiveness as a Teaching-Learning Tool

The 'Effectiveness' rating is given with respect to a specific intended use of the material (e.g., Lecture/Demo, Tutorial, Homework, Lab – group or individual learning or other use) as indicated by the author.

1. Does it increase the potential for enhancing student learning?

a) Do the graphics and/or multimedia content enhance the presentation of the model/s or concept/s?
b) Is it engaging, interactive, and/or entertaining?
c) Is it a learning tool (e.g., not a toy)?
d) Is the user encouraged to generalize concepts or make predictions?

2. Does it develop/increase conceptual understanding?

a) Is the user encouraged to generalize concepts from data or observations?
b) Is the user asked to make predictions or applications using the target concept?

3. Can it be used in a variety of ways to achieve teaching and learning goals?

a) Is the material versatile enough to be used in a variety of settings or contexts (e.g., lecture/demo, group projects, homework assignments, independent study or tutorial)?

4. Are the teaching-learning goals and consequent uses easy to identify?

a) Can instructors readily identify the teaching-learning goals?
b) Can instructors readily identify teaching-learning uses for the software?

Ease of Use

1. Are the interface and general layout consistent and visually distinct?

a) Are the labels, buttons, menus, text, and other user interface elements and layout consistent and distinct?

2. Does the software provide feedback?

a) Is feedback provided about the system's status and the user's responses?

3. Is the software easy to enter, use, and exit from?

a) Is the software easy to enter and exit from?
b) Is the user not likely to get diverted or trapped while navigating the software?

4. Is the software robust?

a) Does the software load quickly?
b) Will ordinary use not cause the system to crash?

Part 5

From the Semantic Web to EML and Instructional Engineering

This final section introduces some of the more complex aspects of LO implementation and delivery. The Semantic Web, in which the Web is made meaningful to machines using XML and RDF, is followed by an introduction to educational modelling languages, which have been referred to in previous chapters. Some of the technical issues involved in the creation of a network of interoperable LO repositories are presented. This is followed by chapters on intelligent agents and knowledge engineering.

In Chapter 22 Sean B. Palmer introduces the principles and applications of decentralized metadata, and some of the techniques supported by the Semantic Web. An explanation of HTML and XML is followed by an introduction to RDF. Vocabulary in terms of ontologies and the RDF Schema and OWL are explained. He outlines the importance of storing learning objects as first class objects on the Web (i.e. as resources with URIs). This enables anyone to say anything about them in RDF assertions.

He argues that the best courses available on the Semantic Web will generally thrive while the lesser courses will not necessarily drop out of existence, but merely receive less recognition. And, by working on small parts of the architecture at a time, but remembering that the goal is always to support access to learning objects, viable systems can be built. He notes that good Semantic Web applications are those that we do not even realize are there.

Anderson and Petrinjak, in Chapter 23, describe some recent work by European educational researchers on a standardized way of describing educational transactions, namely EMLs (Educational Modelling Languages). The authors use a standard musical notational analogy to argue for a similar one for the design, delivery and learning processes in education. They maintain that new structures will usher in a new era of understanding of the processes involved in teaching and learning.

Their chapter illustrates the promise of including components of the educational process: its roles, resources and context, and links them to developments with the Semantic Web. They stress the importance of and need for EMLs, arguing that the difficulties involved in implementation are outweighed by the benefits of accesibility, reusability, search and retrieval, and so on.

In Chapter 24 Richards and Hatala describe the eduSource Canada initative for the creation of a pan-Canadian network of learning object repositories (LORs). Key to the success of such a structure, the authors argue, is the development of easy-to-use tools that interoperate with different LORs and tools. They outline technical issues related to the functional interoperability of such a system, and how it might build upon previous work of projects associated with the CANARIE eLearning Program and other initiatives.

Fuhua Oscar Lin, in Chapter 25, describes an adaptive web-based course generation and delivery structure for distributed learning. This structure supports a system that is capable of assisting students and/or instructors in different subject areas to generate suitable personalized curricula, delivering adaptive learning materials in the form of LOs to the student just-in-time. Based on the ideas from knowledge modelling, knowledge management and intelligent software agents, the author proposes a methodology for modelling knowledge for developing course design agent systems. He suggests some models and mechanisms for knowledge modelling and management that enable and support educational agents' activities, focusing first on knowledge modelling for developing course design agents and second on course design knowledge. Then he introduces an approach to modelling goal-based learning objects (LOs).

In the final chapter, Paquette analyses, from an instructional engineering (IE) viewpoint, the concept of an Educational Modelling Language (EML). He claims that the work on EMLs and its subsequent integration into the IMS Learning Design Specification is the most important initiative to date aiming to integrate Instructional Design (ID) preoccupations in the international standards movement. He suggests that ID has evolved to what can be termed 'IE', integrating ID, software and cognitive engineering processes and principles. Educational Modelling Languages share a software engineering and cognitive science approach. The main difference, he points out, comes from the fact that IE is a methodology mostly concerned with the processes and principles that will produce good specifications of a learning system, in particular, EML specifications. He explores how an IE method can be adapted to and synchronized with a learning design specification standard like EML/IMS-LD and, conversely, how such a method can contribute to the evolution and use of a learning design standard.

Chapter 22

The Semantic Web and metadata decentralization

Sean B. Palmer

This chapter serves as an introduction to the principles and applications of decentralized metadata, and to the techniques thereof fostered by the Semantic Web. An explanation of HTML and XML is followed by an introduction to RDF and NTriples. Ontologies, the RDF Schema and OWL are also discussed.

The Web, HTML and XML

The World Wide Web as a flexible system for storing documentation is revolutionary. As a flexible system for storing data, however, it is inadequate. The principle of hypertext, so well known to millions of people worldwide, was pre-Web, ephemeral. The nascent Web of the early 1990s nearly failed to succeed because of the amount of resistance from people who viewed the Web in terms of then extant documentation and hypertext systems.

The principle that drove the Web, that of a universal information space, was so counter-intuitive that standards bodies actually resisted nomenclature, suggesting that the Web was universal (Berners-Lee, 1999). The Web's axioms took over a decade to be standardized. Moreover, SGML, the application framework of which HTML is an instance, was not considered swift enough for encoding information that could be transmitted via a global computer network and then rendered.

Ten years after the formation of the Web, XML was created (Bray, Paoli and Sperberg-McQueen, 2000). It has been heavily touted as the replacement for HTML for storing information on the Web. Considering its flexibility and the wealth of generic tools available to parse it, it is easy to be convinced that all one has to do is encode data as XML to make it perfectly useful on the Web. That is not so. XML is simply a data structure; to gauge the meaning of an XML instance, one must already have some prior knowledge of the structure's meaning.

When providing metadata for digital content such as learning objects, though it is possible to use XML to store the data, a separate mechanism is required for being able to say what that information means. To illustrate the futility of storing information in XML without a standard data framework, consider the following XML document instance, a piece of metadata for this chapter.

```
<chapterMeta>
<auth>Sean B. Palmer</auth>
<title>The Semantic Web and Metadata Decentralization</title>
</chapterMeta>
```

Here, it may be fairly obvious to a human reader what the meaning of the parts is. The 'auth' element corresponds to the name of the single human author of the chapter, and the 'title' corresponds to the title, in the English original, of the chapter. It is possible to work this out since 'Sean B. Palmer' is clearly a name, and 'auth', most people will be able to quickly work out, is an abbreviation of 'author'; 'title', likewise, is self-explanatory to humans. But machines cannot parse natural languages. If they could, there would be no need for XML: all of the prose in HTML could simply be formalized and searched.

Simple metadata can be said to be comprised of 'atoms' corresponding to concepts, and assertions that link the concepts. Binary assertions and first order predicate logic is good for expressing knowledge on the Web. For example, to say that a certain page has a certain author, we could say, using a property (subject, object) format, authorName (http://example.org/, "Bob B. Bobbington").

Search engines on the Web such as Google are extremely effective for finding text in web pages. They are not so good for answering logical queries: one has to hope that a problem is addressed directly by a web page, and that the phrasing can be guessed.

The Semantic Web

The Semantic Web is for data what the World Wide Web is for documentation. Berners-Lee (2001) claims that for data, the world is still pre-Web. Implemented as a set of formats, frameworks, languages, protocols, software, interfaces, and best practices, the Semantic Web forms a machine processable global decentralized data storage system. The most important of these constituent technologies is the Resource Description Framework.

RDF

The Resource Description Framework was conceived as a generic metadata facility that could be serialized as XML. It has gradually evolved through years of careful standardization work (though often marred by heated personal debates), but generally consists of a model theoretic semantics and XML serialization. It uses binary assertions whose constituent atoms can be any of a URI (Uniform Resource Identifier), a literal, or an existentially quantified blank node.

It is also serializable as XML, though other serializations have been proposed, and one – NTriples – standardized in part. It is a convention to use a slightly augmented version of NTriples as an instructional format for demonstrating RDF, since it is less verbose than XML and requires no knowledge of XML's quirks. It is necessary to learn a serialization of RDF in order to illustrate RDF's ontological capabilities.

NTriples: A straightforward RDF serialization

NTriples files consist of lines of binary assertions in subject property object format, terminated with a full stop (Beckett and Grant, 2003). Each of the terms can be one of a literal (delimited with double quote marks: " "), a URI (delimited with angular brackets: <>), or an existentially quantified blank node (prefixed with _:). For example:

> <http://www.w3.org/> <http://purl.org/dc/elements/1.1/title> "W3C".

Since URIs are often quite long and yet property names often, by convention, have common prefixes, a prefixing facility is also available. A prefix is declared before the rest of the file, thus:-

> @prefix dc: <http://purl.org/dc/elements/1.1/>.
> <http://www.w3.org/> dc:title "W3C".

This binds the prefix 'dc:' to the URI http://purl.org/dc/elements/1.1/ for the file. You can see how 'dc:title' is now equivalent to 'http://purl.org/dc/elements/1.1/title'. When using these abbreviations, which are called QNames, the angular brackets *must* be omitted.

Using RDF for learning objects

Here are some metadata for a learning object in the NTriples serialization of RDF:

> <http://mystudy.example.org/> rdf:type:LearningObject .
> <http://mystudy.example.org/> dc:title
> "A Study of the Phenomic Characteristics of the word 'Gickling'." .
> <http://mystudy.example.org/> dc:subject :Language .
> <http://mystudy.example.org/> dc:subject :Phenomics .

```
<http://mystudy.example.org/> dc:date "2003-01" .
<http://mystudy.example.org/> dc:author "Bob B. Bobbington" .
<http://mystudy.example.org/> dc:lang "en-GB" .
<http://mystudy.example.org/>:suitableAges "16-" .
```

It is useful to make an analogy here to a simple database format. You can take the subject as being the first column, and then the various properties as being the rest of the columns as shown in Figure 22.1. However, the utility of RDF is that:

- Datatypes can be provided. Even basic RDF can distinguish between URIs and string literals. However, there is also a greater functionality that allows authors of RDF to express datatypes using any existing webized repository, such as that provided by XML Schema (Biron and Malhotra, 2001).
- Assertions are binary, not arbitrarily n-ary. This can be a disadvantage in that it can be inefficient, but the sacrifice is made for interoperability.
- Properties are no longer expressed as strings. They are URIs. This is the biggest advantage, facilitating the merging and querying of systems on a global scale. Since learning objects are to be deployed globally, it is a significant advantage to use an interoperable property-naming system.

To expand the last point, on the Semantic Web the system for choosing predicates is very similar to the entire ethos of learning objects itself. For learning objects, course material is chosen by reputation; for the Semantic Web, predicates are also chosen by reputation. But not only that: equivalences between predicates can be expressed so that databases can be merged.

Consider two learning object repositories. Both may use custom database systems, but have a CGI and HTML based Web interface, available via HTTP so that anybody with a browser can access it. This means that someone can query for all learning objects with 'Shakespeare' in the title, and whose contents are suitable for ages 10–11, for example. However, this still means that a person wanting to find materials from both databases must search each one in turn. Now, suppose that at some later take, the two institutions controlling the databases decide that they ought to merge to form a superior database. Since they are using custom database

rdf:subject	dc: lang	dc: date	...
<http://mystudy.example.org/>	"en"	"2003–01"	

Figure 22.1 A simple database format

systems, this merge might take months, and many hours of labour. The advantage of the Semantic Web is that, by using RDF, time can be saved. There will still be work to do on the conversion, but overall, the time can be significantly reduced.

Now think larger. Think about ten database systems being merged, or even twenty, all using different systems and formats. The problem of interoperability is not linear: it is an n^2 problem; viz. that for any n systems, n^2 solutions need to be found to make the data consistent. Whilst this has not been a problem so far due to the relatively anachronistic nature of institutions' approaches towards their data, we cannot apply these principles to a global decentralized future.

Once such databases merge, their utility will increase. Storing learning objects as first class objects on the Web (i.e. as resources with URIs) enables anyone to say anything about them in RDF assertions. The best courses available to all will generally thrive; the lesser courses will not drop out of existence, however, but merely receive less recognition. Exposition of the suitability of a learning object can be done in two ways: either the author(s) of the object can classify it and provide details such as what age groups the object is suitable for, and/or the consumers of the learning object can classify and also rate it. But to be able to be expressive, we need first to be able to create languages in our new semantic world. For this, we require schemata and ontologies.

Schemata and ontologies

One of the most important concepts on the Semantic Web is that of a vocabulary. It is, however, a very loose concept. A vocabulary can be thought of as a set of related terms that can be used for providing metadata for a particular application. All of the terms will, of course, have URIs, and in order to facilitate their use in certain serializations of RDF, they will often share a common prefix.

RDF Schema

One of the first and most important vocabularies for the Semantic Web is RDF Schema, which is a general-purpose language for representing information in the Web (Brickley and Guha, 2003). It was standardized along with the original RDF, and has not changed much in the years since its inception. RDF Schema provides the concepts and URIs for classes and properties. In other words, there is a URI for the class of all classes, and the class of all properties. A class bears great analogy with a class in Object-Oriented Programming: any group that has differentia, such that one can say definitively whether or not a particular individual belongs to it, can be a class. The 'type' property of RDF can be used to show membership of an instance to a class. An instance can belong to more than one class. For example:

```
@prefix rdf: <http://www.w3.org/1999/02/22-rdf-syntax-ns#> .
@prefix rdfs: <http://www.w3.org/2000/01/rdf-schema#> .
_:Animal rdf:type rdfs:Class .
_:Human rdf:type rdfs:Class .
_:Duck rdf:type rdfs:Class .
_:Bob rdf:type _:Human .
_:Bob rdf:type _:Animal .
_:Quacky rdf:type _:Duck .
_:Quacky rdf:type _:Animal .
```

Clearly, Bob is a member of both the Human and Animal classes since Human is a subset of Animal. RDF Schema provides a property called rdfs:subClassOf which allows one to express a sub-classing relationship. For example:

```
:Human rdfs:subClassOf _:Animal.
```

By themselves, classes and properties do not often allow one to express enough information to be able to check how consistent these data are. For example, with RDF Schema one is not able to state that two classes are disjoint, nor can one even express that two classes are equivalent (though by making A a sub-class of B and B a sub-class of A one can express an equivalence of set membership). In order to provide more useful information, we must turn to ontological construction languages such as the Web Ontology Language (OWL) [*sic*].

OWL

OWL is a general language that allows one to express equivalencies, disjunctions, enumerations, property restrictions, property elements, and more. OWL can be used to either describe and formalize an existing system such that it can be used on the Semantic Web, or to develop a new system under the auspices of the benefits inherent to Semantic Web technologies. It is comprised of three different 'layers' of increasing complexity, to facilitate deployment. One often finds that software implementations of an overly complex language have sub-optimal performances when only a subset of that language is used!

Complex systems, first order predicate logic and Notation3

To be able to bring RDF up to a level of First Order Predicate Logic (FOPL) completeness, and therefore to be able to express rules, we need to add two concepts to the language: formulae, and universal quantification. The Notation3 (N3) language was conceived by Tim Berners-Lee (the inventor of the World Wide Web, URIs, HTML, HTTP, and the Semantic Web) and also the director of the W3C, which is the consortium responsible for developing RDF as a testbed for these concepts. Various pieces of running code and toolkits are available for using Notation3.

A formula is a collection of statements, commonly referred to as 'contexts'. They are a hypothetical group of statements; namely, when they are used in a file, they are *not* being asserted by the author. This is a very important note, and has profound legal and other implications. Formulae are represented in N3 using curly braces: {}.

Universally quantified variables, counterparts to the existentially quantified variables that RDF already contains, are indicated using a question mark '?' as a prefix instead of '_:'.

For example, here is a simple rule for querying for learning objects that are suitable for a student given their age:

```
@prefix : <#> .
@prefix log: <http://www.w3.org/2000/10/swap/log#> .
@prefix math: <http://www.w3.org/2000/10/swap/math#> .
{ ?student :age ?age .
?learningObject :suitableForAges (?lower ?upper) .
?lower math:lessThan ?age .
?upper math:greaterThan ?age } log:implies.
{ ?learningObject :suitableFor ?student } .
```

Note how the subject property object syntax is still followed, with the antecedal formula as the subject, log:implies as a property, and the consequential formula as the object. Code exists, which can already apply the above rule to an RDF database.

OWL and FOPL use case: Identifying people

It is important to be able to identify people on the Semantic Web. The authors of works must be able to be determined, and records of students must be able to be kept straight. It is obvious that a name is not a very good unambiguous identifier for a person: names such as 'John Smith' are common enough to cause a problem on a large scale. For that reason, it is common to use e-mail addresses to uniquely identify people on the Semantic Web. It is not a requirement, but since e-mail addresses can be provided cheaply (i.e. for free) and persistently (one e-mail address per person for the time that the server recognizes that address) it is a good choice.

For the purposes of identification, the foaf:mbox property of the Friend Of A Friend (FOAF) vocabulary can be used to provide a person's mailbox.

The documentation for this property is given below. Note the use of OWL (though OWL's predecessor, DAML+OIL, is currently used in the FOAF documentation); specifically, the UnambiguousProperty class.

```
@prefix rdf: <http://www.w3.org/1999/02/22-rdf-syntax-ns#> .
@prefix rdfs: <http://www.w3.org/2000/01/rdf-schema#> .
@prefix foaf: <http://xmlns.com/foaf/0.1/> .
@prefix daml: <http://www.daml.org/2001/03/daml+oil#> .
foaf:mbox rdf:type rdf:Property .
foaf:mbox rdfs:label "personal mailbox" .
foaf:mbox rdfs:comment """"A web-identifiable Internet mailbox asso-
ciated with exactly one owner, the first owner of this mailbox. This
property is a 'static unambiguous property', in that there is (across
time and change) at most one individual that has any particular personal
mailbox.""" .
foaf:mbox rdf:type daml:UnambiguousProperty .
foaf:mbox rdfs:isDefinedBy <http://xmlns.com/foaf/0.1/> .
```

(Note: FOAF's slogan is 'Semantic Web Vapourware for the Masses' (Brickley and Guha, 2003) and was created by one of the authors of the RDF Schema specification as a simple Semantic Web testbed. It is, however, implementable, and many developers are finding applications for FOAF. The FOAF community is numerous.)

The fact that this property is asserted as being a member of the daml:UnambiguousProperty class means that we can apply the following rule:

```
{ ?p a :UnambiguousProperty .
?x ?p ?z .
?y ?p ?z } log:implies.
{ ?x :identicalTo ?y } .
```

This is useful if, for example, one database contains the following data:

```
_:Bob :name "Bob Bobbington" .
_:Bob foaf:mbox <mailto:bob@example.org> .
```

and another:

```
_:b :name "Bob B. Bobbington" .
_:b foaf:mbox <mailto:bob@example.org> .
```

So, by the UnambiguousProperty rule_:Bob and _:b will be declared identical.

The future: Education and the Semantic Web

The term 'killer application' is often applied to an application that realizes the full potential of a system by bringing in a large user base. It is arguable, for example, that the Web was the killer application for the Internet, and that NCSA's Mosaic was the killer application for the Web.

The killer application for the Semantic Web is simply itself, or perhaps even its invisibility. Good Semantic Web applications are those that we do not even realize are there, much like the fundamental axioms of the Web that users do not recognize are there. In trying to make information flow smoothly – in trying to facilitate interoperability between disparate systems – a successful solution is one that the users take for granted or do not even realize is there.

So it is with the Semantic Web, and so it is with education and the Semantic Web. Plans dreamed up on the fly every year by exasperated teachers with budget crises and with no time for customization are not optimal for education. Good education is supported when plans are engineered globally and collaboratively, when they are open to change and augmentation, and when learners and instructors in different regions can select them by simply filling in a profile and/or submitting an electronic form. With information pervasive to the point of ambience, the dreams may become reality sooner than anyone could expect.

References

Beckett, D. and Grant, J. (2003) (accessed 28 April 2003) RDF test cases. W3C working draft, (Online) http://www.w3.org/TR/2003/WD-rdf-testcases-20030123/#ntriples.

Berners-Lee, T. (1999) *Weaving the Web*, Texere Publications, London.

Berners-Lee, T. (2001) (accessed 12 March 2003) Business model for the Semantic Web, (Online) http://www.w3.org/DesignIssues/Business.

Biron, P. V. and Malhotra, A. (2002) (accessed 23 March 2003) XML schema Part 2: Datatypes. W3C recommendation, (Online) http://www.w3.org/TR/xmlschema-2/.

Bray, T., Paoli, J. and Sperberg-McQueen, C. M. (2000) (accessed 13 March 2003) Extensible Markup Language (XML) W3C recommendation, (Online) http://www.w3.org/TR/2000/REC-xml-20001006.

Brickley, D. and Guha, R. V. (2003) (accessed 25 March 2003) RDF vocabulary description language 1.0: RDF schema. W3C working draft, (Online) http://www.w3.org/TR/2003/WD-rdf-schema-20030123/.

Chapter 23

Beyond learning objects to educational modelling languages

Terry Anderson and Anita Petrinjak

Much energy and research to date has been focused on finding, tagging and storing chunks of educational content, referred to as learning objects (LOs). The prime objective of this effort is to enable searching, retrieval and reuse of learning resources by teachers and instructional designers. However, it is somewhat ironic that despite all the effort to define standards and specifications for creating and packaging parts of the educational process such as sequencing LOs, defining objectives and standardizing question formats, there has been only very preliminary work on specifying how to formally describe the complete educational process itself. It is as if we have established means and techniques to identify and measure the ingredients, but have yet to figure out how to combine the ingredients to bake the cake!

Recent work by European educational researchers promises to benefit educators by providing us with a standardized way of describing educational transactions. This effort promises to achieve for education what the invention of a standard notation for music in the fifteenth century did for music production, distribution and performance. Once a formal, standardized protocol was established, musicians of any culture, language or instrument could compare, distribute, perform and study music composition. The emergence of structured formats to describe not only the resources of education use, but also the context, roles and interactions of learners, teachers and content, heralds a new age of describing, storing and most importantly, of understanding the educational process.

The syntax and vocabulary of these formal descriptions of the educational process are referred to as Educational Modelling Languages (EMLs). EMLs provide a formal description of the education process and its expression in XML that allows the educational process, including the objects used in its execution, to be stored in distributed databases that can be searched and harvested by both humans and autonomous or directed agents. These agents are distributed software applications that can be released on the networks to make autonomous decisions related to searching, selecting or harvesting with varying degrees of inferential 'intelligence', relevant information on behalf of their creators (Shaw, Johnson and Ganeshan, 1999; Thaiupathump, Bourne and Campbell, 1999).

Thus, EML serves as a major building block of the educational Semantic Web. This chapter overviews the function of an EML and highlights the particular version developed by Rob Koper and his colleagues at the Open University of the Netherlands (Koper, 2001).

Functions of models

We first introduce the function of modelling in systems and software design generally and education specifically. The *American Heritage Dictionary* defines a model as 'a schematic description of a system, theory, or phenomenon that accounts for its known or inferred properties and may be used for further study of its characteristics'. Generally these descriptions of phenomena are created to simplify and clarify complex features or functions of the process under investigation. Further, models provide a schematic framework within which confusing and complex behaviours, events and interactions can be located and described to facilitate sense-making.

These models can also be used to develop systemic solutions to explain problems and to discern and describe solutions. Most importantly, when these models are described in formal language and expressed in XML they can be made accessible on the Web for search, retrieval and automatic manipulation by both humans and agents.

Models then can also be used to simplify complex educational interactions so that they can be classified, compared and contrasted and used in a variety of testing and experimental applications. In educational application, they can be used to abstract the description, sequence and facilitation of individual and group learning experiences. Finally, formal models allow for effective databasing based upon salient variables and processes identified in the model.

From mental models to formal models

Many critics (and some supporters) of a LO approach to education development and delivery have argued that education is not primarily concerned with delivery of content so much as encouraging, enhancing, structuring and supporting a learner's interaction. This interaction is multifaceted and includes interaction with teachers, with peers and with content (Moore, 1989; Anderson, 2003). LOs are one component of a larger educational context that serves to support these interactions. In most cases actual LO use is left to implementation by individual teachers and becomes more of an obscure art than a visible and sharable process. Typically teachers design and execute a lesson or series of lessons in which learning objectives, student assessment and various forms of interaction are orchestrated. Usually these contextual variables are not formally defined (or tagged) and often not even rigorously described. This meets only the needs of those who feel that teaching is an imprecise art that cannot and should not be detailed. However, such an unstructured approach means that knowledge of teaching and learning can evolve only in an inscrutable style. Such impreciseness leads to only shallow or mystified understandings of the dynamics of teaching and learning and leaves huge 'black boxes' of unarticulated knowledge.

Educational knowledge in this context can then only be grown and sustained through implicit learning techniques such as teacher apprenticeship. Further, such imprecise identifications of key variables are generally insufficient to guide development of educational models in which students create their own learning contexts and objectives and where humans and automated agents navigate and use an educational and meaning-filled Semantic Web. Hence the need to move beyond imprecise mental models to formal models of the educational process.

Educational modelling languages clearly and explicitly define, in formalized language, the activities, activity structures, roles and resources of the full educational context. These reusable components are then scripted for execution in real time. It is useful to think of EML as a script for a play in which teachers, students, set and props interact in order to produce learning outcomes.

The educational Semantic Web

The vision of the second major evolution of the World Wide Web was described by the original architect of the Web, Tim Berners-Lee, as the addition of meaning to content display – thus creating the Semantic Web (Berners-Lee, 1998). The Semantic Web is populated with information that is aware of itself. Through tags and organizational structures known as ontologies, tools can be created to deduce and infer relationships between separate chunks of information located anywhere on the Web.

In educational terms, this means that content for use on the Web will not be described only in terms of the display characteristics it should exhibit, but learning variables (such as content, context, evaluation, etc.) will also be aware of what function they play in the provision of an educational experience. For example, on today's Web, a learning objective for a web-based course or unit is usually described or tagged for display with a set of format tags telling the web browser to display the text in a bold font, of a certain size and colour and perhaps with a particular bullet or sequential numbering format. On the Semantic Web, the words could be described with a tag identifying it as a unit level learning objective. Further, the objective will contain implicit and explicit links to the content, activities, assessment, ownership, authorship and a host of other attributes that define and describe the objective's role and function within the educational sequence.

In other words the LO and its context are endowed with semantic information giving it meaning far beyond its display characteristics. Of course, the tagged objective could also be rendered so as to determine the colour, font size and other display characteristics and could, with knowledge of the display medium selected, format the objective for display on paper or screens of various sizes down to very small mobile displays for m-learning.

The added value of semantic information to educational content and context is just beginning to be explored. At one of the simplest levels semantically tagged content or knowledge objects can be searched, sorted and harvested across any machine connected to the Internet. This function alone will revolutionize the cataloguing, search and retrieval of educational content or objects such as textbooks, audio and video files. Further, formal learning objectives can be classified within a structured ontology (see for example IMS learning objectives). Thus, a student, parent, teacher or administrator will be able to request the display of learning objectives for any unit of study. These can be linked to any content or suggested learning activities that accompany them. Efficient rights management systems will monitor the use of content and be capable of restricting access, metering, or supporting payments for the right to access any components of the educational transaction.

The formalized structure of knowledge is being developed in many fields and applications in order to benefit from treatment on the Semantic Web. An extensive list of markup languages from a very wide variety of industry, commerce and non-commercial applications is provided at the Physical Markup Language Web Site at the Massachusetts Institute of Technology <http://www.mit.edu/afs/athena/org/m/mecheng/pml/standards.htm>. A few examples from this list include Human Resources Markup Language, Liturgical Markup Language and Earth Science Markup Language. Thus, education is not alone in seeing the need for a formal description and modelling language that can be expressed in XML and applied on the Semantic Web.

We can expect that the expression of the educational experience in formalized terms on a distributed network will allow us to describe and compare not only the experience, but also the critical context in which it operates. As never before, educational researchers will be able to describe, manipulate, extract and document their activities in ways that can be analysed and amalgamated by machine intelligence.

At its most profound level the educational Semantic Web provides a means towards the vision that inspires all teachers. This is a capacity to provide education that is uniquely configured to support the entire social, intellectual and spiritual needs of each learner. This includes not only the technical capacity of the content to respond to a dynamic understanding (or model) of the individual learner, but also allows learners to willfully configure content as networked mind tools (Jonassen and Carr, 2000). Further, it allows us to describe, measure and set objectives for student–student and student–teacher interaction. This is a capacity that takes advantage of the full complement of possible learning activities including virtual and face-to-face social interaction, individual tutoring, collaborative construction of knowledge, authentic problem-solving and immersive learning experiences.

The Semantic Web does not exist at the beginning of the twenty-first century. But very significant steps are being made towards this goal. None are more important than the development of Educational Modelling Languages.

Educational Modelling Languages

An educational modelling language is defined as 'a semantic information model and binding, describing the content and process within a "unit of meaning" from a pedagogical perspective in order to support reuse and interoperability' (Rawlings *et al.*, 2002).

The capabilities of an educational modelling language are described by Koper (2001) as:

- *Formalism*. In a computer science sense, formalism allows ideas, expressions and ideas to be explicitly described using structured format and usually controlled vocabularies to make their content visible and scrutable by self and others. Additionally, the formal expression of ideas greatly enhances storability, communicability, and testability. Heylighen (1999) has argued that formal expressions are invariant across contexts – an unachievable goal, but none the less an aspiration that formal expression should be defined in such detail that their meaning can be deduced with some elements of consistency by agents (both human and non-human) across varying contexts. Obviously, from this information new meaning can be generated by cognition (humans) or computation (machines).
- *Pedagogical flexibility*. The EML must not be confined to or prejudiced towards or against any particular pedagogy or learning theory. By focusing on activity, EML describes what students and teachers do, and how these activities are measured and evaluated. In this respect, it has a behaviourist capacity, but it also can be used to describe affective and cognitive goals and activities to achieve these goals. This focus allows EMLs to describe diverse forms of education from individual drill and practice to collaborative knowledge construction that takes place at a distance in a classroom or some other combination.
- *Integration of learning objects*. Much talk and effort is being expended in the design and development of LOs and repositories for their storage

and distribution (see for example MERLOT <www.merlot.org> or CAREO <www.careo.org>). These efforts are not obviated by EML, but rather serve as essential components of the content upon which educational activity is modelled and executed. Further, EML deals with the criticism of LOs that they are lacking in essential description of context and application. An EML approach allows the use, context, assessment and valuation of the object to lie outside of the object – thereby facilitating reuse in multiple contexts.

- *Completeness*. EML does not imply that education or learning is contained within the description of the process, but it does argue that it is possible to describe the activities, prerequisites and assessment of the complete educational transaction, thus creating the conditions under which learning can arise and roles, functions, resources and context of the learning transaction can be described.
- *Reproducibility*. The completeness of the description allows the learning sequence to be reproduced at another time and perhaps within another context. Of course no two learning contexts are identical, but the EML description should be complete enough to allow the learning sequence to be reproduced and further to model any contextual changes that arise to be formally described.
- *Personalization*. Personalizing education has long been the quest of educational technologists, especially those concerned with artificial intelligence in education. In computer science parlance, this usually takes the form of the development of dynamic student models that are informed by individual learning desires, competencies, styles and aspirations. In EML these individual (or group) profiles are stored as dossiers, which can be used to direct the flow of tasks, selection of environments or tools. Personalization can also affect other actors including peers and teachers as their prerequisite skills attitudes can be used to modify the unit of learning as it is expressed at run-time. Personalization has been a long-sought and very illusive goal of educational technologists. Some have argued that the inherent unpredictability and complexity of the learning context is such that effective models of complex students or teachers can never be simplified to the point where they provide meaningful guidance to sequencing and content selection (Earle, 2002). Others have argued that what must be modelled is the learning process (Akhras and Self, 1997) or context within which individuals or groups of learners operate. Certainly the complexity of creating an infinite set of personalized learning outcomes has stalled rapid development of effective personalized learning solutions, but newer tools, understanding and technique such as those being developed on the educational Semantic Web promise a fruitful area to continue this effort.
- *Medium neutral*. The inherent flexibility of XML as a definition language of structure, not one of display, means that activities and

content formatted and encapsulated in EML as a particular application or XML can generally be displayed in multiple formats. Text and graphics will be configured to operate within the constraints and capacities of whichever technology is used to execute the EML at run-time. However, this does not preclude use of particular media or very specific formats. EML is designed with the multimedia Web in mind, such that the inclusion of video, audio or graphic learning sequences is presumed, but not required.

- *Distributable*. Naturally, an EML must be distributable for direct application in instructional settings, but as importantly must be searchable and retrievable across the Semantic Web.
- *Interoperable*. EML is designed to enhance reusability of both educational content and scenarios and learning activities. Thus, it is critical that the expression of EML be interoperable across diverse machines, technologies and media.

Types of educational modelling languages

Work done in software engineering has created an open standard for creating models of complex processes known as Unified Modelling Language (UMLs) (Rational Software, 1998). These general principles of UML have been adopted to create a variety of Educational Modelling Languages. The CEN/ISSS Educational Technology Working group (2002) has produced a very interesting comparison of six non-proprietary EMLs developed in Europe. Four of the six have limited scope and the report concludes that they can be used to model educational content and structure but they are generally incapable of expressing the way the content is used in a pedagogical sense. The Spanish PALO system <http://sensei.lsi.uned.es/palo/> can currently be used only to model individual tasks and thus the report concludes that the Dutch product is the most complete and full-featured of the six products reviewed.

The Open University of the Netherlands' EML design was also used as the basis for the IMS Learning Design Specification (see <http://www.imsglobal.org/learningdesign/index.cfm>) and thus seems to have a growing international community of support. It is likely to be the specification most extensively developed in the near future.

Components of EML

In order to understand how EML achieves overall flexibility and the other features mentioned in the previous sections, we will look into its structure (see Figure 23.1). The topmost component is Unit of study (Unit-of-study). It represents the aggregate of different aspects of the learning process. As described by Koper (2001):

a unit of study can not be broken down to its component parts without loosing [*sic*] its semantic and pragmatic meaning and its effectiveness towards the attainment of learning objectives. . . . In practice you see units of study in all types, sorts and sizes: a course; a study program; a workshop; a practice; a lesson could all be considered to be a unit of study.

Components of the unit of study are designed to formally describe the full learning process within a particular context. This learning situation can contain prerequisites (e.g. needed resources) and objectives of the learning process, the resources such as instructions, LOs, books, or means of communication for collaborative work. The learning process itself can contain sequences of actions that lead to the achievement and evaluation of specific learning objectives. This structure is reflected in the design of the unit of study. All components are not required parts of the unit of study. Some are optional and therefore provide flexibility when developing a particular unit of study's objectives. As described by Koper (2001), the unit of study consists of the following components:

* Metadata
* Roles
* Learning objectives
* Prerequisites
* Content
* Method.

Metadata contains information about the unit of study. The metadata contains information such as *Title, Creator, Description, Keywords* and *Copyright*. As in similar tagging systems, elements can be mandatory, optional or multiple instances allowed within a well-formed unit of study. This information can be used for search and retrieval of objects. Metadata and their component titles are the only required fields in this section.

What kind of a role a person involved in the learning process (an actor) can have is determined by the component Roles. An actor can be classified as Learner or Staff. Each of two role categories can have more precise sub-classifications. At least one Learner is required within a unit of study. Koper (2001) suggests that the whole unit of study should be modelled from the perspective of the actor in the Learner role. Actor(s) in the Staff role are usually responsible for the learner support activities.

The learning objectives element consists of individual learning objectives. The same structure is used to describe prerequisites. Activities within the unit of study can also have individual learning objectives and prerequisites.

The Content element contains two other elements: Environment and Activity. The Environment element represents the learning environment

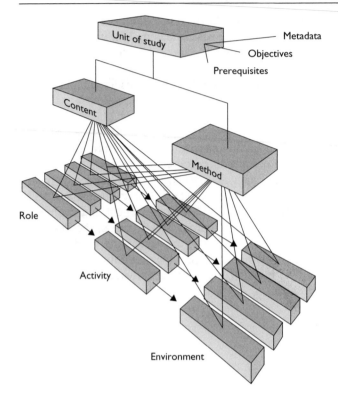

Figure 23.1 Conceptual model of an EML unit of study

available for the learning process. It can contain different types of objects including knowledge objects and communication objects. Knowledge objects can represent a wide range of resources including LOs, books, video clips and articles. Communication objects represent tools and environment to support communication between actors such as e-mail, conferencing facilities or face-to-face classrooms. Activity elements represent a unit of learning activity that will be used in the Method component as part of the larger learning scenario. Content can contain one or more Activity elements. Since it is a building block for the learning process, Activity is one of the crucial sub-elements of the unit of study.

The Method element contains the key activity components of the learning process. It contains both the Activity structure and Play elements. The Activity structure element is used for putting activities from the Content into specific sequences. The Play element delineates the scenario for learning events, that is, it specifies which role will engage in which activities or activity structures, and it models the interplay of roles. Play is the core element of the unit of study design.

EML and XML

All XML records are formally defined and constrained by a formal description of the structure and perhaps the semantics characteristics of a valid file. An EML record is defined by a Data Type Definition (DTD) file. XML files may also be defined using XML schema that provide more precise control of the type of data and constraints on valid entries within the XML tags; however, a formal EML schema has not yet been released. The DTD defines the types of tags and the structure of the documents that are permitted within the file. Each unit of study is expressed as an XML file that is an instance of the EML DTD.

Figure 23.2 illustrates a valid EML file as expressed in XML. This file models a problem-based unit of learning used in the author's graduate course.

EML applications

The Open University of the Netherlands (OUNL) built a prototype of an electronic learning environment in 1997 as the first test for EML. It was applied and tested within two programmes at OUNL: the Maastricht School of Hotel Management and the Public Administration degree programme. In 2000, Edubox, a complete version of the system, was built and further deployed within OUNL programs and the University of South Africa (UNISA), another open university. There are also reported projects and courses using EML from the Austrian Tiroler Bildungsinstitut and the Dutch Digital University. According to the CEN/ISSS survey of educational modelling languages (CEN/ISSS, 2002) EML was used for delivering more than 20 courses. In summary, OUNL EML is the most applied educational modelling language today, and its use in actual courses confirms that it is robust enough to deal with practical learning situations.

Creating an Educational Modelling Language unit

Using EML is a two-part process. First an XML file is created in which the educational activity is explicitly defined or modelled. Koper has designated the smallest unit of EML as a Unit of Learning. Each Unit has an actor that performs a function within an environment using a variety of tools.

XML is designed to be read and interpreted by both machines and humans, so it is quite possible to open a text editor (Word, Notepad, etc.). Creating EML files using a text editor is, however, very tedious work and prone to error. Using a general purpose XML editor has some advantages including the capacity to test the file against the DTD or schema that is used to describe or validate the file. A number of dedicated EML editors and other production tools are currently under development. They promise

```xml
<Unit-of-study Link-name="Athabasca distance learning project" Id="c0001" Type="PBL problem">
  <Metadata>
    <Title>SaveMore College Case Study</Title>
  </Metadata>
  <Roles>
    <Learner Id="student"/>
    <Staff Id="teacher"/>
  </Roles>
  <Content>
    <Activity Link-name="Initial learning" Id="step1">
      <Activity-description Type="task">
        <What><P>Learning to how to use the technology</P></What>
        <How><P>Follow Initial learning instructions.</P></How>
        <Completed><User-choice/></Completed>
      </Activity-description>
    </Activity>
    <Activity Link-name="Planning" Id="step2">
      <Environment Link-name="step2 environment">
        <Knowledge-object Link-name="Planning instructions">
          <Metadata><Title>Planning group work (collaborative)</Title>
          </Metadata>
          <Source><P>          1) discussing what the case requires of the group.
                              2) identifying any individual strengths of group
              members that apply to the case.
                              3) deciding on the steps that will be taken and the
              amount of time that will be allotted to each one.
                              4) assigning group roles (e.g.: moderator, analyst,
              recorder, timekeeper, synthesizer, skeptic, ombudsman,
          peacemaker
          </P></Source>
        </Knowledge-object>
      </Environment>
      <Activity-description Type="task">
        <What><P>Planning group work (collaborative)</P></What>
        <How><P>Get acquainted with Project instructions and then follow Planning
        instructions.</P></How>
        <Completed><User-choice/></Completed>
      </Activity-description>
    </Activity>
    (...)
    <Environment Link-name="Student environment" Id="env1">
      <Knowledge-object Link-name="Project instructions">
        <Metadata><Title>Information Sheet for Participants</Title>
        </Metadata>
        <Internet-source Url="instructions.html" Link-name="Project instructions"/>
      </Knowledge-object>
      <Communication-object Link-name="Project team communication"
      Id="communication_channel1" Reusability="Reusable">
        <Metadata><Title>Project team communication</Title>
        </Metadata>


        <Asynchronous-conference>
          <Participant><Role-ref Id-ref="student"/></Participant>
          <Conference-manager><Role-ref Id-ref="student"/></Conference-manager>
        </Asynchronous-conference>
      </Communication-object>
    (...)
    </Environment>
  </Content>
  <Method>
    <Activity-structure Id="teacher_structure1">
      <Activity-sequence Link-name="Introduction">
        <Activity-ref Id-ref="teacher_step1"/>
        <Activity-ref Id-ref="teacher_step2"/>
      </Activity-sequence>
    </Activity-structure>
    <Activity-structure Id="student_structure">
      <Activity-sequence Link-name="Student activities">
        <Environment-ref Id-ref="env1"/>
        <Activity-ref Id-ref="step1"/>
        <Activity-ref Id-ref="step2"/>
        <Activity-ref Id-ref="step3"/>
        <Activity-ref Id-ref="step4"/>
        <Activity-ref Id-ref="step5"/>
        <Activity-ref Id-ref="step6"/>
        <Activity-ref Id-ref="step7"/>
      </Activity-sequence>
    </Activity-structure>
    (...)
    <Play Link-name="Project workflow">
      <Role-ref Id-ref="teacher"/>
      <Activity-structure-ref Id-ref="teacher_structure1"/>
      <Continue><When-completed/></Continue>
      <Role-ref Id-ref="teacher"/>
      <Activity-structure-ref Id-ref="teacher_structure2"/>
      <Role-ref Id-ref="student"/>
      <Activity-ref Id-ref="student_structure"/>
      <Continue><When-completed/></Continue>
      <Role-ref Id-ref="student"/>
      <Activity-ref Id-ref="student_teleconference_structure"/>
      <Role-ref Id-ref="teacher"/>
      <Activity-ref Id-ref="teacher_teleconference_structure"/>
      <Role-ref Id-ref="teacher"/>
      <Activity-ref Id-ref="marking_structure"/>
    </Play>
  </Method>
  Unit-of-study>
```

Figure 23.2 Problem-based learning example represented in EML

to further aid in file construction by providing pop-up menus that will facilitate the selection of appropriate tags and content. As with similar developments in the creation of Web HTML documents, we are likely to see rapid development of EML editing capacity. A goal will be the creation of WYSIWYG interfaces that allow new and legacy content to be developed and tagged as EML Units of Meaning.

Once the EML file is created, it can be run by an EML player to create run-time presentations of EML units of learning. Further, the EML can be stored in a database for later incorporation into larger play units or stored in larger repositories for search and retrieval on any of the fields for reuse by others. Perot Systems with the OUNL is currently developing an EML player known as EduBox that is scheduled for release in 2003.

Conclusion

The preceding discussion illustrates the promise of EML to move beyond a formal description of content, to a description of the complete educational process – including its components: roles, resources and context. It is also apparent that work is just beginning in this important area and like most of the Semantic Web, is not yet operational. There is a pressing need for an educational modelling language or a set of specifications and tools to build the educational Semantic Web. The problems of implementation are great, but the benefits of accessibility, reusability, search and retrieval and much deeper understanding of the educational process will, in the hopefully not too distant future, allow us to grow far beyond our current limited and limiting understanding and use of LOs.

References

Akhras, F. and Self, J. (1997) (accessed 23 April 2003) Modelling learning as a process, (Online) http://cbl.leeds.ac.uk/~fabio/home.html.

Anderson, T. (2003) Modes of interaction in distance education: Recent developments and research questions, in *Handbook of Distance Education*, ed. M. Moore, pp. 129–44, Erlbaum, Mahwah, NJ.

Berners-Lee, T. (1998) (accessed 29 April 2003) Realising the full potential of the Web, World-Wide Web Consortium, (Online) http://www.w3.org/1998/02/Potential.html.

CEN/ISSS (2002) (accessed 28 April 2003) Information Society Standardization System – Learning technologies workshop, (Online) http://www.cwnorm.be/isss/workshop/it/.

Earle, A. (2002) (accessed 18 December 2002) Designing for pedagogical flexibility – Experiences from the CANDLE project, *Journal of Interactive Media in Education*, 4, (Online) http://www-jime.open.ac.uk/.

Heylighen, F. (1999) (accessed 4 December 2002) Advantages and limitations of formal expressions, *Foundations of Science*, 4 (1): 57–82 (Online) http://pespmc1.vub.ac.be/Papers/Formality-FOS.pdf.

Jonassen, D. and Carr, C. (2000) Mindtools affording multiple knowledge representations for learning, in *Computers as cognitive tools: No more walls*, ed. S. Lajoie, pp. 165–96, Earlbaum, Mahwah, NJ.

Koper, R. (2001) (accessed 28 June 2002) Modeling units of study from a pedagogical perspective: The pedagogical meta-model behind EML, Heerlen, Open University of the Netherlands, (Online) http://eml.ou.nl/introduction/docs/ped-metamodel.pdf.

Moore, M. (1989) Three types of interaction, *American Journal of Distance Education*, **3** (2): 1–6.

Rational Software (1998) (accessed 14 December 2002) Conceptual, logical and physical design of persistent data using UML, (Online) http://www.rational.com/media/whitepapers/logical.pdf.

Rawlings, A. *et al.* (2002) (accessed 14 December 2002) Survey of educational modelling languages, *CEN/ISSS Learning Technologies Workshop*, (Online) http://eml.ou.nl/forum/docs/EML%20Survey%20version%201.pdf.

Shaw, E., Johnson, W. L. and Ganeshan, R. (1999) (accessed 23 April 2003) Pedagogical agents on the Web, *Third International Conference on Autonomous Agents*, (Online) http://www.isi.edu/isd/carte/publications/agents99/agents99.htm.

Thaiupathump, C., Bourne, J. and Campbell, J. (1999) Intelligent agents for online learning, *Journal of Asynchronous Learning Network*, **3** (2).

Chapter 24

Semantic cobblestones

An interoperability mechanism for learning object repositories

Griff Richards and Marek Hatala

The wholesale adoption of Internet technology as a channel for education and training has resulted in an abundance of learning resources in web-ready digital format. These digital learning objects (LOs) may be lesson content, stored as text, audio-visual or interactive media files (Wiley, 2002), or simply learning activity templates expressed in educational markup language EML (Koper, 2000). Despite their apparent ubiquity, the locating and reuse of LOs is hampered by a lack of coordinated effort in addressing issues related to their storage, cataloguing and rights management. Intensive efforts have been made to create portal repositories by communities such as MERLOT, SMETE and, in Canada, by TeleCampus and CAREO. Not surprisingly, each entity produces a rather individual reflection of its own perceived organizational needs, and the concept of making all these repositories work together, while laudable, has received less attention.

This chapter discusses general problems of repository interoperability and describes our proposed mechanism for 'cobbling' together individual LORs as well as large networks, into a globally scalable pool of LORs. We call our method 'semantic cobblestones'.

Typical functionality of learning object repositories

By-passing the traditional debate on what is or is not a 'learning object', we will pragmatically constrain ourselves to discussing those digital learning resources which can be made available over the Internet (Richards, 2002). As a wider variety of non-textual LOs have appeared, and as LOs are retrieved from databases or constructed on demand, less and less of the potential LO pool is locatable using text-based search engines such as Google. Digital libraries and object repositories solve this problem by using explicit metadata schemas to catalogue or 'index' learning objects. Metadata usually contain the name, location and physical attributes of the file, as well as fields containing keywords and other descriptive information that is pertinent to the community of interest. Once the LOs are 'tagged' with metadata, a search engine can be used to search the database of metadata in order to identify potentially useful LOs and determine their location and other information such as availability, file size and type and cost. A successful search may yield several LOs from which a selection can be made by either best-fit algorithms, or by previewing the object. Thus LORs not only serve as a place to store digital learning resources, but as an efficient means to enable the sharing of educational materials for use in new and different contexts.

At their core, LORs function as rather simple databases of metadata that point to physical locations of digitized learning resources. Primary repositories are digital libraries that store the actual object, while secondary repositories or meta-portals facilitate the collation and searching of metadata, and point to the primary location. Some LORs may offer ancillary services to facilitate transactions in the exchange of information, and associated functions of control of access and security of the transactions. A media production house might also integrate workflow functions dealing with task management, rights management, life-cycle and credits for the production team. Generally, a LOR is designed, developed and configured in response to the needs of its intended user community, although an off-the-shelf solution with reasonable functionality would appeal to many – particularly those with less technical aspirations.

Since LORs reflect the needs of their sponsoring organization, it is not unusual for the metadata records to be mixed with other information about internal workflow, intellectual property and copyright. This internal information needs to be protected from accidental release. Security of LOs and their metadata may also be of concern. Typically, individuals or organizations allowing searching by external users will want to control the degree of access to their collection. For these reasons, even a simple repository such as SPLASH <http://www.eduSplash.net> offered a selection of three primitive protection levels: Public, Metadata only, and Local access.

The goal of repository interoperability is to facilitate discovery and reuse of LOs. With completely independent LORs, anyone wanting to search for a particular LO would have to first identify each repository of potential interest, and initiate a separate search through each site. One of the basic goals of interoperability is to automate this search process, so a repository search command could be repeated or relayed to other repositories and the results would reflect the larger global pool of LORs rather than simply those objects available at the local level. This is especially important if we want to expedite a search and discovery process using an autonomous software agent.

Centralized, distributed and peer-to-peer repositories

To frame the discussion on interoperability, it is useful to look at three basic approaches to building repositories: centralized, distributed and peer-to-peer networks. To demonstrate how these basic approaches might operate, we use the example of the Province of New Brunswick's TeleCampus <http://www.telecampus.edu>, a repository that collects world-wide information about online course offerings, and allows these metadata to be searched by those seeking learning opportunities in almost any discipline. Once harvested into a centralized location, these second-order metadata pose a maintenance problem for those who must ensure that the metadata are accurate and up-to-date.

A centralized solution to this maintenance problem would be to enable or require institutions to maintain their own metadata at the TeleCampus. The metadata would follow a standard format input through web forms, or uploaded from a tailored metadata editing tool such as ALOHA <http://aloha.netera.ca>. Alternatively, a distributed solution might require each institution to maintain their own repository, and TeleCampus could simply relay search requests to the member institutions. The metadata that are searched are native to the repositories actually holding the objects, and are locally maintained by each institution and will vary in quality with the local priorities and available resources.

In a Napster-style peer-to-peer network, learning object repositories such as SPLASH (Hatala and Richards, 2002) can directly query other portals in the network. In a pure peer-to-peer network both control and storage of the learning object assets are decentralized – there is no central control node governing access. Search requests are simply relayed until objects are found or the network is exhausted.

It should be noted that repositories are built of layers of technology – objects are wrapped with metadata (which in turn can refer to ontologies) and placed in a database with a web interface, protocols and transport layers. Object sharing and exchange can succeed only when we consider interoperability at all levels.

Lessons from POOL

In Hatala and Richards (2002) we described our tiered network of LORs as POOL, POND and SPLASH, based on our peer-to-peer application <http://www.edusplash.net> and our use of semantic technologies for mapping metadata fields when searching disparate LORs, that is matching local metadata schemes to a more global metadata schema such as IMS LOM, or its subset, CanCore <http://www.cancore.org>.

A peer-to-peer (P2P) network such as Napster or Kazaa is built of local nodes, essentially applications that are installed on the computer desktop and can send out and relay search requests to other nodes. After a flurry of searching, metadata about the objects found are relayed back to the searcher, and ultimately a LO is selected and transferred to the requesting machine. We extended this ability to search other peers to search targeted repositories that were not intrinsically part of the P2P network. To search non-SPLASH repositories such as CAREO <http://www.careo.org> required the installation of the P2P application on a computer topologically close to CAREO, and then customizing the commands to match the XML-RPC expectations of the CAREO database. (This approach is commonly known as 'wrapping'. We discuss wrappers in later parts of this chapter.)

Since both SPLASH and CAREO use the CanCore metadata application profile, there was a direct semantic mapping. In other words, every field such as title, name, or date used in the SPLASH metadata had a corresponding title, name or date field in the CAREO metadata. In the case of AVIRE, an Australian architectural repository, the dedicated SPLASH machine required mapping as many fields as possible to the non-CanCore metadata, and a custom interface to translate SPLASH commands to the search and access commands used by AVIRE.

As we mapped and translated SPLASH to various repositories of interest, we realized the obvious conclusion that it would entail much less work if:

A. as many repositories as possible used common protocols and meta-data, and
B. customization could be done through a user-configurable toolset.

In condition A we could expect to automate much of the inter-repository transactions and under condition B we expected to pass along the burden for interoperability by enticing third parties with an open set of easy-to-use user-configurable tools.

We dubbed the tool that would pave the way for interoperability as 'cobblestones' and, by using semantic technologies for the mapping between the sub-level ontologies, we propose to build a set of 'semantic cobblestones' for this purpose.

Interoperability: Goals and mechanisms

With the LORs being created rapidly to support the immediate needs of the individual institutions or consortia, interoperability came to many as an afterthought. For the educational audience the problem of interoperability may be perceived as a new phenomenon emerging as a result of dynamic negotiations around the standard metadata fields for describing LOs. Although this is true to some extent, the problem is well known in other fields, such as digital libraries, agent systems, and so on. Before trying to address the interoperability issues in the context of LORs and the current state of Internet technologies, we first examine what we can learn about the problem and approaches to interoperability from other domains.

Although Paepcke *et al.* (1998) couch their examination of the inter-operability issues in the context of digital libraries, their framework is

Table 24.1 Criteria for evaluating interoperability solutions

Criterion	Description
High degree of component autonomy	Provides more local control over implementation and operation of components
	Makes it easier to include legacy systems as participating components
	High autonomy can lead to solutions that allow only the lowest common denominator of functionality
	Can require expensive construction of component descriptions or translation facilities
Low cost of infrastructure	Can be difficult to asses, especially if development is distributed
Ease of contributing components	Incremental cost of enabling the interoperability when building a new component
	Higher cost may be justified if provides other engineering advantages or makes it easier to use
Ease of using components	Has two aspects: the complexity of creating client component and complexity of interacting with the component at run time
Breadth of task complexity supported by the solution	Variance of supported services
	Ease of adding a new service during system operation
Scalability in the number of components	Number of components the solution can effectively support

suitable for the analysis of interoperability for any heterogeneous distributed resources and services. To evaluate interoperability solutions Paepcke *et al.* define six criteria as shown in Table 24.1.

The *autonomy* refers to compliance with pre-set global rules: the higher the autonomy, the more local control is possible. Typically the autonomy is limited to some degree with respect to protocols and data exchange formats, or the system may require a component to participate in transactions and adhere to only one predefined schema.

The *cost of infrastructure* criterion is one aspect dealing with the total cost of investment to support the solution. The incremental cost of building new components is covered by the *ease of contributing components* criterion. This can involve both hardware costs and the complexity of software development. The *ease of use* criterion recognizes two aspects: the ease of using an infrastructure and creating a client using this infrastructure and the complexity of interacting with the components in the run-time. The *breadth of task complexity* criterion refers to the functionality supported by the solution. Finally, *scalability* is measured as the number of components the solution can effectively support.

Paepcke *et al.* (1998) classified possible interoperability solutions into five families: strong standards, families of standards, external mediation, specification-based and mobile functionality.

1. *Strong standards* provide for the easiest way to achieve interoperability. Using this approach, all the components have to adhere to predefined standards and protocol. A good example of this approach is the Z39.50 standard from the library community <http://lcweb.loc. gov/z3950/agency/>, or the Open Archive Initiative (OAI, www. openarchives.org) specifying its Protocol for Metadata Harvesting (PMH) and the Dublin Core schema as standards. Adding a new repository into such a framework means to implement defined protocol and use the metadata schema defined for the framework.

2. The *families-of-standards* approach builds the framework around the idea of a set of standards the repositories can use for communication. Once two repositories agree (preferably automatically) on the standard they want to use, all the following communication uses those standards. This approach can be used at several communication layers as specified in the Open System Interconnection (OSI) standard defined by the International Standards Organization (ISO).

3. The *external mediation* method externalizes the functionality supporting interoperability from the participating local systems. The mediators provide translations between formats and interaction protocols. Two main types of mediators are *gateways*, which are most commonly used for translating between interaction protocols, and *wrappers* for translating between schemas. Gateways typically connect two different networks while wrappers connect an individual component with different schema to the network.

4. *Specification-based interaction* is an interoperability mechanism more common in autonomous agent systems. Here each component describes its own services and provides this description to others. The communication between two components starts with downloading the mutual specifications. The following communication is based on the reasoning about participants' abilities. This highly autonomous technique has great potential in creating adaptive systems supporting community building, but it is very complex and difficult to implement.

5. Finally, the *mobile functionality* depends on the system's ability to exchange a whole application code. The interoperability is achieved by retrieving the code that is able to communicate with other systems. Java applets are a good example of this approach. This method makes it difficult to incorporate local needs (low autonomy) but it makes it easier to contribute new components. Table 24.2 lists some of the major advantages and disadvantages of the outlined interoperability solutions.

Significant interoperability efforts

The e-learning community has seen fruitful initiatives in the standardization of LO metadata by IEEE and towards the standardization of other

Table 24.2 Advantages and disadvantages of interoperability solutions

Solution	Advantages	Disadvantages
1. Strong standards *Z 39.50, TCP/IP, HTTP*	Appropriate standard is a powerful tool Wide availability of the modules and services Supports infrastructure investments	Difficult to agree on, i.e. result being a complex combination of features Hinders site autonomy, bans to introduce local optimizations and local preferences
2. Families of standards *OSI, online payments, DRI*	Layered architecture enables to address problems at different levels independently Alleviates the problem of autonomy infringement	Standards might not be available
3. External mediation *Wrappers, gateways, global schema translation*	Very high level of autonomy Ease of use Good scalability	Mapping not always easy Mismatch in interaction models Contributing a new component requires corresponding mediation facility (can be alleviated by family of standards)
4. Specification-based interaction *KIF, agent communication*	High autonomy Good scalability	Assumes that all components use same knowledge exchange facilities High complexity
5. Mobile functionality *Applets*	Easy to contribute new components Ease of use if security resolved	Low autonomy due to same execution model Expensive because of the latency, bandwidth consumption, risk management

aspects of LOs and learning processes by organizations such as IMS and ADL. More recently, the e-learning community is focusing on the ability to connect and use resources located in distributed and heterogeneous repositories. This process closely resembles the initiatives in the domain of digital libraries. In this section we examine how the interoperability is handled in four major projects: the National Science Digital Library project, the IMS Digital Repository Interoperability group, our recent POOL project, and our current approach to interoperability in the eduSource Canada project.

NSDL

The National Science Digital Library (NSDL) project <http://www.nsdl.org> is a major project funded by the National Science Foundation with the goal of building a digital library for education in science, mathematics, engineering and technology. The potential collections have a wide variety of data types, metadata standards, protocols, authentication schemes and business models (Arms *et al.*, 2002). The aim of the NSDL interoperability is to build coherent services for users from technically different components. NSDL aims to support three levels of interoperability: federation, harvesting and gathering.

The *federation* implements the strong standards approach with libraries agreeing to use specific standards. The *harvesting* allows higher autonomy. The only requirement is to enable a limited set of services via a simple exchange mechanism. NSDL is using Protocol for Metadata Harvesting (PMH) developed by the Open Archive Initiative. To support the metadata harvesting from the repository, a relatively simple wrapper communicated via PMH and providing metadata based on the Dublin Core standard has to be implemented. Third, *gathering* uses the web crawler technique to collect information from the organizations that do not formally participate in the NSDL program.

NSDL has selected eight preferred metadata element sets to store metadata in. Preferably, the libraries should store the metadata in their original format but they have to be able to serve the metadata in Dublin Core format. Effectively this solution establishes Dublin Core as the lowest common denominator for the NSDL.

IMS DRI

The IMS Digital Repository Interoperability Group, in its public draft specifications for the digital repository interoperability (IMS DRI, 2002), provided a functional architecture and reference model for repository interoperability. Aiming at very broad application of the specification, the document makes a recommendation only at a certain level, leaving the resolution of more operational issues to the system implementers. Five basic functions defined by IMS DRI are: search/expose, gather/expose, submit/store, request/deliver, and alert/expose. For the *search* function, the specification recommends using XQuery <http://www.w3c.org/XML/Query> with SOAP protocol or Z39.50. For the *gather* function, the OAI's harvesting protocol is recommended. No recommendation is made for other functions in the current version of the specification.

The specification does not explicitly deal with repositories that might be storing metadata in different formats, as it implicitly assumes metadata to be in the IMS LOM format. The IMS DRI in its current version does not explicitly deal with heterogeneity of the repositories and it is up to the implementers to ensure the format compatibility. The DRI Group recommends development of a 'minimal search grammar' and suggests use of the Dublin Core metadata as a lowest common denominator for cross-domain searches.

POOL

The POOL project ran from 1999 to 2002. One of its major goals was to build an infrastructure for connecting heterogeneous repositories into one network. The infrastructure used a peer-to-peer model in which nodes could be individual repositories (called SPLASH) or community or enterprise repositories (PONDs). PONDS were connected to the POOL network using a specialized peer performing both functions of a gateway and wrapper. The POOL network used the JXTA peering protocol <http://www. juxta.org> and followed the CanCore/IMS metadata profile/specification to exchange metadata. Connected PONDs communicated using wrappers either via HTTP and CGI or XML-RPC protocol. The wrapper also performs the metadata schema translation functions that are needed. The network supported a high autonomy for the repositories, but this required creating a specialized wrapper translating between the metadata schemas and communication protocols.

eduSourceCanada

The eduSource project <http://www.edusource.ca> brings together major LOR players in Canada to create an open infrastructure for linking interoperable LORs. The infrastructure will support a wide range of services (autonomy and breadth of functionality) with ease of connecting a new system into the infrastructure and ease of use of existing systems. EduSource aims at creating a system that is both open to new services becoming participants in the system and existing systems connecting to the EduSource. For example, a repository using PMH protocol and Dublin Core metadata can either communicate with the eduSource network as a whole via gateway mechanisms or can become a participant with access to a wider range of services via the interoperability connector called semantic cobblestone.

Semantic cobblestones: Interoperability in eduSource

The interoperability solution for the eduSource project aims to provide an effective and expandable infrastructure that conforms to the IMS DRI specification and provides a generic solution for connectivity to other major initiatives such as OAI, NSDL and the Edutella project <http:// edutella.jxta.org>. The solution builds on open standards and enables any interested party to connect to the eduSource network and access its services. The eduSource project uses the lessons learned from other projects and specifically (in the area of interoperability) the POOL project (Hatala and Richards, 2002).

The backbone of the interoperability is the eduSource Communication Language (ECL), which implements the core functions defined in the IMS Digital Repository Interoperability reference model. A primary communication protocol in eduSource is SOAP, and ECL is implemented as asynchronous SOAP messages. The default metadata standard selected for the eduSource is CanCore/IEEE LOM.

The eduSource infrastructure makes no assumptions about the format of metadata stored in the repositories participating in the network. The repositories store metadata in their local format and metadata are available and can be used by other services and tools in original form or mapped into other supported standards.

Such a high level of autonomy typically makes it difficult to add a new component into the network. In eduSource we alleviate this problem by providing a highly configurable connector, the semantic cobblestone, with predefined mapping mechanisms for the most common metadata schemas along with the ability to expand its functionality by defining additional mappings.

In addition to mapping between metadata schemas, the connector enables users to define mapping at the deeper semantic level. This is necessary for mapping between taxonomical or ontological structures used as sources of values for the metadata elements, for example in the classification element. The ability to map between two ontological structures is essential for allowing individual repositories to expand metadata schema with elements supporting local community needs.

The third function of semantic cobblestone is to translate between repository native communication protocol and ECL. We do not consider this function to be as essential as implementation of the ECL over the SOAP protocol, which is supported with libraries simplifying the process.

The internal eduSource infrastructure is being implemented using a web services model with the envisioned semantic web services extension (Ankolenkar *et al.*, 2002). The initial set of services available in the eduSource network are repositories for storing LOs, metadata repositories for storing LO metadata, tagging tools for creating metadata records, search tools for searching LOs, aggregation tools for aggregating LOs into lessons and a digital right management component for handling copyrighted materials. Similar to POOL, the eduSource infrastructure supports organizational and individual (peer-to-peer) repositories.

Gateways: Interoperability outside of eduSource

Although the eduSource internal protocol provides a flexible and efficient solution, it is unlikely that well-established repositories and resources will invest resources and convert their protocols to the ECL. However, the ability of the eduSource project to connect to other established protocols and major initiatives is of the utmost importance to the project participants. EduSource addresses the problem of outside interoperability by providing a second type of mediator simply called eduSource gateway. EduSource gateway is modelled after the design patter of an adapter (Gamma *et al.*, 1995) functioning at the network level. The range of the functionality is similar to that of the semantic cobblestone, but the main function of the gateway is to mediate between ECL and communication protocols used by the outside systems. Two protocols being implemented at the beginning are OAI PMH and Z39.50. The gateway component is being developed as an open source product by the eduSource community with a clearly defined architecture of chained handlers, which makes it easy to incorporate a new functionality or update an existing one.

Another specific functionality the gateway may perform is a selector of internal eduSource services for the incoming requests. This functionality has been identified as important but will require more attention in the near future. Figure 24.1 illustrates the interoperability model for the eduSource network.

The implications of interoperability for your organization

Any organization willing to invest resources into building a LOR is addressing some specific organizational needs. The selected solution has to fulfil as many needs as possible while leaving possibility for the future

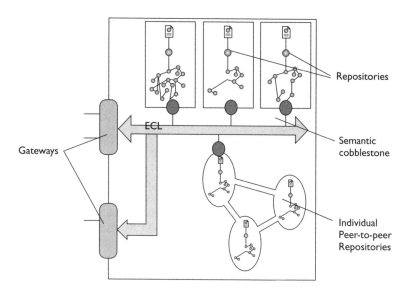

Figure 24.1 Proposed eduSource interoperability framework

growth widely open. Probably the most pressing need is to maintain a collection of LOs to support the operation of the organization. Although this requirement can be very prescriptive for the selection of the system with the proper set of features, it does not provide any guidance for selection of the best solution for sustainable growth. Being able to seamlessly discover and manipulate both internal and external resources, the solution has to provide an appropriate level of interoperability.

The criteria outlined in the beginning of this chapter are a good starting point for understanding the required minimum interoperability level. The analysis should consider not only individual organizational needs but should also include the major potential sources of the LOs and established and emerging standards. Repository interoperability is a rapidly evolving area and several promising solutions outlined in this chapter should provide an initial understanding of the main issues.

For background information on e-learning standardization bodies and processes read Friesen's (2002) gentle overview of the area. Latest standards, specifications, and reference implementations are available from the websites of IMS <http://www.imsglobal.org>, Dublin Core <http://dublincore.org>, IEEE LTSC (ltsc.ieee.org), SCORM <http://www.adlnet.org> and OAI <http://www.openarchives.org>. Significant initiatives and projects always provide a valuable source of technical information on how to deal with specific issues: NSDL (Arms *et al.*, 2002), eduSource <http://www.edusource.ca>, Australian Learning Federation <http://www.thelearningfederation.edu.au>, and Edutella <http://edutella.jxta.org>.

As with any system, it is probably more important to examine the needs of the users rather than adapt a pre-existing solution. Flexibility is going to be important, perhaps more so than control.

References

Ankolenkar, A. *et al.* (2002) DAML-S: Web service description for the Semantic Web, in *International Semantic Web Conference 2002*, eds I. Horrocks and J. Hendler, pp. 348–65, Springer.

Arms, W. Y. *et al.* (2002) (accessed 23 January 2003) A spectrum of interoperability: The site for science prototype for the NSDL, *D-Lib Magazine*, **8** (1), (Online) http://www.dlib.org/dlib/january02/arms/01arms.html.

Friesen, N. (2002) (accessed 23 May 2003) E-learning standardization: An overview, (Online) http://www.cancore.org/e-learning_standardization_overview.doc.

Gamma, E. *et al.* (1995) *Design patterns*, Addison-Wesley, Reading, MA.

Hatala, M. and Richards, G. (2002) Global vs. community metadata standards: Empowering users for knowledge exchange, in *International Semantic Web Conference 2002*, eds I. Horrocks and J. Hendler, pp. 292–306, Springer, Berlin.

IMS DRI (2002) (accessed 23 January 2003) Core functions information model, *IMS Digital Repositories Interoperability*, (Online) Http://Www.Imsglobal.Org/Digitalrepositories/Driv1p0/Imsdri_Infov1p0.Html.

Koper (2000) (accessed 28 March 2003) Educational modelling language reference manual, Open University of the Netherlands (Online) http://eml.ou.nl.

Paepcke, A. *et al.* (1998) Interoperability for digital libraries worldwide, *Communications of the ACM*, **41** (4): 33–43.

Richards, G. (2002) The challenges of the learning object paradigm, *Canadian Journal of Learning and Technology*, **28** (3): 3–10.

Wiley, D. A. (2002) (accessed 1 May 2003) The instructional use of learning objects, Agency for Instructional Technology and the Association for Educational Communications and Technology, (Online) http://www.reusability.org/read/.

Chapter 25

Knowledge modelling for designing learning objects

Fuhua Oscar Lin

Over the past few years, universities and colleges have demonstrated substantial progress in using the Web to deliver courses. Educators generally agree that in any educational setting, the ability to tailor courses and course materials to individual students' needs is desirable, and that these needs are determined by such factors as students' previous knowledge of the subjects, their learning styles, their general attitudes, and their cultural and linguistic backgrounds. A skilled teacher will be able to achieve this goal in one-to-one interactions with learners, but not, as a rule, in the lecture hall/classroom settings typical of higher education. As well, a developer of traditional course materials will not be able to cater to an individual learner's needs to any great extent. Web-based educational materials can potentially be much more flexible than traditional course materials because e-learning has the potential advantage of rapid access to distributed educational repositories for course authors and students.

Problems

Ongoing research, standardization efforts, and the increasing availability of electronic educational resources have all paved the way towards building adaptive course generation and delivery systems. At the same time, the number of college-level courses delivered over the Internet and the number of students enrolled in distance education courses are increasing continuously. Problems of efficiency and cost-effectiveness have developed and will become more serious unless novel mechanisms are implemented to support educators in the development of web-based courses through knowledge sharing and reuse.

Life-cycle of e-learning courses

The life-cycle of an e-learning course starts with the course planning. The next stage is course development, when the course is designed and developed by a team of course developers consisting of subject-matter experts, editors, and visual designers. Then, the course package is delivered to students via the Web under the coordination and facilitation of an instructor. One or more instructors may be needed to provide a tutoring service for the course, depending on the size of the class. The course continually goes through course evaluation and course revision until it is closed.

To be successful in e-learning, we should implement emerging technologies to develop software tools to reduce the workload of educators and to provide advanced learning services, such as adaptive curriculum sequencing, problem-solving support, adaptive presentation, and student model-matching.

The agent-based approach

A software agent is a software package that carries out tasks for others autonomously without direct intervention by its master once the tasks have been delegated. The researchers at Intelligent Software Agents Lab at Carnegie Mellon University's Robotics Institute <http://www-2.cs.cmu.edu/~softagents/> define an 'agent' as 'an autonomous, (preferably) intelligent, collaborative, adaptive computational entity'. What is important in designing e-learning courses is the ability to gather relevant knowledge and to generate personalized courses. In other words, we emphasize agents' autonomy and local knowledge about learning design tasks.

Using the agent-based approach

First, distributing tasks to numerous specialized agents lets new services come and go without disturbing the overall system. Second, limiting the complexity of an individual agent simplifies control, promotes reusability, and provides a framework for tackling interoperability. Third, the use of agents, because of their autonomous nature, begets a 'fire-and-forget' approach. We do not need to remember to invoke them explicitly at the right point. They are able to react for themselves if they have access to the right data. The central feature of software agents is their ability to independently carry out tasks delegated to them by users or by other software applications. For example, the robust marketplace-like educational resources available today (or tomorrow) simply could not function unless we were able to delegate to software the multitude of tasks that would otherwise be left to armies of people to handle. Fourth, agents are more robust than conventional software. If conditions and environments are less than ideal, agents should be able to degrade gracefully rather than just failing and perhaps bringing down another process.

The obstacles

The use of agent technology in designing web-based courses faces two main obstacles. One is the difficulty of understanding and interacting with digital educational resources and systems. The other is the difficulty of modelling agent knowledge, such as experience knowledge, when designing domain-specific courses. Here, knowledge modelling can be characterized as a set of techniques focusing on the 'specification' of static and dynamic knowledge resources.

The goal

In response to these problems, the goal of this chapter is therefore to propose some models and mechanisms for knowledge modelling and management to enable and support educational agents' activities, focusing first on knowledge modelling for developing course design agents and second on course design knowledge. Then an approach to modelling goal-based learning objects (LOs) will be introduced.

Literature review

Since 1990, a number of studies have been made of knowledge modelling for adaptive learning environments and web-based adaptive educational systems (Brusilovsky, 1996). For example, McCalla and Greer (1990) described the curriculum from a computational perspective, while Harley (1992) described the curriculum from a more traditional educational perspective. Paquette, Aubin and Crevier (1999) proposed a knowledge-based method for the engineering of learning systems to solve problems with the existing computerized tools intended for pedagogical design. Vassileva (1997) developed a tool, DCG (Dynamic Course Generation), which uses 'concepts structure' as a road map to generate the plan of a course. Murray (1998) described a distributed curriculum model using a topic server architecture. This allows a web-based tutorial to include a specification for another tutorial, so that the best fit to this specification will automatically be found at run-time. Carey et al. (1999) developed a Learner-Centered Design (LCD) Idea Kit that supports the design process with information and a structure for creating learner profiles, scenario narratives and a design visualization of high-level design issues.

Considering the needs of learner-centred design and the distributed nature of e-learning, many researchers have opted for agent-based architectures (Boticario and Gaudioso, 2000; Chan, 1995; Frasson, 1996; Greer et al., 2001; Johnson, Rickel and Lester, 2000; Lin and Holt, 2001) to construct intelligent distributed learning environments. For example, Greer et al. (2001) developed and deployed the I-Help agent-based peer-help learning support system.

A current trend in e-learning involves the development and adoption of learning standards such as SCORM (Sharable Content Object Reference Model) <http://www.adlnet.org/>, the IEEE Learning Technology Standards Committee (LTSC) Learning Object Metadata (LOM) standard <http://ltsc.ieee.org/wg12/>, and the development of Extensible Markup Language (XML)-based educational metadata repositories.

Course design knowledge

Course design process

In e-learning environments, in addition to being able to find digital educational resources, the system is able to assist instructors and learners in organizing and scheduling learning activities. LOs will be assembled into lessons and courses designed to enable students to achieve specific learning goals, subject to constraints on pedagogy, quality, cost and duration.

As illustrated in Figure 25.1, the development of a new e-learning course usually occurs in two phases. One involves designing a course structure and planning a set of learning tasks according to the learning goals and initial knowledge of a student. The other involves organizing the course content according to the learning style and preference of the student. Experience has shown that developing a new e-learning course is costly and time-consuming and that delivering a personalized one is even more difficult.

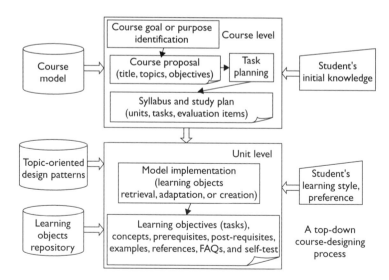

Figure 25.1 The process of designing e-learning courses

Knowledge of course structure design

We formulate course design knowledge by using the following elements:

- learning goals and goal-trees;
- goal-course plan mapping rules;
- course plans;
- constraints on the educational dimensions;
- rules and algorithms for curriculum patterns management;
- rules and procedural knowledge for curriculum pattern realization; and
- goal-based LOs.

Learning goals

A course must have an aim or purpose. Purposes and goals are formulated on many levels. A learning goal can be divided into sub-goals and
represented by a tree. Figure 25.2 illustrates an example of learning goal
decomposition in a 'Software Engineering' course.

Here, the goal G1 'To learn "Software Engineering"' is divided into
four sub-goals: G11 'To learn the theoretical foundations for "Software
Engineering"', G12 'To learn the conventional methods for "Software
Engineering"', G13 'To learn object-oriented "Software Engineering"',
and G14 'To learn advanced topics in "Software Engineering"'. G11 can
be further decomposed into two sub-sub-goals, G111 'To learn the concepts
of the product and the process' and G112 'To learn software project
management'.

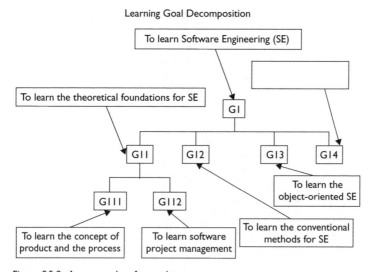

Figure 25.2 An example of a goal-tree

Goal-course mapping rules

To enable a course design agent to find a course plan enabling the achievement of the learning goals selected by learners, the goal-course mapping knowledge is represented in the form of 'IF-THEN' rules which describe a mapping from a learning goal space to a course plan space. Table 25.1 provides some examples of such rules for the Software Engineering course.

Petri Nets-represented course plan

To represent course plans and enable adaptive decision-making in curriculum planning, we adopt a formal specification model – the Petri Nets model (Reisig, 1985). Petri Nets is a formal and graphically appealing computer language, which is appropriate for modelling systems with concurrency <http://www.daimi.au.dk/PetriNets/>. Petri Nets enables us to describe simultaneous and asynchronous events, which are typical of distributed learning activities, and to specify how the system state changes as a consequence of learner actions. The Petri Nets model allows for the possibility of representing systems whose behaviours are varied according to the context, and therefore it is particularly suitable for formalizing learner-adapted curriculum plans.

In the Petri Nets model for representing course plans, transitions denote learning tasks, while places denote preconditions and post-conditions. Arcs represent the relations among places and learning tasks. Figure 25.3 shows an example of a Petri Nets-represented course plan, namely course plan SE2 'Design course for Software Engineering'. An instructor teaching a one-semester (or one-quarter) sequence covers *B1* (the theoretical foundation), then starts *B3* (the life-cycle). *B1* can then be taught in parallel with *B3* or at the end of the course, while the students are doing the term project (*TP*). When teaching the two-semester sequence, the blocks of the course are taught in order. The students will then be fully prepared for the term-based team project that they will do in the following semester.

In Figure 25.3, Places *P1, P2, . . ., Pn* are used to represent the selection status. If the marking of place *Pi M(Pi)* has a value 0, the task *Bi* is not selected. If it has a value 1, then *Bi* is selected.

Rules for course plan selection

A course plan is further determined according to the level of the students and the duration of the course to be offered. From the example given

Table 25.1 Examples of rules for software engineering courses

Rule #1: G111 and G112	→	SE 1 (Software Project Management)
Rule #2: G12 and G13	→	SE 2 (Design Course)
Rule #3: G13 and G14	→	SE 3 (Method Course)

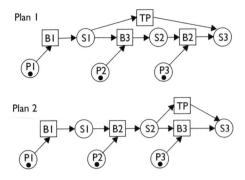

Figure 25.3 Examples of course plans represented by Petri Nets

earlier about Software Engineering courses, we can have the two Course Plan Selection rules listed in Table 25.2.

Topic tree and concept map

A topic tree is a way of representing or organizing a body of knowledge, being a simplified version of a concept map. A concept map goes beyond the typical outline in that it shows relationships between concepts, including bi-directional relationships. Concept maps can thus illustrate faulty views individuals may have and help us understand how students may misconstrue meanings from subject matter. Concept maps can be used as excellent planning devices for instruction, as shown in Figures 25.4, 25.5 and 25.6.

The course structure model as a fuzzy constraint mathematical model

Based on the concepts and ontology of a domain, a 'curriculum pattern' can be formulated. A curriculum pattern is a goal-oriented instructional plan that can be represented as a group of quantitative and qualitative constraints and sequential relations among a set of topics. The parameterized constraints of the course structure describe the curriculum design

Table 25.2 Two course plan selection rules

Rule #001: If course _ID=SE2 and the curriculum is for one semester for four-year undergraduates, select Plan SE2_001;

Rule #002: If course _ID=SE2 and the curriculum is for two semesters for four-year undergraduates, select Plan SE2_002.

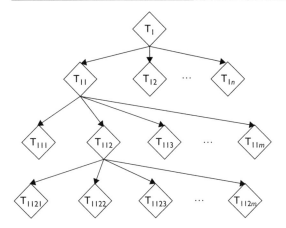

Figure 25.4 The architecture of topic trees

dimensions. They can be acquired by using knowledge engineering methods directly from domain experts' teaching experiences through converting the latent and tacit knowledge of subject-matter experts into articulated knowledge. The sequential relations can also be obtained by using information retrieval methods from the semantic expression of LOs, and other descriptions of the resources.

Let T denote the targeted total amount of learning time (duration) for the course for a typical target audience, and ΔT the error of the total time.

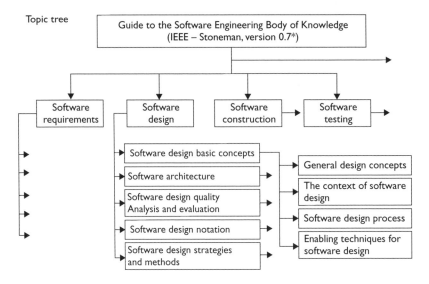

Figure 25.5 An example of topic trees

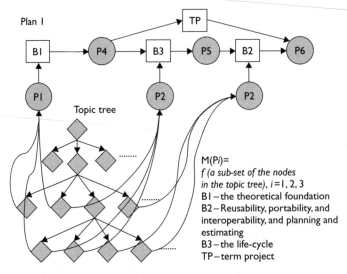

M(Pi)=
f (a sub-set of the nodes
in the topic tree), i=1, 2, 3
B1 – the theoretical foundation
B2 – Reusability, portability, and
interoperability, and planning and
estimating
B3 – the life-cycle
TP – term project

Figure 25.6 Course plan Petri Nets adaptation according to the topics in a topic tree

Let $TT(i)$ $(i = 1, 2, \ldots, n)$ denote the percentage of ith topic $(i = 1, 2, \ldots, n)$, $\Delta TT(i)$ $(i = 1, 2, \ldots, n)$ allowed errors in duration about $TT(i)$ $(i = 1, 2, \ldots, n)$, $CT(i)$ $(i = 1, 2, \ldots, m)$ the time percentage of ith competency type, $\Delta CT(i)$ the error limit of $CT(i)$ $(i = 1, 2, \ldots, m)$. Let $X(i)$ $(i = 1, 2, \ldots, n)$ denote the current learning time for the ith topic $(i = 1, 2, \ldots, n)$ of a course. Then, we have the total-time constraints:

$$T - \Delta T \leq X(1) + X(2) + \ldots + X(n) \leq T + \Delta T, X(i) \geq 0, i = 1, \ldots, n. \ (1)$$

the topic-time distribution:

$$TT(1) + TT(2) + \ldots + TT(n) = 100, \ (2)$$

with error limit distribution:

$$\{\Delta TT(1), \Delta TT(2), \ldots, \Delta TT(n)\}, \Delta TT(i) \geq 0, i = 1, \ldots, n.$$

competency-time distribution:

$$CT(1) + CT(2) + \ldots + CT(m) = 100, \ (3)$$

with error limit distribution:

$$\{\Delta CT(1), \Delta CT(2), \ldots, \Delta CT(m)\}, \Delta CT(i) \geq 0, i = 1, \ldots, m.$$

The competency can be classified in terms of cognitive classification. For example, a type set of competency for a subject can consist of the following elements: Knowledge, Comprehension, Application, Analysis, Synthesis, and Evaluation.

Other distributions, such as constraints involving 'total cost', which is the sum of the costs of all LOs, distribution for 'interactivity level – time', distribution for 'learning source type – time', and so on, can be formulated in a similar way.

Procedural knowledge of curriculum pattern realization

We formulate the problem of dynamically generating a curriculum plan as a process of dynamic curriculum pattern construction. The process of course generation can be viewed as a mapping from a customized curriculum pattern in a knowledge structure space to a subset of a LO space. Course generation is a process of heuristically solving a goal-directed multi-objective dynamic programming and planning model in (1) ~ (3) through searching for and selecting LOs.

The model of goal-oriented learning objects

The notion of 'learning objects' makes a major contribution to modelling and managing electronic educational resources, releasing task knowledge that was once confined in the heads of specialized human educators. A model of goal-oriented LOs defines their structure and includes LO topics, learning tasks and evaluation items. The tasks are predefined and correspond to the LOs assignments that a student is supposed to complete.

The evaluation items correspond to different forms of student evaluation over the timeline of the course, such as instructor's tests and the student's self-evaluation of his or her knowledge of domain terms. These evaluation items are used for a run-time evaluation of the current learner's knowledge of a specific topic and for consecutive adaptation of the student's behaviour.

Learner model

The purpose of building a learner model is to capture and specify the learner's goals and initial knowledge at the beginning of the course, to track the changes in the learner's knowledge, and to maintain a record of the changes in the learner's understanding of concepts as they evolve and change. Therefore, we represent the learner model with a tree of learning goals and a tree of topics, enhanced with tags indicating the learner's knowledge, interests and mastery status.

Agents for course design knowledge management

The system's intelligence should be represented and mediated via a set of intelligent software agents. They appear to be a very convenient tool for implementing the system architecture's processes. Intelligent, task-centred user interfaces can provide intelligent assistance to end-users and increase productivity in e-learning.

A knowledge management agent with three graphical editors (domains, courses and educational resources) is being developed and used by domain experts as a means for dynamically creating, modifying and testing the course design knowledge. With this agent, the knowledge base can obtain new and complex knowledge continuously during the course of application. For the domain knowledge management agent, a method is being developed to maintain the ontological knowledge autonomously when needed or with human supervision when desired. Some mechanisms for the curriculum pattern classification, curriculum pattern identification, pattern indexing, pattern storage and retrieval, pattern verification, and pattern learning are being developed.

Knowledge in goal-based adaptive learning objects

Goal-based learning

Goal-based learning is one of the most commonly used pedagogical approaches for optimizing e-learning (Naidu, 2001). It utilizes educational environments in which goal-based learning scenarios are used to anchor learning. Hence the 'goals' in this context refer to the successful completion of the task at hand. In order to achieve this goal, the learner needs to acquire particular skills and knowledge and make informed decisions.

Goal-based learning scenarios

A goal-based learning scenario is a simulation in which there is a problem to resolve or a mission to complete. This scenario serves both to motivate learners and also to provide them with the opportunity to learn by doing, by making mistakes, and by receiving feedback.

E-learning course materials can potentially be much more flexible than traditional course materials. They offer a unique opportunity to achieve the above-mentioned goal through personalization, where both the selection and presentation sequence of the units of educational material making up a LO or course are determined by a dynamically updated learner model. To model goal-based LOs, we use the Petri Nets theory as a tool for specifying learning activities (plans) and learning scenarios. Learning tasks are the basis of the learning scenario modelling and are constructed and organized towards some learning goals of the LO.

LP-nets

First, in order to achieve a certain learning goal, a set of learning tasks is organized into a plan called the 'Learning Plan' *(LP)*. A learning plan can be specified as a specialized Petri Net *(LP-net)*. A *LP-net* represents non-sequential causality among tasks that is used to personalize a *LP-net* by adapting to the student's learning status. A *LP-net* is a special kind of Petri Net defined with the following restrictions: (1) only one transition may be 'fired' at a time; (2) a *LP-net* is a safe Petri Net; (3) all arcs are weighted by 1. In addition, the following rules are applied to represent a learning plan by using the Petri Nets model described earlier: each learning task or well-established group of learning tasks is represented by a transition. For each transition T_i, we create one precondition-place input place PP_i representing the conditional predicate for triggering T_i. The markings of these places are determined by the *LP-net* adaptation described later. For every PP_i, after one token has been removed from it for firing the corresponding transition, the place cannot receive another token. The removal of a token indicates that the transition has already been fired and cannot be fired again. For each successor transition T_m of a transition T_i $(1 \leq i, m \leq n)$, we use one place CP_{im} so that (T_i, CP_{im}) and (CP_{im}, T_m) are two arcs of the LP-net. This kind of place in a *LP-net* represents the sequential relationship constraint between learning tasks (see Figure 25.7).

The learning process using a LO is a process of executing an adapted *LP-net*. For example, the goal of the LO might be '*to become familiar*

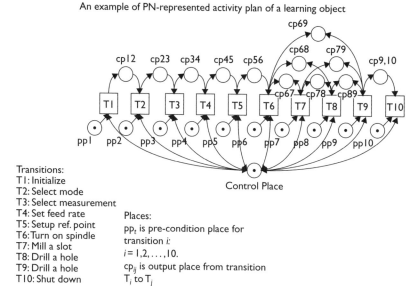

An example of PN-represented activity plan of a learning object

Transitions:
T1: Initialize
T2: Select mode
T3: Select measurement
T4: Set feed rate
T5: Setup ref. point
T6: Turn on spindle
T7: Mill a slot
T8: Drill a hole
T9: Drill a hole
T10: Shut down

Places:
pp_i is pre-condition place for transition i:
$i = 1, 2, \ldots, 10$.
cp_{ij} is output place from transition T_i to T_j

Figure 25.7 An example of LP-net

with the manual operations of CNC milling'. The tasks planned are to start the CNC milling machine, to mill a slot and drill two holes at the specified positions, and to shut down the machine. The *LP-net* for this learning is shown in Figure 25.8.

Task-oriented learning scenario models

To reduce the complexity of goal-based learning scenario modelling and analysis, a goal-based learning scenario is conducted for each task. From the *LP-net*, the whole learning scenario model for a given learning goal can be obtained. A task-oriented learning scenario model can also be represented by a Petri Net that consists of places and transitions representing knowledge about simulation, interface, instruction and evaluation (see Figure 25.9).

Simulation knowledge

In this architecture, a simulation module controls the objects in the learning environment. Each textual or graphical object in a simulated world is represented internally as an object with attributes. Some attributes control its visual appearance, while others control its behaviours. Rules and constraints that propagate changes from one object to the other determine object behaviour.

Interface knowledge

According to the learning task from the learning task-planning module, the simulation module generates learning scenarios in the learning environment to provide an interface that lets learners interact with the objects. A learning scenario model should be used to generate scenarios that give the learner experience when the learner performs various possible actions, including erroneous actions. To this end, an Expert Model is constructed

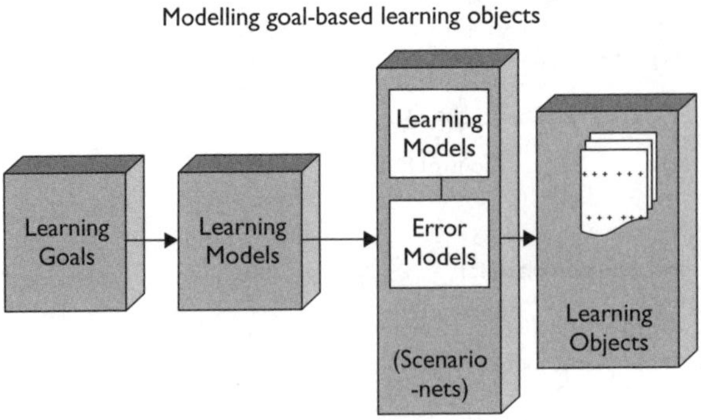

Figure 25.8 Learning scenario modelling

Specifying task-driven training scenarios — Error Model

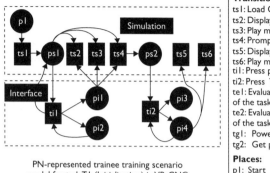

Transitions:
ts1: Load CNC machine model
ts2: Display the power button red
ts3: Play machine sound #01
ts4: Prompt Ready?
ts5: Display the power button blue (off)
ts6: Play machine sound #02
ti1: Press power ON button
ti2: Press YES
te1: Evaluate the trainee s performance of the task
te2: Evaluate the trainee s performance of the task
tg1: Power on first
tg2: Get physical setting ready

Places:
p1: Start
ps1: The CNC graphical model is loaded
ps2: Ready? appeared
pi1: ON button is pressed
pi2: One of the other buttons is pressed
pi3: YES button is pressed
pi4: One of the other buttons is pressed

PN-represented trainee training scenario
model for task T1 (Initialization) in VR-CNC

Figure 25.9 An example of task-driven learning scenarios

first by decomposing the tasks in a *LP-net*. From the Expert Model, an Error Model is extended by considering various possible violations, such as goal violation, plan violation and an action constraints model.

The most difficult task in constructing *Error Models* is that various possible violations should be forecast, and effective dilemma-resolution plans should be given. Typically, a learner may perform the following three types of actions: *correct* actions, *allowed but useless* actions, and *wrong* actions. The concept of 'bandwidth' is used to present a rough categorization of the amount and quality of the learner inputs. The learner's mental state in problem-solving is most important for the definition of 'bandwidth'. During learning, the learner passes through problem-solving from the beginning to the end of the learning task in the 'problem state spaces'.

On-line instruction, knowledge and impasse recognition

From the learning scenario models, the knowledge required for on-line instruction can be built by expanding the models. The action transitions for providing on-line instruction information in the nets are activated according to the input of the learner (error type) and the situation of the learning.

Evaluation knowledge

The function of the evaluation module is to provide information about learner performance to the task-planning module and the instruction modules by maintaining learner models. Learner models are described by using evaluation knowledge, which consists of a set of learning performance evaluation criteria. A learner model is key to individualization when planning learning tasks and providing on-line instruction, and refers to the information that a system keeps about individual learners. In our approach, a learner model in a LO is a set of task-related learning performance historical data. The learner model is updated after each learning session of an individual.

To represent the learner models, the *LP-net* is used, and for each transition representing a learning task in the *LP-net*, a pointer is added to the transition link of the learner performance data for this task. For a specific learner model, the personal history of learning about the learner is linked to it. The learner models are described by the following quantitative and qualitative parameters:

- task completion time, *time*(t_i), $(t_i \in T)$, refers to the latency associated with a transition for a task;
- proficiency level of transition t_i, is denoted by *level*(t_i) $(t_i \in T)$. One of the commonly-used ways to calculate the proficiency level of task or action *ti* about a learner is *level*$(t_i) = \rho(t_i) \times \mu(t_i)/v(t_i)$, where $\mu(t_i)$, $v(t_i)$, and $\rho(t_i)$ denote the number of the trial, the number of the correct actions, and the coefficient respectively; and
- the coefficient can be given by domain experts, based on error type and the proficiency levels of connecting nodes.

In the context of evaluation, error type *type*(t_i) could be (1) plan dependency violation, (2) action situational warranted, (3) goal failure, and (4) action constraint. Other types of errors might be identified in different tasks for performance measurement.

Probability, denoted by *prob*(t_i), refers to the odds of taking one path in the net versus other paths outputted from the same 'switch' transitions representing actions and transitions leading to alternative task selection in the *LP-net*. Probability allows one to think of an individual's performance on two performance dimensions: (1) effectiveness (optimal vs. non-optimal) and (2) efficiency.

Other learner behaviour measurements may be set for the specific purposes of different learning domains

Conclusion

Agent and LO technologies can support adaptive course planning and delivery adaptive course materials. Since agent knowledge modelling is a bottleneck in agent revolution, we proposed models for specifying the knowledge necessary for course design. Also, we developed a Petri Nets

(PN) model as a tool for specifying goal-based LOs. The process and model of agent knowledge modelling for e-learning may be interesting to those who are agent developers or LO authors. The notion of Petri Nets hierarchy in the learning scenarios facilitates the modelling and simulation for verification. We will convert the course design knowledge specification to a universal knowledge representation by conforming to the World Wide Web Consortium (W3C) standards such as Educational Modelling Language (EML), XML-based Petri Nets (PNML), and other international standards.

References

Boticario, J. G. and Gaudioso, E. (2000) A multiagent architecture for a web-based adaptive educational system in *2000 AAAI Spring Symposium*, pp. 24–7, AAAI Press, Madrid.

Brusilovsky, P. (1996) Methods and techniques of adaptive hypermedia, *User modeling and user adapted interaction*, **6**: 87–129.

Carey, T. T. *et al.* (1999) Scaling up a learning technology strategy: Supporting student/faculty teams in learner-centred design, *Journal of the Association for Learning Technology*, **7** (2): 15–26.

Chan, T. W. (1995) Artificial agents in distance learning, *International Journal of Educational Telecommunications*, **1** (2/3): 263–82.

Frasson, C. (1996) An actor-based architecture for intelligent tutoring systems, in *ITS '96 Conference, Lecture Notes in Computer Science*, Springer-Verlag, Hamburg.

Greer, J. *et al.* (2001) Lessons learned in deploying a multi-agent learning support system, in *AIED 2001, The I-Help Experience*, San Antonio.

Harley, J. R. (1992) The curriculum and instructional tasks: Goals, strategies, and tactics for interactive learning, *Adaptive learning environments: Foundations and frontiers*, ed. M. Jones, C. Tubman and P. Winne, pp. 123–46, Springer-Verlag, New York.

Johnson, W. L., Rickel, J. W. and Lester, J. C. (2000) Animated pedagogical agents: Face-to-face interaction in interactive learning environments, *International Journal of AI in Education*, **11**: 47–78.

Lin, F. and Holt, P. (2001) Towards agent-based online learning, in *(CATE 2001) Fourth IASTED International Conference on Computer and Advanced Technology in Education*, Banff, Canada.

McCalla, G. and Greer, J. E. (1990) SCENT-3: An architecture for intelligent advising in problem-solving domains, in *Intelligent tutoring systems*, eds C. Frasson and G. Gauthier, pp. 141–61, Norwood, NJ.

Murray, T. (1998) (accessed 30 November 2003) A model for distributed curriculum on the WWW, *Journal of Interactive Media in Education*, **5**, (Online) http://www.jime.open.ac.uk/98/5/.

Naidu, S. (2001) Designing and evaluating instruction for e-learning, in *Designing Instruction for Technology-Enhanced Learning*, ed. P. L. Rogers, pp. 134–59, Idea Group Publishing, Hershey, PA.

Paquette, G., Aubin, C. and Crevier, F. (1999) A knowledge-based method for the engineering of learning systems, *Journal of Courseware Engineering*, **2**: 63–78.

Reisig, W. (1985) *Petri Nets: An introduction*, Springer-Verlag, Berlin.

SCORM (2001) (accessed 21 February 2003) Advanced distributed learning initiative. Section on SCORM, *OASIS* (Online) http://www.adlnet.org.

Vassileva, J. (1997) Dynamic course generation on the WWW, in *Artificial intelligence in education: Knowledge and media in learning systems*, eds B. D. Boulay and R. Mizoguchi, pp. 498–505, IOS, Amsterdam.

Chapter 26

Educational modelling languages from an instructional engineering perspective

Gilbert Paquette

The accelerating evolution of learning technologies has multiplied the number of decisions one must take to create a Distributed Learning System (DLS). While it is true that a majority of the first web-based applications have been mostly ways to distribute information, more and more educators have become aware of the need to go beyond these simple uses of information and communication technologies. This context has created a much-needed interest in pedagogical methods and, more generally, the field of instructional design (ID).

In American literature, this discipline is known as 'instructional design' (ID), 'Instructional System Design' (ISD) or 'Instructional Science' (Reigeluth, 1983; Merrill, 1994). In Europe, one of the pioneers in the field used the term 'Scientific Pedagogy' (Montessori, 1958). The origin of ID goes back to John Dewey, who, a century ago, claimed the development of an 'interlinked science' between learning theories and educational practices (Dewey, 1900). His demand was heard at the beginning of the 1960s, when we can speak of the beginning of a new discipline. In the 1970s and the 1980s, *instructional theories* have blossomed, but today, it seems necessary to renew the ID methodology to support the creation of distributed learning systems in order to operationalize the theoretical foundation.

Previously, this author has proposed a new approach to ID (Paquette, 2001a). This approach is founded on cognitive science and labelled as *instructional engineering* (IE), which is defined as a method that supports the planning, analysis, design and the delivery of a learning system, integrating the concepts, the processes and the principles of ID, software engineering and cognitive engineering.

Software engineering brings some interesting solutions to this goal. From a technical point of view, a DLS is an information system, a complex array of software tools, digitized documents and communication services. By adapting software engineering principles to ID, IE proposes well-defined processes and principles that help produce 'deliveries', precisely describing the products of these processes. Moreover, multi-agent systems offer a good way to represent a DLS at delivery time as a set of agents, persons and computerized objects, interacting to help some of the agents to learn and others to facilitate learning.

Knowledge engineering is a methodology developed in the field of expert systems and artificial intelligence over the past thirty years. It helps to identify and structure knowledge, to explain it, to represent it in a symbolic or graphic language, facilitating its subsequent use by persons and computer systems. Knowledge engineering has been applied in education to build intelligent tutoring systems (Wenger, 1987), and also support systems for designers (Merrill, 1994; Spector, Polson and Muraida, 1993). There is now a renewal of interest in the integration of knowledge representation in the form of ontologies, as a basis for a new generation of the Web, the Semantic Web (Berners-Lee, Hendler and Lassila, 2001). In an IE method, the knowledge engineering processes can help designers define content and objectives, instructional scenarios and instructional materials, as well as the delivery processes of a learning system.

A knowledge engineering approach is a response to the increased need for the reuse of knowledge resources and the interoperability of e-learning systems that has led to a vast movement towards international standards for learning objects (LOs) (Duval and Robson, 2001).

The work on Educational Modelling Languages (Koper, 2001), and the subsequent integration of a subset into the IMS Learning Design Specification, is the most important initiative to date to integrate ID into the standards movement. In particular, it describes a formal way to represent the structure of a Unit of Learning and the concept of a pedagogical method, specifying roles and activities that learners and support persons can play using LOs. Instructional Engineering, as defined above, and Educational Modelling Languages have much in common. They put the main emphasis on pedagogy and ID. They share a software engineering approach, EML being represented using the UML software modelling methodology.

In this chapter, an IE Method, MISA (méthode d'ingénierie d'un système d'apprentissage [Learning Systems Engineering Method] (Paquette, 1999) that shares similar goals with EML/IMS-LD will be presented. Our goal is to study how an IE method could be extended and synchronized with a learning design specification standard like the IMS-LD and, conversely, how such a method as MISA could contribute to help designers using a learning design standard.

EML and the IMS Learning Design Specification

EML is described by Anderson and Petrinjak in Chapter 23. As in the MISA method that we will present later in this chapter, the central concept of EML is that of a learning unit, an Educational Modelling Language being essentially a notation for learning units or units of study.

The IMS learning design conceptual model

The Educational Modelling Language has served as a basis for the IMS Learning Design (LD) Specification – Version 1.0 (IMS, 2002). The approach in IMS-LD has been to define a complete core that is as simple as possible, with some extensions.

The Level A specification contains all the core vocabulary needed to support diversified pedagogical models. Level B adds properties and conditions enabling personalization. And Level C adds notification between actors involved in the learning unit. Figure 26.1 (reproduced from the IMS – Learning Design Specification document, version 1.0, p. 10) presents a conceptual model of these three levels.

When activating a unit of learning, the method element is central. This unique element and its sub-elements control the behaviour of the unit of learning as a whole, coordinating the activities of the players in their various roles and their use of resources. The Method, Plays, Acts and Role-parts are all nested within each other, as displayed in Figure 26.2 (reproduced from the IMS – Learning Design Specification document, version 1.0, p. 73).

There are three levels in a Method. At the first level, we find two elements, a list of plays and a complete-method object. The latter holds both the condition for completion of the unit of learning and optional actions to be taken when it is. The plays represent logically independent parts of the learning design as they are always run concurrently. They can be used to provide alternative scenarios for the same unit of study for

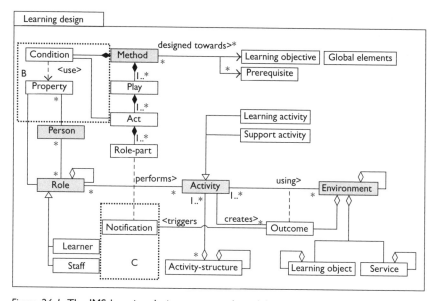

Figure 26.1 The IMS learning design conceptual model

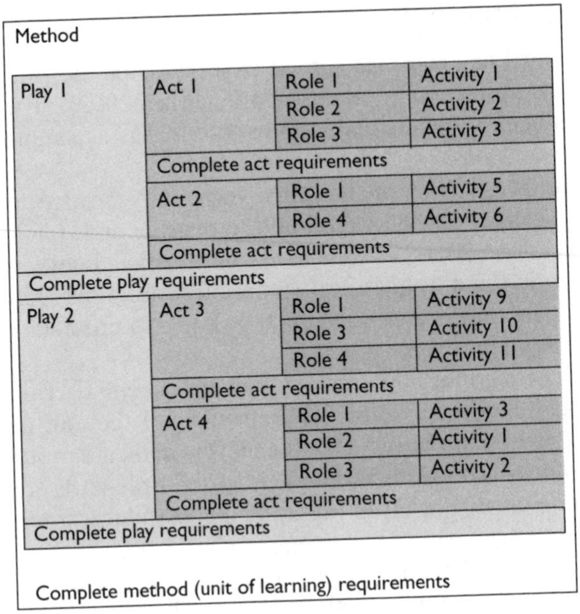

Method			
Play 1	Act 1	Role 1	Activity 1
		Role 2	Activity 2
		Role 3	Activity 3
	Complete act requirements		
	Act 2	Role 1	Activity 5
		Role 4	Activity 6
	Complete act requirements		
Complete play requirements			
Play 2	Act 3	Role 1	Activity 9
		Role 3	Activity 10
		Role 4	Activity 11
	Complete act requirements		
	Act 4	Role 1	Activity 3
		Role 2	Activity 1
		Role 3	Activity 2
	Complete act requirements		
Complete play requirements			
Complete method (unit of learning) requirements			

Figure 26.2 Structured method in a learning design

Source: IMSI – Learning Design Specification document, version 1.0, p. 73.

different target populations or for different delivery models (e.g. classroom-based vs distance learning).

An act brings together one or more role-parts to allow more than one role to perform at the same time or asynchronously in a certain time period. Therefore, role-parts within an act always run in parallel. Each role-part associates exactly one role with exactly one activity or environment. The same role can be associated with different activities in different role-parts and conversely. However, the same role may be referenced only once in the same act.

Instructional engineering with MISA

Figure 26.3 presents a high-level view of the main components of the MISA 4.0 IE Method and its relation to the Explor@ delivery system. In short, MISA supports designers in formulating the design of an instructional system. This learning design can then be used to produce a run-time instructional system that can function within a delivery system such as Explor@ which is described in Chapter 20 (see also Paquette, 2002), or another Learning Management System (LMS) or Learning Content Management System (LCMS). Figure 26.3 presents also the interrelations between the four main models created using MISA 4.0 as presented in Figure 26.1.

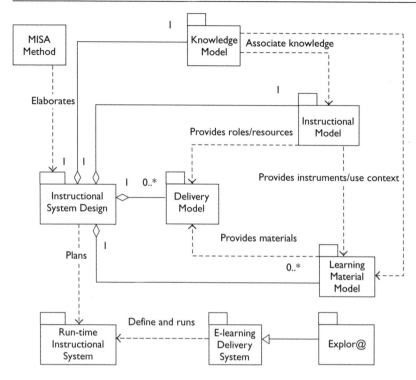

Figure 26.3 Interrelations between MISA 4.0 design specifications and Explor@

The MISA 4.0 instructional engineering method

We have used a knowledge modelling approach to define the IE method itself, its concepts, its processes and its principles. This effort started in 1992 and has led to MISA 4.0 (Paquette, 2001a, 2002a) and a web-based support system for designers, ADISA (un atelier distribué d'ingénierie d'un système d'apprentissage) (a distributed engineering workshop for a learning system) (Paquette *et al.*, 2001).

The root task – 'To produce a model of a learning system' – is distributed into six phases, each phase progressively developing four design models and their objects' descriptions.

- The *Knowledge Model* is a graphic representation of the content domain of a learning system. In this model, target and prerequisite competencies are associated to units of knowledge providing learning objectives to the Instructional Model.
- The *Instructional Model* is essentially a network of learning units (LU) and events, to which knowledge and target competencies are associated. Each LU is described by a graphic learning scenario describing

learning and support activities linked to resources. Resources holding content (called instruments) are associated with a subset of the knowledge model.

- The *Learning Material Models* are optional. Each model groups instruments into a material (or LO), describing the media components, the source documents and some presentation principles and other specifications to build or aggregate LOs.
- These learning materials and the other types of resources such as tools, communication links, services and locations, described in the Instructional Model, can be organized in one or more delivery model. Each delivery model is a multi-user workflow process where actors use or produce resources while adopting different roles.

MISA 4.0 comprised 35 basic sub-tasks, each producing one design element. In a manner similar to software engineering methods, each model definition starts with a statement of orientation principles. In each of the four axes, one or more graphic models are built. Graphic modelling is the backbone of the method. It is done by a designer using a knowledge representation technique and tool called MOT. It was developed in-house and is commercially available through COGIGRAPH Inc., a spin-off company of Télé-université du Québec.

Most of the other tasks in MISA describe properties of objects in these models. For example, target and prerequisite competencies are properties of objects in the knowledge model. Learning activities and learning instrument design elements are properties of the objects in the learning events network or in the learning scenarios. MOT models and object properties all translate to XML. ADISA uses the corresponding XML files for data propagation and export, providing an XML binding for MISA design specifications.

The Instructional Model in MISA

As shown by the UML class diagram on Figure 26.4, at the highest level, an Instructional Model is a *network of learning events*. 'Learning Event' is a generic term to describe a module, a course, a training program, and so on. A network of learning events is composed of learning events, resources, links and rules. Composition (C) links build the hierarchy of learning events, while precedence (P) links describe prerequisites between them. Resources or products are related to learning events using input/product (I/P) links. Rules governing the use of learning events are connected to each other using a regulation (R) link. This is where, for example, it is possible to specify that there is a choice between three alternative learning events or units or that evaluation take place in a certain way in a learning event.

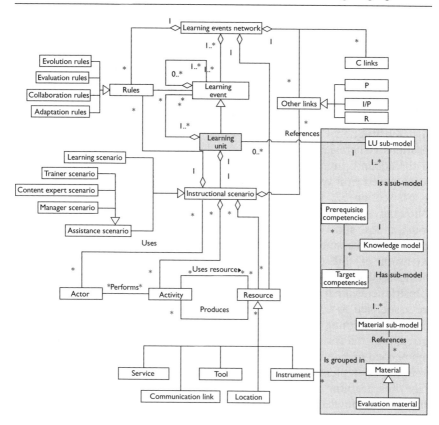

Figure 26.4 A class diagram of the MISA 4.0 instructional model

A second step in the elaboration of the instructional model is to build a *learning scenario* for each *learning unit*. A learning unit is a learning event that is not decomposed into other learning events. It has learning objectives and prerequisites, provided by target and prerequisite competencies defined in the Knowledge Model.

A learning unit references exactly one Instructional Scenario grouping actors, resources, activities and links. Actors rule activities (R link) that use or produce resources (I/P links). Activities can also be linked by precedence (P) links but no composition (C) links are allowed. As for a learning event, execution, evaluation, collaboration and adaptation rules can be R-linked to activities. The subset of the scenario grouping activities performed by a learner and their associated resources is called the Learning Scenario. The subset grouping activities performed by all the other actors (called facilitators) and their associated resources is called the Assistance Scenario.

Further subsets of the Assistance Scenario are possible for different types of facilitators; we could obtain a Trainer Scenario, a Content Expert

Scenario, a Manager Scenario, and so on. In the Virtual Learning Center Model on which the Explor@ web-based learning delivery system is based, we have distinguished five main types of actors: learner, trainer, informer, manager and designer, but the system itself accepts other actor typologies (Paquette, 2002b). In MISA, the possibility is there but it has not yet been implemented in the ADISA support system.

Five types of resources can appear in the learning events network and in any instructional scenario in a learning unit: instruments, tools, services, locations (where learning is carried out) and communication links (such as 'broadband', mail or face-to-face). These categories have been further decomposed in a typology expanding the IEEE LOM typology. In IEEE LOM, section 5.2 where the learning resource types are presented. The following are listed: exercise, simulation, questionnaire, diagram, figure, graph, index, slide, table, narrative text, exam, experiment, problem statement, self-assessment and lecture. Of course the IMS LD permits the extension of this typology, for example including learning units and methods (IEEE, 2002).

Instruments are the only resources that hold content. More precisely, they are associated to a sub-model of the Knowledge Model. We distinguish them from learning materials because they can, in general, be produced in different media formats. Usually, instruments are small pieces of information needed or produced in the activities of a learning scenario that will be grouped and implemented in a certain media format to create learning material. Thus, learning materials, described in another model, are also associated with a knowledge sub-model. In particular, evaluation material, such as a questionnaire, an exam or an essay, is also associated with a knowledge sub-model and the competencies linked to knowledge in that submodel. These competencies are the basis on which evaluation takes place.

The author has shown elsewhere (Paquette 2001a) that it is possible to derive a learning scenario from a generic skill involved in a target competency, in the context of different educational models. For example, if a target competency states that learners should learn to diagnose equipment failures, the generic diagnostic process provides a workflow or task model composed of the individual diagnostic tasks with their inputs, products, and control principles. This approach is similar to the KADS software engineering methodology (Breuker and Van de Velde, 1994). An instructional scenario is created when a pedagogical model is added to this basic flow of tasks. In an expository approach, an instructor will use the workflow model to present or demonstrate segments of the diagnostic process. In a discovery approach, diagnostic problems in the field of equipment failure will be proposed to the learners, an instructor (or a learner) using the workflow model for assistance with the tasks.

Figure 26.5 presents an example of a MISA diagnostic learning scenario. In a MOT graphic model, ovals represent activities that are performed by actor roles (L for learner or F for facilitator). Rectangles represent resources labelled I for instruments, T for tools, S for services, C for communication or L for location. Unmarked resources are outcomes produced during an activity. Hexagons represent rules: X for execution, E for evaluation, C for collaboration and A for adaptation.

In the learning scenario subset (in white on black), learners rule six activities, starting with the analysis of an electronic system to diagnose for faults. A collaboration rule (C) states that they work in teams of two. Execution rules (X) define iteration between activities until the complete system has been analysed. Through these cycles, using LOs as inputs, each team produces intermediate outcomes and, finally, a list of defaults components. Using an assistance scenario, a facilitator (F at top of Figure 26.5) distributes systems to teams, provides feedback using a forum and document transfer, providing evaluation services to learners, trainers and training managers.

Comparing MISA and IMS-LD ontologies

As can be ascertained from the figures, there are many similarities between the main concepts of MISA and those of IMS-LD. Although some of the terminology differs, the IMS-LD subset of EML has approximately the same scope as the Instructional Model in MISA.

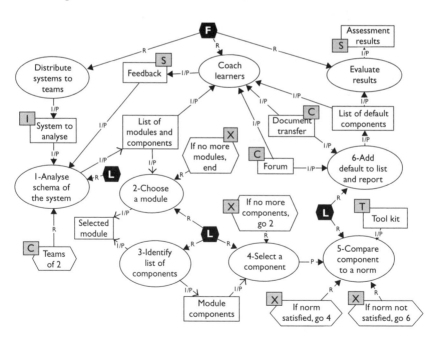

Figure 26.5 An example of a MISA diagnostic learning scenario

MISA as an educational modelling language

In a study of Educational Modelling Languages, Rawlings *et al.* (2002, p. 10) defined EML as a 'semantic information model and binding, describing the content and process within a "unit of learning" from a pedagogical perspective in order to support reuse and interoperability'.

It is clear that the MISA Instructional Model constitutes an EML according to this definition. The set of MOT models grouping the Network of Learning Events, plus the Instructional Scenarios of each learning unit, and their associated knowledge models constitute a semantic information model that describes the content and process of any learning event from a pedagogical perspective. The translation of these MOT models into a set of XML files constitutes a semantic information binding that serves the same reusability and interoperability purposes as the XML files in the IMS-LD specification.

Most of the differences between the two approaches lie in their different roles in the design–development–delivery general process. MISA is a method similar to software engineering methods. It describes processes and principles of IE that help define design elements, not only the resulting specification of a DLS. IMS-LD, being such a specification, is more focused on delivery, content packaging and run-time implementation issues that are not really considered in an IE method like MISA.

For those aspects, it will be more interesting to compare it to designs produced using the Explor@ delivery system. If we go back to Figure 26.3, MISA should produce an XML specification of a learning system in a way compatible to IMS-LD. Then a delivery system like Explor@ should be able to process these XML specifications, whether they have been produced using MISA or in other ways.

These different viewpoints explain why MISA addresses a larger set of subjects and preoccupations, but does not include concepts such as Property, Global Elements, Conditions and Notification found in IMS-LD, which are closer to run-time issues. For the same reason, MISA does not separate services from the other resources because conceptually they are included in the IEEE definition of a LO, while IMS-LD considers that Services are not LOs because they have to be initiated at run-time.

Terminology correspondences

To better identify the frontiers of the IMS-LD specification, a synthesis of the correspondence between the main concepts of both ontologies is presented. The concept of a unit of learning in IMS-LD corresponds better to the MISA concept of a learning system because it can include quite elaborate activity structures as large as a complete training programme or as small as a module lasting a few hours. The learning design of a learning unit thus corresponds well to the MISA instructional model.

Although competencies might play a similar role to learning objectives and prerequisites in EML, they are defined in a structured way in the knowledge model as a skill applied to a knowledge unit in a certain performance context. Each learning unit is associated with exactly one subset of this knowledge model and the associated target and prerequisite competencies are linked. It might be interesting to compare this approach to the original OUNL-EML and the IMS Competency specification, and to consider it in future versions of the IMS-LD specification.

Learning Events and Learning Units both correspond to the *activity* concept in IMS-LD. The network of learning events in MISA is similar to an *activity structure*, but a learning event network can be more complex because different kinds of links can be added between learning events (for example prerequisite links) and between learning events and input or product resources. Also, rules can be associated to learning events to describe execution paths, collaboration requirements, evaluation requirements, or adaptation possibilities.

Methods and instructional scenarios

The ontology differences between IMS-LD methods and MISA instructional models is a central question because both ontologies put a strong emphasis on the representation of pedagogical methods enacted as processes.

The concept of instructional scenario is the closest equivalent to the IMS-LD concept of a method, with the difference that there is only one play in a scenario because there is only one scenario in a MISA learning unit. Is this a limitation of MISA? Not really, because to build alternative plays in MISA, it is only necessary to build different alternative units of learning addressed to different target populations or enacting different delivery models. Thus, an instructional scenario in MISA corresponds to a play in IMS-LD but a play is a linear sequence of acts, while a MISA scenario can be any network of activities and resources, in particular a linear sequence, a tree structure, or a workflow model with iteration.

Figure 26.6 shows a MISA scenario corresponding to the first play of the IMS-LD method presented earlier in Figure 26.3. It captures the sequential nature of acts and the concurrency of role-parts associating roles to activities, which is the essence of an EML method. The role-part being an association between a role and an activity, the R link in the MOT model represents this association. This scenario is not a totally general play because activities can be complex activity structures. But if such activities are replaced by a local graph corresponding to an activity structure, an equivalent conceptual representation will be formed.

There appear to be limitations because of the hierarchical nature of the method concept. A precise definition of an Activity Structure is available in the IMS Learning Design information model (pp. 31–32) and the IMS Learning Design XML binding (pp. 26–28) documents (IMS, 2003a,

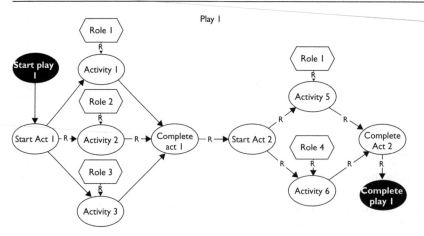

Figure 26.6 An example of a MISA role play scenario

2003b). These are most probably in order to ease the implementation of a specification for current LMS and LCMS. An activity structure can nest references to any number of smaller activity structures up to any number of levels, which is the definition of a tree. The leaves can be a reference to a single learning activity or support-activity, or a reference to another IMS-LD unit of learning. In that last case, the organization of the method of a learning unit is structured in the same way as represented in Figure 26.6.

It is difficult to represent a more general MISA scenario like the one in Figure 26.5 because of its non-hierarchical nature and the presence of explicit links between its resources and activities. For example, you might want to show that a learner produces homework that is sent to a tutor, who evaluates it and sends the results to both the learner and a trainer. In IMS-LD, you could, of course, separate these activities in different acts and relate them through references to LOs, but it might look unnatural to a non-technical instructional designer.

Another difficulty might lie in the MISA rules that can be integrated both in the network of learning events and in instructional scenarios. IMS-LD includes the possibility to use textual activity descriptions for this and so does MISA. However, on certain occasions, it might be important to add rules for the iteration of activities, important collaborations, evaluation features, or part of the scenario that can be adapted at run-time. IMS-LD level B properties and conditions might be an answer to this, but this analysis exceeds the scope of the present chapter.

Generality of the theatrical metaphor

According to the instructional design literature, an instructional method should have the following components: (a) the activities or the phases through which the learning/teaching process unfolds; (b) a social system, the roles and relationships between learners and staff, including collaboration; (c) feedback from the instructor through his/her analysis of learners' performing activities; (d) a support system including materials and resources, as well as services given by instructors and other facilitators; and (e) expected outcomes, that is the target learning that the strategy is supposed to support (Joyce and Weil, 1980).

All these elements are present in both the MISA learning scenario and the IMS-LD play concepts, but it seems that an IMS-LD play, being more constrained than a MISA Scenario, is, at least theoretically, less general. The theatrical metaphor, on the other hand, favours synchronization points. An IMS-LD play can probably cover most of the situations, but we think that it is important at design time, to leave open a large set of possible instances. It still remains to be seen if there are implementation difficulties that would prevent a description of a method as a general workflow model.

Any metaphor has its limits and other metaphors have been proposed for LO aggregation, for example a molecule-atom metaphor (Wiley, 2002) or an 'organic metaphor' (Paquette and Rosca, 2002; see also the Introduction to this book). From one or the other of these viewpoints, we can ask ourselves what is the 'smallest structured component'. In IMS-LD, it is the individual learning or support activities that are a sequence of steps or task elements similar to the activity concept in MISA. These are the atoms of a method. Adding a structure to the atoms (or the cells) creates molecules (or tissues). In IMS-LD, there are no intermediate molecules that structure atom-activities.

In MISA, the learning unit concept and its associated learning scenario serve that purpose. Following up on Romiszowski (1981), the first version of MISA had a four-level hierarchy of learning events: curriculum, course, learning unit and learning activities. We abandoned this approach for the one described earlier, not only to add flexibility on the number of levels, but mostly because it was hard to keep consistency between the different levels. If we accept that knowledge and competencies at higher-level learning events are the sum of those appearing in their components, we need only to associate knowledge and competencies to learning units. At that level, it is easier to see if some are missing, to add them up in the learning unit sub-model and to automatically propagate the new elements in the models of all parent learning events.

Any learning design should contain a well-defined *smallest molecule concept* such as the MISA learning unit. Learning units, as defined in MISA 4.0, are large enough to be significant, in particular to support constructivist strategies, but not so large that they could not be reused in other situations. Furthermore, in practice, an instructional strategy or method is rarely decided at a programme or even at a course level, but rather at the level of smaller modules such as a MISA learning unit. Non-technical instructional designers need simple graphic tools to elaborate a method. It might be that a more open approach, in terms of a general workflow mode, turns out to be easier for them to use, provided that graphic tools are available to describe general activity process models.

Conclusion

This chapter is written based on a design point of view. It argues that implementation and delivery issues might put constraints on learning design that are not helpful and unnecessary. Also, since the aim of IMS-LD is to provide a widely accepted specification, it should not be too detailed so that everybody is caged into a tight uniform model. In that respect, the IMS-LD specification does present a sound, non-restrictive and quite general solution.

An IE method such as MISA can help support the use of such a specification by providing well-defined and systematic processes and design principles to support designers building LD specifications. It can also provide productivity tools embedding these processes and principles, especially graphic tools to elaborate learning event networks and instructional scenarios to build domain knowledge and competency models, as well as distributing these into learning units and learning events. Finally, some of the MISA concepts, such as competencies, can be viewed as skills applied to knowledge. The learning scenario workflow model might bring useful extensions to the specification, without restricting its usability and flexibility.

Educational Modelling Languages and the IMS-LD specification bring an important innovation to the e-learning toolset. In particular, the proposed methodology leads directly to delivery models of a DLS that are multi-actor process models. In Paquette and Rosca (2002) we have developed this idea, termed as functions models, to provide a solution to the inherent complexity of a distance learning system. The new specification should encourage evolution of the delivery systems towards greater flexibility and descriptions, not only of the anatomy of a learning system, but also of its physiology, as a dynamic set of interactions.

For our part, our next work will be to analyse the specification from a delivery point of view to adapt our Explor@2 system so that it can fully process all three levels of the IMS-LD specifications. This work will be conducted as part of the eduSource project, which is a pan-Canadian project that aims to implement a functional network of learning object repositories, based on international standards, providing a software suite of tools to find, reference and use learning objects in educational applications. Within this project, we will also define generic services that any delivery system should provide to fully exploit XML-based specifications.

References

Berners-Lee, T., Hendler, J. and Lassila, O. (2001) (accessed 1 December 2003) The Semantic Web, *Scientific American* (Electronic version), May, (Online) http://www.sciam.com/article.cfm?articleID=00048144-10D2-1C70-84A9809EC588EF21.

Breuker, J. and Van de Velde, W. (1994) *CommonKads library for expertise modelling*, IOS Press, Amsterdam.

Dewey, J. (1900) Psychology and social practice, *Psychological Review*, **7**: 105–24.

Duval, E. and Robson, R. (2001) Guest editorial on metadata, *Interactive Learning Environments: Special issue: Metadata*, **9–3**: 201–6.

IEEE (2002) (accessed 16 March 2003) Draft standard for Learning Object Metadata (LOM), Learning Technology Standards Committee (LTSC), (Online) http://ltsc.ieee.org/doc/wg12/LOM_WD6_4.pdf.

IMS (2002) (accessed 23 January 2003) IMS specifications, (Online) http://www.imsglobal.org/specificationdownload.cfm.

IMS (2003a) (accessed 28 March 2003) IMS Learning design information model, (Online) http://www.imsglobal.org/learningdesign/ldv1p0/imsld_infov1p0.html.

IMS (2003b) (accessed 28 March 2003) IMS Learning design XML binding, (Online) http://www.imsglobal.org/learningdesign/ldv1p0/imsld_bindv1p0.html.

Joyce, B. and Weil, M. (1980) *Models of teaching*, Prentice-Hall, New York.

Koper, R. (2001) (accessed 28 June 2002) Modeling units of study from a pedagogical perspective: The pedagogical meta-model behind EML, Heerlen, Open University of the Netherlands, (Online) http://eml.ou.nl/introduction/docs/ped-metamodel.pdf.

Merrill, M. D. (1994) *Principles of ID*, Educational Technology Publications, Englewood Cliffs, NJ.

Montessori, M. (1958) Pédagogie scientifique, in *The Montessori Method*, ed. D. D. Brouwer, Schocken Books, New York.

Paquette, G. (1999) Meta-knowledge representation for learning scenarios engineering, in *9th International Conference on Artificial Intelligence in Education (AI-ED)*, LeMans, France.

Paquette, G. (2001a) Designing virtual learning centers, in *Handbook on Information Technologies for Education and Training*, eds H. Adelsberger, B. Collis and J. Pawlowski, pp. 249–72, Springer-Verlag, Heidelberg, Germany.

Paquette, G. (2001b) TeleLearning Systems Engineering: Towards a new ISD model, *Journal of Structural Learning*, **14**: 1–35.

Paquette, G. (2002) The Explor@-II system for learning resource management, in *Second Canadian National E-Learning Workshop*, Montreal.

Paquette, G. (2002a) *La modélisation des connaissances et des compétences, pour concevoir et apprendre*, Presses de l'Université du Québec.

Paquette, G. (2002b) *L'ingénierie pédagogique, pour construire l'apprentissage en réseau*, Presses de l'Université du Québec.

Paquette, G. and Rosca, I. (2002) Organic aggregation of knowledge objects in educational systems, *Canadian Journal of Learning Technologies*, **28** (3)**:** 11–26.

Paquette, G. *et al.* (2001) Web-based support for the IE of e-learning systems, in *WebNet'01 Conference*, Orlando, FL.

Rawlings, A. *et al.* (2002) (accessed 14 December 2002) Survey of educational modelling languages, *CEN/ISSS Learning Technologies Workshop*, (Online) http://eml.ou.nl/forum/docs/EML%20Survey%20version%201.pdf.

Reigeluth, C. (1983) *Instructional theories in action: Lessons illustrating selected theories and models*, Lawrence Earlbaum, Hillsdale, NJ.

Romiszowski, A. J. (1981) *Designing instructional systems*, Kogan Page/London Nichols Publishing, New York.

Spector, J. M., Polson, M. C. and Muraida, D. J. (1993) *Automating ID – Concepts and issues*, Educational Technology Publications, Englewood Cliffs, NJ.

Wenger, E. (1987) *Artificial intelligence and tutoring systems: Computational and cognitive approaches to the communication of knowledge*, Morgan-Kaufmann, San Francisco.

Wiley, D. (2002) Connecting learning objects to instructional design theory: A definition, a metaphor, and a taxonomy, in *The instructional use of e-learning objects*, ed. D. Wiley, pp. 1–35, Agency for Instructional Technology, Bloomington, IN.

Appendix
International metadata standards

Definitions

Some of the following definitions have been adapted from Webopedia (http://webopedia.internet.com).

1. *Specifications*: Less evolved than standards and attempt to capture a rough consensus in the user or implementer community. They enable people to get on with the job of system and content development. It can take a long time before specifications are finally approved as standards.
2. *Standards*: Definitions or formats that have been approved by a recognized standards organization, or are accepted as *de facto* standards by the industry. Standards serve a regulatory function and have been created for programming languages, operating systems, data formats, communications protocols and electrical interfaces.
3. *Application Profile*: A simplified and interpreted version of a standard or specification that is created to serve the needs of a particular community of users or implementers. Application profiles can combine elements from more than one specification or standard into a single profile, but should not modify these in such a way that would have a negative impact on interoperability.
4. *Metadata*: Simply put, metadata are data 'about data'. Like a card or record in a library catalogue, metadata describe a resource (a book, document, video clip, application), but unlike a library record, metadata can either be embedded in the resource they describe, or be located separately from it. Metadata can be generated either manually or automatically, but are most often structured according to semantically understood elements – access points such as author, title and location.
5. *Interoperability*: The ability of systems or components to work together, without unnecessary human intervention. In the case of metadata, interoperability refers specifically to the ability to exchange information and to process information that has been exchanged. True interoperability would allow users to search and otherwise make use of systems in a seamless manner – despite their location, origin or internal operation.

6. *XML*: Extensible Markup Language is a specification defining syntax for tagging that superficially looks similar to HTML. Unlike HTML, XML allows developers to create their own custom tags. This makes it possible to label the purpose of particular elements in a document – instead of simply specifying the way these elements might appear in a web browser, as is the case with HTML. A set of tags or elements created in XML that specify the kind and format of permitted data is known as a DTD (Document Type Definition) or Schema. XML documents that actually contain this data are known as XML records.

Specifications organizations

1. *Dublin Core* (http://purl.oclc.org/dc/; named for Dublin, Ohio, not Ireland). Dublin Core has been described as the most broadly based metadata specification. It coexists comfortably with the other metadata sets and is intended to facilitate interoperability between the semantics of metadata specifications. Dublin Core metadata is syntax-independent, and can be encoded in a number of ways – in metatags in the header of an HTML document, in XML documents or in RDF/XML markup. Dublin Core consists of only fifteen optional elements such as Title, Description, Creator, Subject, etc.

2. *IMS* (http://imsproject.com). The IMS (Instructional Management System) was established by EduCom (now EduCause) in 1994. Its mandate is to serve as a catalyst for the development of instructional software, the creation of an online management infrastructure for learning, the facilitation of collaborative learning activities and certification. Its members include Apple, Cisco, IBM, Industry Canada, Microsoft, Oracle, Sun, and the US Defense Department. The IMS has been developing a number of specifications for the community of e-learning developers: for example, content packaging, digital repository interoperability, and learning design. Included with these is a metadata specification that both incorporates and extends the Dublin Core. Bindings or encodings are available for IMS metadata in both XML and RDF/XML. Although the IMS metadata schema represents an important activity, the IMS is *not* just a metadata schema. The IMS is involved in the development of other learning application specifications.

3. *ARIADNE* (http://ariadne.unil.ch/). The Alliance of Remote Instructional Authoring and Distribution Networks for Europe (ARIADNE) has fostered the sharing and reuse of electronic pedagogical material by universities and corporations. It attempted to create a Europe-wide repository for pedagogical documents called the Knowledge Pool System. It has also acted as a co-author of the IMS metadata specification.

4. *ADL SCORM* (http://www.adlnet.org/Scorm/). The Advanced Distributed Learning Network Sharable Content Object Reference Model, supported by the US Department of Defense and the US government. It combines and interprets a number of interrelated technical specifications built upon the work of the AICC, IMS and IEEE to create a unified content model. This model specifies the behaviour and aggregation of modular, interactive learning components, and makes extensive use of XML. Like IMS, SCORM is *not* simply concerned with metadata, but combines metadata with a number of other specifications that deal with a variety of aspects of learning content and management

Standards organizations

1. *IEEE LTSC* (http://ltsc.ieee.org). The Institute of Electrical and Electronics Engineers Learning Technology Standards Committee creates and supports standards and best practices related to the technical aspects of e-learning. The IEEE LTSC has released the Learning Object Metadata, referred to as IEEE LTSC LOM P1484.12, as an approved standard. This standard is almost identical to the IMS metadata specification, and is compatible with Dublin Core metadata.

2. *ISO* (http://jtc1sc36.org/#terms_of_reference). The ISO (International Standards Organization) is a network of the national standards institutes of some 130 countries that is responsible for coordinating the development of international standards of all sorts. The Information Technology for Learning, Education, and Training Committee of the ISO supports the standardization of information and communications technologies for learning. This sub-group liaises closely with the IEEE LTSC.

Application profiles

There are other organizations working on metadata that conform to international metadata specifications. Because the purpose of metadata is to enable interoperability, everyone wants to conform to emerging standards. For example, the Canadian Core Metadata Application Profile, or CanCore, is an attempt to interpret and simplify the elements of the IMS model.

1. *CanCore* (http://www.cancore.ca). The Canadian Core Learning Resource Metadata Application Profile is primarily concerned with the semantics associated with LOM metadata elements. Users of the CanCore application profile know that their data will conform to the emerging international standard for educational metadata based on and fully compatible with the LOM standard. CanCore has defined a sub-set of data elements from the LOM data model for the purposes of the

efficient and uniform description of digital educational resources. It is intended to facilitate the interchange of records describing educational resources and the discovery of these resources. CanCore is at the leading edge in providing semantic guidance to the implementation of the IEEE Learning Object Metadata specifications.

2. *Heal* (http://www.healcentral.org/documents.htm). The Health Education Assets Library is creating a national repository of free, web-based multimedia teaching materials in the health sciences, as a component of the National Science Digital Library, an initiative of the National Science Foundation. As a part of this work, Heal has developed an application profile of the LOM, including element extensions for health education, an XML schema and XML documentation.

3. *SingCORE* (http://www.ecc.org.sg/cocoon/ecc/website/singcore-17jan-03.pdf). SingCORE is an application of the metadata specification for the labelling of digital learning resources in Singapore. It is based on the IMS metadata specification version 1.2.2 and follows the IEEE LTSC Learning Object Metadata (LOM) Standard. It defines a subset of elements from the LOM.

Related organizations

1. *AICC* (http://aicc.org/). The Aviation Industry CBT (Computer-Based Training) Committee created early guidelines and recommendations for online learning systems. It provides guidelines for interoperability using metadata and protocols.

2. *ALIC* (http://www.alic.gr.jp/). The Advanced Learning Infrastructure Committee (Japan) works with other international standards bodies for metadata. It facilitates interoperability within Japan and outside.

3. *CEN/ISSS* (http://www.cenorm.be/isss/). The European Committee for Standardization Information Society Standardization System provides for both formal and informal standardization. This includes guides to best practice as well as full standards. It works by consensus among industry and consumer groups. It covers a broad constituency and is quite flexible in its methods.

4. *Cisco Systems RLO/RIO* (http://www.cisco.com/). Reusable Learning Objects/Reusable Information Objects are based on chunked reusable objects that form a complete lesson. The objects incorporate metadata that conform to the IMS/SCORM specifications.

5. *CLEO* (http://www.cleolab.org/). Customized Learning Experiences Online is a one-year research collaboration between corporations including Cisco Systems, Click2Learn, IBM Mindspan Solutions, Microsoft and NETg. Using the ADL SCORM specification, CLEO focuses on applied research on technical and pedagogical issues.

6. *GESTALT* (http://www.fdgroup.co.uk/gestalt/partners.html). Getting Educational Systems Talking Across Leading-edge Technologies is

constructing an online training demonstrator using tools and technologies previously developed. These include discovery services capable of offering users the ability to search, locate and access online interactive multimedia vocational training courseware; and online training through delivery of courseware materials. The demonstrator includes a number of elements from the GESTALT Architecture. These include a web-based client interface and web server technology. It is the intention of the project to publicize both the object descriptions and the metadata syntax, and wherever possible, to align these with related developments both within Europe and globally, thus maximizing the possibility of their widespread adoption.

7. *MARBI* (http://www.ala.org/alcts/organization/div/marbi/marbi.html). The Machine-Readable Bibliographic Information Committee is the body within the American Library Association responsible for developing official ALA positions on standards for the representation in machine-readable form of bibliographic information. MARBI focuses its attention on the development of the MARC format.

8. *MARC 21* (http://lcweb.loc.gov/marc/). The Machine-Readable Cataloging record is a library standard for the representation and communication of bibliographic and related information in a machine-readable form. It is comprised of three elements: the record structure, the content designation, and the data content of the record. It is supported by the Library of Congress Network Development and MARC Standards Office. MARC consists of dozens of metadata elements, yet is generally not considered flexible enough for the cataloguing of Internet resources. Dublin Core is perceived by many as a substitute for MARC in this area of distributed digital resources.

9. *Microsoft LRN* (http://www.microsoft.com/elearn/support.asp). The Learning Resource Interchange is a specific implementation of the IMS content packaging specification, v 1.0. It incorporates the IMS metadata and provides a toolkit.

10. *OAI* (http://www.openarchives.org/). The Open Archives Initiative advances interoperability standards that facilitate the propagation of content, increasing accessibility to intellectual content. Among the most important of its initiatives is the metadata harvesting protocol, a means of systematically sharing metadata records across distributed databases or repositories. The OAI is supported by the Digital Library Federation, and the Coalition for Networked Information.

11. *Warwick Framework* (http://www.dlib.org/dlib/july96/lagoze/07lagoze.html). The Warwick Framework has not been widely accepted, but still remains significant for metadata generally. It provides a higher-level context for Dublin Core, nesting components or packages of information in 'containers', thus facilitating interoperability. It allows for the selective manipulation of data.

12. *Z39.50* (http://www.loc.gov/z3950/agency/). The International Standards Maintenance Agency and the Library of Congress Network Development and MARC Standards Office supports this information retrieval protocol, that facilitates communication among different information systems. It allows users to search multiple, heterogeneous databases from a single interface or point of access in real time. It is widely used in libraries and it supports MARC records and other types of metadata.

Learning object repositories

The metadata employed by the repositories listed here may not conform fully to the international standards. They are given here as working examples of learning object repositories.

1. *CAREO* (http://www.careo.org). The Campus Alberta Repository of Educational Objects has as its primary goal the creation of a searchable, web-based collection of multidisciplinary teaching materials for educators across Alberta and beyond. CAREO is a project undertaken jointly by the Universities of Alberta and Calgary in cooperation with BELLE (Broadband Enabled Lifelong Learning Environment), CANARIE (Canadian Network for Advanced Research for Industry and Education), and the University of Calgary Health Education Cluster project.

2. *GEM* (http://www.thegateway.org/). The Gateway to Educational Materials is learning object repository housing uncatalogued educational materials. It is supported by a consortium of more than 200 organizations and individuals under the aegis of the US Department of Education and ERIC.

3. *JA-SIG* (http://www.mis2.udel.edu/ja-sig/). Java in Administration Special Interest Group is a collection of interactive online learning materials written in the Java computer language. It was created before the emergence of international specifications in the area of educational metadata.

4. *MERLOT* (http://www.merlot.org). The Multimedia Educational Resource for Learning and Online Teaching is a project of the California state university system under the Distributed Learning and Teaching, and Multimedia Repository initiatives. It houses a collection of high-quality interactive online learning materials, many of which have been evaluated by professionals.

5. *TeleCampus Online Course Directory* (http://telecampus.edu). The TeleCampus metadata repository has a data structure that conforms to the international specifications. It consists of web links to more than 55,000 courses, modules, and lessons in over 30 countries. Note

that it houses only the metadata and not the actual lessons, modules, and courses. It links to the institutions that own them.

6. Edutella (http://edutella.jxta.org/servlets/ProjectHome). Edutella is a peer-to-peer exchange network for metadata. It is based on the well-known GNUtella open source application, and its development is supported by the Wallenberg Global Learning Network, a partnership of organizations in Sweden and Germany.

7. *EML* (http://eml.ou.nl/introduction/). The Educational Modelling Language is a system for codifying pedagogical experiences that has been created by the Open University of the Netherlands in partnership with CISCO. It defines a document type in XML that allows for the modelling of units of study in terms of roles, relations, interactions and activities.

8. *PALO* (http://sensei.lsi.uned.es/palo/). PALO is a Spanish initiative similar to EML. It is expressed in XML and has different levels for content, activities, structure, sequencing and management.

This listing has been adapted from a list created by Norm Friesen and Rory McGreal and originally published in the *International Review of Research in Open and Distance Learning*, **3** (2), 2002; http://www.irrodl.org/content/v3.2/tech11.html.

Index

In the index *f* and *t* following page numbers refer to figures and tables respectively